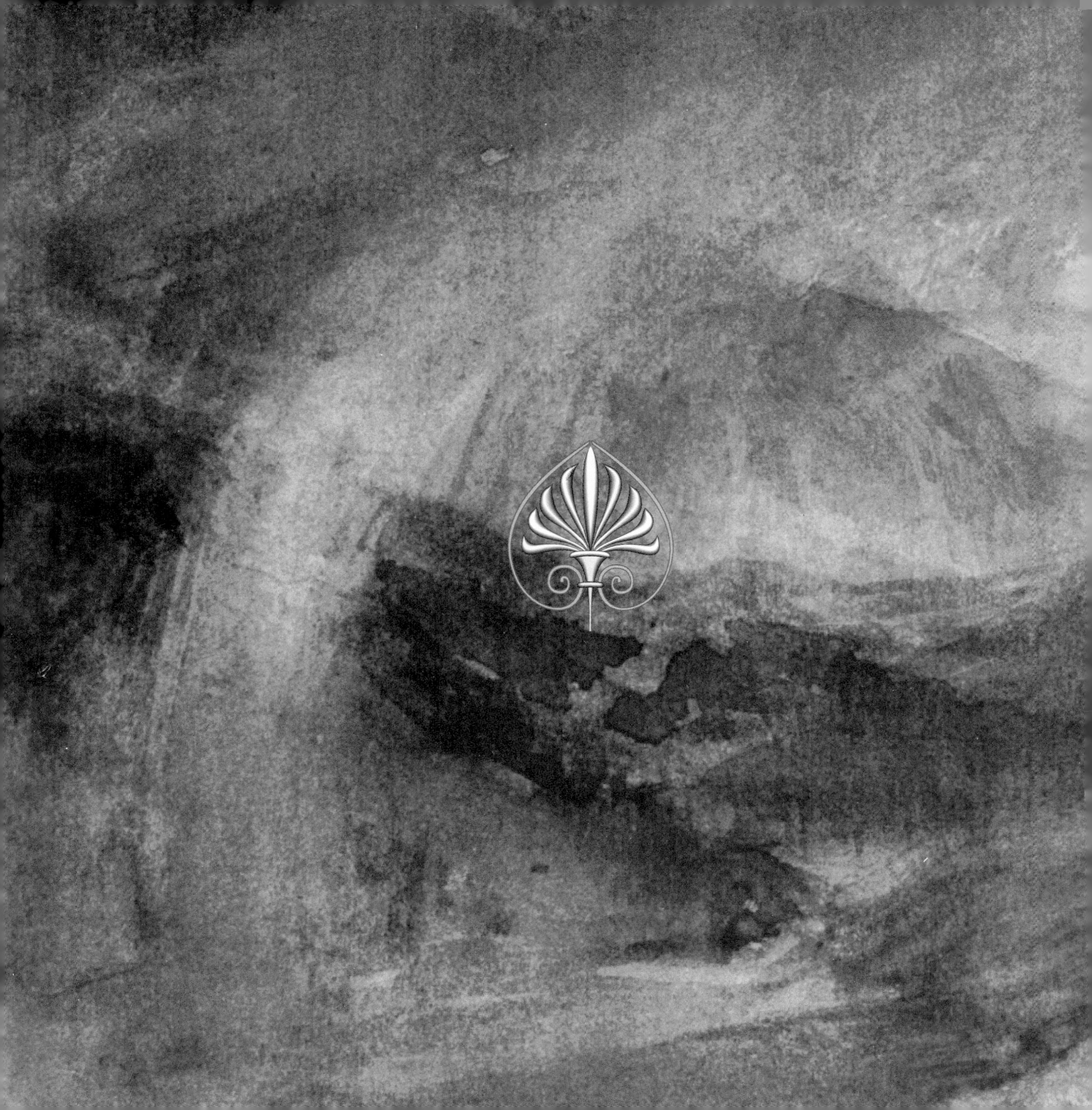

Clarence Whaite and the Welsh Art World

The Betws-y-coed Artists' Colony 1844-1914

Manweb

A ScottishPower Company

Clarence Whaite
and the Welsh Art World

The Betws-y-coed Artists' Colony
1844-1914

Peter Lord

with a foreword by
David Mortimer-Jones

The National Library of Wales

First published by
the National Library of Wales,
Aberystwyth, 1998

The National Library of Wales wishes
to thank Manweb plc for its generous
sponsorship of this book and Mr Roy Luff,
Deganwy, for his good offices.

ISBN 186225 0081

Designed by Olwen Fowler
Set in Gill, Garamond and Gwendoline

Printed by Cambrian Printers,
Aberystwyth

Contents

Foreword

This book came about as an offshoot of Peter Lord's broader and far ranging studies of Welsh visual culture. Certainly it is about the Victorian artist Henry Clarence Whaite, but more than that it concerns a considerable number of artists who, leading up to the mid-nineteenth century and beyond, demonstrated a significant shift in their attitude to Wales, its people and landscape, in the lives they led and through their art. It is also about the magnetism of Betws-y-coed and a *plein air* tradition which appealed to a younger generation of artists who by the 1850s were no longer just passing through Wales.

Whereas Turner progressed from the highlands of Scotland and the mountains of Wales to the grandeur of Switzerland as his aspirations and vision as a painter evolved, the reverse was true of Clarence Whaite. Even though his first works as a young painter to be hung in the Royal Academy were both of Swiss subjects, a fortuitously cancelled second trip to Switzerland in 1851 led him to visit Betws-y-coed instead. This was the start of a career and a gradual migration which took him over the next twenty years from Betws-y-coed and Capel Curig to Trefriw, Conwy and finally Tyddyn Cynal where he established a home and studio, which he occupied for the rest of his life. The choice of Tyddyn Cynal with its ancient thatched farm cottage, close to the broad bend in the Afon Conwy leading up to Tal-y-cafn, was not accidental. It was, for him, an important icon through which he was able to experience and express in his work both a romantic ideal and the more down to earth realities of Welsh rural life.

While I was growing up at Tyddyn Cynal in the 1950s I gradually became familiar with the existence of Henry Clarence Whaite (who had died nearly four decades before I was born) not as a remote, white bearded figure as he appears in later photographs, but more as a real and believable person. His personality, energy and enthusiasm still seemed to permeate the house in which he had lived and painted for over forty years and where he died in 1912. There were two reasons for this sense of continuity with the past which I experienced.

Firstly, not a great deal had changed at Tyddyn Cynal over the years, and day to day life was remarkably similar to the way it must have been when Whaite was alive. For the first ten years of my life electricity had not reached us so that days were governed by the rising and setting of the sun and winter evenings were characterised by the light of candles, oil lamps and flickering firelight. It was another five years before running water in the house put an end to the daily chore of carrying water from the well and taking baths in the tin bath in front of the open fire. It also meant the end of those visits, whatever the weather, to the detached *tŷ bach* with its wide wooden plank seat and two circular openings side by side, one large and one small, each with its heavy lid and the niche in the wall with its solitary candle, which on windy nights never seemed to stay alight for very long.

Looking back now, it seems strange that the place should have felt so remote. Modern civilisation only made its presence felt when the sound of the steam train, making its way up or down the far side of the Conwy, broke the silence as it came round the sweeping bend in the river. Its hoot echoed across the whole valley. I remained unaware of the consternation caused over a hundred years earlier when the tentacle of this branch line had made its way up the valley as far as Betws-y-coed. The river itself had in the past provided a much more significant means of transport and easier access to Tyddyn Cynal than the hilly potholed lane which eventually came out not far from Conwy at Gyffin. Anything bulky, such as heavy oak furniture, would have arrived by sloop. I frequently imagined Whaite loading up his large paintings from the studio at Tyddyn Cynal onto a boat for their journey down the river to Conwy and then by horse and cart to the station at Llandudno Junction, destined for exhibitions far and wide and on occasions as far as the other side of the world.

The proximity of the river also meant regular deliveries of flatfish and the occasional salmon which I remember my *nain*, Clarence Whaite's daughter, Lily, paying for at the back door. The fish would be kept fresh by being placed, sometimes still flapping, on the cold wet slate slabs in the darkness of the pantry. My *nain* told me about how late one summer evening, at high tide, when she and her father were being rowed up the river to Tal-y-Cafn, a salmon leapt right into the boat. The event almost repeated itself when, as a child, the rowing boat which was taking us up river at dusk passed Meddiant. The river was like a sheet of glass and a salmon made a startling leap over one of the oars, shattering the surface of the water.

The second reason for my strong sense of a link with the past was the fact that my *nain* was the dominant and most influential person in the household when I was growing up. She had been very close and devoted to her father and had been thirty-six years old when he died. She was the source of endless stories and anecdotes, often very amusing, about her father's life. Although I have forgotten many of the factual details, through her I came to sense that a powerful artistic tradition in the Conwy Valley had at one time dominated life at Tyddyn Cynal. However, it was difficult to define and the saddest thing for me was that what must have been a rich visual enterprise involving very many artists now only existed as part of a fading oral tradition.

When I started to study art history myself it was not surprising that Wales did not figure a great deal. I soon realised that the tradition I had first been made aware of was going to remain at best elusive and at worst a permanent myth. Apart from the stereotypical role that art in Wales was given in the history of English art there were no other points of reference - no history of the art of the Conwy Valley for example to take down from the library shelf, and a dearth of images to explore and bring the thing to life. When I was very young there were the openings of the Annual Summer Exhibitions of the Royal Cambrian Academy in Conwy, which strangely were less significant to me as contemporary events than as after-images through which one aspect of the past was, if not exactly brought to life, at least made more believable. However, one recurring message which accompanied this strong flavour of the art world in the late Victorian period was Whaite's own determination and commitment as an artist and his aspirations for Welsh art - exemplified by his long involvement with the Royal Cambrian Academy, his support for a National Museum of Wales, the development of Welsh art through the Eisteddfodau and the encouragement of younger artists.

It is easy to caricature the formation of the Royal Cambrian Academy as the way a few artists based in north Wales created for themselves a kind of private artists' club, which brought with it an essentially conservative ethos and self-congratulatory entrenchment. Whaite was, after all, in his mid-fifties by the time the Academy gained momentum, and the pattern of his working life as an artist in Wales was firmly established. However, I believe that the motivation of Whaite and the Welsh artists who were involved in the early days of the Academy was somewhat different and more radical. For them it would have been natural to see the creation of a national academy of art as a necessary and progressive step in the development of a nation's art activity - not least through an educational programme and 'schools' within the academy to foster a younger generation of artists. Other nations within Britain had academies which received Royal patronage, as well as their own national galleries and museums. In the late nineteenth century it was these institutions which were seen as ensuring that art had a status and an acknowledged position in the cultural life of any civilised nation. The absence in Wales of such institutions made it difficult to focus on a national cultural identity in the visual arts, rather than simply acknowledging the activities and achievements of individual artists. I feel confident that Whaite intended the Academy to celebrate and value these activities as part of the cultural life of Wales in a way which might free artists from having to subject their work continually to the judgement of the dominant English, or rather London-based, art establishment.

For several decades after Whaite died the slumbering nature of life at Tyddyn Cynal and a certain devotion to his memory meant that his studio and its contents remained largely untouched and no doubt this would have continued had it not been for the intrusion of the Second World War. The need for more storage space for farm produce meant that the contents of the studio had to be pushed to one side to make way for the storage of grain. From this time on rats and a badly leaking roof caused untold damage in the studio and it is sad to contemplate how much was destroyed. Fortunately sufficient survived, especially in the form of letter books and dusty correspondence, for it to be possible to make an informed appraisal of Whaite's position in a general sense in the Welsh art world of the nineteenth and early twentieth centuries. Perhaps someday a more comprehensive account will be written.

I believe that Clarence Whaite's drawings also reveal a great deal. They show in a very modern way how important the drawing process was to him. More often than not it was simply an end in itself, rather than a preparation for some subsequent stage - an almost unavoidable way of thinking about and responding to the environment of which he felt a part. Although clearly a romantic, in the main Whaite was not drawn to the heroic individual in these studies, made directly from life, but rather he demonstrated an almost tireless desire to record collective social activities, which frequently seem to involve all the members of many families. Groups of figures sheep washing, sheep shearing, harvesting, building haystacks, collecting mussels, dredging oysters or at fairs and markets were drawn, time and time again with untiring enthusiasm in what became a highly developed notational style. He depicted all the principal secular activities which demonstrated the social cohesion of nineteenth century rural Wales, which was about to change dramatically with the coming of the First World War.

The author and I would like to acknowledge the support of the many individuals and institutions who have contributed to this reassessment of the importance of Clarence Whaite and his colleagues in the development of Welsh visual culture. The book was written at the University of Wales Centre for Advanced Welsh and Celtic Studies at Aberystwyth, and we thank the Director, Professor Geraint H. Jenkins for his encouragement. Mr Paul Harries, research assistant to the Welsh Visual Culture Research Project at the Centre, made a substantial contribution in the form of detailed work on individual artists, statistics and topography. Many public and private collections of pictures and documents have been consulted, and in particular we would like to thank the Royal Cambrian Academy, Mr Simon Fenwick, archivist of the Royal Water Colour Society, and the Martyn

Gregory Gallery, London. The National Library of Wales is both publisher of this volume and organiser of the exhibition of the work of Clarence Whaite which accompanies its launch, and we thank the many members of staff who have given generously of their time and expertise. In particular, we thank Mr Gwyn Jenkins and Mr Huw Ceiriog who are responsible for the Library's publications programme, Dr Huw Owen and Mr Michael Francis of the Department of Pictures and Maps, and the photographer Mr Gareth Lloyd Hughes, for their support. Finally, we extend our thanks to the many individuals living in Dyffryn Conwy who have helped us with our work, and in particular Mr and Mrs Schärer of Plas Muriau.

David Mortimer-Jones
Tyddyn Cynal
August, 1997.

Introduction

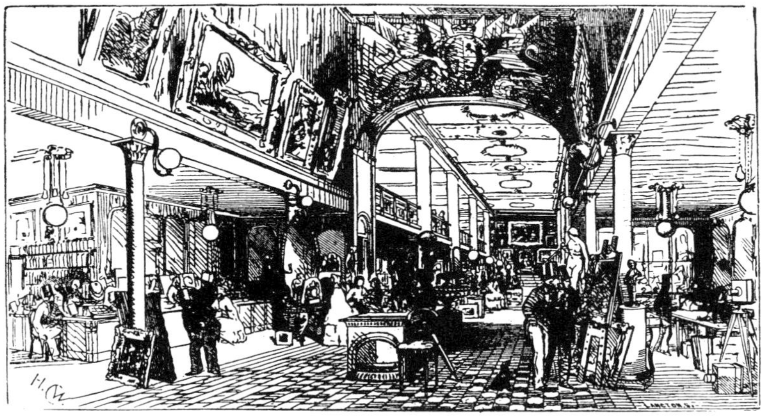

Clarence Whaite, *Interior of Whaite's Fine Art Gallery, Bridge Street, Manchester,* 1857.

Henry Clarence Whaite was born in Manchester in 1828. His father, Henry Whaite, had established an art gallery and picture framing business in the town, which also supplied trade unions, friendly societies, Sunday schools and many other organisations with painted banners for display at their meetings and rallies. The whole family participated in the development of the business, including Clarence who learnt to paint in this artisan tradition. Like the children of many other artisan painters, Clarence Whaite developed an ambition to become an art painter and the prosperity of the family business enabled him to attend the Manchester School of Design. In 1850 he travelled to the continent. He went through Switzerland and down the Rhine, enjoying himself sufficiently to plan a second trip for the following summer. However, his intentions were frustrated and instead Clarence Whaite came to Wales to paint, apparently for the first time.[2] On 23 August 1851 he was at work near Llanberis:

> *'On going to my sketch, there was another artist sketching where I am, he is staying at Bettws y coed, and come this far for a work. He says there are ten artists there, amongst others is D.Cox.'*[3]

[1] Both William Jones, son of a painter and decorator at Beaumaris, and Penry Williams, son of a painter and decorator at Merthyr, went to the Royal Academy Schools. For these and other examples, see Peter Lord, *Artisan Painters* (Aberystwyth, 1993).

[2] He appears to have been let down by a friend who was to accompany him on the Continental tour.

[3] Diary of Clarence Whaite, 23 August 1851, Whaite archive, private collection.

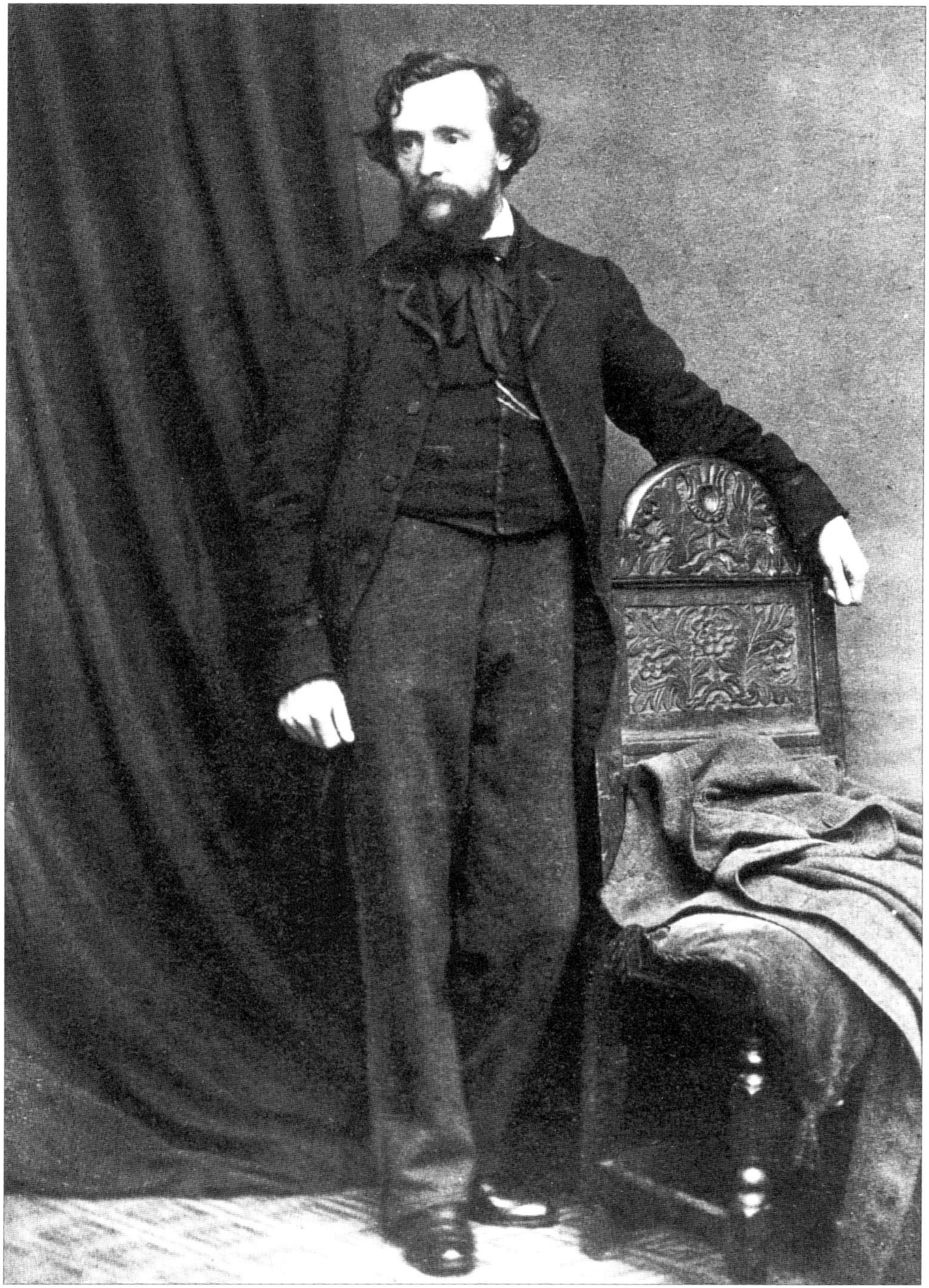

Unknown photographer,
Henry Clarence Whaite,
1863.

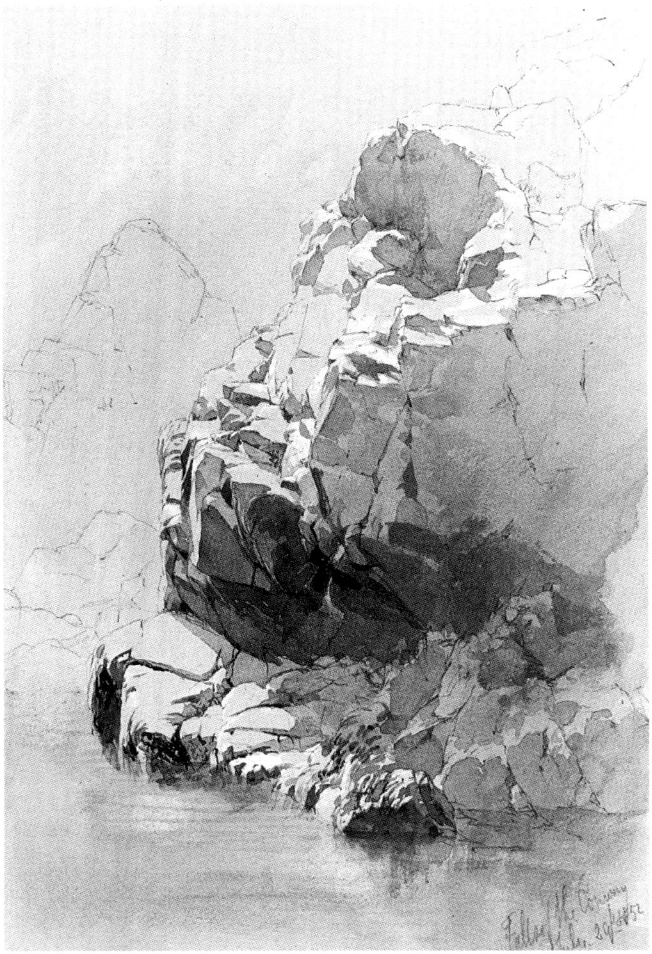

Clarence Whaite,
Falls of the Conway, 1852.

The presence of David Cox at Betws-y-coed would not have come as a surprise to Whaite since the painter's annual visits there, begun in 1844, were famous and already a part of the fabric of the English art world. Nevertheless, his proximity to the great man and to the place celebrated by association with him must have excited the young painter. He returned to Manchester for the winter where he was obliged to assist in the family business as well as pursuing his own painting, which probably included working up sketches made in Wales into more finished pictures. Clarence Whaite had been moved by the drama of the mountainous landscape, and in the summer of 1852 he returned, noting in his diary:

> *'I am now in Wales, and thankful do I feel for the change from banner painting (which I am forced to do) - to the finest scenery of Wales - how its grandeur overpowers me - if I could paint the extent of my feelings...'*[4]

He was again informed of the presence of David Cox at Betws and on 3 September 1852, he met the great man:

> *'David Cox called to see my drawings - and expressed his delight. He liked my picture for the atmosphere I had got into it but said the tone and depth I had in my sketch from the old road was much finer - so it is but my oil picture has not the tone yet about it - the studies at the bed of the river he said was excellent. He liked them much.'*[5]

[4]Ibid., 16 July 1852.

[5]Ibid., 3 September 1852.

This kind of encouragement to a young painter was typical of the generosity of Cox, who enjoyed the presence of young admirers about him. Given the status of the old man in the early Victorian art world, second only to that of Turner (who had died the previous year), his support must have had a strong effect on Whaite. It is not difficult to detect technical and stylistic elements in the young painter's works which reflected those of the Master. Furthermore, the presence of a group of other painters in the area, many of them from Manchester and Liverpool, intensified Clarence Whaite's enjoyment of working in Wales. Over the succeeding twenty years he travelled in England, Scotland, and as far as Italy to paint, as well as to other parts of Wales, but he always returned to the Conwy Valley and eventually set up home there. His meeting with David Cox put him in contact with a tradition of art about Wales which extended back through the eighteenth century. Whaite lived until 1912 not only to see parts of the Conwy Valley physically changed beyond recognition, but also to witness a change of comparable degree in the artistic life of Wales as a whole. He made a considerable contribution to that change, both by his painting and by his work in institutional development. His meeting with David Cox in 1852 not only marked a crucial moment in his own career, therefore, but can be understood as a symbolic moment of change in the wider context of Welsh art. Cox, like generations of English painters before him, had come to Wales as a visitor. Clarence Whaite, and others of his generation, came to stay. Their images and the development of their relationship with the culture of the country, its indigenous painters and intellectuals, would be an important factor in the emergence of a national art world in Wales in the period before the Great War.

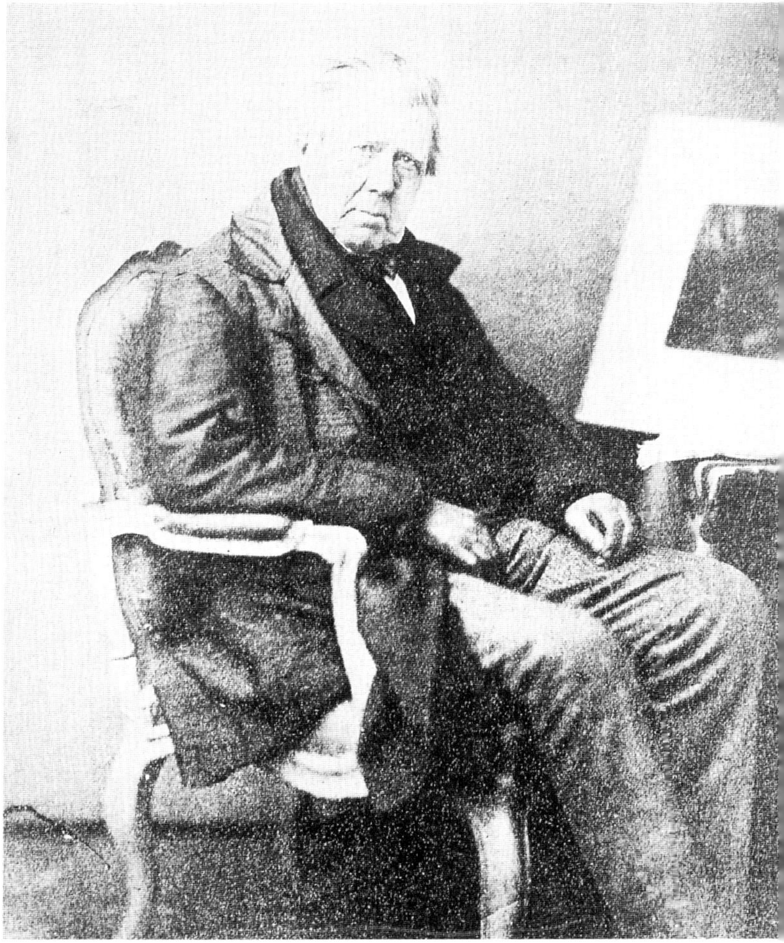

Unknown photographer, *David Cox*, c.1855.

1

The Conwy Valley and Betws-y-coed

Wenceslas Hollar,
Archbishop John Williams, 1642.

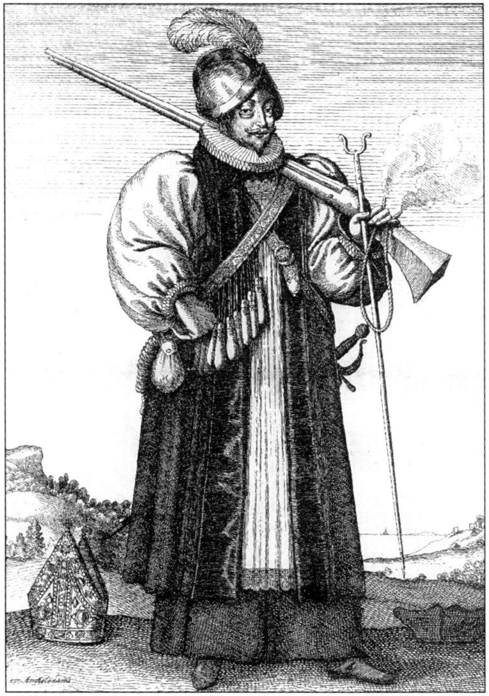

Conwy had been visited by artists from an early date.[6] The background to Wenceslas Hollar's engraving of *Archbishop John Williams*, made in 1642, showed the castle with Aberconwy and the land to the east side of the river, and is the earliest known topographical view of the area of a modern kind. It was taken exactly a century before the Buck brothers, the most productive of the early topographers, visited Conwy and struck inland to record Dolwyddelan Castle. They probably travelled up the river valley from the town to the tiny village of Betws-y-coed (about thirteen and a half miles to the south), where the river Llugwy converged with the Conwy. Even then Betws was an ancient site, marked by a medieval church and by a bridge, Pont y Pair, built - according to tradition - in 1468. A mile further up, the Conwy was joined by the Lledr, in the valley of which stood Dolwyddelan. It was reputed to have been the birthplace of Llywelyn Fawr, and guarded the valley, five miles to the west of Betws, with Moel Siabod looming behind. Most early depictions of north Wales concentrated on such antiquities, though generally on the Edwardian Castles. John Boydell, for instance, published a view of Conwy Castle in 1749. As the first publisher on a large scale of landscape

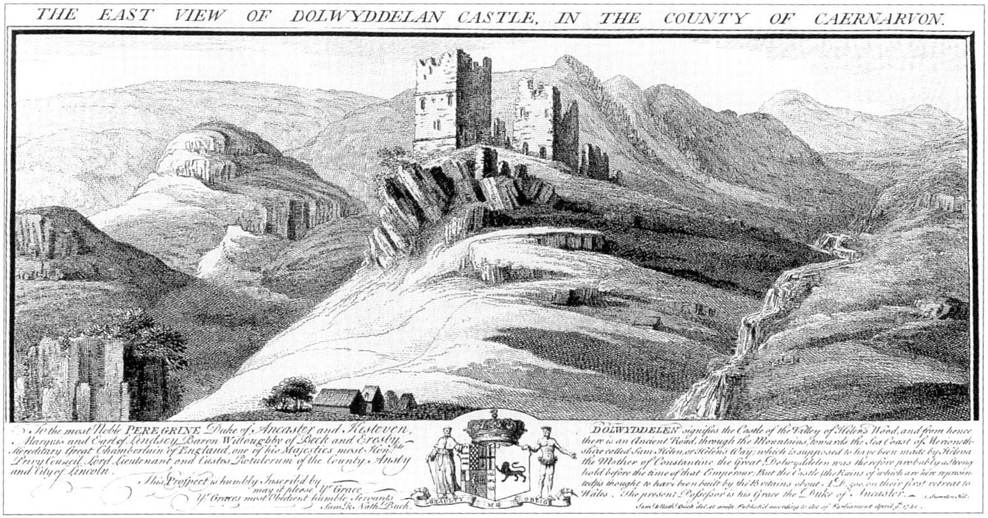

Left: Samuel and Nathaniel Buck, *The East View of Dolwyddelan Castle, in the County of Caernarvon*, 1742.

prints, Boydell contributed greatly to the emerging fashion for Wales in England, but he had no view of scenery in the Conwy Valley.[7] There was no castle at Betws and few early views taken in the immediate vicinity of the village survive. Whether the cataracts and falls of the area were frequented by travellers and painters who came to Snowdonia in the first half of the eighteenth century is unclear. John Dyer and, subsequently, Richard Wilson visited in that period, and Dyer certainly liked waterfalls. In 1728, he had 'a surprising escape on horseback, on a very narrow wooden bridge in North Wales, about fifty feet above rocks and a great torrent of water, which frightened the horse', but the precise location of this mishap is not recorded in the incomplete records of his travels.[8] Wilson worked nearby in Dyffryn Nantlle, but no view taken in the Conwy Valley has survived.

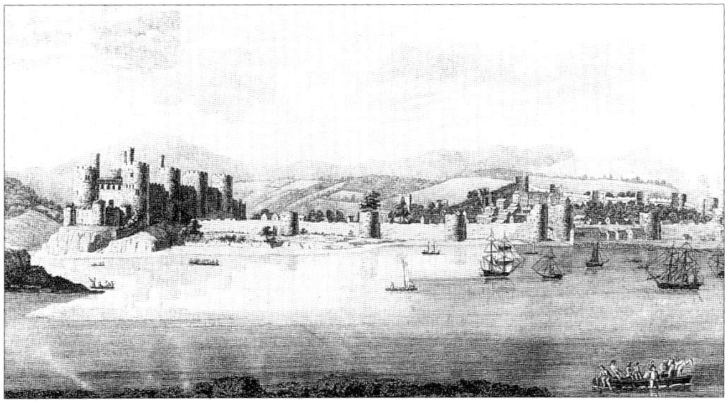

Below: John Boydell, *A West Prospect of Conway Castle, in Caernarvonshire*, 1749.

[6] A bird's-eye view drawing of Conwy Castle on a manuscript of c.1600, in the possession of the Marquess of Salisbury, is among the earliest surviving attempts to depict a particular Welsh site.

[7] John Boydell, *Castles and Mountainous Views in Wales* (London, 1749-50).

[8] Quoted in J.P.Hylton Dyer Longstaffe, 'John Dyer as a Painter', *Montgomeryshire Collections* (1878), p.401.

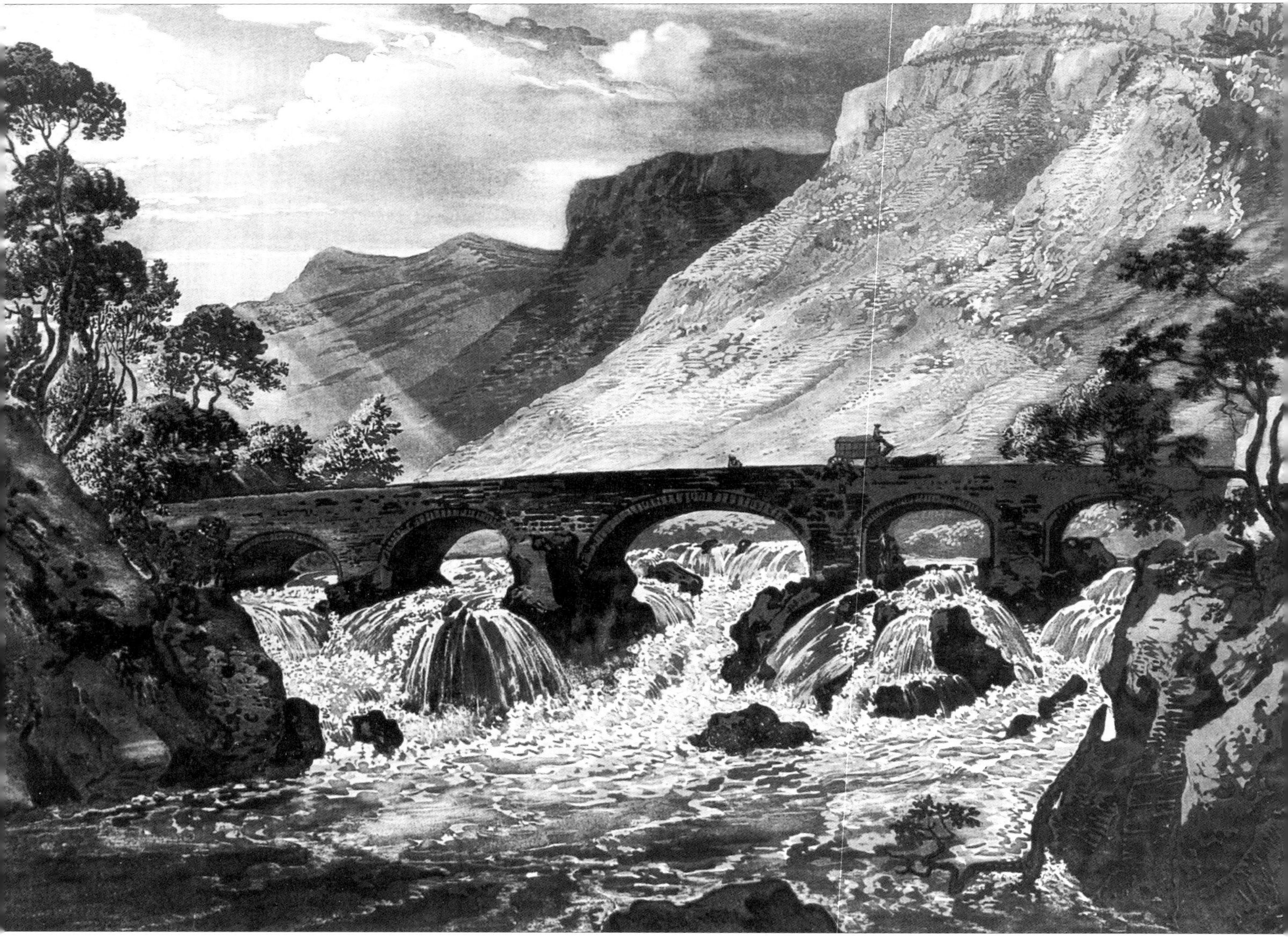

Paul Sandby, *Pont y Pair*, 1776.

By the 1770s interest in natural scenery for its own sake was the height of fashion. Edmund Burke is reputed to have had a high regard for the Conwy Valley[9] and both Welsh and English intellectuals among the *avant garde* began to visit. Sir Watkin Williams Wynn took Paul Sandby on tour, and his view of Pont y Pair with the river in spate and a dramatic shaft of light striking down through the clouds was published in the *XII Views in North Wales* in 1776. At about that date Thomas Pennant was in the area, and - as was his habit - he commented at length on the antiquities he saw. On this occasion, however, he was struck also by the natural beauty of the area. Pont y Pair was 'a most singular bridge' and 'The scenery beyond, of rocky mountains, fringed with woods, is very striking'.[10] Pennant's artist, Moses Griffith, made a fine, large drawing of the bridge, dated 1776. Proceeding up the river Llugwy, he visited Rhaiadr y Wennol and the unusual enthusiasm of his description of the scenery there impressed some later travellers who, using the *Tours in Wales* as a guidebook, had come to regard Pennant - however worthy - as rather dull:

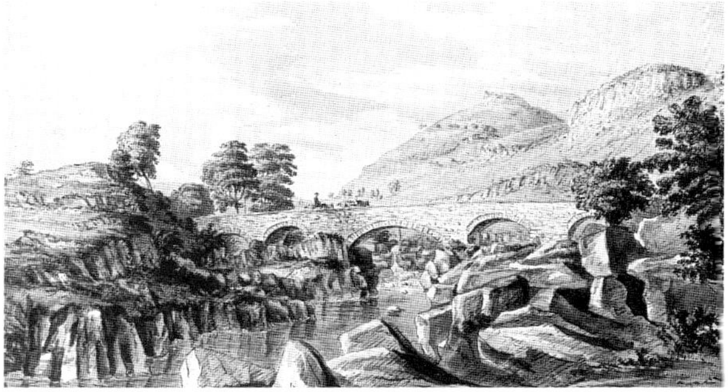

Moses Griffith,
Pont y Pair, 1776.
Reproduced in
colour on p.41.

> *'The river runs along a strait stony channel, for a considerable way, amidst narrow meadows, bounded by majestic Alpine scenery; then falls into an amazing hollow. The bottom is difficult of access; but when arrived at, exhibits a wonderful scene of mountain and precipice, shaded with trees, which fringe the top, and start even from the fissures of the sides.'*[11]

The publication in 1757 of Thomas Gray's poem, *The Last Bard*, had provided antiquarians with an additional reason to visit the area. Ultimately on the authority of the Gwydir Manuscripts,[12] Gray set the suicide of the mythical Bard in the Conwy Valley, and artists - irrespective of whether or not they had first-hand knowledge of the topography - set about painting the subject. Paul Sandby exhibited a picture in London in 1760, which almost certainly predated his first visit to Wales to see for himself. Even the Welshman Thomas Jones of Pencerrig, who painted his *Last Bard* in 1774, had probably never been to the Conwy Valley. Similarly, Philippe de Loutherbourg could not have claimed first hand experience when his famous bardic image was published in Edward Jones's *Musical and*

[9] Burke's admiration for the area was reported by William Hall, *David Cox, Artist. A Biography* (London, 1881), p.80.

[10] Thomas Pennant, *Tours in Wales*, ed.John Rhys (London, 1883), II, p.292.

[11] Ibid., p.296-7. Pennant's reference to the alpine nature of the scenery was based on direct experience as he had travelled through Switzerland.

[12] Gray's immediate source was Thomas Carte's *General History of England*. For the use of the Bard legend in visual culture, see Peter Lord, 'The Bard - Celticism and Visual Culture', *Gwenllian - Essays on Visual Culture* (Llandysul, 1994), pp.103-128.

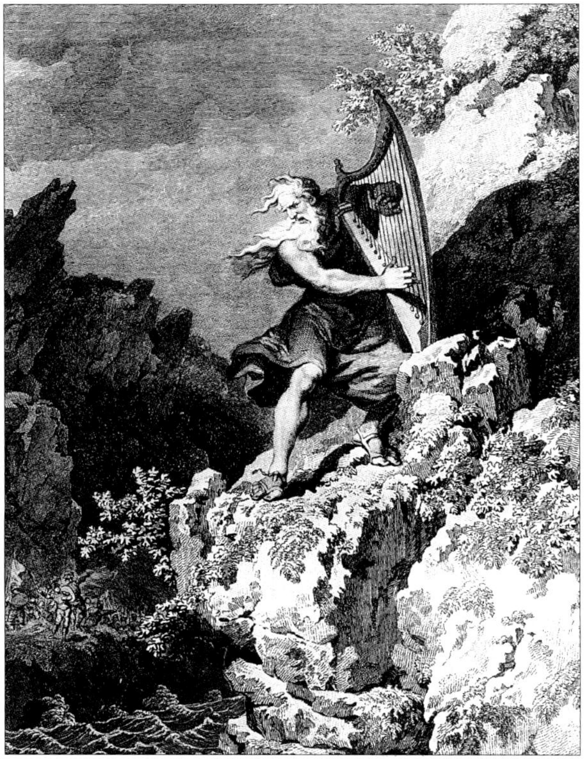

Philippe de Loutherbourg,
The Last Bard, 1784.

Poetical Relicks of the Welsh Bards in 1784. However, two years later he came on a Welsh tour which included a visit to waterfalls in the Conwy Valley. In his *Cataract on the Llugwy* he portrayed himself and his wife, suitably impressed by the boiling waters below, to which they were led by primitive descendents of the Ancient Britons:

> *'After we had struck out of the high road, we came to a hovel, not unlike one of those of Oonalashka, as delineated in Cook's Voyages, where we found a man and his daughter, who conducted us to the spot. By this man we were informed, that it was the place to which the devil conveys the souls of bad stewards...'* [13]

The search for the exact location of the bardic suicide fascinated travellers, among them the Welsh painter Edward Pugh, who felt he had found it in Craig Lwyd. Pugh believed that 'Mr Gray... without doubt meant no other rock than some of those near Pont y Pandy, as there are no others from Llyn Conwy to the Irish Sea that are so consistent with his description'.[14] Pugh was clearly under the misapprehension that the poet had visited the place.

By the time of de Loutherbourg's visit, therefore, Betws-y-coed was on the tourist route, though not yet a destination. Many early visitors had approached the village from the north, entering Wales through Chester and sometimes being forced to submit to the extortionate rates extracted by the notorious ferrymen who carried them across the Conwy at the estuary. They usually travelled up the river valley on the Caernarfonshire side through Trefriw to Gwydir, the ancient house built for Sir John Wynn. Nearby they could cross the famous bridge, which they were informed (probably erroneously) was the work of Inigo Jones, and put up for the night in Llanrwst. Joseph Cradock took this route

[13]Philippe de Loutherbourg, *Romantic and Picturesque Scenery in England and Wales* (London, 1805), no pagination. The text was bilingual in English and French although the extent to which the book was distributed in French-speaking countries is not clear.

[14]Edward Pugh, *Cambria Depicta* (London, 1816), p.416.

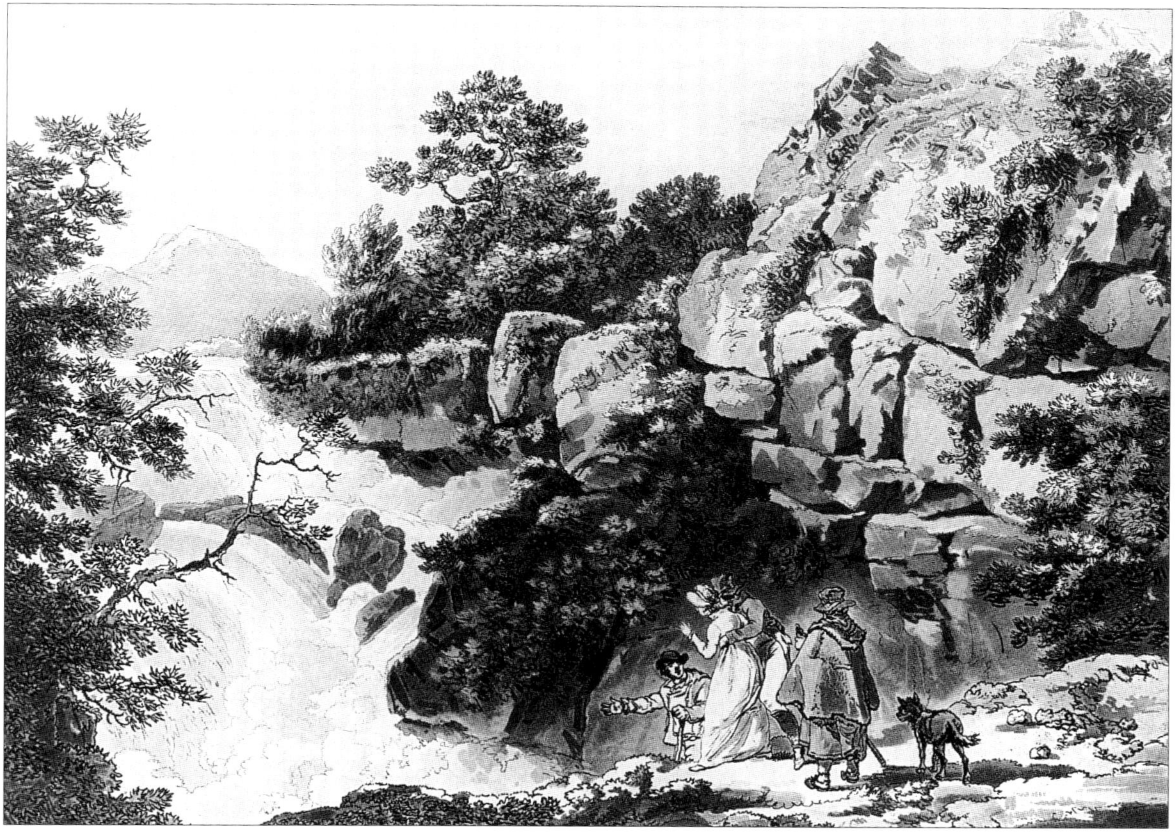

Philippe de Loutherbourg, *Cateract or the Llugwy*, 1806.

and in one of his *Letters from Snowdonia*, published in 1770, he reported elegantly that 'The town of Llanrwst is about ten miles distant from Conway; the road to it leads through a beautiful little vale, environed by mountains that scale the heavens.'[15] Cradock's tour map, published in a second volume in 1777, did not mention Betws by name, but the ancient church of Saint Garmon was marked as the southernmost point of the road from Conwy.[16] However, before long, visitors would pass through Betws and on to Bangor via Capel Curig, many of them pausing to make an excursion to Dolwyddelan. Some visitors made the circular trip in the other direction, in order first to experience the famous

[15]Joseph Cradock, *Letters from Snowdonia* (London, 1770), Letter IV, p.23. Cradock believed that Wales had 'a kind of hereditory claim on me', presumably because of his name, a corruption of Caradog.

[16]Joseph Cradock, *An account of some of the most Romantic Parts of North Wales* (London, 1777).

Henry Thompson, *Richard Pennant, Lord Penrhyn*, c.1800.

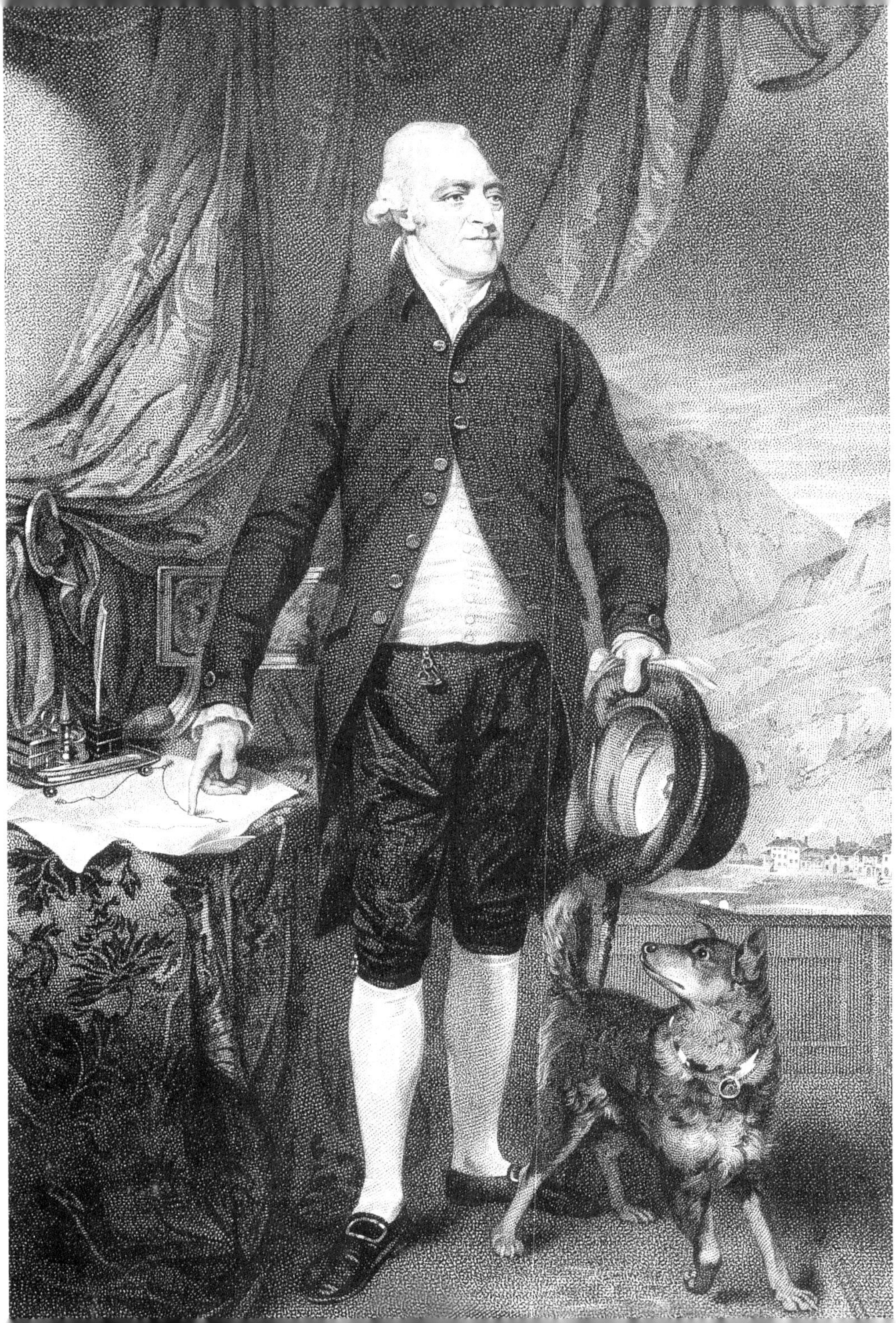

[17]C.D.R.Jones and D.Parry, *Telford in the Dee Valley* (Mold, 1989), p.23.

[18]Edward Pugh, op.cit., p.111.

[19]Henry Wigstead, *Remarks on a Tour to North and South Wales in the year 1797* (London, 1800), p.22. Müller referred to Betws as the 'English Switzerland', see N.Neal Solly, *A Memoir of the Life of W.J.Müller* (London, 1875), p.22.

hazards of Penmaenmawr on their way along the north coast to Bangor. A more direct inland route through Betws from Shrewsbury was gradually improved in the years after 1779. Robert Lawrence, a Shrewsbury innkeeper, encouraged the building of inns along the road in order to attract trade away from Chester, and by 1787 the new route to Holyhead was marked on published maps.[17] In 1791-2 Lord Penrhyn built a new section of road where the route crossed his land, and at Capel Curig opened a hotel. The route became of greater strategic importance for the English after the Act of Union with Ireland in 1800, and the Royal Hotel flourished. It had been built in modern style from designs by Wyatt, including a castellated Gothic bay, and soon it had 'no less than twelve handsome rooms added to it'.[18] The Royal Hotel became a stopping point for many travellers entering or leaving the Betws area in the early nineteenth century. In Henry Thompson's fine portrait, Lord Penrhyn was portrayed standing before the mountains, his new hotel in their shadow, pointing to the location on a map. Henry Wigstead went that way in 1797 with Thomas Rowlandson, and in his account of the place made a comparison with Switzerland which would become proverbial in the mid-nineteenth century:

> *'From hence [Cernioge] to Llanrwst, a most sublime extent of scenery unveils itself, the most luxuriant vale, embracing every where the basis of cloud-capped mountains, constitutes the general feature. We, in contemplating this beautiful burst, considered it as comparable to any of the most admired situations in Switzerland, or in the environs of Tivoli.'*[19]

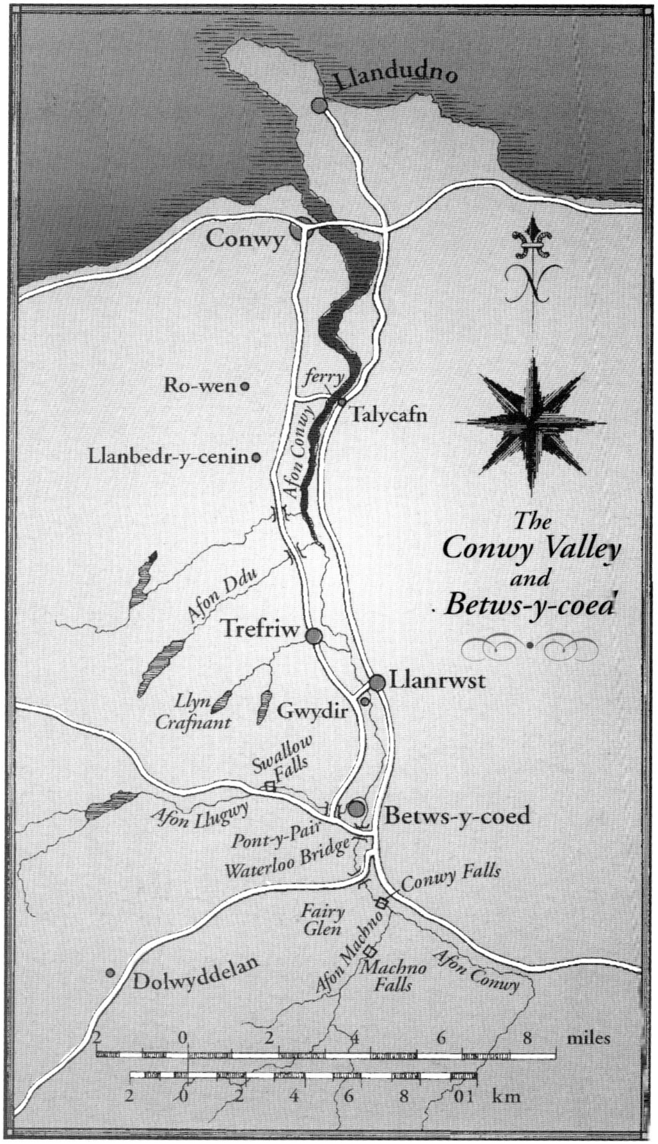

The area was becoming fashionable, and attracted favourable comment in an increasing number of guide books. Typical of them was *The Beauties of England and Wales*, published in 1812, in which the Rev.J.Evans remarked that:

> *'... the late Lord Penrhyn erected, for the accomodation of the public, a handsome inn; so that travellers through this dreary region may now meet with good entertainment, and very excellent lodging. Since this inn and hotel has been occupied, it has become a fashionable resort. During the summer months, numerous genteel families, and others, make a temporary residence at Capel Cerrig, to enjoy the numerous diversified and interesting walks and rides, amidst the magnificent objects of the surrounding scenery.'*[20]

Richard Colt Hoare,
The Inn at Capel Curig, 1810.

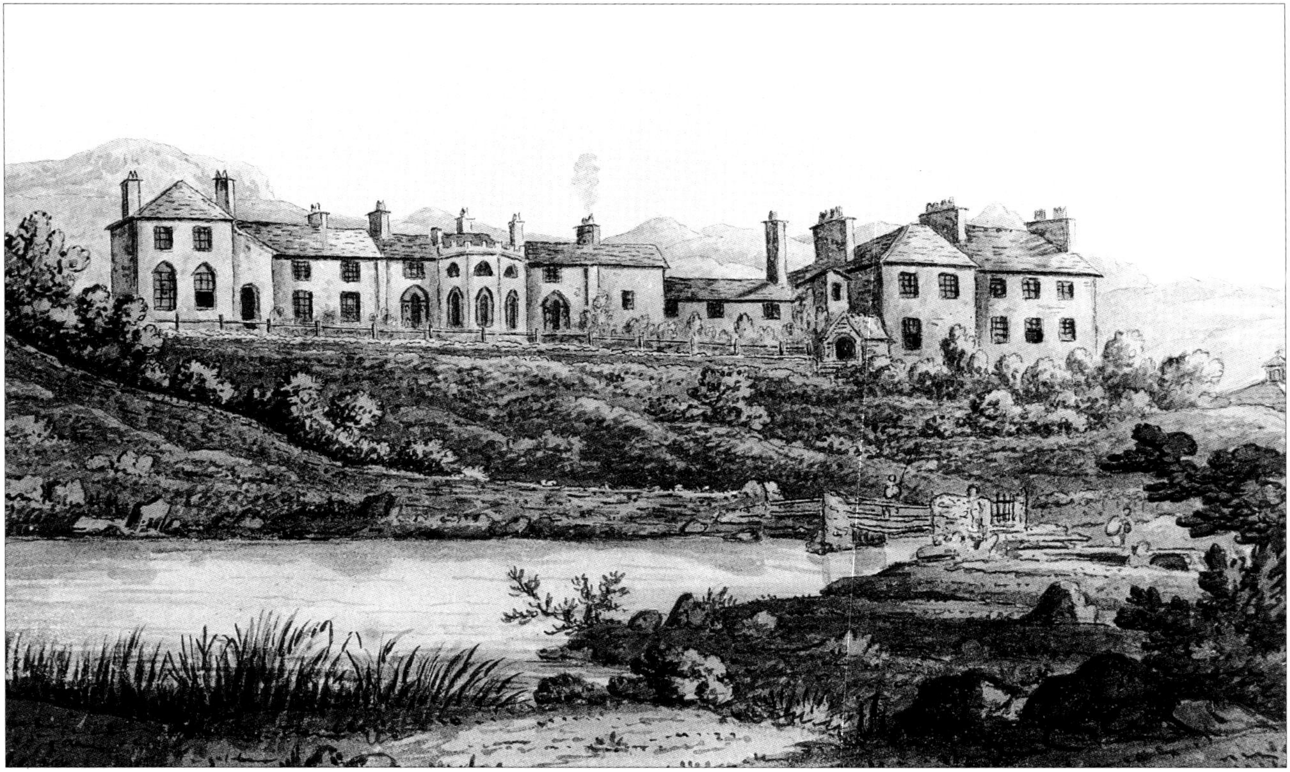

From 1808, mail coaches ran regularly but the road stood in need of further improvement and in 1811 the engineer Thomas Telford submitted a report commissioned by Parliament. In 1815 work commenced under his direction and the Betws section was among the first to be rebuilt. The opening up of the village to the world was completed by the construction of the Waterloo Bridge over the Conwy, opened in 1816, on whose ironwork the symbols of the four nations of the United Kingdom were cast.

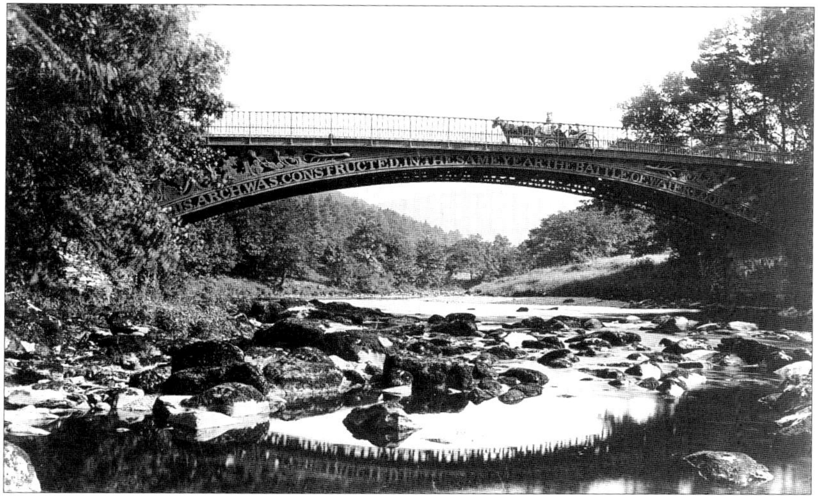

Unknown photographer,
The Waterloo Bridge,
c.1880.

The expanding reputation of the Betws area in England was the result not only of its strategic position on the route through Snowdonia from the east but also to developments in aesthetics in the English art world which made its particular combination of scenic features fashionable. As we have seen, early visitors were motivated by antiquarian ideas as much as by a love of the visual quality of the landscape, and many of their products were strictly topographical - that is to say, concerned with recording the appearance of a place of interest with almost a map-making objectivity. However, towards the end of the eighteenth century the use of landscape imagery as a vehicle for the expression of theories about the nature of beauty and its effect on human emotions took hold. Betws itself had not been an ideal site for those in search of the sublime experience of 'delicious terror' in the mountains, but the village and the river valleys surrounding it could offer much to meet William Gilpin's requirements for the picturesque. Gilpin's *Observations on the River Wye*, written in 1770, and his other manuscripts had a profound influence on a small but influential circle of intellectuals even before they were available in print, years later. He came to Conwy in 1773 but unfortunately was in such haste that he

[20]Rev.J.Evans, *The Beauties of England and Wales* (London, 1812), North Wales p.460. Evans' use of the word 'dreary' was complimentary, meaning likely to inspire feelings of melancholy, rather than perjorative, in the modern sense.

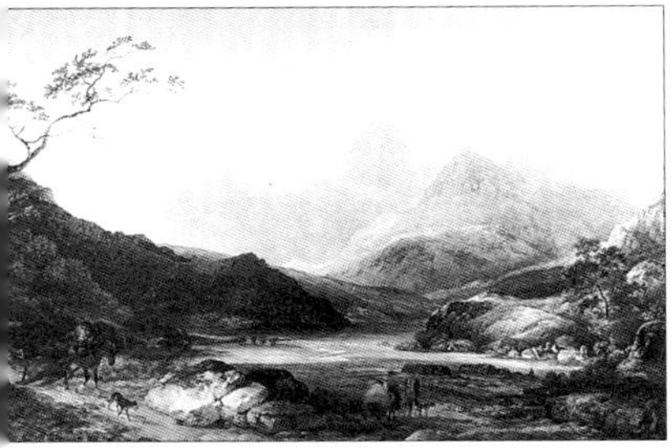

Philippe de Loutherbourg, *Snowdon from Capel Curig*, 1787. Reproduced in colour on p.41.

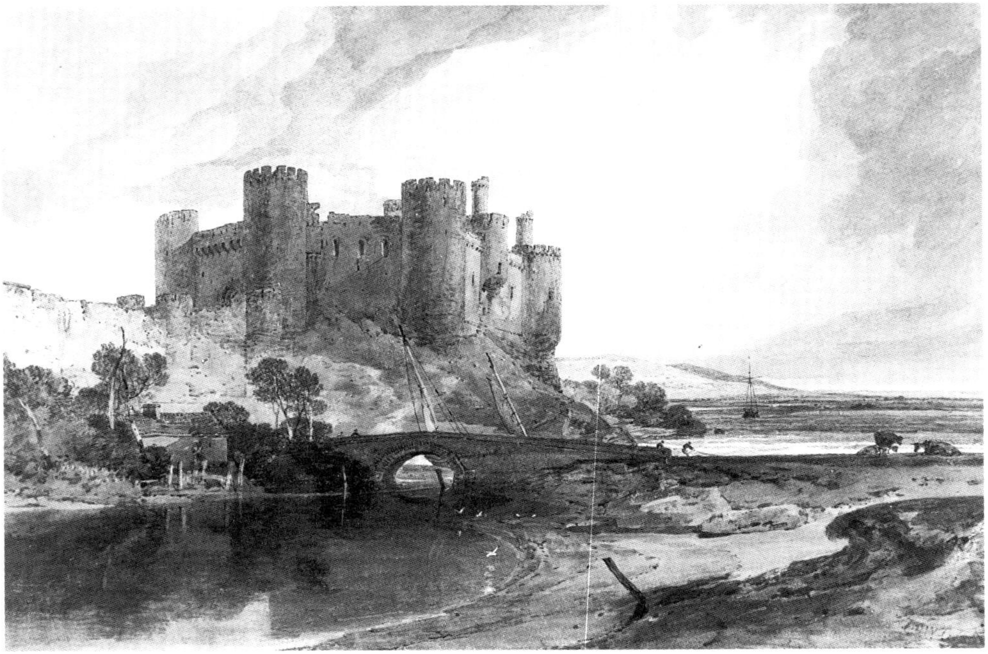

J.M.W.Turner, drawing for *Conway Castle*, 1802.

did no more than glance up the river as he crossed the estuary in a ferry boat. Nevertheless, he was assured by others that 'The woods, and rocks and sweeping mountains... were equal to any thing we could see in Wales', information which Gilpin passed on to his readers.[21] He proceeded speedily to Anglesey, with which he was not impressed, but it did not take long for painters and aesthetes to discover in the Conwy Valley the combination of various features which Gilpin admired in other places.

In the *fin de siècle* period, watercolour became a fashionable medium for the exploration of the new aesthetics. A number of English artists, linked together by a complicated network of teacher-pupil relationships and personal friendships, travelled to landscapes with desirable characteristics all over the British Isles and continental Europe. In 1804 many of the new school of painters came together as the Society of Painters in Water Colours, and the catalogues of the first twenty years of their exhibitions reveal that

[21] William Gilpin, *Observations... on several parts of North Wales* (London, 1809) p.123.

north Wales was by far the most important site for their activities. In the first exhibition in 1805 there were fifty-two Welsh views, compared with ten from Scotland, nineteen from Yorkshire and one from the Lake District of Cumbria. Subsequently, the English Lake District increased significantly in popularity but only in three years did Cumbrian views outnumber those from Wales. Almost all the English watercolourists of the period came to Snowdonia on their Welsh tours, and most visited the Conwy Valley.

Although he was young and little known at the time, ultimately the most famous of all the English artists who came to Snowdonia was J.M.W.Turner. It was in Wales, initially under the strong influence of Richard Wilson, that he laid the foundations of his art. In 1794, on his first visit to the north, Turner got no further west than Llangollen, but in 1798 he passed through Betws-y-coed. The following year, Turner returned to produce a large body of work which he developed in the studio when he got back to London. The results were exhibited over a period of several years after his visit. Among his rivals in London at this period was de Loutherbourg, who exhibited magnificent atmospheric mountain landscapes painted in oils in the studio but based on drawings done on the spot. The north Wales works of the two artists showed marked parallels. De Loutherbourg exhibited a *View of Conway Castle from the Ferry* at the Royal Academy in 1801, for instance, a picture which was matched by Turner's *Conway Castle* of 1802.[22] Again, like his rival, it is clear that Turner's experience of the Conwy Valley and the continuing vogue for its supposed historical associations led him to develop ideas for a Bardic picture. However, they were not carried through, and the large-scale historical subject which emerged, based on his Welsh experience, was the *Dolbadarn Castle*, presented as his Royal Academy diploma work in 1802.

Welsh painters made little direct impact on the English art world early in the nineteenth century. The work of Thomas Jones of Pencerrig has come into vogue in the late twentieth century, but in his lifetime he was regarded as a very minor figure and his pictures were not widely exhibited. Moses Griffith was known only as Thomas Pennant's visual emanuensis. Edward Pugh moved on the periphery of fashionable art circles in London, where he was well known to Boydell, and he provided some original drawings which were published in Henry Wigstead's account of his Welsh tour. Nevertheless, a number of

[22]Not shown at RA. For the picture and its preparatory drawings, see Andrew Wilton, *Turner in Wales* (Llandudno, 1984), pp.30, 71.

better-known English artists had been encouraged in their interest in Wales by personal acquaintance with Welsh people. John Warwick Smith had shared lodgings with Thomas Jones in Italy, where he was presumably informed about the beauties of his friend's native country. Jones was a pupil of Richard Wilson, which must have given his recommendation an added authority. Certainly, Smith became the most enthusiastic of all Welsh tourists, visiting at least a dozen times between 1784 and 1806. His most important tour was that of 1792, when he conducted Julius Caesar Ibbetson and Robert Fulke Greville around the country, like a *cicerone* in Rome. Among Thomas Jones's contemporaries in Wilson's studio in 1763 had been Joseph Farington. Unlike Jones, Farington became a highly influential figure in the London art world, sought out by young painters for his support. For instance, on his return to London from Wales in 1798, Turner visited Farington, who noted in his diary that 'William Turner called on me. He has been in South and North Wales this summer - alone and on horseback - out 7 weeks. Much rain but better effects - one clear day and Snowdon appeared green and unpicturesque to the top'.[23] Farington's first love was the English Lake District but he came to Wales himself on several occasions in the 1790s. In 1801 the poet

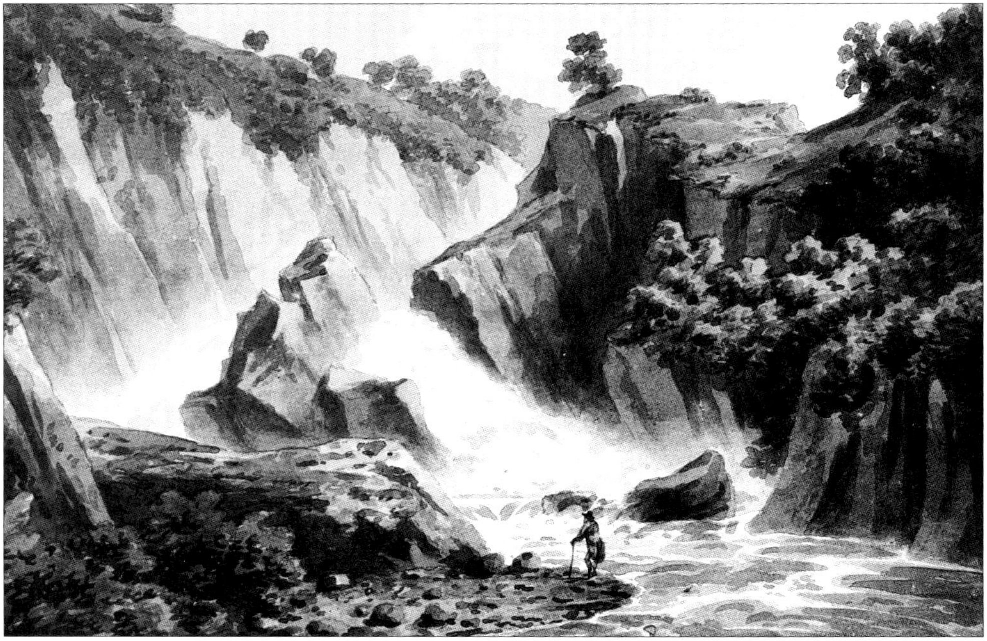

John Warwick Smith, *The Falls on the Conway River*, 1790.

[23]Farington's diary for 26 September 1798, quoted in Wilton, *ibid.*, p.52.

[24]Rogers to Gilpin, 12 January 1801, quoted in C.P.Barbier, *Samuel Rogers and William Gilpin. Their Friendship and Correspondence* (London, 1959), p.57.

[25]See Sydney Kitson, *The Life of John Sell Cotman* (London, 1937).

Samuel Rogers met him by chance in Conwy, in the company of his friend George Beaumont. He reported that 'Their port-folios were full of rocks & cateracts & ruin'd Castles'.[24] Between 1799 and 1806 Sir George took Benarth House as a summer base for his explorations of the Conwy Valley. Like Farington, Beaumont's importance was less as a painter than as an arbiter of taste in the London art world and as a collector. Nevertheless, he exhibited Welsh views at the Academy between 1804 and 1811. His temporary residence in the Conwy Valley attracted other artists. Cotman seems to have stayed with him and it has been suggested that it was at Benarth that he met Girtin, who would have a considerable influence on his work.[25] Cotman made a second visit to the area in 1802, bringing with him Paul Sandby Munn, who exhibited drawings based on this experience for several years. John Varley, another influential figure in this extensive network of English artists, made his first Welsh tour in either 1798 or 1799 with George Arnald, and returned several times. While in Wales he met, among others, William Havell and Joshua Cristall, who painted not only the landscape but also made portraits in which the common people of the area emerged not as stereotypical peasants but as individual personalities.

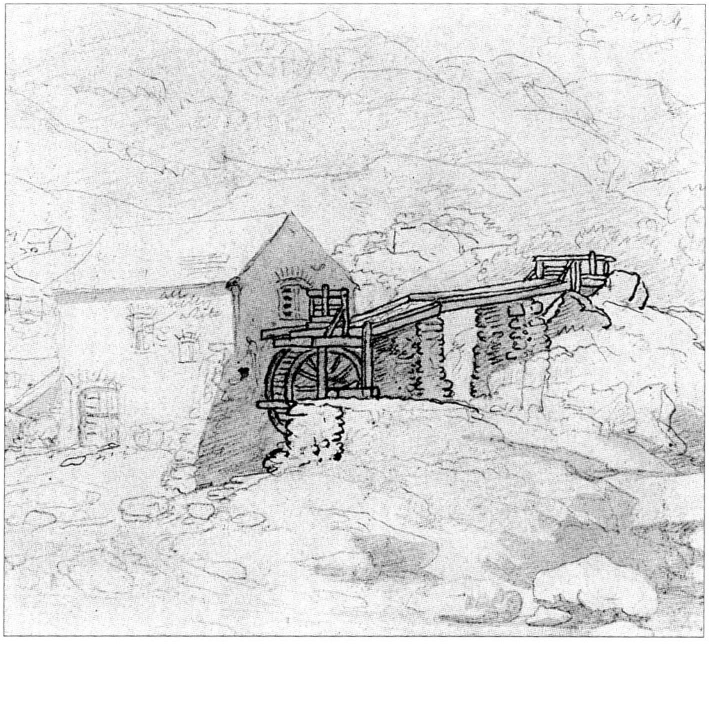

Joseph Farington, *Trefriw*, 1800.

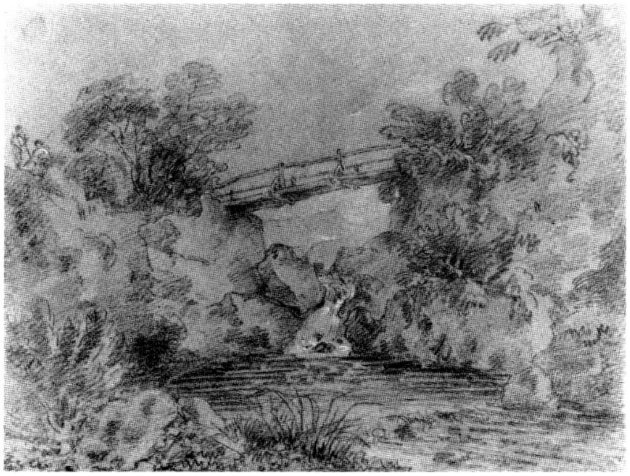

George Beaumont, *Bridge over a Pool at Llanrwst*, c.1805.

Joshua Cristall,
Girl with a Pitcher,
1831.

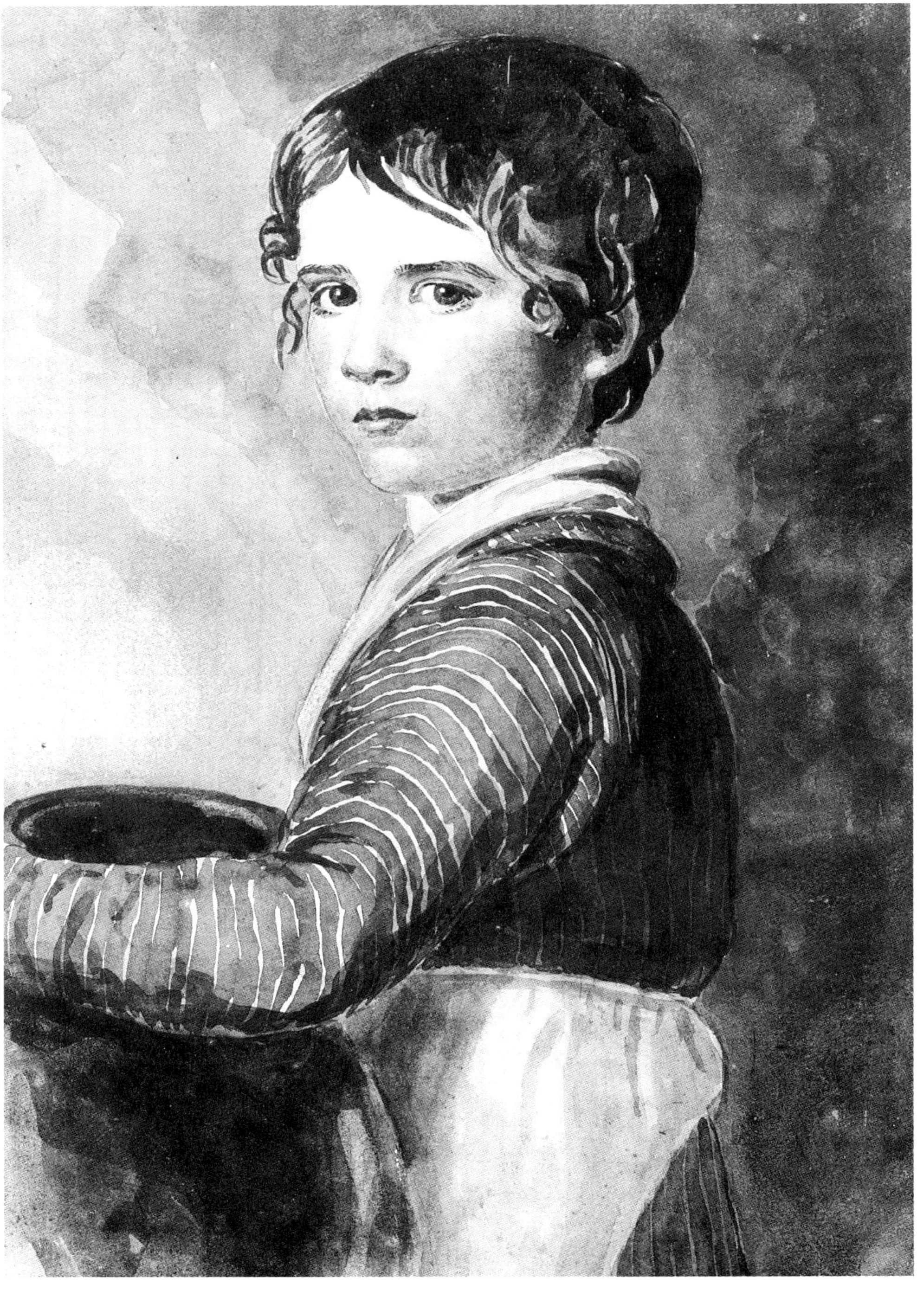

Edward Pugh's main contribution to the English art world came in the form of his *Cambria Depicta*, a volume that he was initially encouraged to write by Boydell and which was published posthumously in 1816. It was intended as a guide book for foreign artists on tour and certainly helped to sustain the interest of outsiders in Wales in the early nineteenth century. The author visited Betws at least twice during the nine years in which he researched and prepared drawings for the work, and - like Pennant - was particularly impressed by Rhaiadr y Wennol, 'a mighty torrent rushing down a precipice about eighty or a hundred feet high, between two wood-covered rocks; exhibiting, in my estimation, subject for a noble picture'.[26]

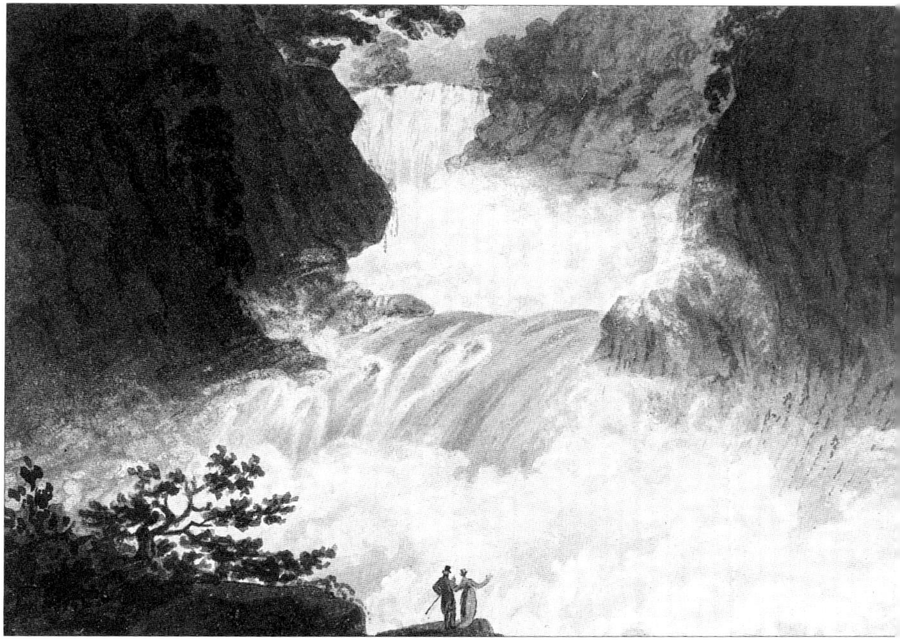

Edward Pugh, *Rhaiadr y Wennol*, drawing for *Cambria Depicta*, 1816.

Pugh's volume was published shortly before another Welsh artist, Hugh Hughes, began work on his book of wood engravings, *The Beauties of Cambria*. Hughes was certainly the earliest Welsh painter to work regularly in the Conwy Valley, because of his strong family connection with the area. He was born at Llandudno but his mother's family home was Y Meddiant, Glan Conwy, where he spent time as a child and which he later came to regard as his family home. He engraved many of the blocks for *The Beauties of Cambria* in the house. Among them was Pont y Pair, published with the first part of the volume in 1819. In his diary for 5 July of that year Hughes recorded his impressions of a ride along the banks of the Conwy near Llanrwst at six o'clock in the morning:

> *'The serenity of the atmosphere this morning, with the brightness of the sun shining nearly horizontal between still heavy clouds upon the hills and fields recently washed with heavy rain, and the stillness [and] crystaline brightness of the gliding stream made the meanest object appear magnificent and the magnificence inexpressibly grand and awful.'*

[26] Pugh, op.cit., p.112.

Unfortunately, Hughes had nothing to say of Betws in his diary, although he passed through it on several occasions and he certainly worked there, since his first oil painting exhibited in London was a Betws view, *The Miners' Bridge, North Wales*. This site, where a wooden bridge had been thrown over the turbulent waters of the river to facilitate the journey of miners to their work, would subsequently become one of the most popular in the area with painters and photographers.

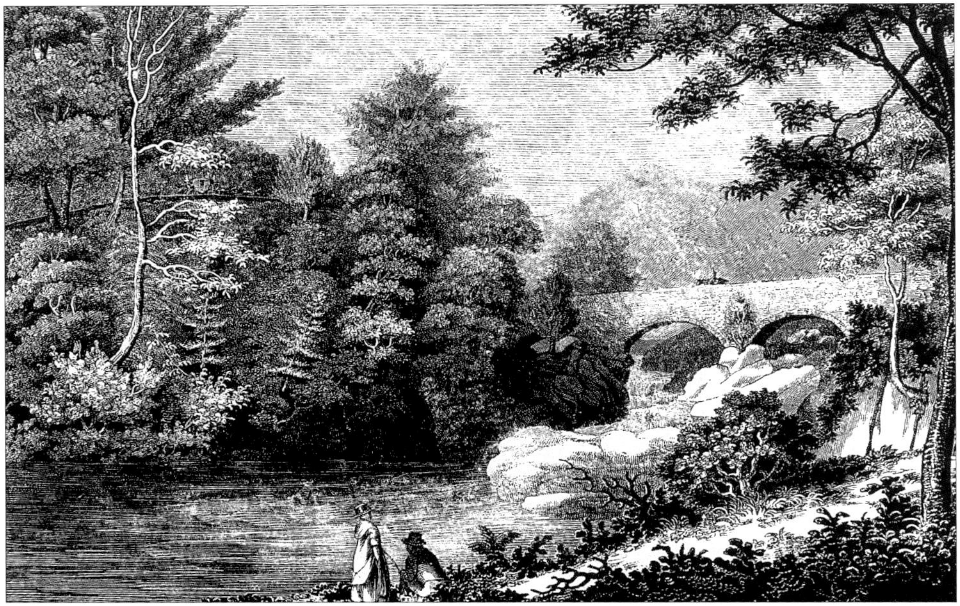

Hugh Hughes,
Pont y Pair, from
The Beauties of Cambria,
1819-23.

The Beauties of Cambria established a considerable reputation for Hughes as a wood engraver, both in London and in Wales. While he was working on the book, he established relationships with printers throughout Wales, enabling them to produce illustrated books and pamphlets in larger numbers than before. The earliest of these relationships was formed with John Jones of Trefriw, who subsequently moved his business to Llanrwst. By the early 1830s John Jones was by far the largest producer of popular illustrated prints in Wales. The activities of Hughes and Jones are a reminder that the reality of the indigenous culture in towns such as Llanrwst was rather different from that perpetuated in the images of Cambria presented by visiting artists in London exhibitions, whether they were de Loutherbourg's Ancient Britons or the picturesque peasants of the members of the Society of Painters in Water Colours. A modern culture of both the printed word (in the Welsh language) and the printed image was developing rapidly, supported by a thinking middle class, which was of little interest to English painters. Hugh Hughes was unusual by virtue of the fact that he was in touch not only with this energetic indigenous culture, but also, in a peripheral way, with the London art world. When he wrote his description of the Conwy Valley, Hughes had been living in London

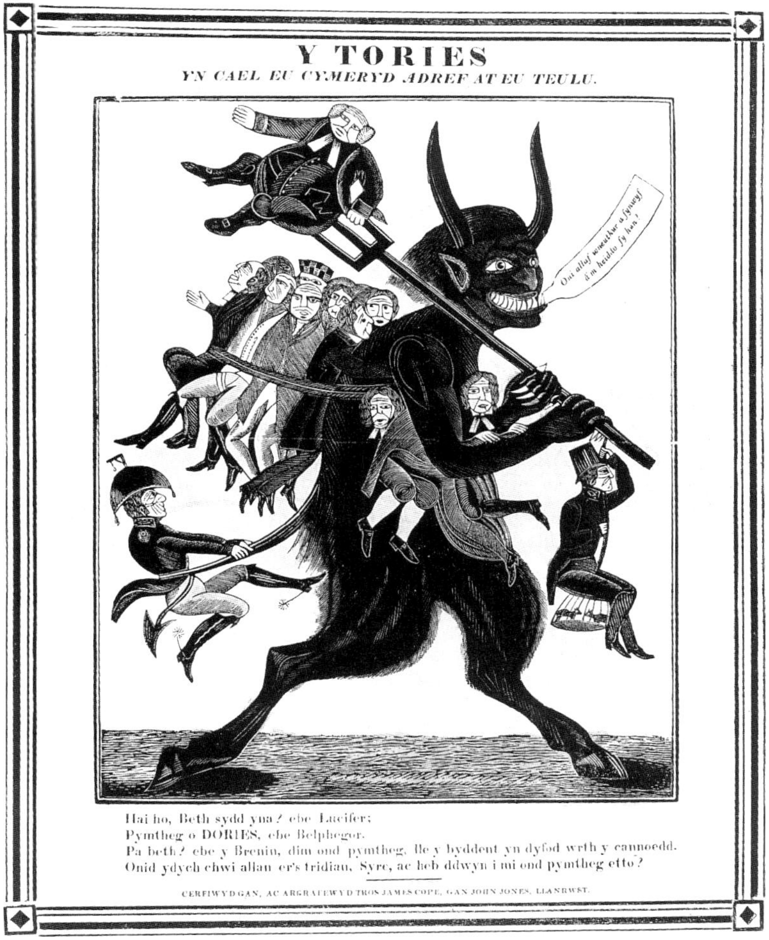

James Cope, *Y Tories*, political cartoon published by John Jones, Llanrwst, c.1832-42.

for six years, and his comments reflected an awareness of the language of high-art aesthetics in the period. In general, this owed more to his familiarity with art literature and exhibitions than to direct contact with English artists and intellectuals. Nevertheless, in 1827, when he ventured to show his *Miners' Bridge, North Wales*, at the Suffolk Street gallery of the Royal Society of British Artists, he was engraving views for John Glover, the first treasurer of the Society, who had worked in north Wales. Furthermore, in the same year, Hughes was engaged to engrave views of Hereford drawn by David Cox.[27]

[27]Hughes was in direct contact with Glover in respect of his commission. William Owen Pughe saw the distinguished English painter in Hughes's studio and noted the event in his diary. The engravings after drawings by Cox were commissioned to illustrate W.J.Rees, *The Hereford Guide* (Hereford, 1827). In this case it is unclear whether or not the two men met. For these commissions, see Peter Lord, *Hugh Hughes, Arlunydd Gwlad* (Llandysul, 1995), pp.144, 151, 156, and for Hughes's involvement with John Jones and the development of illustrated popular prints, see Peter Lord, *Words with Pictures, Images of Wales and Welsh Images in the Popular Press, 1640-1860* (Aberystwyth, 1995).

2

David Cox and the Origins of the Artists' Colony

In 1836 what would become the most influential illustrated guidebook to Wales in the middle of the nineteenth century was published. Thomas Roscoe's *Wanderings and Excursions in North Wales* has been described as 'the pinnacle of design and reproductive engraving in England, alongside the illustrative work of Turner and his engravers'.[28] In his book Roscoe correctly observed that the Conwy Valley was a place for artists, one of whom he saw at Llanrwst, 'probably desirous of fame... studiously portraying the enchanting objects around'.[29] The flow of already well-known visitors had not abated since the turn of the century. In 1833 the Bristol painter William James Müller visited for the first time with Skinner, Prout and Jackson, staying two nights at Betws and Capel Curig. Samuel Palmer was in the area three years later, painting magnificant romantic watercolours of Conwy and other sites. Thomas Roscoe's *Wanderings and Excursions in North Wales* was illustrated by several artists of such stature, including George Cattermole and Thomas Creswick, but the main contributor was David Cox. Little is known of the genesis of Roscoe's book, and in particular of whether Cox was involved at a deeper level than simply as illustrator. However, among Cox's half dozen images of the Betws area, scattered through the text, was the *Vale of the Llugwy*, which showed a woman blowing a cow's horn to summon the workers. This 'singular custom' was also described by Roscoe, which suggests a close co-operation between author and illustrator.[30]

[28] Stephen Wildman, *David Cox* (Birmingham, 1983), p.64. Thomas Roscoe's *Wanderings and Excursions in North Wales* (London, 1836), was followed in 1837 by a guide to south Wales by the same author. The volumes were issued in parts, chapter by chapter. Thomas Roscoe (1791-1871) was the fifth son of William Roscoe of Liverpool, first patron of John Gibson (who was born at Gyffin, near Conwy).

[29] Roscoe, ibid., 1844 edition, p.200.

[30] Ibid.

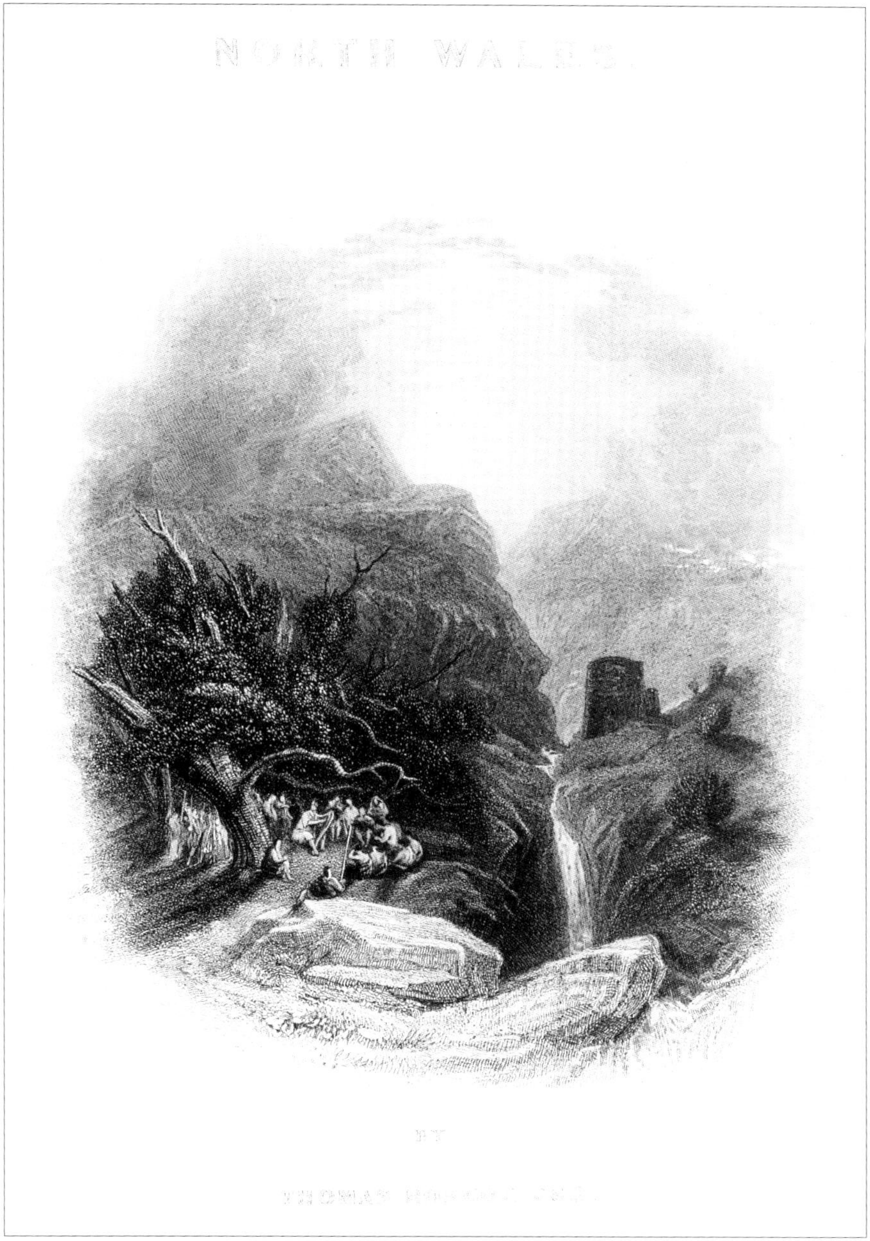

Thomas Roscoe, Frontis to *Wanderings and Excursions in North Wales*, 1836.

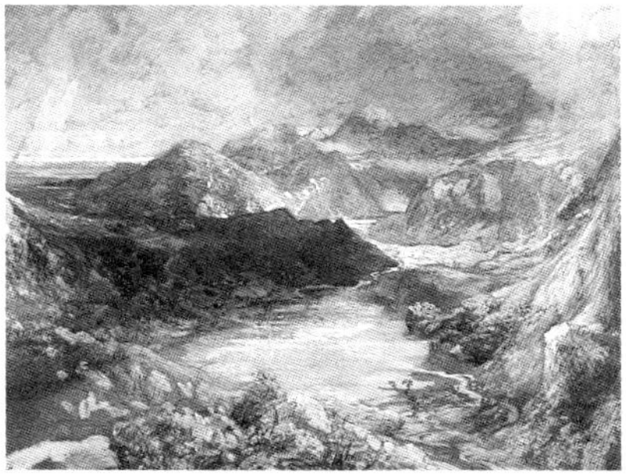

Samuel Palmer, *Llyn Gwynedd*, c.1835.
Reproduced in colour on p.42.

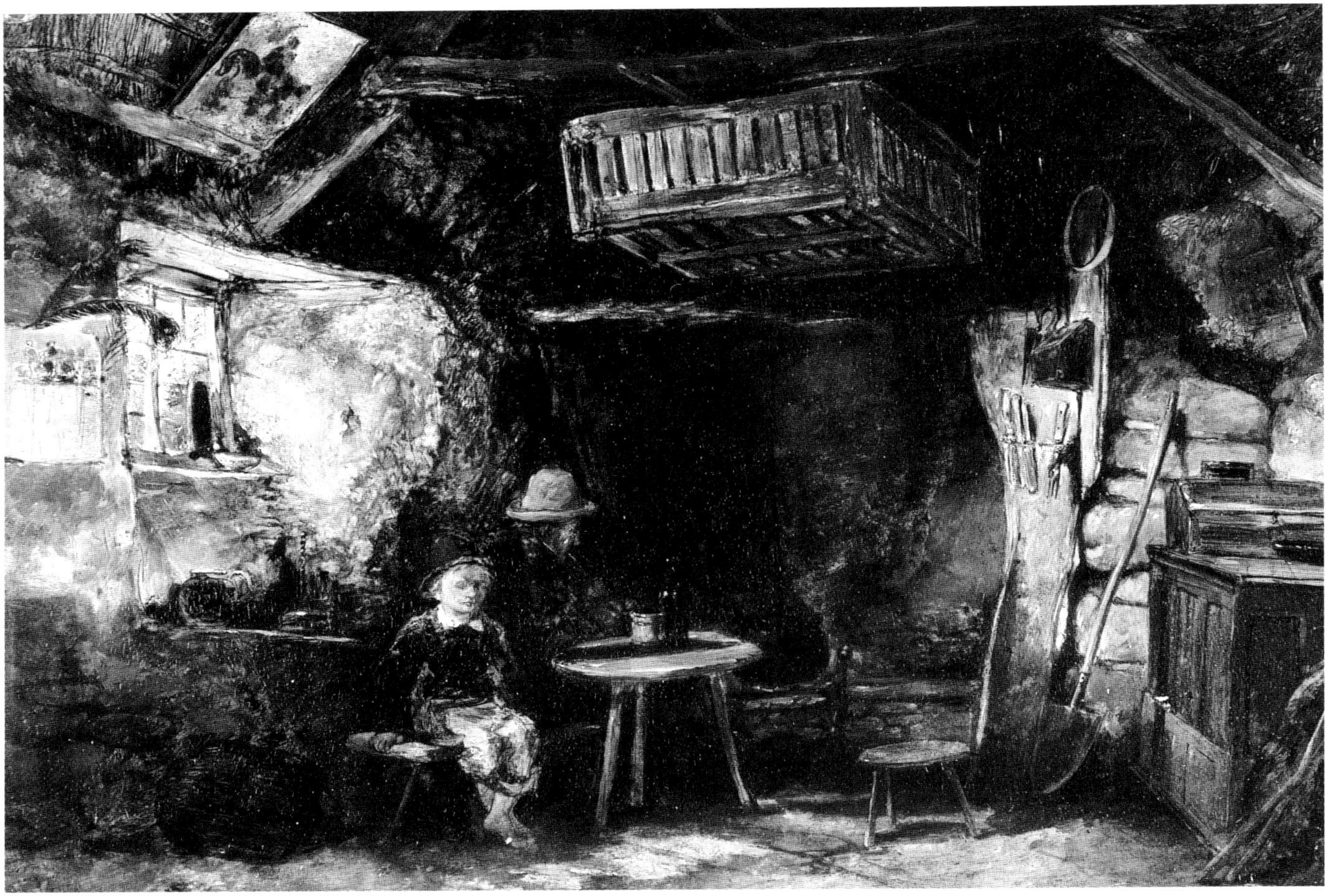

William James Müller,
Interior of a Welsh Cottage,
c.1843.

David Cox had first come to Wales in 1805 on a tour with Charles Barber, the son of his teacher in Birmingham, and returned the following year. He soon became a part of the network of English landscape painters familiar with the country. From among them, he considered asking Glover or Havell to teach him, but settled on John Varley. He made frequent visits to Wales over the first thirty years of his career and must have passed through Betws on several occasions.[31] However, he seems to have paid it little particular attention and his list of exhibits at the Society of Painters in Water Colours in London suggest that Roscoe's commission to illustrate the *Wanderings and Excursions* may have

[31]In 1834, for instance, he exhibited *Near Cernioge, North Wales*, at the Society of Painters in Water Colours. The list of his exhibits at the Society is given in N.Neal Solly, *Memoir of the Life of David Cox* (London, 1873), Appendix I.

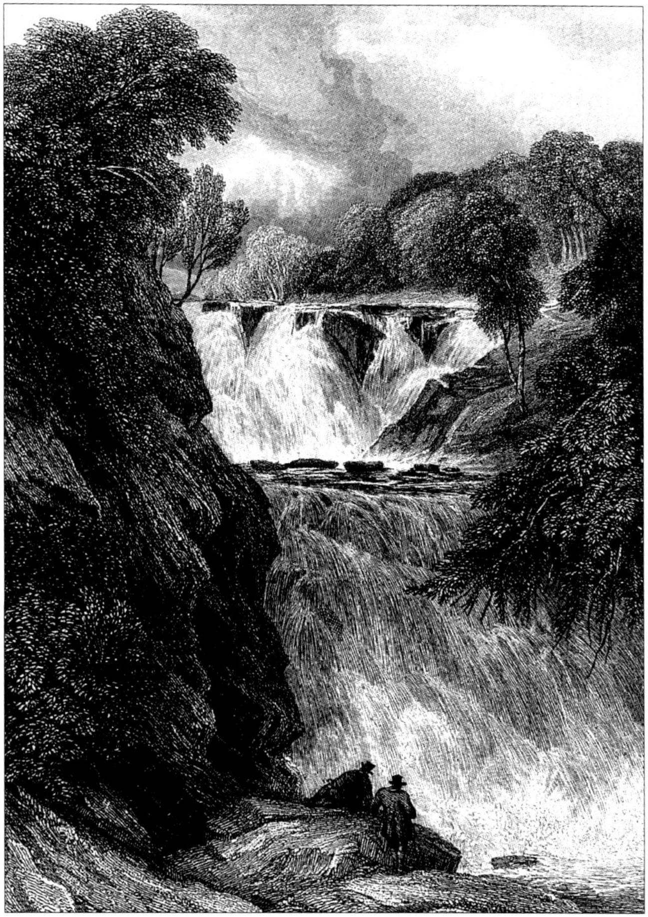

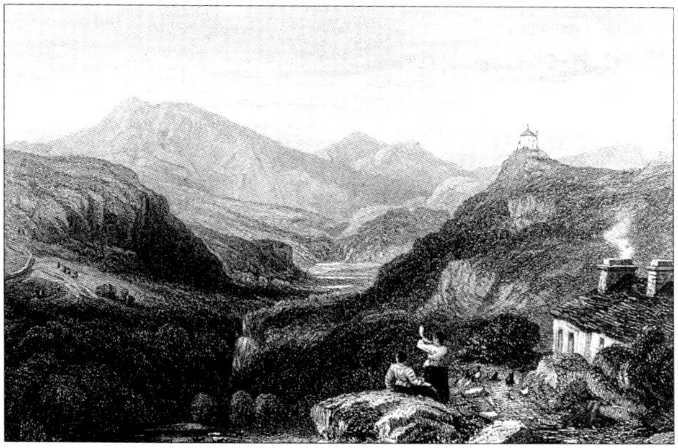

David Cox,
Vale of the Llugwy, from
Wanderings and Excursions in North Wales, 1836.

David Cox,
Rhaiadr y Wennol, from
Wanderings and Excursions in North Wales, 1836.

been the occasion for his first working visit to the village. *Waterfall of Pont-y-pair, North Wales* (perhaps the original of the picture engraved for Roscoe) was shown in 1835, along with *On the River Llugwy, North Wales*, and the following year he showed *Cottages near Bettws* and two other pictures of the area. These were his earliest exhibited Betws views.

Thomas Roscoe liked the 'pretty village' of Betws well enough, and devoted a paragraph to its description.[32] However, in 1844 a second and substantially rewritten edition of the *Wanderings and Excursions* was published in which the mildly complimentary paragraph was expanded into a eulogistic chapter about Betws.[33] The six pictures of the

[32]Roscoe, op.cit., p.199.

[33]A third edition was issued in 1853 and seems to have been the most popular of all.

area by Cox were concentrated around the new text, along with the delightful view of the main street of Betws itself by Creswick. It was also in 1844 that Cox made the first of his annual summer sojourns in the village which became so celebrated a part of the English art world. It seems certain that the start of Cox's particular association with Betws and Roscoe's heightened opinion of it were related.

Thomas Creswick, *Bettws y Coed*, from *Wanderings and Excursions in North Wales*, 1836.

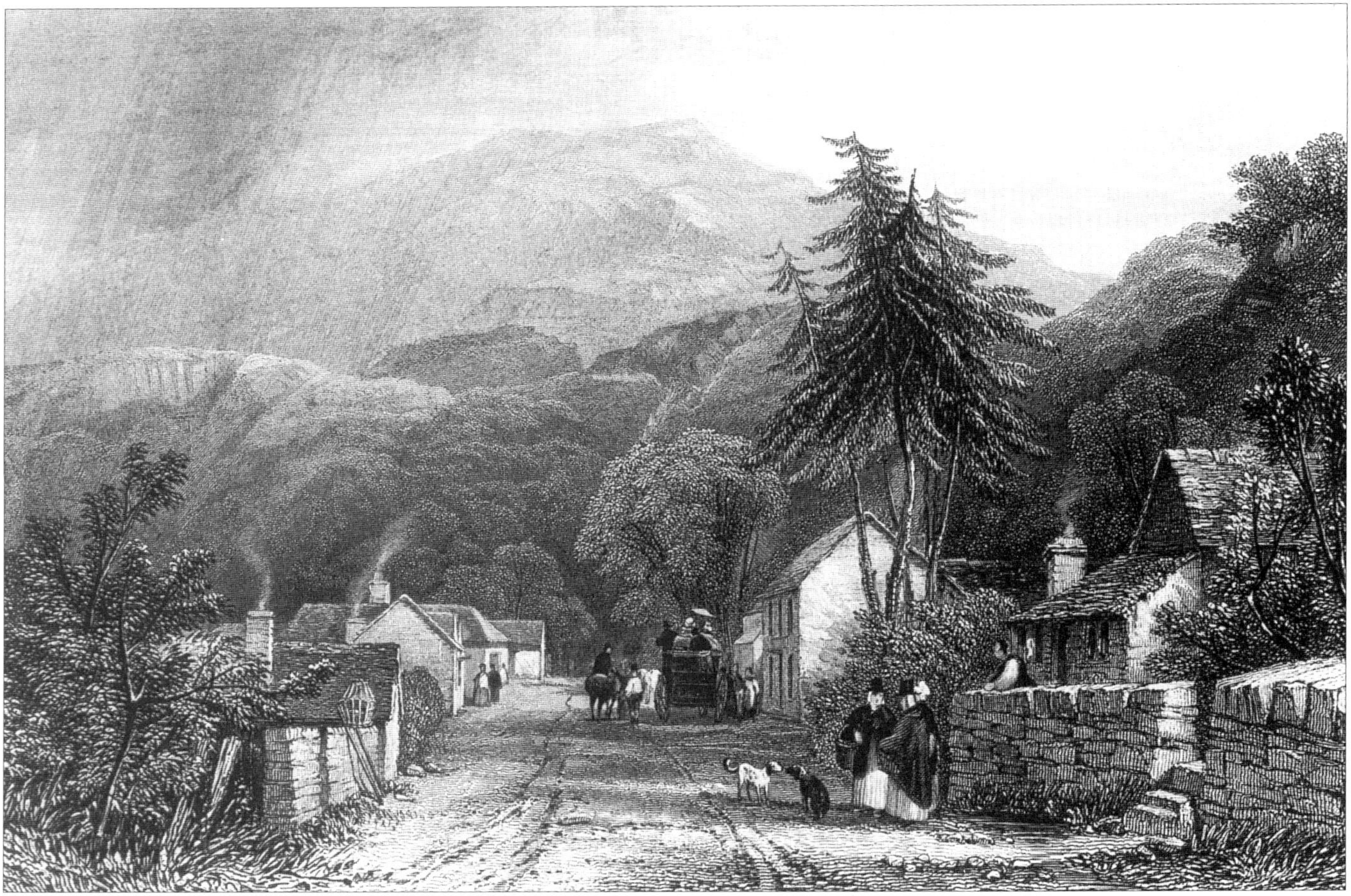

Thomas Creswick,
Bridge at Bettwys Coed,
c.1827.

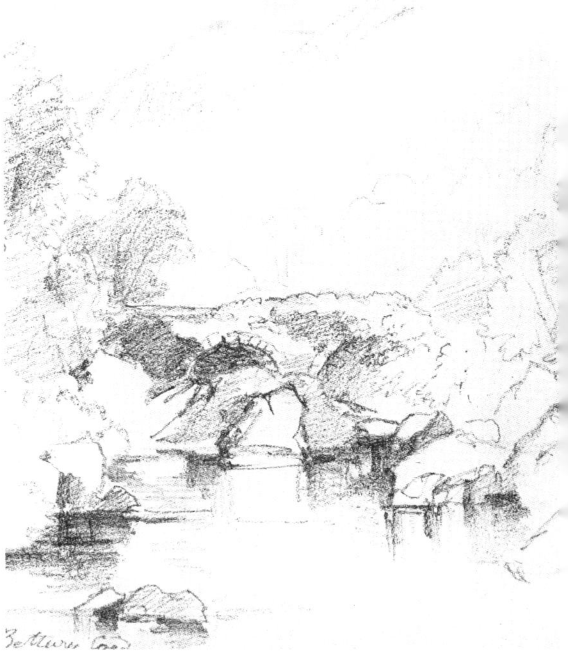

After 1844 Betws-y-coed became a destination for artists rather than a place at which to pause briefly before passing on, a development for which the writer of the guide and the artist who illustrated it were largely responsible. Other painters were staying to work by that time, notably Thomas Creswick, whose association with Betws was longstanding. An early notebook, possibly dating from a first visit in 1827 or 1828, demonstrates how he encountered Betws from the north, visited Dolbadarn, and passed on to Corwen and Llangollen in the classic manner. By 1844 he had returned many times to stay in the village, and three other artists were about to take up permanent residence. Nevertheless, all contemporary observers agreed with the young painter William Hall, that 'Until David Cox honoured it with his visits, and brought his genius to bear upon its numberless charms, it was comparatively unknown'.[34] Precisely what happened to change the perception of Betws in these men's minds between 1835 and 1844 is difficult to say, but Thomas Roscoe's descriptions, published in the second edition of his work, leave no doubt as to his infatuation with the place. On the first morning of his stay, 'The sun rose with a June splendour over the village of BETTWS-Y-COED, dispersing the light haze which hung over those far-stretching plantations of larch-trees, that distinguished it from every other place I had seen in the Principality'.[35] Setting out over the Waterloo Bridge, Roscoe proceeded up the valley of the Lledr:

> *'Nothing that I had witnessed can be compared to the seclusion of this romantic glen; even the occasional dwelling-place of man, perched on the table of some frowning cliff, or the solitary animal that browsed upon the scanty herbage of the hollows, or looked wistfully from the topmost crag, seemed to confirm the loneliness of the place.'*[36]

[34]William Hall, *A Biography of David Cox* (London, 1881), p.30.

[35]Roscoe, op.cit., p.205.

[36]Ibid., p.210.

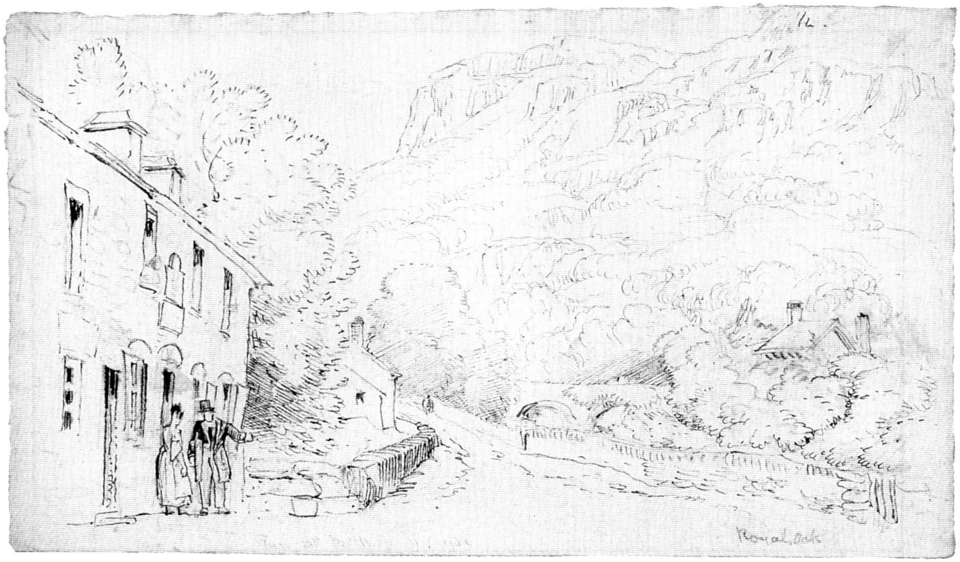

David Cox,
Royal Oak Inn,
c.1850.

Roscoe stayed at the Royal Oak inn, which he recommended for 'its homely comforts, and the active services of the little obliging *grisette* who never lets the traveller wait long for his savoury breakfast of eggs and ham'.[37] This was Mary Roberts, daughter of the landlord, Edward Roberts, to whom many flattering comments were addressed in the visitors book of the inn. The Royal Oak was described as it was in 1846, before the first of a number of reconstructions, by William Hall:

> *'Like other humble houses in the Principality, the door opened with a thumb-latch, when it was closed, which was not very often, admitting visitors to the kitchen, the better class passing through it, and likewise through the group of farm-labourers and other rustic guests, smoking pipes and drinking their ale by the fire-side, along a short, dark passage into the parlour, reserved for the company of "the higher order." On entering the front door the eye caught a glimpse of the bedroom staircase, very steep and very narrow, the sides of which from bottom to top were decorated with saddles and harness, requiring occasionally dexterous steering by visitors on the way to bed, to avoid a blow in the face from some unduly projecting piece of horse-furniture. Bacon and hams hung from the kitchen ceiling, ripened and mellowed, no doubt, by the clouds of smoke from the peat fires.'*[38]

[37]Ibid., p.206.

[38]Hall, op.cit., p.83.

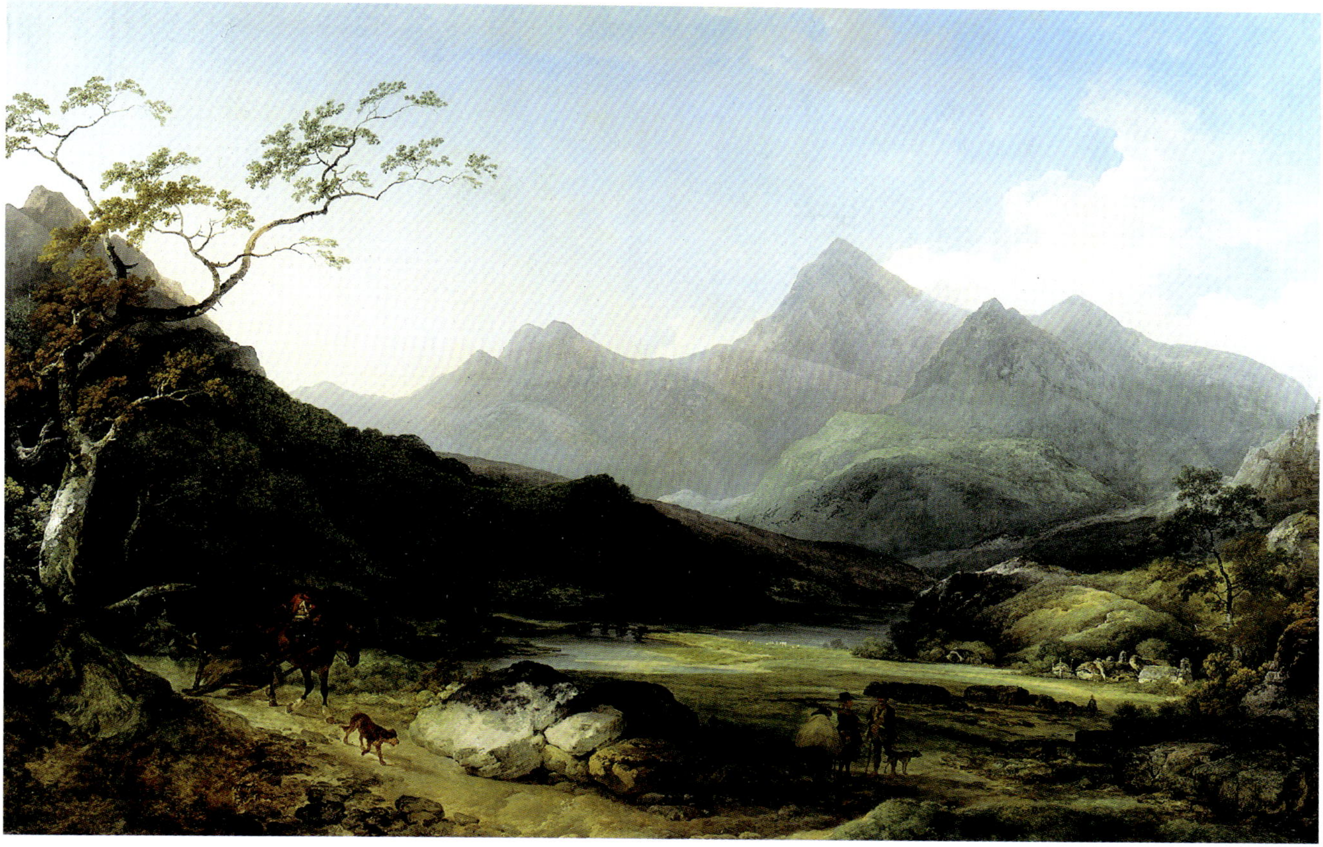

Philippe de Loutherbourg,
Snowdon from Capel Curig,
1787.

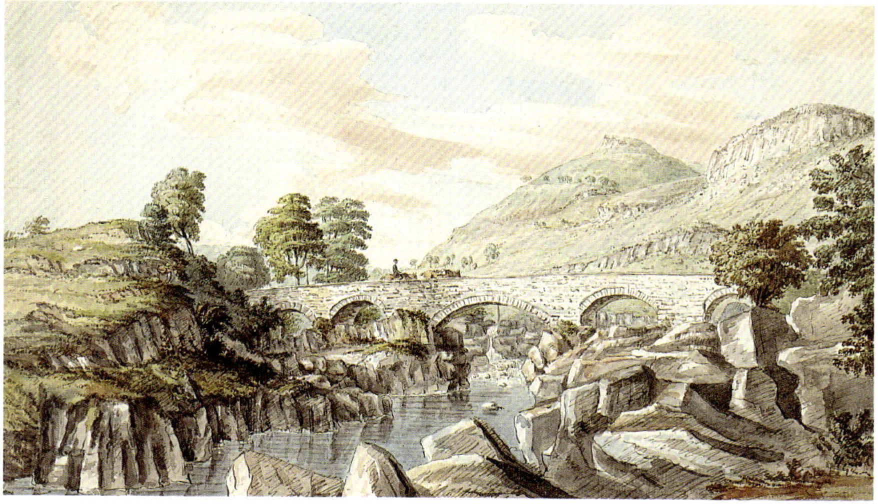

Moses Griffith,
Pont-y-pair,
1776.

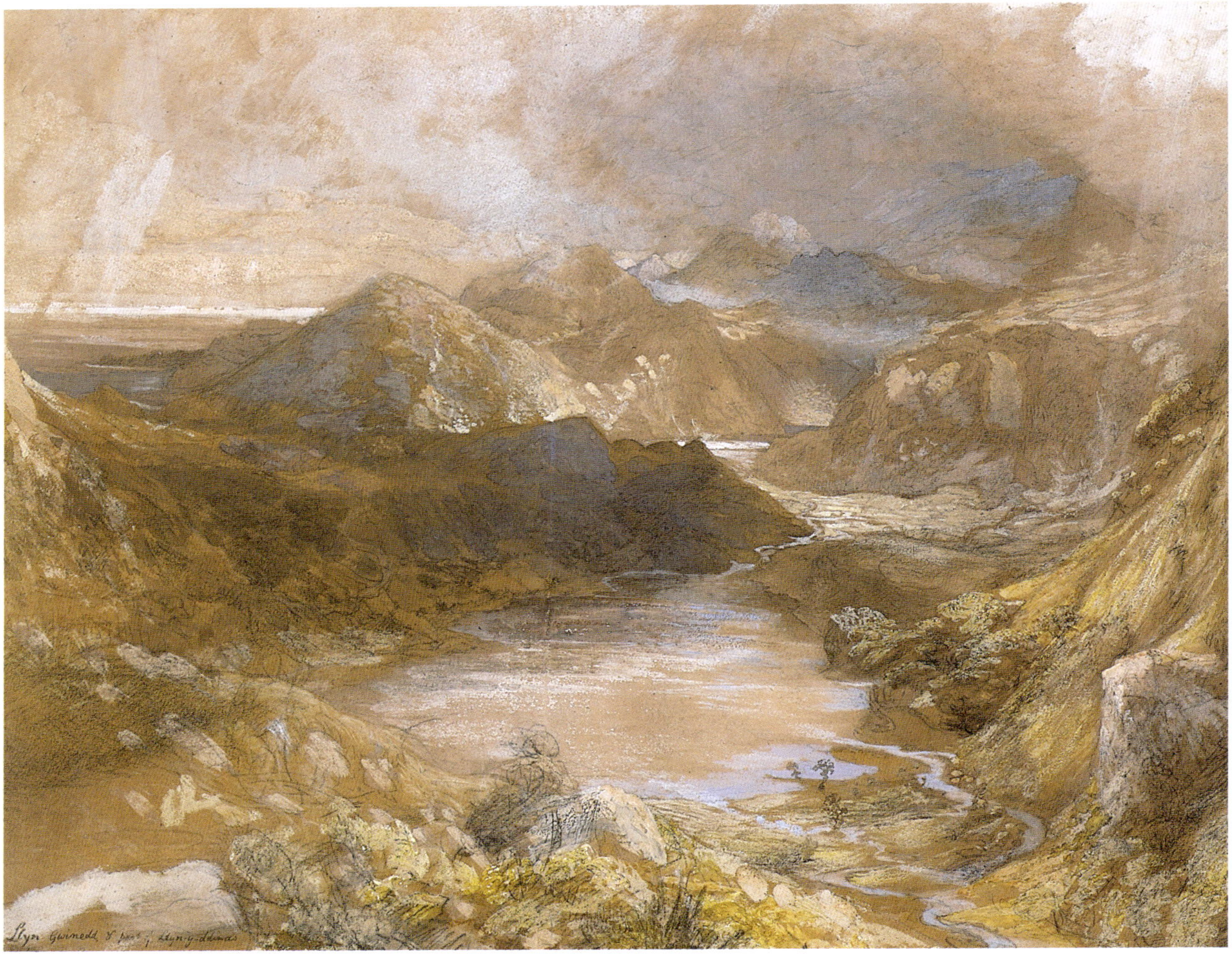

Samuel Palmer,
Llyn Gwynedd, c.1835.

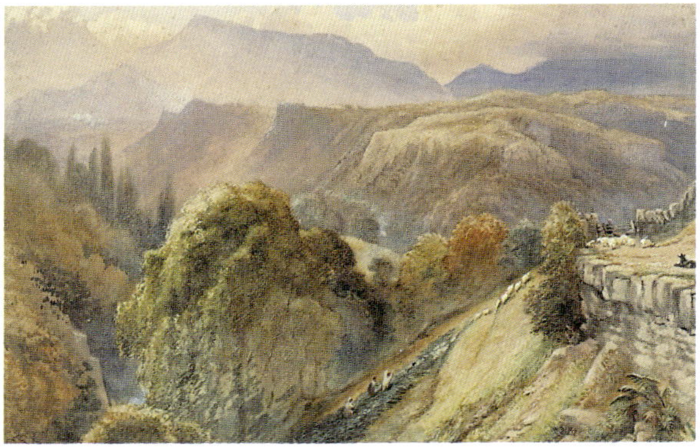

George Popkin,
The Valley of Dolwyddelan,
c.1846.

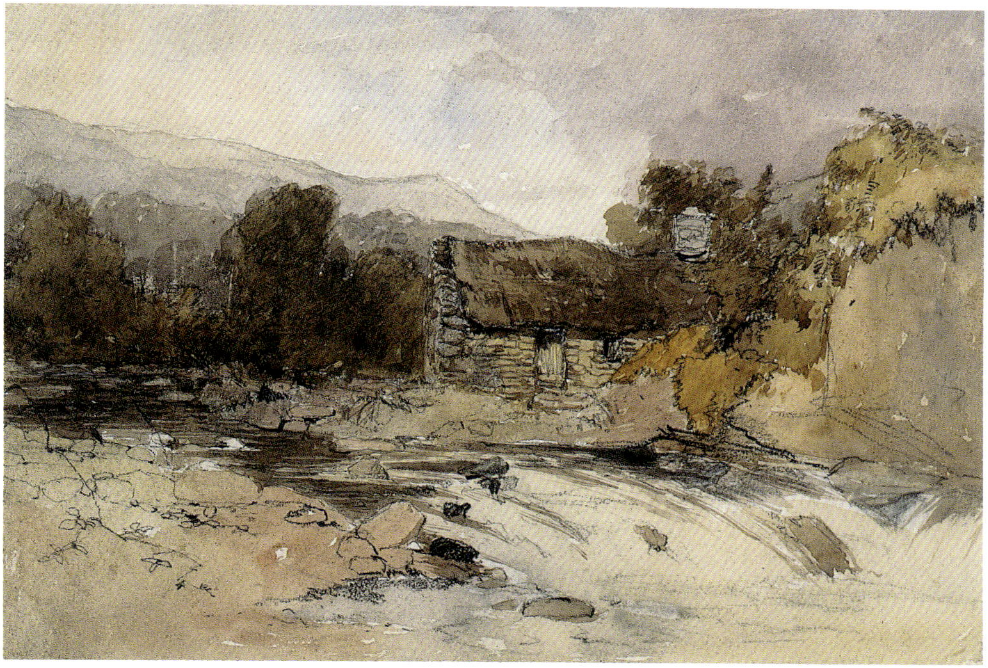

William Evans,
Cottage near Betws-y-coed,
c.1844.

William Evans,
Autumn Landscape, north Wales,
c.1844.

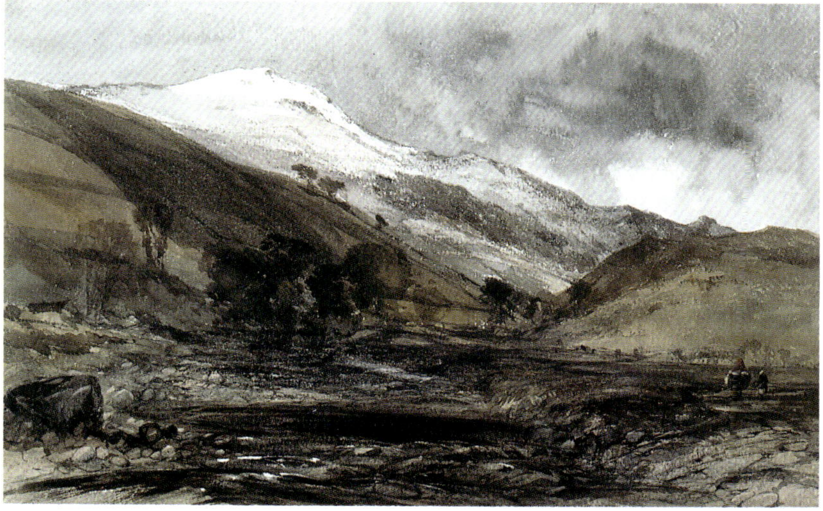

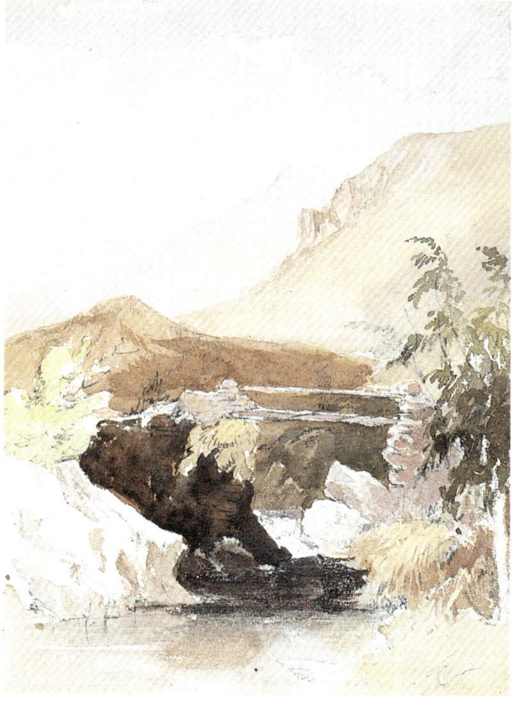

Richard Bond,
Footbridge in north Wales,
c.1830.

David Cox,
Capel Curig, Caernarvonshire,
c.1845.

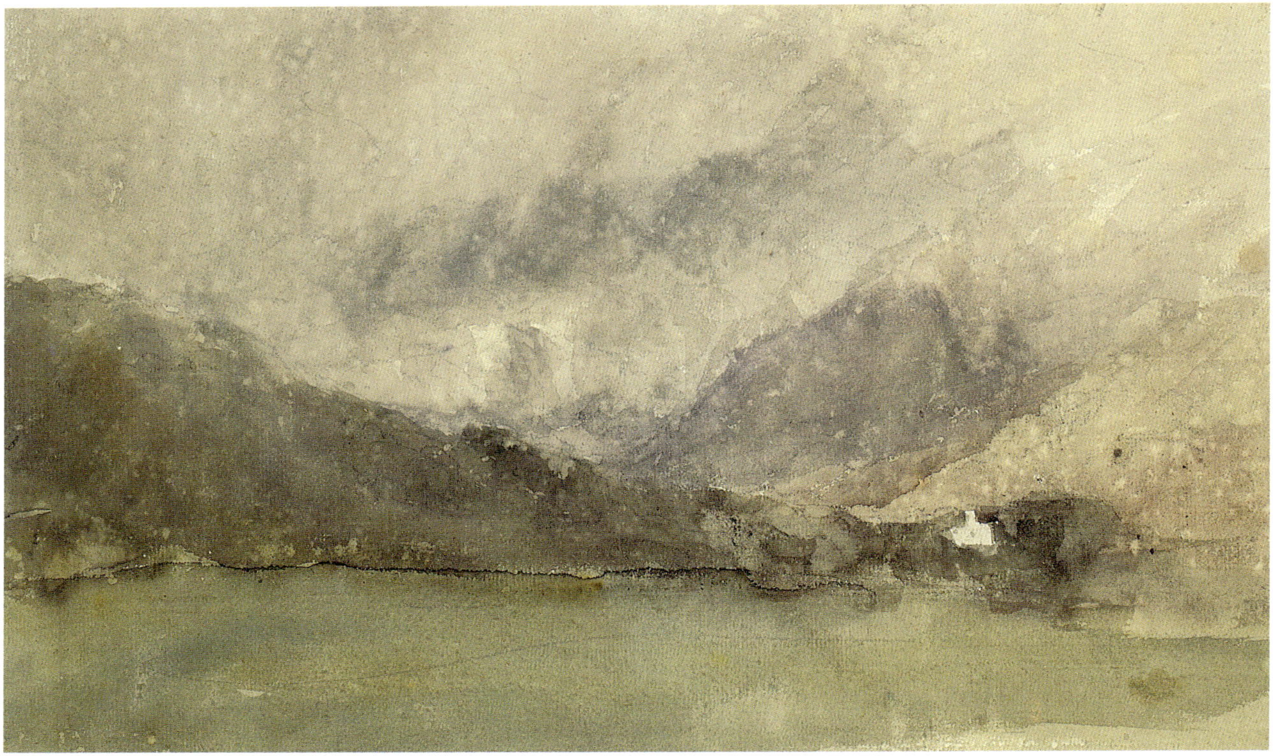

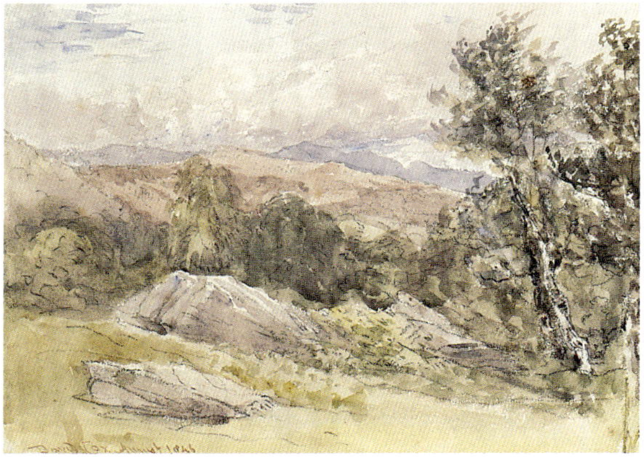

David Cox,
Near Penmachno Mill, north Wales,
1846.

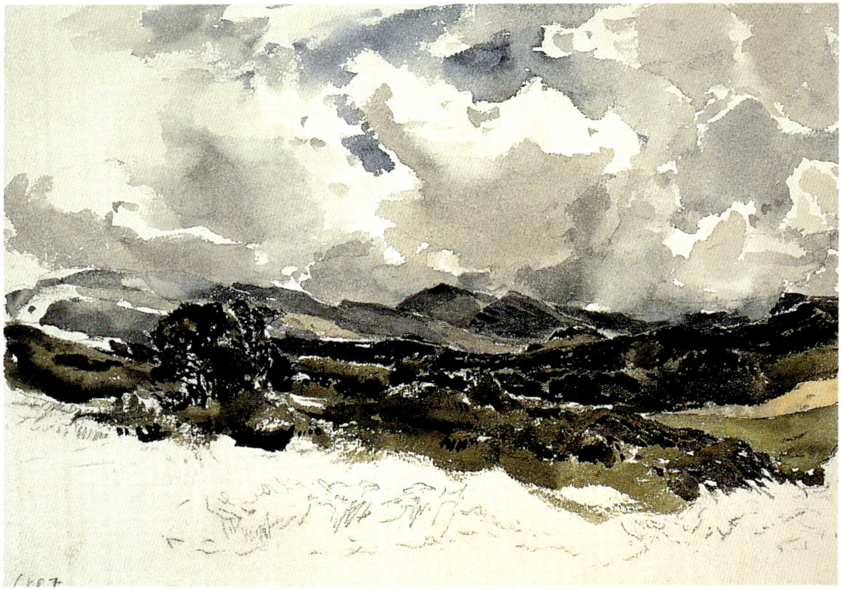

Thomas Collier,
Hilly Country with Clouds,
c. 1887.

The Royal Oak provided a sociable place to stay, but it was also within easy walking distance of romantic solitude. This was an important consideration for Cox who was entering into old age - he was 61 when he stayed at Betws in 1844. On the other hand, Cox liked people as much as he liked solitude, and the potential offered by Betws not only for work but also for keeping summer company with associates from London appealed to him. When Cox arrived at Betws in 1844, accompanied by a young acolyte, Harry Johnson, they found Thomas Creswick already installed, either at the Royal Oak or at its chief rival, the Swan.[39] Cox remarked significantly that Creswick was 'communicative'.[40] George Popkin, one of the first artists to take up permanent residence, described the social life of the small community that began to collect around Cox at this time:

> *'In the evening he sat on the sofa in the parlour of the Royal Oak inn which in those days was an artist's club pur et simple. Here he took his cigar (he smoked no pipe) and his pint of ale, with one or two cronies by his side, willing to listen and willing to teach. There was no racket, no shouting, no fastness or slang; it was an intelligent, rational, pleasant evening's amusement and I have heard French, German, Hungarian, English, and Welsh flowing on like a polyglot stream at the same time in that dingy parlour.'*[41]

Cox did not teach formally at Betws but encouraged his acolytes with critiques and demonstrations. Sometimes he donated the results to the younger artists, such as Hall, who had met Cox in the village for the first time in 1846 and soon became a regular companion. Hall wrote the fullest and most vivid descriptions of Betws in this period to have survived. The village was still small and physically unaffected by the attention of the artists: 'It could boast of only one small shop - a mere cottage, with a little window, in which a few useful articles were exposed for sale... Much Welsh and a little English, was spoken.'[42] Nevertheless, among the items kept at the shop was turpentine, and Hall remembered that, as early as 1846, 'During the sketching season, Bettws, as it became better known, was often filled to overflowing with amateurs and artists':

> *'Their white tents and umbrellas, to be seen in whichever direction the eye turned, suggested to the visitor the encampment of an invading army. In every road or lane, on every eminence or river-bank, the artist was encountered, bearing his paraphernalia to or*

[39] According to Hall, ibid., p.82, early visitors had stayed at an inn called the Hand, 'a wretched house, with miserable accomodation'.

[40] Letter to his son, 15 July 1844, published in Solly, op.cit., p.162.

[41] Ibid., p.172.

[42] Hall, op.cit., p.91.

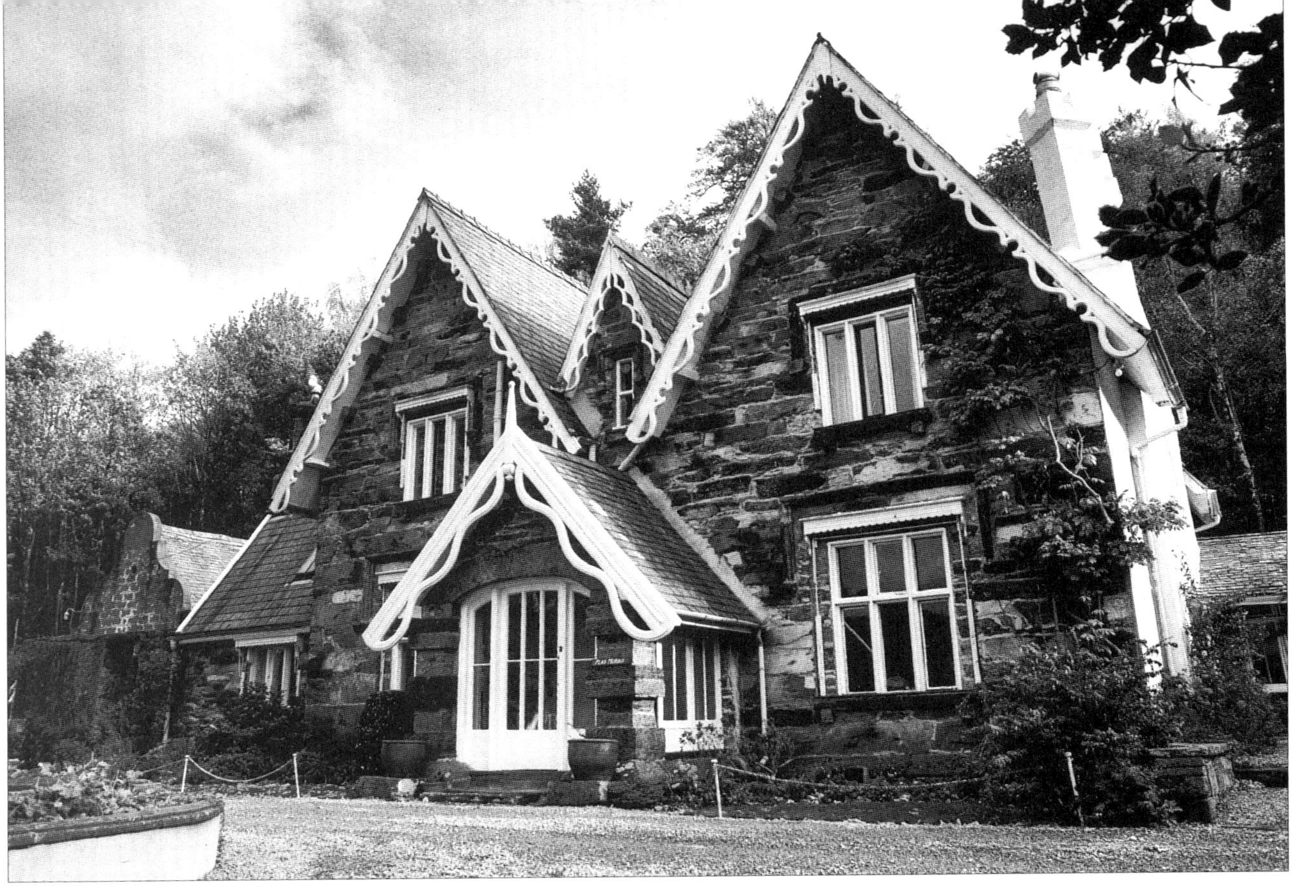

Plas Muriau, Betws-y-coed.

from the sketching-ground, or beheld busily at work transferring to canvas the beautiful objects before him; whilst in the evenings, after the labours of the day, he was seen chatting with his fellows at the inn door, smoking pipe or cigar, and enjoying the delicious calm of the closing day.'[43]

David Cox had greeted Hall as his carriage drew up at the Royal Oak for the first time in the summer of 1846: 'And this was Bettws-y-coed, about which we had heard so much! "And you'll like it," said Cox, as we descended from the car to enter the humble little hostelry, "I hope, as well as I do".'[44] Cox was 'a sort of little king at Bettws, was waited on, respected, and beloved by all who came into contact with him. Lord Willoughby might be the owner of the soil, but David Cox was lord of the people's affections':[45]

[43]Ibid,. p.85.

[44]Ibid., p.78.

[45]Ibid., p.94.

'He was quite at home there. Everybody was kind to him; everybody was studious to please and make him happy. From the landlord [Edward Roberts], Miss Mary Roberts, and the son, who often drove him to his painting ground, down to the lad who carried his traps, and the old woman who knitted his winter stockings, all were delighted to see him... There was generally a great contention among the village lads as to which should be his "tiger," to carry the sketching apparatus for the season; and "Mr Cox's boy" always looked upon himself as in the proudest tradition of them all. Not even the lad who carried the easel and colour-box for Mr. Thomas Creswick, the great R.A., felt so elated and raised above his fellows, as did "little John," who, with canvas on back and sketching-stool in hand, trotted in the rear of David Cox, the veteran artist and kind-hearted man, who gave himself no airs of greatness, but went about humbly and unpretendingly, and had a good-natured word for everyone he met.'[46]

It is clear that Cox intended to buy a property in the Conwy Valley, probably near Llanrwst. On 23 April 1845, he wrote to his friend William Roberts:

'I am thankful I am able to go about; and when I can get off into Wales I hope to breathe the sweet mountain air. I have made some inquiries about the little property in Wales, and hope in a week or nine days to hear more, as it is necessary for the person to write down for all particulars. I have seen one or two who have resided there in the winter, artists, who agree that it is a great deal warmer in Bettws than in London... This all tends to give me a better idea of the place, and I hope I may be able to purchase the place I wish for within a moderate sum.'[47]

Cox did not carry through this project; neither did he name the artists who had stayed over the winter at Betws, though his friend 'Fat' Hoyle, fisherman and painter, who resided for long periods at the Royal Oak, may have been one of them. The census returns for 1841 recorded no artists living at Betws or, indeed, in the Conwy Valley as a whole. However, by 1846, George Popkin was living at Castell Pwt, on the eastern side of the road to Llanrwst, where his first child was born. By 1850 he had moved a few hundred yards to the south to a fine new house, Plas Muriau, opposite Muriau Farm, although it is not entirely clear whether or not it was built by him.[48] Popkin showed Betws views at the Royal

[46]Ibid., p.87, p.94.

[47]Solly, op.cit., p.133.

[48]Given as 'Plas Myria' by Solly, ibid., who quoted Popkin at length on the subject of Betws at the time of Cox's summer visits. Popkin's father, George Parr Perry Popkin, was an attorney living in Dean Street, Soho. He died in 1834 leaving £8,000 and land to his son and younger sisters, suggesting that George Popkin could certainly have afforded to build Plas Muriau.

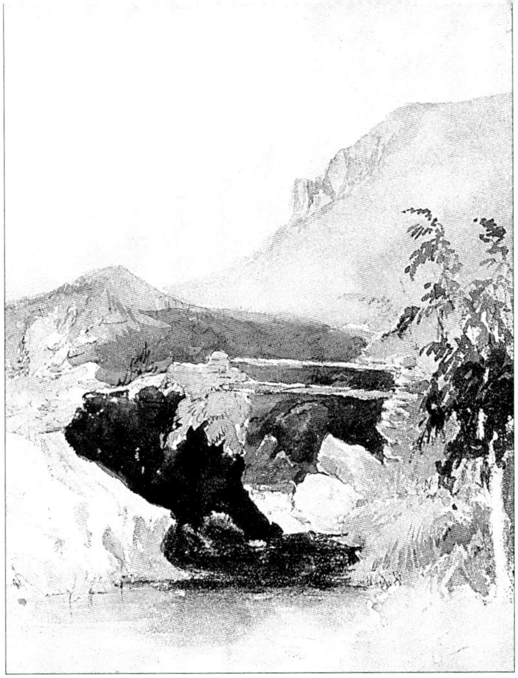

Richard Bond,
Footbridge in north Wales, c.1830.
Reproduced in colour on p.43.

Society of British Artists in London from 1850. About a mile away to the south of the village, above the Fairy Glen, the painter Richard Bond was living at Wernfawr. Bond was born in 1808 in Liverpool and trained there. His association with Wales extended back considerably further than that of Popkin, since he is known to have visited at least as early as 1830,[49] though he did not exhibit Betws views in London until 1846, at the British Institution. The census recorded that his son, John Lloyd Bond, was born in Llanrwst parish in that year. Popkin and Bond were almost certainly the earliest English artists permanently resident in the area, and both knew Cox well. Bond was mentioned several times in Cox's correspondence,[50] and at least one painting, *The Salmon Trap*, is known to have been worked on by both artists. Bond's wife, Sarah, was Welsh, the daughter of a minister at the small village of Ro-Wen, between Trefriw and Conwy. Ro-Wen was frequented by artists, notably Müller, from an early date, which may suggest how Bond came to meet his wife.[51] Their life together at Betws seemed to be idyllic to George Wightwick, a tourist who visited them in 1856:

> *'"Love in a cottage" is a proverbial sentiment; and I trust it is here a practical fact. Here lives the... "Landscape Painter", with the finest woman I ever saw in Wales for a wife, and three children "beautiful exceedingly". The Lady brought me out a chair, wheron to sit and take these views. The gentleman fed me with oat-meal cakes, rendered delectable by butter, and facilitated by Whiskey. The Lady is of the blood of Glendower, - "serene, - imperial". The Gentleman is an Englishman, blessed in his wife at all events; though I opine, rather content with his fate, than favoured by Fortune, in respect of what should be the monied estimate of his skill and feeling as an artist.'*[52]

[49] Birmingham City Art Gallery has a signed and dated watercolour of 1830.

[50] Solly, op.cit., p.149, for example - a letter from Cox to William Roberts, dated 30 April 1847, which reported that Bond had sold a picture at the British Institution for 50 guineas, either *A Mountain Stream* or *Yr Allt Wyllt*.

[51] The virtues of Ro-Wen had been advertised by Pugh, op.cit., p.26: 'Here are several ivy-covered cottages, which would gratify the artist. One of them would entice me twenty miles to see it.'

[52] George Wightwick, 'A Week's Sketching in North Wales', 1856, National Library of Wales DV17. Wightwick did not name the artist but there can be little doubt that it was Bond. Wightwick (1802-1872) was born near Mold but was educated in England, and subsequently articled to a London architect. He worked for Sir John Soane but developed his own practice in Plymouth before retiring to Clifton. He wrote extensively about art. On his visit to Betws he stayed with a relative, R.P.Collier, probably with Mrs Hughes at Llugwy Cottage, later frequented by the painter Thomas Collier and many others.

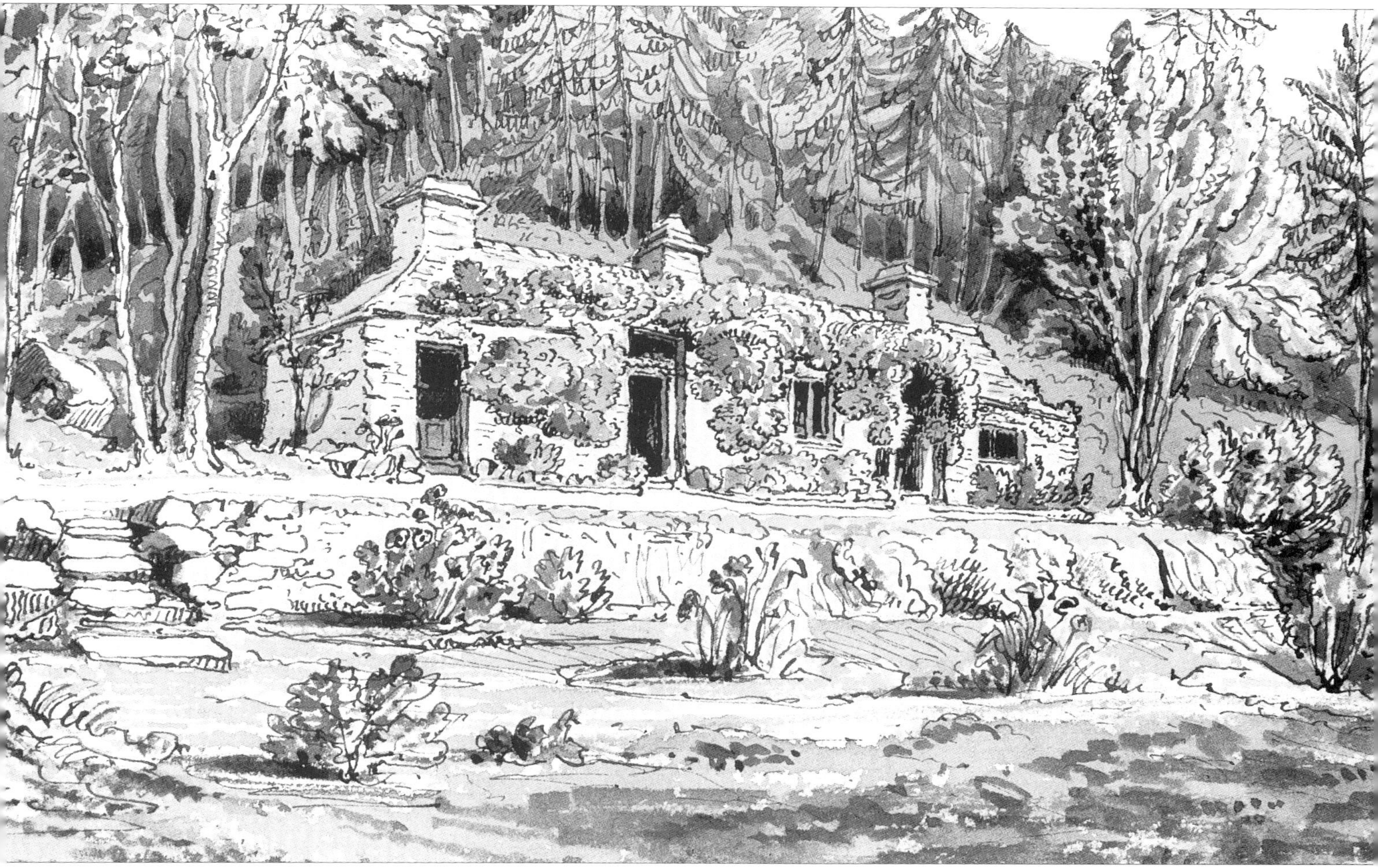

George Wightwick,
View of an Artist's House,
(Wernfawr, Betws-y-coed),
1856.

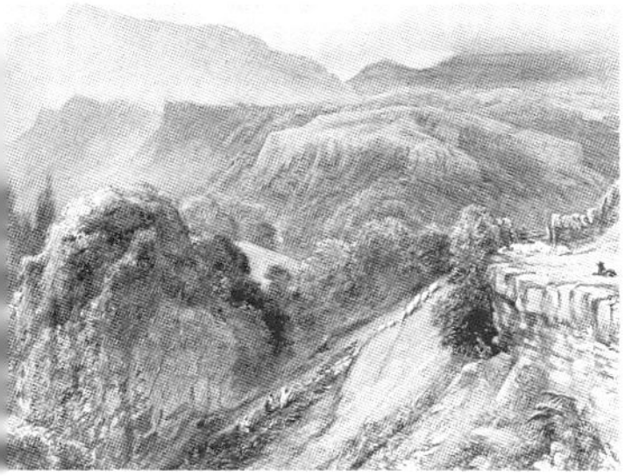

George Popkin,
The Valley of Dolwyddelan, c.1846.
Reproduced in colour on p42.

Bond took pupils, one of whom, William Morgan Williams, forms the earliest known link between indigenous painters and the immigrants. Williams was the son of William Williams, Caledfryn, an Independent minister and prominent radical associate of the painter Hugh Hughes. As a child in Caernarfon in the 1840s, ap Caledfryn had his first lesssons in drawing from Hughes. In 1850 his father moved to a ministry in Llanrwst and at some time between then and 1856 ap Caledfryn was introduced to Bond and 'engaged to him as a pupil in landscape and figure painting':

> *'I had to start at once from nature. I had the advantage of seeing the renowned David Cox work, and in figure I and W.Underhill... I had to study from the antique at the same time and from models [and] in about twelve months Mr.Bond pronounced me able to make my own living...'*[53]

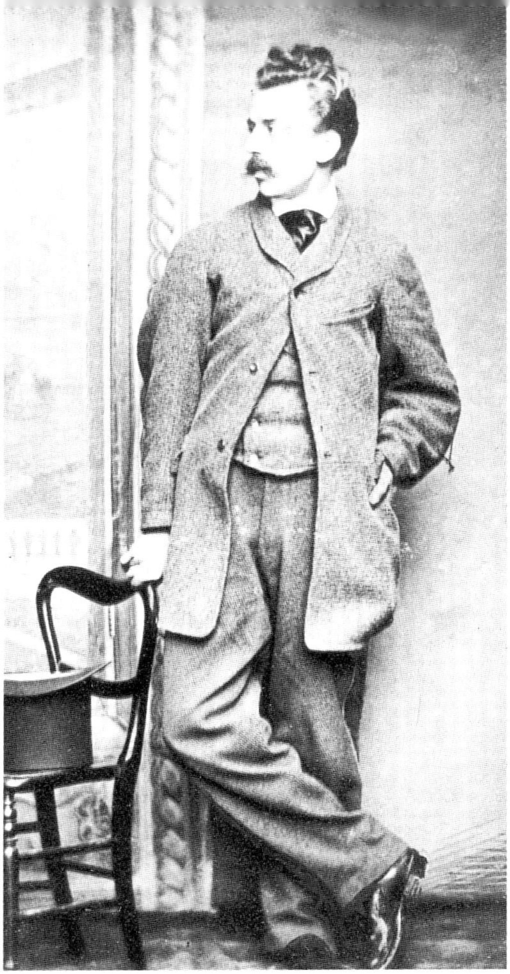

Unknown photographer, *William Morgan Williams, ap Caledfryn*, c.1865.

George Popkin sold up and left Plas Muriau in 1860, but Richard Bond remained at Betws until his death in 1886. His son, John Lloyd Bond, also became a landscape painter and lived on at Wern Fawr into the 1890s with his sister Mary, ten years his junior, who practiced as a portrait artist. The only painter from a Welsh family to take up residence at Betws in this period was William Evans, known variously as 'Welsh Evans' or 'Evans of Bristol', since he was born there in 1809.[54] He rented Ty'n-y-cae, in the fields between

[53]Cardiff Central Library MS Cardiff 1.194 (4/6), no.31. I am indebted to Professor Geraint H.Jenkins for this reference. 'I' Underhill may be a mistake for Frederick Charles, brother of William Underhill. Ap Caledfryn won first prize at the Conwy Eisteddfod of 1861 for 'a landscape from nature', and contemporary reports speak highly of such pictures, but few have come to light. However, his portraits are numerous and it was in this branch of painting that he earned a living. Ap Caledfryn was active in the development of art in the National Eisteddfod as both exhibitor and judge from 1862. See Peter Lord, *Y Chwaer-Dduwies - Celf, Crefft a'r Eisteddfod* (Llandysul, 1992). For Hughes and Caledfryn, see Peter Lord, *Words with Pictures*, op.cit.

[54]T.Mardy Rees, *Welsh Painters, Engravers and Sculptors* (Caernarfon, 1912), p.46, says he was a north Walian and gives his date of birth as 1811, but without authority. Information concerning his father was given in John Lewis Roget, *History of the Old Watercolour Society* (London, 1891), pp.295-6. Josiah John Jenkins was the source of this, and much of the other information given in Roget. See also Francis Greenacre, *William Evans of Bristol* (1809-1858), (London, 1987).

Bond's Wern Fawr and the Fairy Glen. Like his neighbour, he may already have been familiar with the village for some time. He had been in Wales in 1842, when he met up with Müller who he knew well in Bristol.[55] The following year he exhibited a *View of Snowdon* at the Royal Society of British Artists and he had certainly visited Betws by 1844.[56] According to his un-named obiturist, Evans' cottage at Betws was 'Cyclopean', and indeed, only one window faces from the back of the single storied house which stands, virtually unaltered, above the river:

> *'While accomodating himself to the habits of its primitive inmates,*[57] *his mind became more and more unaccommodating to any but the impressions furnished by the stern features around him. Isolated thus from schools, and studios, and exhibitions, it was only to be feared that he might fall into the trite, circumscribed or minute, or have evaporated into the unreal and the flimsy; but his original impulse never left him, and during this period of his career he produced what must perhaps be considered his finest works...'*[58]

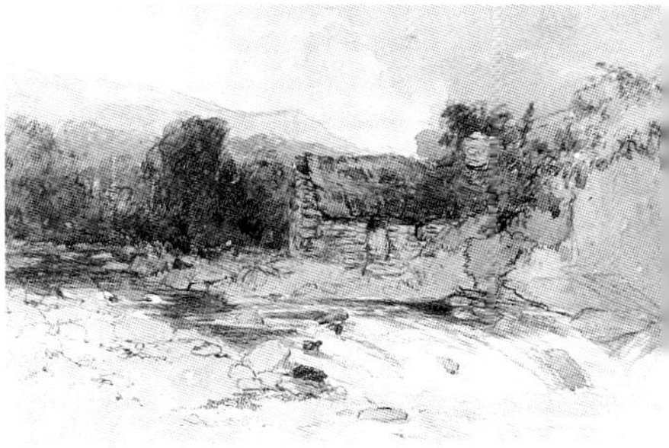

William Evans, *Cottage near Betws-y-coed*, c.1845. Reproduced in colour on p.43.

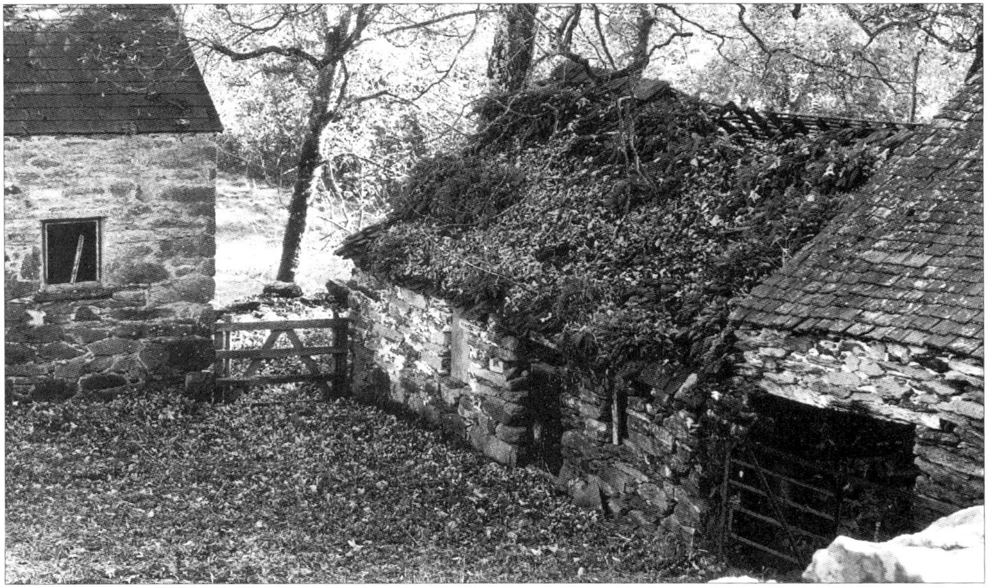

Ty'n-y-cae, Betws-y-coed.

[55]Ibid., p.5.

[56]A watercolour, *The Interior Court of Old Parliament House, Dolgelly, North Wales*, is inscribed 'Given me Sunday Novr. 4th 1844 - at Waterloo Inn, Bettws y Coed N.W.' See *English Watercolours and Drawings, Agnew's 124th Annual Exhibition* (London, 1977).

[57]Presumably Thomas or Owen Williams, owners both of the cottage and Ty'n-y-cae farm.

[58]Anon., 'Mr.William Evans', *Art Journal*, 1859, p.135. This obituary and the shorter notice on p.29, are clearly the source of the limited information given by Mardy Rees, op.cit.

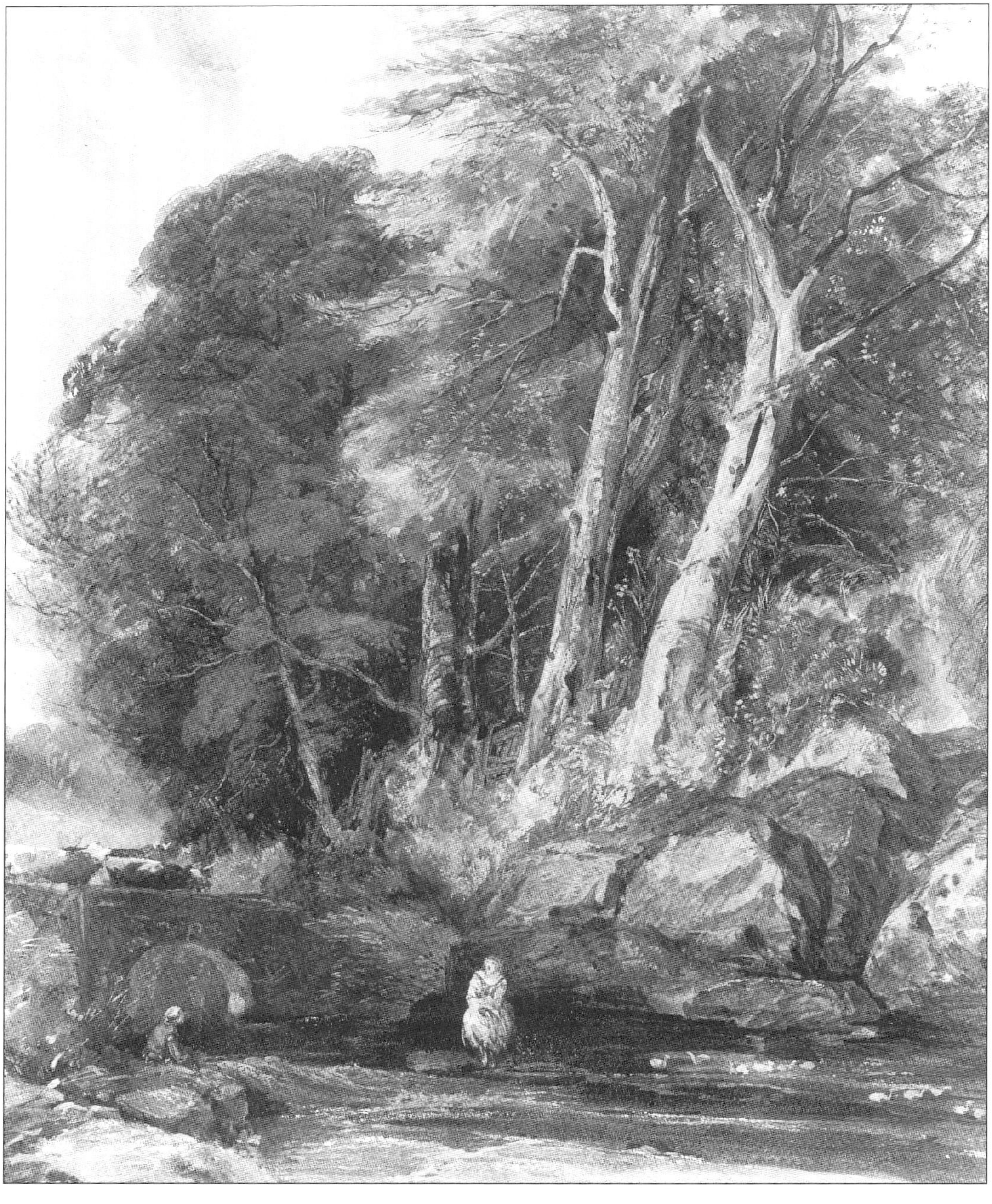

William Evans,
Landscape with Cattle,
c.1845.

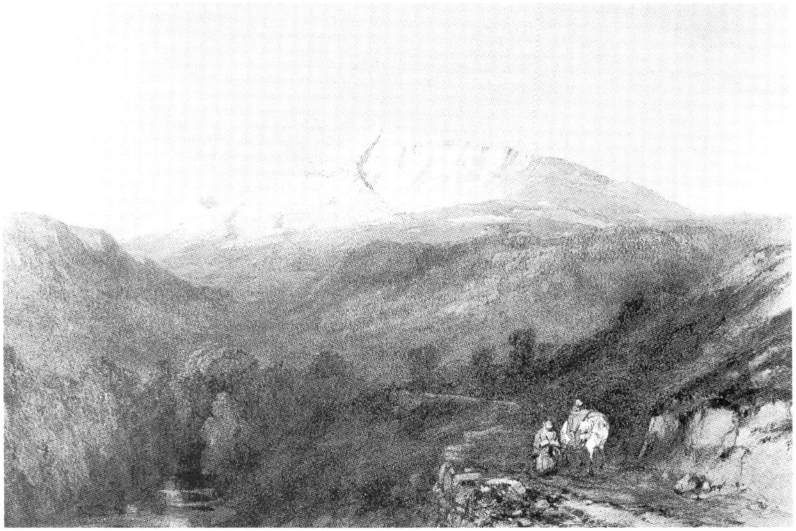

William Evans,
View of Snowdon, 1843.

Despite his extreme life-style, his contemporaries thought highly of him, an opinion born out by the small number of surviving works which are among the most lucid and elegant of the period. He was in Italy between 1852 and 1854, and then in London, but he may also have returned to Wales since he subsequently exhibited a Welsh view along with his Italian works. His obiturist believed that he was 'felicitous in grappling with the true characteristics of the torrents that stir the gloom of these dreary regions, threading their downward course in a thousand more or less defined rills, collecting themselves into tranquil pools, rushing with darkening force through gloomy gorges, fretting their margins amongst minor impediments, and leaping with surging bound the larger obstructions to their career, at once trammelled and impetuous. Nothing can be imagined much finer than his occasional treatment of the cottage scenery of the same district; and not limited to exteriors, but frequently furnished by the views of their interiors, which rival, in force, colour, and light and shade, some of the finest works by the great Dutch masters...'.[59] Evans died in London in 1858, and some years later the biographer and friend of many of the watercolourists of the period, Josiah John Jenkins, made a pilgrimage to Ty'n-y-cae where he 'was shown into the hovel of a room in which Evans slept. It was full of holes and open cracks; swarming with rats, which are said to have continually disturbed him by coursing over his bed in the night. No wonder he set up a chest complaint, from cold and exposure in such a place, which terminated his life'.[60]

[59] Ibid.

[60] Royal Watercolour Society Archive.

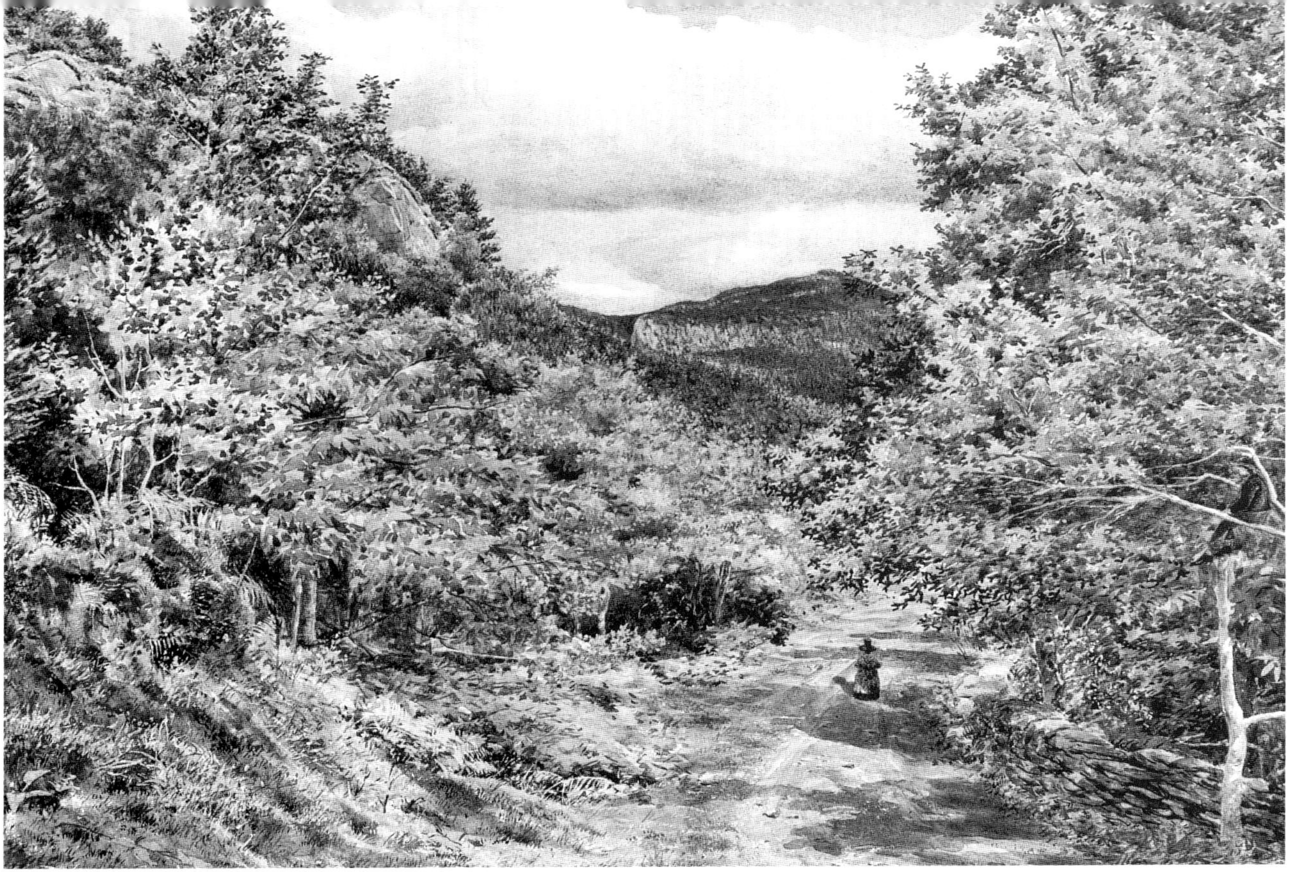

George Price Boyce,
A Road near Betws-y-coed,
1851.

Opposite:
Unknown photographer,
Frank Topham at work
in north Wales, c.1865.

It seems, therefore, that Evans, Bond and Popkin all began their close relationship with Betws at about the time of Cox's first annual visit in 1844. Whether they were drawn there by the recommendation of Roscoe or the reputation of the Master is unclear. It seems unlikely that any of them was introduced to the village by Cox in person. Although he brought many artists to Betws, encouraging them from London and Birmingham to visit him, others found their own way and began their acquaintance with him in Wales. The watercolour painter George Price Boyce, for instance, met Cox in this way. In August 1852 Boyce was out sketching near Betws when the sociable Cox approached and shook hands with him. Boyce immediately came under his influence, noting in his diary that 'After dinner I made an evening sketch on grey wrapping-up paper'.[61] This was Cox's idiosyncratic choice of paper, for which he became celebrated.

[61]'Extracts from the Diaries of George Price Boyce, 1851-75', *Old Water Colour Society's Club*, 19 (1941), p.10.

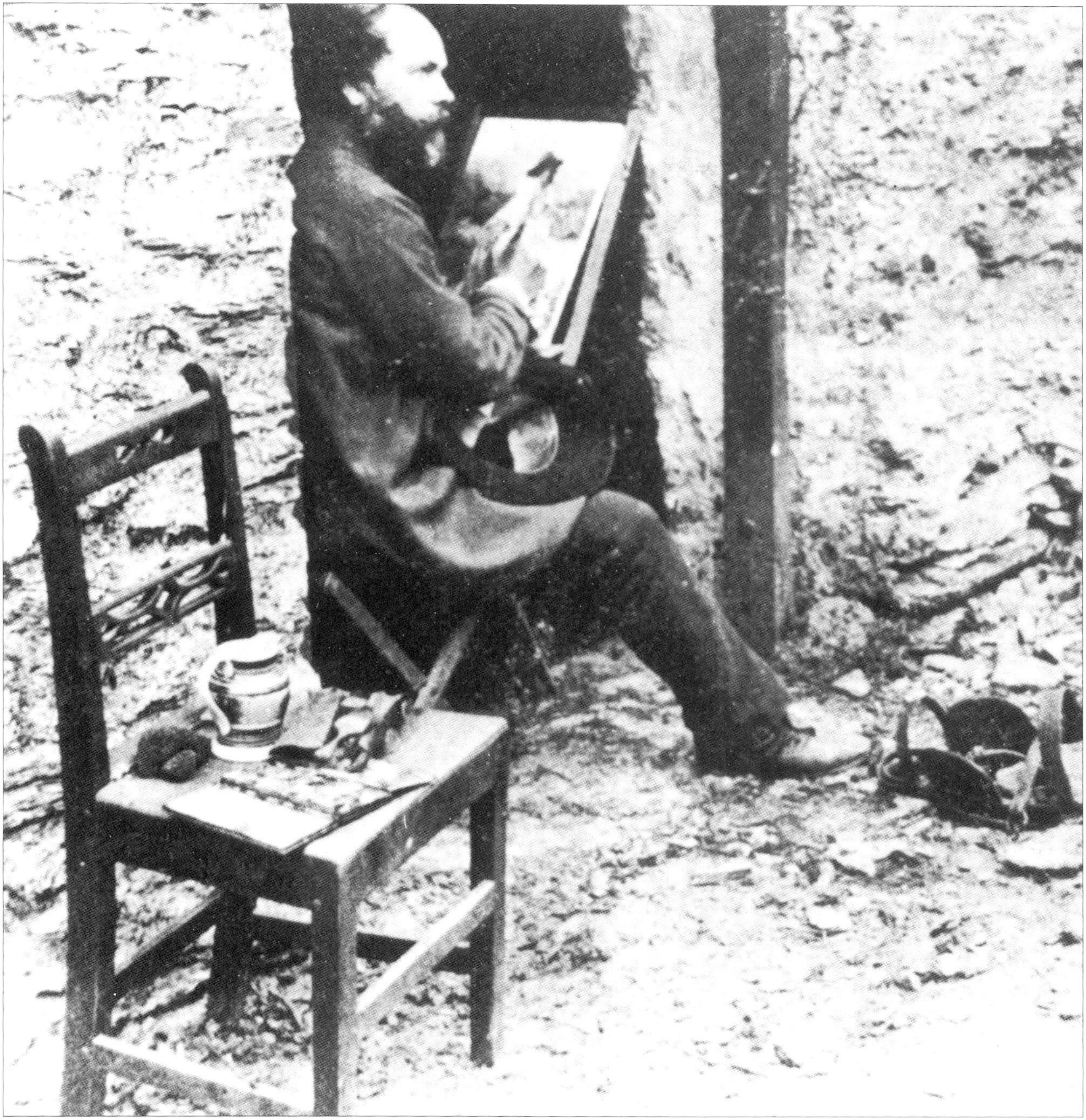

A month later, the painter Francis William Topham arrived at Betws, entertaining the company with conjuring tricks and 'by relating Irish adventures and characters met with in Galway'.[62] Topham painted landscape but specialised in portraits and groups of the peasantry of various parts of the British Isles. By 1861 he had taken Dinas Hill, a house built as a hunting lodge by the Penrhyn Estate, a little further out of Betws than Bond at Wern Fawr. On the day of the 1861 census, Frank Topham himself was absent, but his six children, including his eldest son, Francis William Warwick, also a painter, were all in residence in the substantial house. Topham's visits to Ireland had been taken in the company of other painters, notably Alfred D.Fripp, who, like his friend, specialised in scenes of peasant life, Mark Anthony (who had grown up in Wales) and Frederick Goodall. Alfred Fripp was also an aficionado of Betws, having worked in the area at least as early as 1844, when he exhibited *Welsh Girl Crossing the Style* and *Girls of Moel Siabod, North Wales*, at the Society of Painters in Water Colours. On a visit to Betws in 1852, Topham and Fripp painted interiors in the company of Boyce, who particularly noted in his diary the presence of one Ellen Pritchard, 'a very pretty and interesting girl' from Pwllheli, who posed in a chimney corner for the three men.[63]

It is not difficult to understand the attraction for these young artists of a stay at Betws. In addition to its picturesque scenery and natives, it offered the friendship and free advice of the most famous living painter in England. After Cox introduced himself to Boyce in 1852, they spent many hours together. On 27 August, for instance, Boyce reported in his diary one of the impromptu demonstrations of watercolour technique given by the Master, in this case 'in the presence of Messrs. Poole, Bond, Roberts, Hoyle, Back and myself'.[64] Cox and Roberts regaled the younger painters with anecdotes about the great names of the past whom they had known, such as Turner, Cotman and Chrome. At Betws the young painters could feel that they were close to the centre of the English art world. It was not, however, simply a matter of looking back. They themselves were developing new ideas which would take English painting, and the watercolour in particular, forward from the hiatus upon which critics were commenting in the early 1840s, as the older generation of painters came to the end of their careers.[65] The aesthetics and techniques of De Wint, Copley Fielding and even Cox himself came under critical scrutiny as the younger painters sought

[62]Ibid., p.11.

[63]Ibid.

[64]Ibid. Poole was probably James Pool (1804-86). He did not exhibit in London but evidence from salerooms shows that he painted for many years in Wales and in particular in the Betws area (for instance, *Near Capel Curig, North Wales*, 1854, sold at Sotheby's in 1987). He also painted landscape in Scotland. Back may have been the W.H.Back who exhibited *Moel Shabod, Valley of Dolwyddelan, North Wales*, in 1845 at the Royal Society of British Artists.

[65]See Scott Wilcox and Christopher Newall, *Victorian Landscape Watercolours* (New York, 1992), p.17.

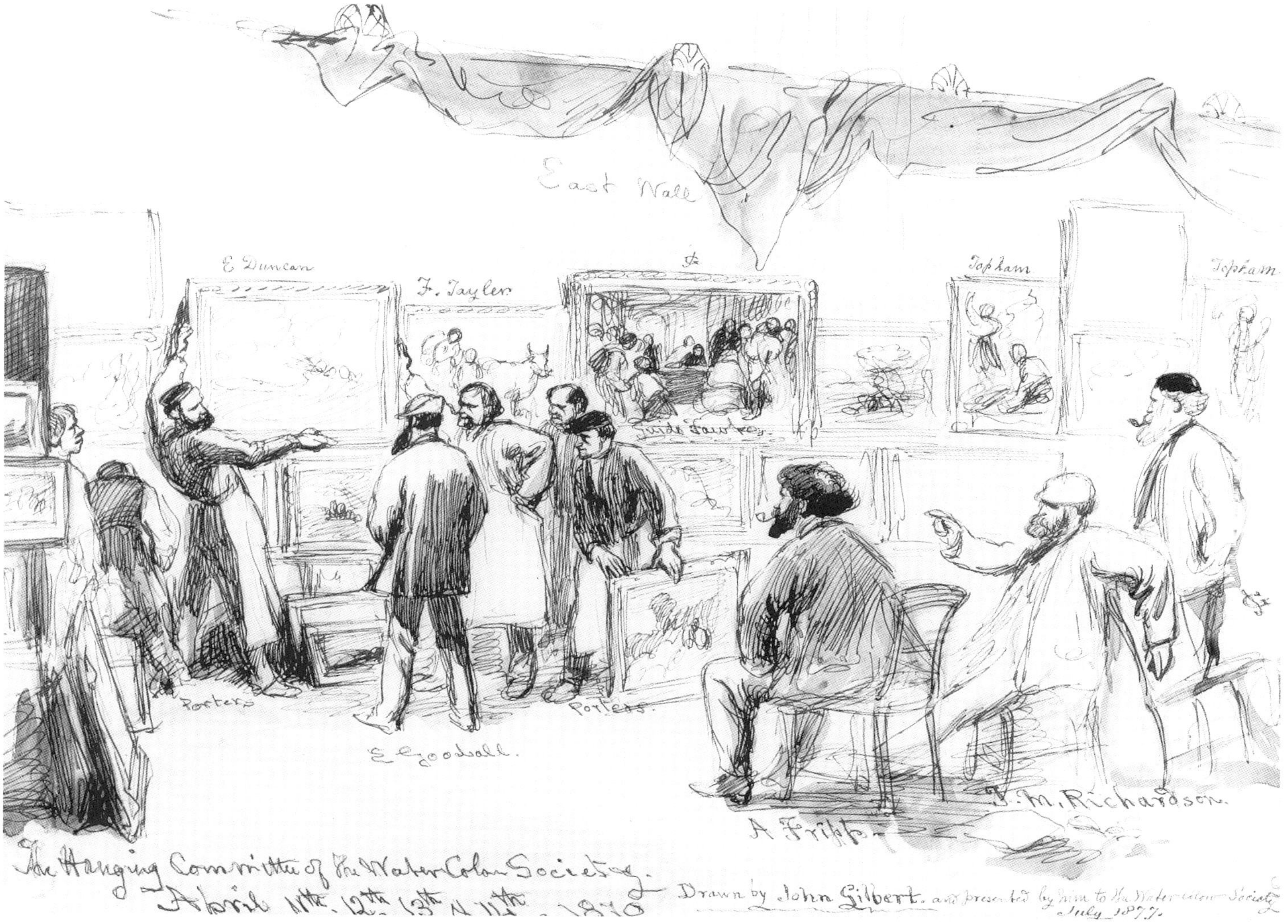

John Gilbert,
The Hanging Committee of the Water Colour Society, 1870.

Frank Topham, *Welsh Girl*, 1874.

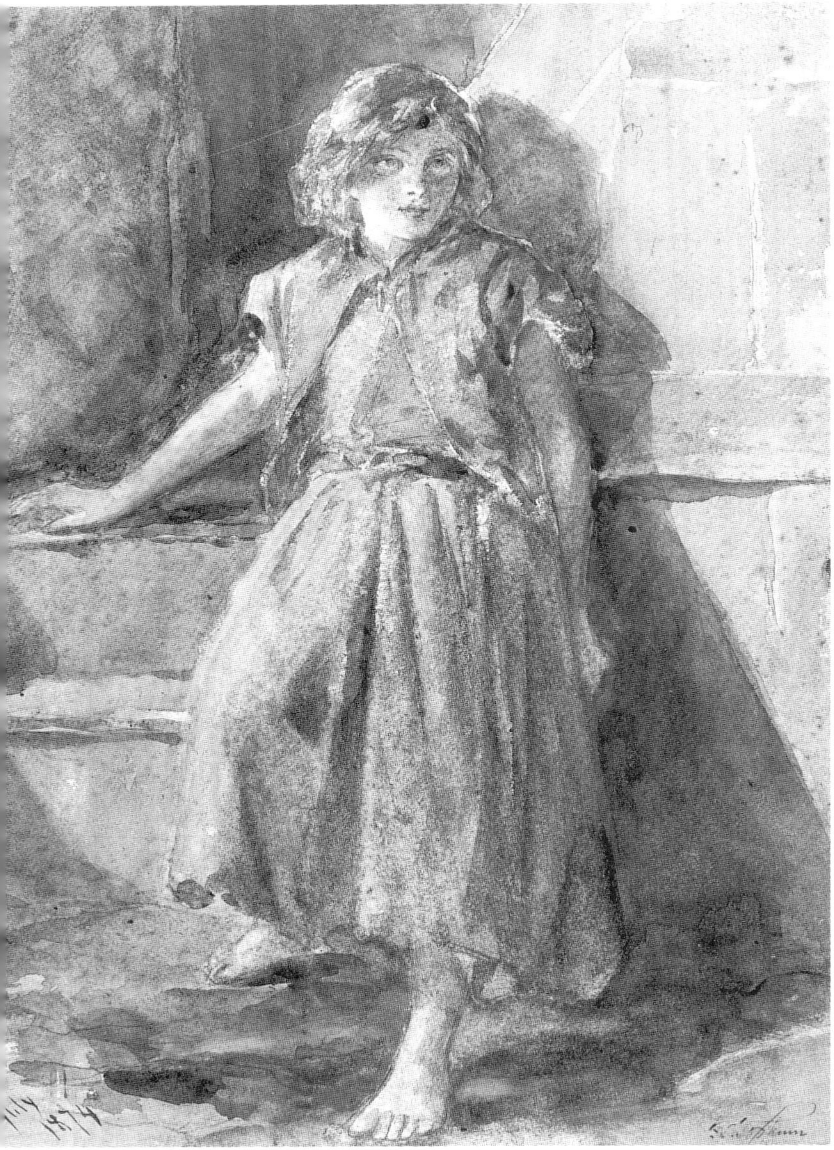

a fresh way forward. The new generation found its voice in 1843 when the first volume of John Ruskin's *Modern Painters* was published. Although Ruskin usually excepted Cox himself from his criticism, he proposed the need for greater particularity in finished works and for the study of detail in nature, as opposed to the fluid generalisation of the old school. In 1852, while painting Welsh peasants in the dark kitchen of the thatched cottage at Betws, Boyce, Fripp and Topham discussed the aesthetics of Ruskin, and the arty social round of the Hampstead Conversazione and the Graphic Society. In Topham's opinion, Ruskin 'was a very clever writer but no artist, and not having any pretension to constituting himself a judge in art matters'.[66] No doubt the aesthetics of the Pre-Raphaelite Brotherhood also figured prominently in their debates. Cox had remarked of a drawing of the church at Betws by Boyce that it 'looked like a Pre-Raffaelite [sic] drawing'.[67]

The immediate environs of Betws suited the demand for particularity in painting better than many of the open upland sites which had attracted romantics in search of the sublime experience. It offered a landscape of immense variety condensed into a small area, with its cluster of houses, the church, the bridges, and the mixture of indigenous and larch trees. Furthermore, the very fact that it was a village with a resident population appealed to the developing English taste for picturesque peasants. In Roscoe's *Wanderings and Excursions*, and in the writings reflecting on Cox's visits to Betws, there was a marked change of tone in the description of local people from that prevalent up to the end of the eighteenth century. Indeed, de Loutherbourg's observations on the primitive nature of the Welsh people, who he compared with natives observed in the South Seas by Captain Cook, had been made as late as 1805. By the 1830s the taste was more for simple and friendly country people, living lives unaffected by the urban industrial background from which so many of the artists emerged in Manchester, Liverpool, Birmingham, Bristol and London. On his way to Dolwyddelan, Thomas Roscoe had celebrated in conventional fashion the seclusion and mountainous scale of the landscape he observed. However, on his return from the castle in the evening, he indulged a ruralism that might equally well have been applied to the peasantry of Kent:

> *'The road was now animated with moving and voluble life. Substantial farmers, on foot or horseback, were returning to their secluded homes, after a day of chaffering, buying and selling, in that exhilerated condition well known in the rural districts as "market-merry." The comely dames of the neighbourhood were mounted singly on well-fed palfreys, and the humbler peasants were driving before them on the dusty road flocks, and herds, and noisy litters.'*[69]

Cultural difference and the exotic retained their attraction to Regency and early Victorian travellers, but became fashionably expressed by a milder form of 'national character' than the threatening cultural otherness of the barbarous mountain dweller, which had complimented the exhilaration of the sublime sentiment in the eighteenth century. Ancient Britons were no longer sighted in Betws. William Hall described the place in terms of peat-gatherers, fern-gatherers, shepherds leading their flocks, drovers, ruddy-cheeked girls, farm labourers and fishermen, all of whom sat comfortably and charmingly within the high Victorian Britain from which he looked back.[69] The fashion on the London market for portraits expressive of benign national character from Wales and Ireland sustained many artists whose careers extended through the Victorian era, such as Topham and Fripp.

[66]Boyce op,cit.

[67]Ibid.

[68]Roscoe, op.cit., 1844 edition, p.210.

[69]Hall, op.cit., p.81-2. Hall was quoting an untraced source.

3

Clarence Whaite: the Conwy Valley between 1850 and 1880

J.P.Seddon, *Rocks by a River*, and the signature of Cox's biographer William Hall, from the visitor's book of the Royal Oak Hotel, Betws-y-coed, 1848.

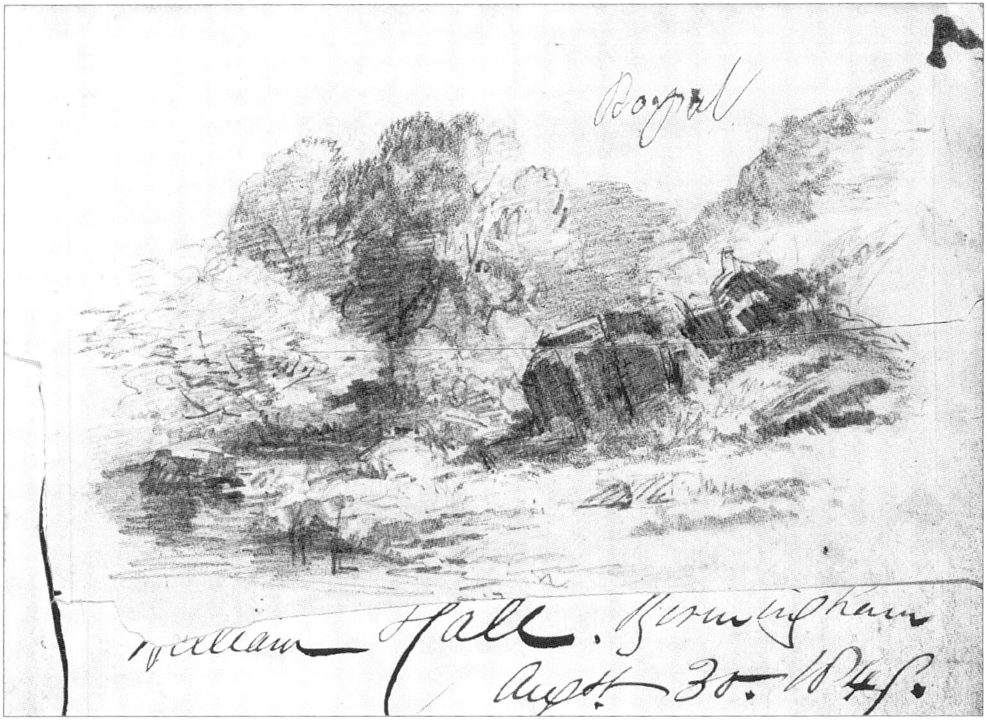

[70]J.J.Jenkins, 'An Artist's Haunt', *Brighton Gazette*, 23 October 1856.

The period 1850-80 saw the consolidation of the fashion for the Conwy Valley among the new generation of English landscape painters, and especially those coming out of the north-west and the midlands of England. The combination of regular visitors and an increasing number of residents had turned Betws into the first British artists' colony, and in 1856 the earliest account of the village to describe it in these terms was published. It was written by Josiah Jenkins, and was significant not only for its description of the village and of the role of David Cox, but also because it revealed a desire to create a school on the French model, associated with a particular place:

> *'English artists do not, like their brethren on the continent, form a class apart, and are not like them gregarious in their habits. English artists have no such places of rural rendezvous as the French meet with in the forest of Fontainebleau, at Barbizon. Perhaps the nearest approach to these continental assemblages which Great Britain affords, is at Bettwys, where "The Oak" occasionally shelters at one time ten or a dozen artists. This distinction is entirely owing to David Cox. It is his pencil that first made the little village known to the world of art; it is the fame he has acquired which has induced others to visit this district, and for the many solid advantages which result from this succession of visitors, the inhabitants are indebted to the friendly, warm-hearted artist who enjoys the happiness of doing good to others. What Walter Scott did for the Highlands, and Wordsworth for the Lake district, David Cox has done for Wales - attracting there not only the younger aspirants for artistic honours, but the admirers of wild, uncultivated, and picturesque scenery, and even the ordinary tourist, who hurries from place to place in search of that mental excitement he is incapable of feeling.'*[70]

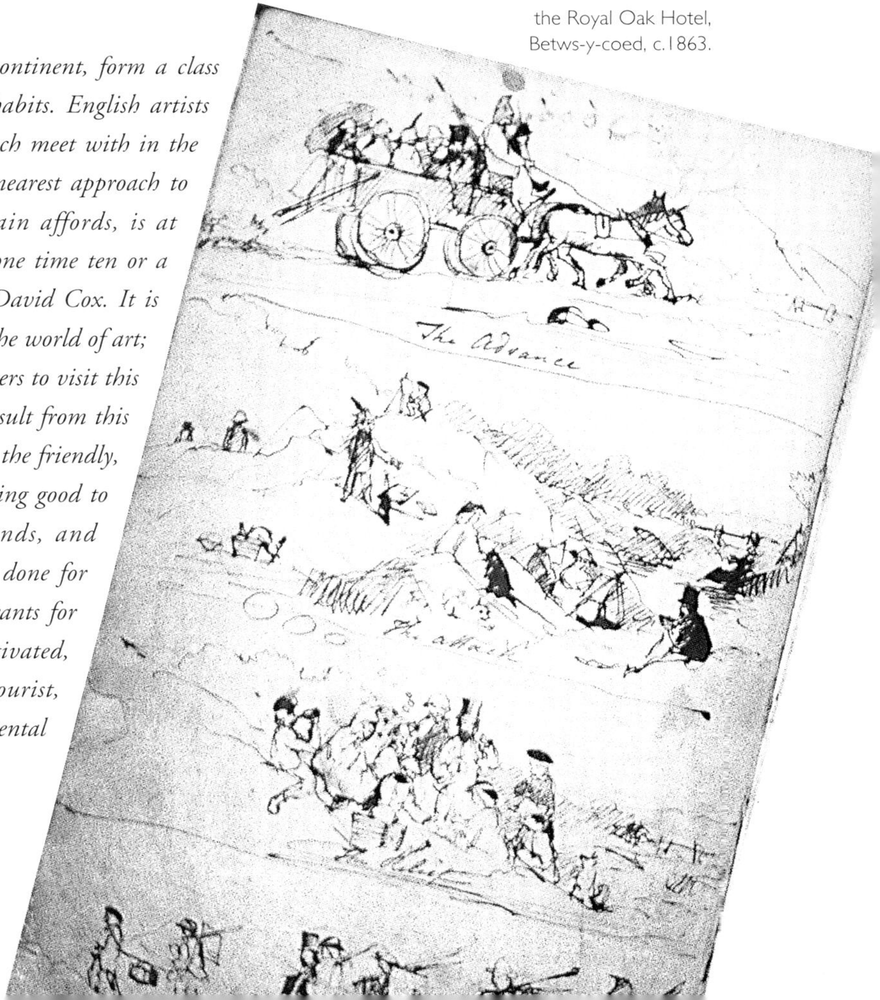

Unknown artist,
The Invading Army,
from the visitor's book of
the Royal Oak Hotel,
Betws-y-coed, c.1863.

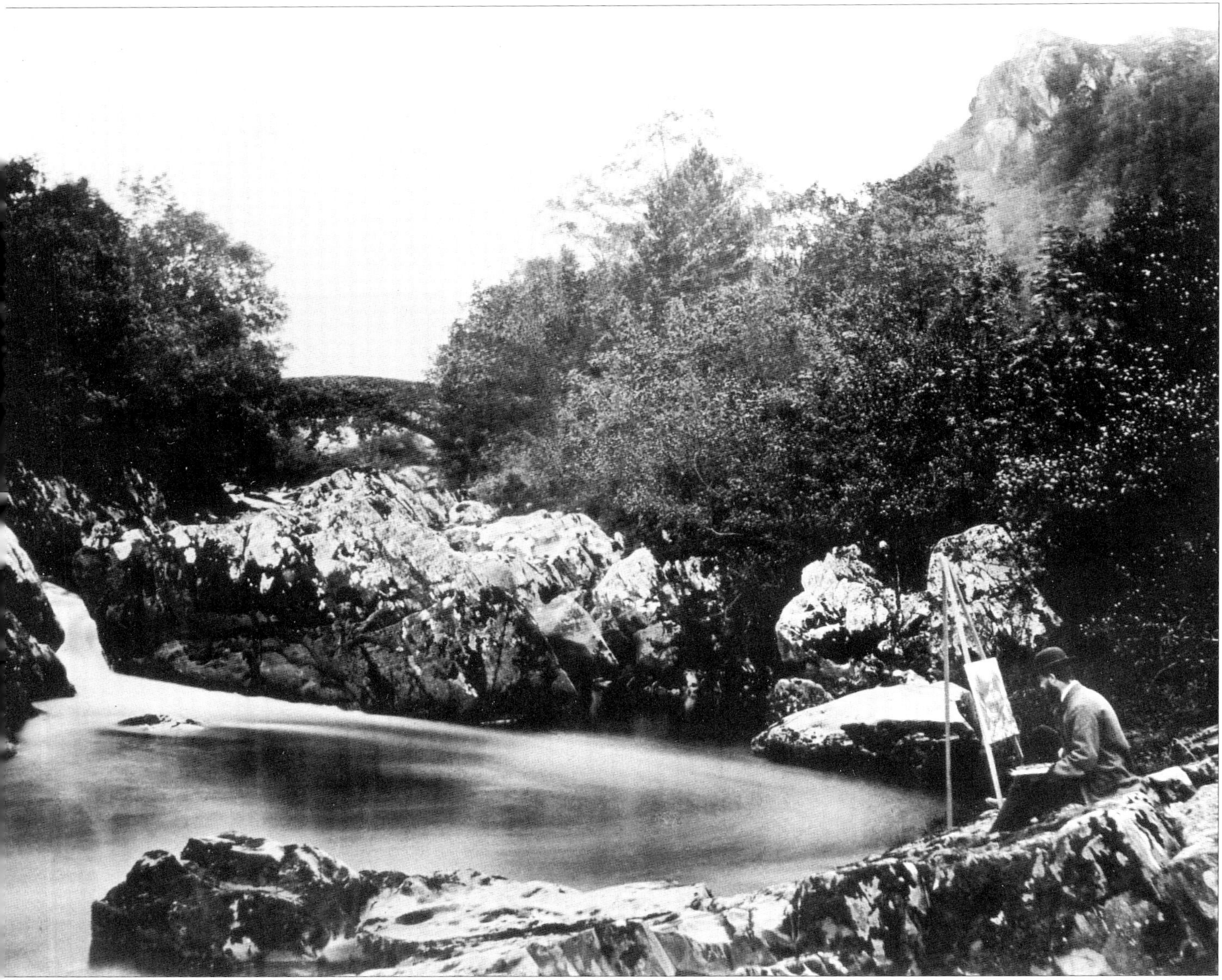

Henry White,
View from the Lledr Bridge,
Betws-y-coed, c.1855-60.

The visitors books of the Royal Oak show that these 'ordinary tourists' were not as homogenous and insensitive a group as Jenkins suggested. While the majority were English, there was also a certain amount of internal tourism, and the names of a number of Welsh poets and intellectuals, most notably William Williams, Caledfryn, father of the painter ap Caledfryn, who stayed in 1854, appear on the register. Among tourists from beyond England, Americans outnumbered any other nationality.[71]

On his first visits to Betws in 1851 and 1852 Clarence Whaite was quickly drawn into the sophisticated company of urban devotees of pious peasants and picturesque landscape around Cox. On 15 August 1852 he was with Cox's friend 'Fat' Hoyle, who introduced him to George Popkin. The following day he was 'brought into one of the most picturesque houses I was ever in. It was a farm house near the junction of the Ledder and the Conway - a Mr.Bedule and two other artists lodging here.'[72] On 20 August, he made the acquaintance of one of the earliest photographers recorded at Betws, a Mr Field. Whaite entered into a long discussion with Field about his 'Talbotype machine'. Field told him that Mark Anthony was using photographs in his work which did not surprise Whaite who felt that 'his pictures have that look'. Whaite was impressed by Field's photographs: 'He has a few pictures with him which are really wonderful and their usefulness to the Artist, I think, we cannot question.' Two days later he went to the falls with the photographer and John Bell,[73] a London painter staying at the Swan, and soon after had a demonstration of the fixing process of the Talbotype. Field's work is untraced, but a few years later the distinguished English photographer Henry White visited Betws, and took pictures using the new wet collodion process. A number of White's photographs showed painters at work near the Lledr Bridge. White would be followed by many more visiting photographers, including Francis Frith and Francis Bedford, both of whom built successful businesses supplying pictures singly or bound in albums. Bedford was probably the most prolific producer of books of Welsh views, and his *Photographic Views of Bettws-y-Coed and Neighbourhood* was among the most popular albums. The purchase of such works became an essential part of the visitor's stay in Betws.[74]

[71]The visitors book for 1847-51, with some later additions, is kept at the National Museum of Wales. Subsequent books are in a private archive.

[72]Diary, Whaite Archive, op.cit. Bedule is untraced. The house may possibly have been Wern Fawr Farm, on the opposite side of the road from Bond's Wern Fawr.

[73]John Bell (fl.1847-61) showed works from the Betws area at the British Institution and at the Royal Society of British Painters in 1854.

[74]Some visitors added their diaries and jottings to the photographic albums. John Severn, who bought Bedford's *Views* on a visit in 1883 bound in extra pages on which he kept a diary of his visit: 'Of the beauties of Bettws-y-coed I had heard much, and my anticipations were not disappointed...' NLW Llyfr Ffotograff 293.

James Whittaker, *View on the Road between Capel Curig and Llyn Ogwen, North Wales*, 1863.

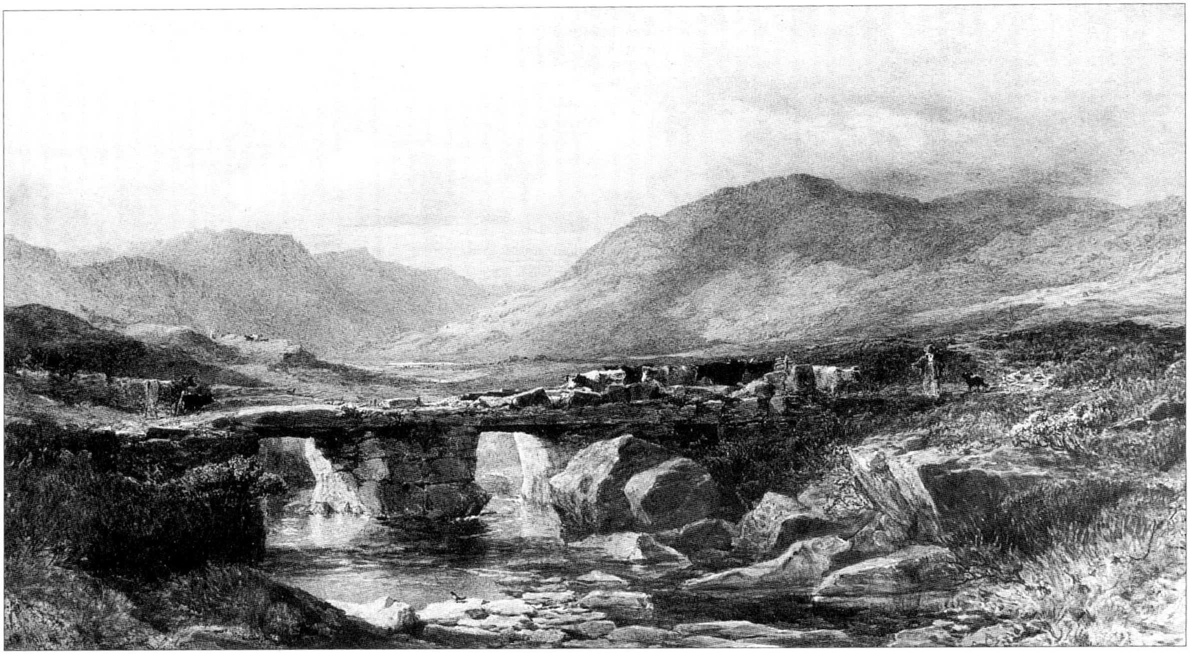

Whaite soon developed personal friendships with the painters around him and began to gain a reputation as his work was exhibited in London and favourably noticed by the critics. Notable among the permanent residents at Betws who Whaite quickly came to know was James Whittaker. He lived at Ffridd on the east bank of the Conwy near its junction with the Llugwy from about 1857. This was the site originally occupied by Popkin, when it was known as Castell Pwt. Whittaker had worked as an engraver to a firm of calico printers in Manchester by which means he saved enough money to set up home in Wales. His neighbour, Frank Topham, admired his work and encouraged him to stand for membership of the Society of Painters in Water Colours, of which he became an associate in 1862.[75] By this time Clarence Whaite knew him well. In a letter written to his father from Capel Curig in 1862, Whaite noted a visit he paid to Whittaker:

[75]'For some time he [Whittaker] sold his watercolours at a low price to a Manchester dealer. Francis William Topham, however, saw and admired them when on a visit to Wales, and recommended Whittaker to try to join the Society of Painters in Watercolour.' C.R.Grundy and F.G.Roe, *A Catalogue of the Pictures and Drawings in the Collection of Frederick John Nettlefold*, Vol IV, p.128.

[76]Whaite archive, op.cit., letter dated 8 December 1862.

'I was at Bettws yesterday in the afternoon - the morning was wet, so did not go to church but attended the Welch at Capel Curig. I called to see Whittaker; saw the baby (such a little one); it is quite well and also Mrs W. I dined with my friend Mr Luke at the Oak - I called to see some drawings by Mr Eddington and met five Manchester artists at his house, or rather four, for I made the fifth and another from Cheshire - so you see Manchester is still well represented at Bettws.'[76]

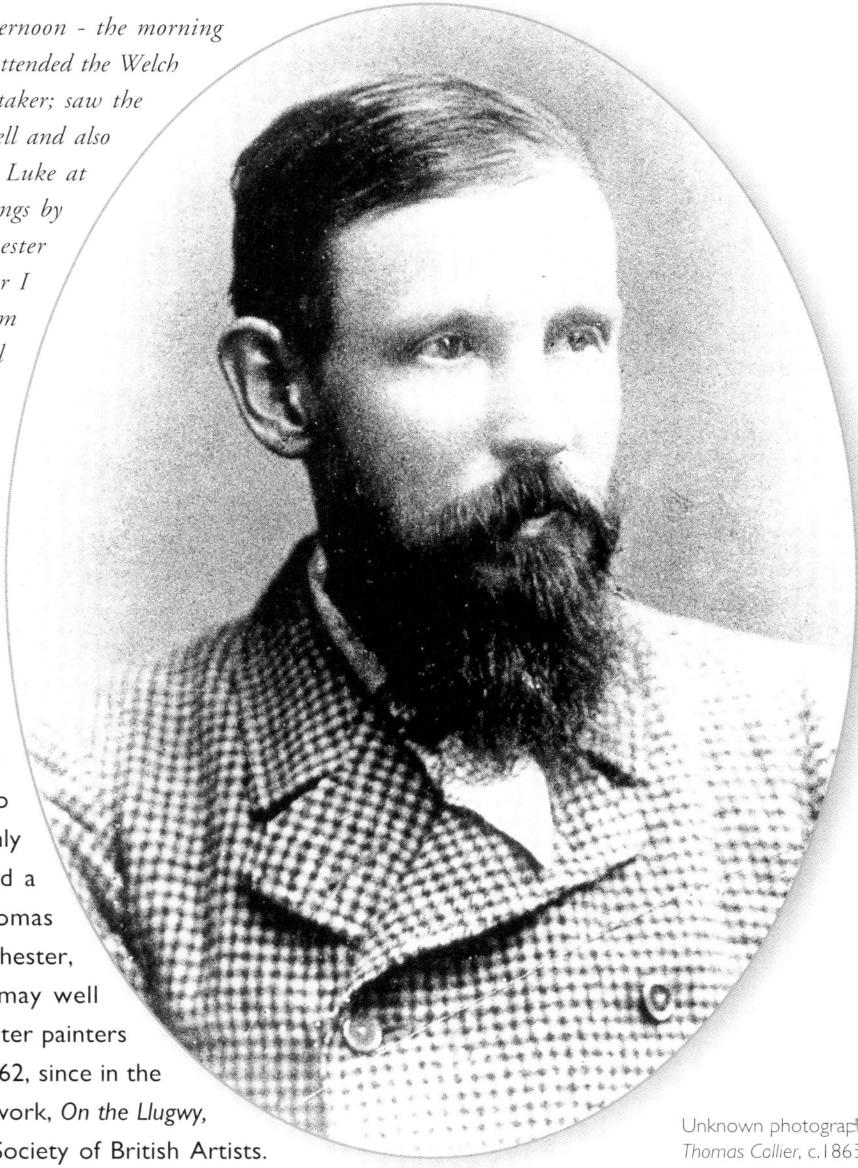

This letter was written on 8 December, and the presence of artists in such numbers out of season suggests that the companionship and hospitality offered by the resident painters swelled the number of visitors all year round. Whittaker travelled to Italy in 1864 and on his return Whaite again visited him, noting that 'he has not done much work but I think it will do him good'. This comment almost certainly referred to the fact that Whittaker had a drink problem. In the same year, Thomas Collier, another painter trained in Manchester, took up residence in Betws. Collier may well have been among the group of Manchester painters mentioned by Whaite in his letter of 1862, since in the following year his first exhibited Betws work, *On the Llugwy, North Wales*, was shown at the Royal Society of British Artists.

Unknown photographer,
Thomas Collier, c.1865.

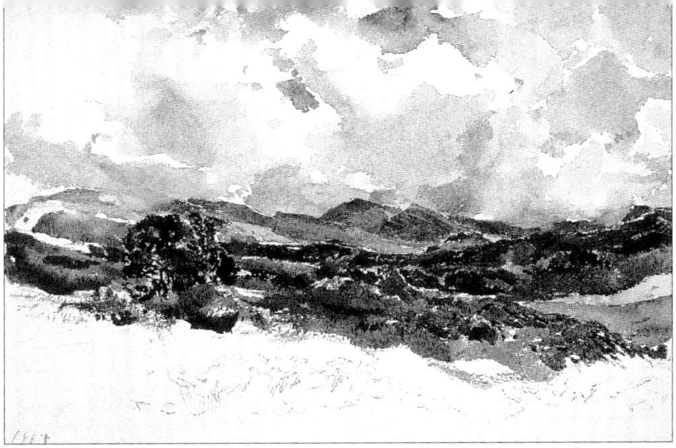

Thomas Collier,
Hilly Country with Clouds, 1887.
Reproduced in colour on p.44.

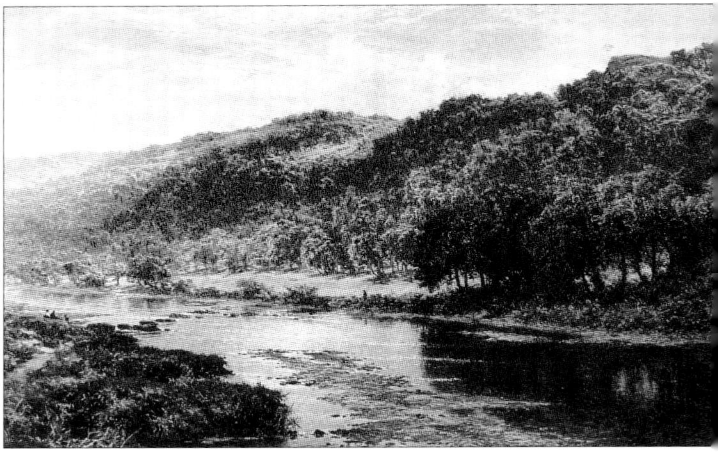

B.W.Leader,
View on the Llugwy, below Capel Curig, 1903.
Reproduced in colour on p.152.

In 1864 Collier took lodgings with Mrs Hughes at Llugwy Cottage where he stayed for long periods. Mrs Hughes was among the first local residents, apart from the publicans, to take advantage of the increasing amount of artistic tourism by letting rooms, and became host to many artists. Collier's progress in London was frustrated by the success of Whittaker, his neighbour over the river. It seems that some members of the Society of Painters in Water Colours argued that both Collier and Whittaker were exponents of Cox's open style of work. Since Whittaker was already a member, the Society had no need of the newcomer, whatever his talent. The Society refused him membership and so Collier turned to the Institute of Painters in Water Colours (the rival 'New Society'), which granted him associate membership in 1870.[77] Collier's circle at Betws included a number of moderately successful painters such as John Syer, but also Benjamin Williams Leader, who was at the beginning of a career which would lead to the top of the English art world. Leader, who was of Welsh descent on his father's side, stayed at the Royal Oak for the first time in July 1859, and exhibited Betws views at the Royal Academy in the following year, when he was 29 years old.

[77]See Adrian Bury, *The Life and Art of Thomas Collier*, R.I. (London, 1944), p.25. Whether Whittaker was a party to the campaign against his neighbour is unclear.

[78]Among several accounts of the death was one given by the agent of the Voelas estate: 'He [Whittaker] was found in the Llugwy, a little below the Miners' Bridge on Thursday evening, and it appears he must have been drowned and in the river for nearly 48 hours as he was missed the previous day - an enquiry was held on Saturday and "accidental death" was the verdict of the jury. He had gone to the river bank to sketch and was I fear slightly intoxicated at the time, and in some way or other he must have fallen over and was washed 400 or 500 yards down the stream when some rocks prevented his going further.' NLW Voelas Estate Papers, B9 159, letter from A.H.Trethewy to Sir Charles Wynne Finch, 12 Sep 1876.

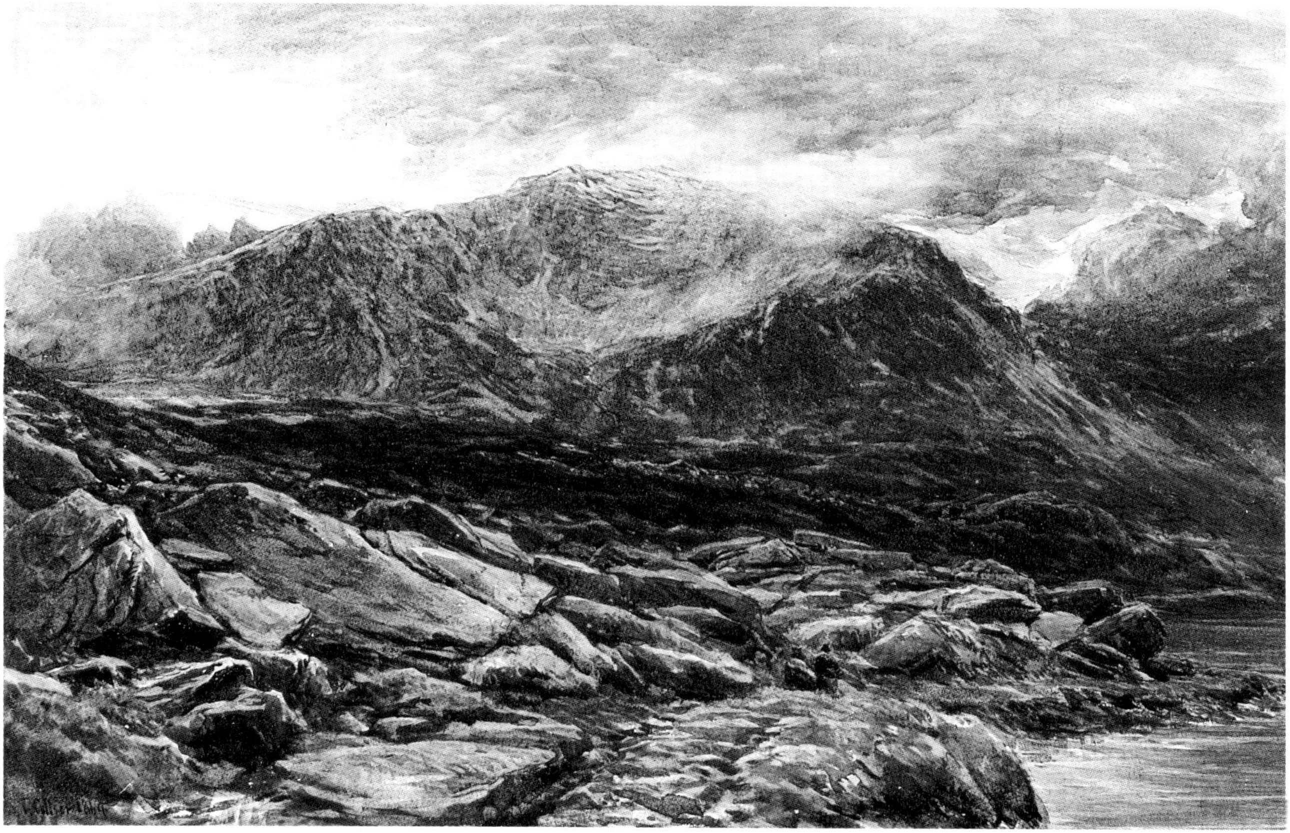

Thomas Collier
Welsh Mountain Landscape, 1869

Collier seems to have given up his lodgings at Betws in 1869, although he continued to visit for many years. Whittaker's career in the area came to a more decisive end in 1876 when he slipped from rocks by the Miners' Bridge on the Llugwy and was killed. The two ladies who discovered his body in a stream also recovered two empty spirit-bottles.[78] Whittaker had finally succombed to the demon drink which had cast the only shadow over an otherwise successful career. Of more long-term importance in the development of the artists' colony was the arrival in the early 1860s of George Harrison from Kent.

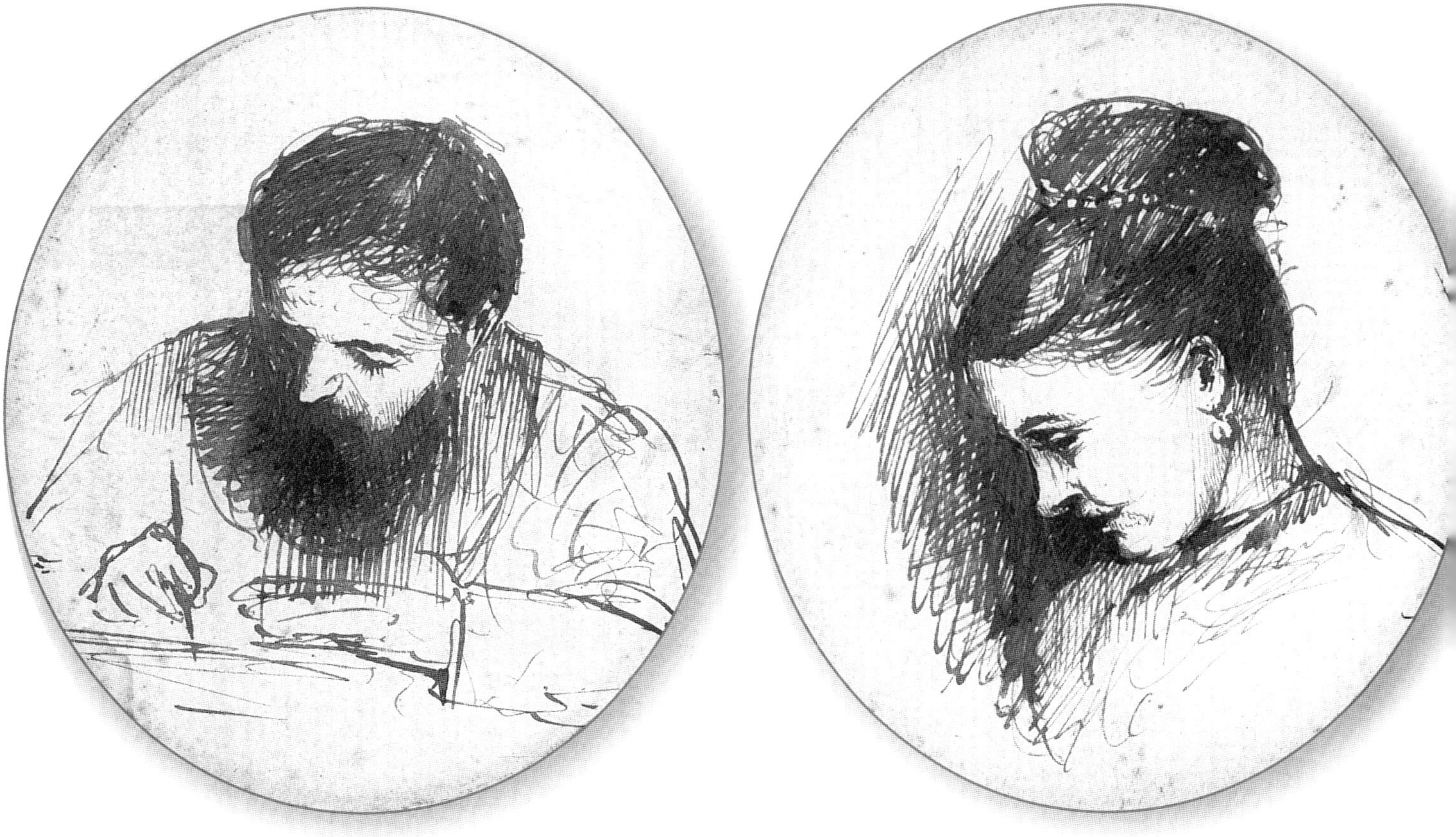

Above:
Unknown artist,
George and Catrin Harrison, c.1865.

Opposite:
Francis Frith, *Distant View of Betws-y-coed*, c.1868.

[79]Bury, op.cit., p.23.

Harrison was forced to run away from his bourgeois family in Canterbury in order to pursue his career as an artist. He was still in his early twenties when he arrived at Betws and his attatchment to the place was secured by a romantic involvement with a local woman. He married Catrin, daughter of the blacksmith at Betws, in 1863 and they set up home at Tŷ Gwyn, a small cottage by the Waterloo Bridge. George Harrison became a friend of Clarence Whaite, although it is not clear at what date they met.

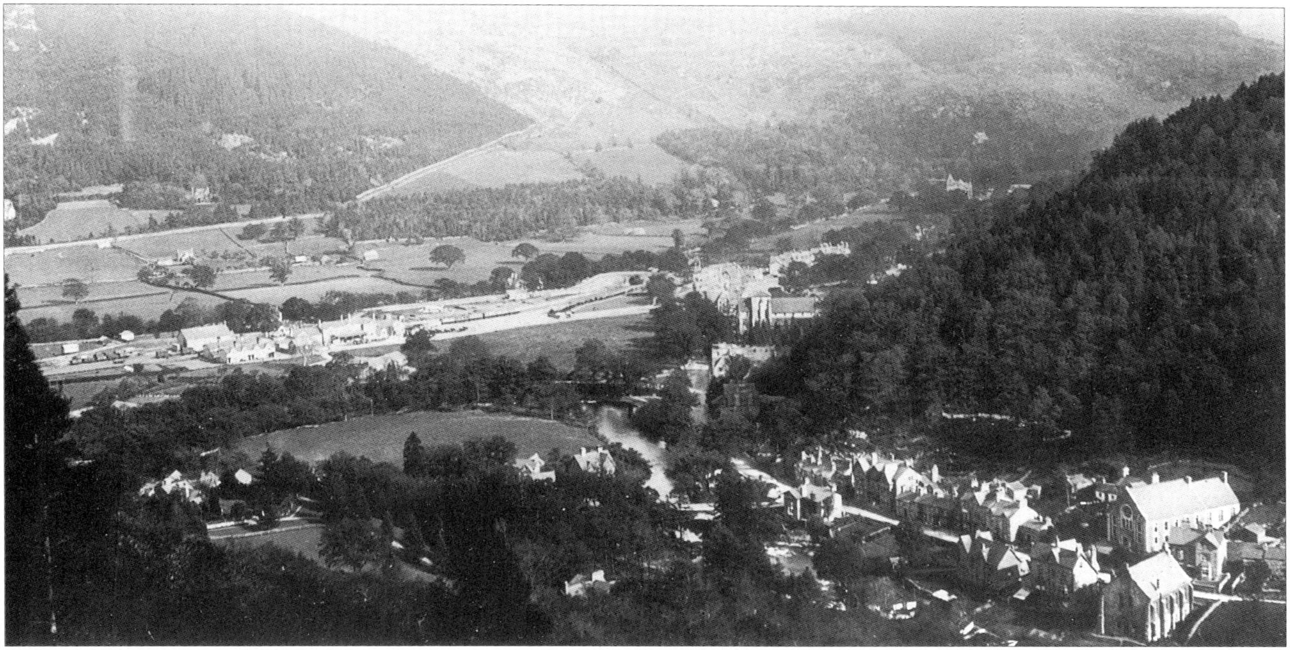

The building of the railway up the Conwy Valley in the 1860s was responsible for further stimulating the number of artists visiting the area. However, some of the residents viewed its impending arrival with trepidation. In 1864, Collier remarked that: 'There is some talk of the railway coming up here, which will be an awful nuisance, and I am afraid quite spoil the place'.[79] The railway had reached Llanrwst in the previous year and was extended to Betws, as Collier predicted, in 1868. In 1879 a further section was built through Dolwyddelan to Blaenau Ffestiniog. The artists were becoming the victims of their own publicity, and older aficionados of the village such as William Hall were deeply offended:

> *'Horror of horrors! a stone bridge with several arches carries this railway across the famous Heron Pool, which many will remember at a bend of the river just beyond the little 'Fish Inn' (now turned into an office), once a convenient halting place for artists desirous of painting the scenery of the valley.'*[80]

[80]Hall, op.cit., p.90. Hall further remarked that 'Bettws, in the season, is overrun with tourists; and artists, male and female, are to be seen on every hillside and under every green tree'. Such comments, written in the 1880s and 90s, are legion. In 1887, for instance, Owen Owen, recalling Hugh Hughes in the 1820s, remarked that he was "a rather tall and thin man, an artist, which was not common in those days, as it was before all the artists came in to the Conway Valley; they are here now thick as bees'. T.H.Thomas, 'A Welsh Bewick', *Red Dragon* 11, 1887, p.462.

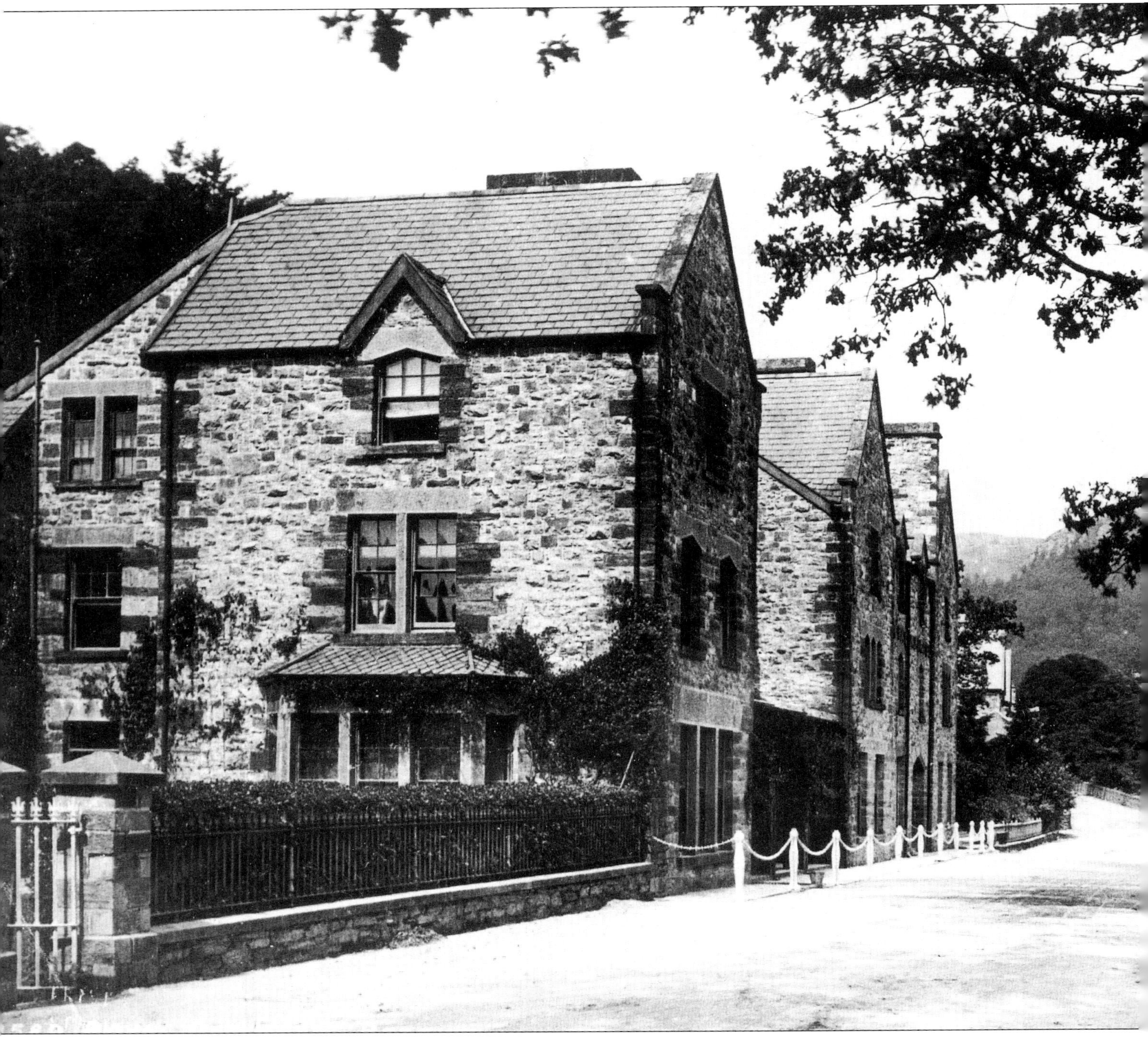

To local landowners, the increase in visitors was a mixed blessing. The Voelas Estate began to charge for admission to the Fairy Glen and, when the weather was bad, the lack of tourists caused a depression in business of sufficient importance for the agent to inform his employer of the losses to the lodging house keepers. On the other hand, he reported that 'some of the excursionists have been actually pulling up by the roots the young larch trees in the Conway Falls plantation under the impression that they have come upon a rare kind of fern. I saw 6 or 8 young trees that had been thus treated and were about to be taken away. Unfortunately I could not find the depradators'.[81] The Victorian fashion for collecting ferns was much practiced at Betws, to the extent that some guide books included lists of the varieties to be found in the area.

Opposite:
Unknown photographer,
The Royal Oak Hotel
(as rebuilt in 1861).

In the village itself, David Cox's 'humble home' at the Royal Oak was rebuilt in 1861 as a three storey gabled structure:

> '*...now crowds of tourists may be seen any fine day in the season, promenading in front of the windows of the grand new hotel; playing croquet in the garden, or sitting down in the evening to a luxurious repast at its* table d'hôte.... *The old church has been found too*

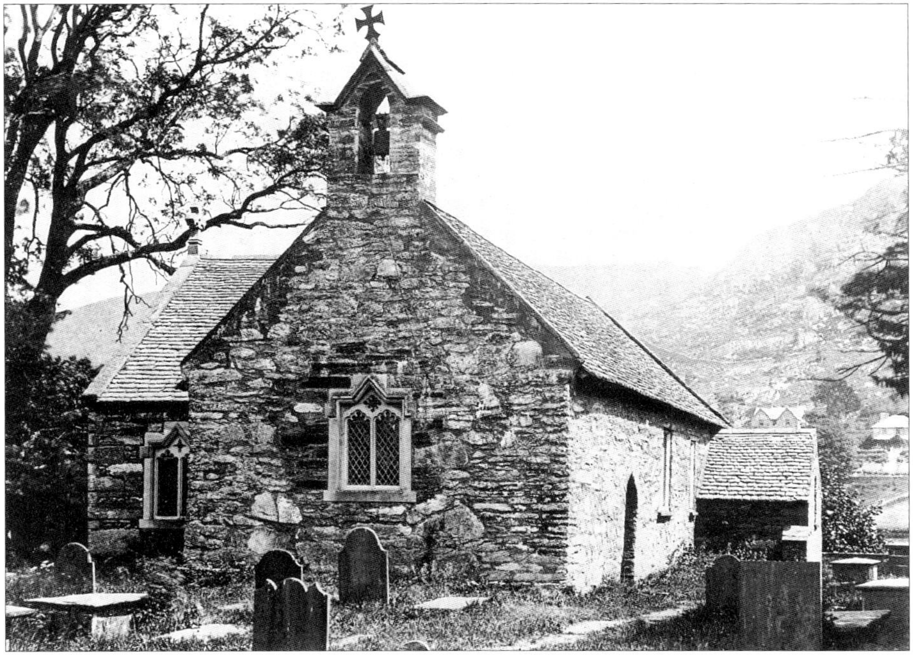

Unknown photographer,
The Church at Betws-y-coed and Ty'n-y-fron (far right - the home of Lawrence Coppard) c.1870.

[81]NLW Voelas Estate Papers, B9 244, letter from A.H.Trethewy to Sir Charles Wynne Finch.

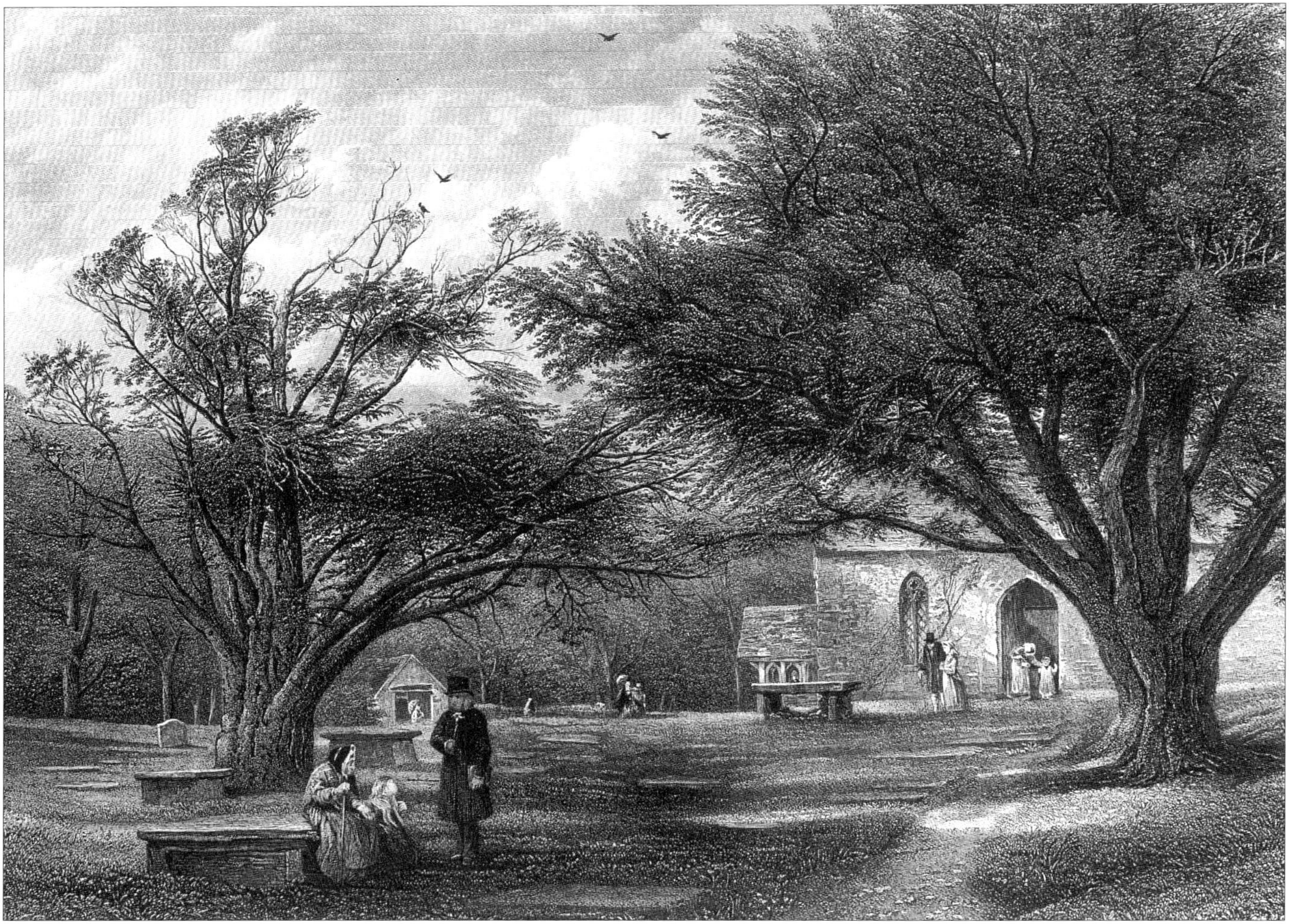

Thomas Creswick,
The Church at Bettws y Coed,
from *The Art Journal*, 1870.

small to accomodate the visitors who crowd into Bettws during "the season," and a new one has been erected, devoted to the English-speaking community entirely. More surprising still! at the back of the old church, and near the side of the "sweet-flowing" river Conway, the visitor may behold in all its ugliness an unsightly gasometer, placed there for the very desirable purpose of lighting "dear old Bettws" with gas! The railway station, with its shrieking engines and multitudinous noises, almost abuts upon the wall of the old churchyard, with its venerable yews, once sacred to quiet, and sweet with the repose of its secluded position amid the mountains that screened it from the world; and a wide thoroughfare now conducts the traveller to the railway platform, near the very spot, and almost over the very ground, where of old might have been seen, on a Sabbath morning, groups of pious villagers wending their ways, in twos and threes, to that sacred fabric where for generations their forefathers had assembled to offer up their prayers.'[82]

Collier's early fears were confirmed by events. In 1870 he found Betws changed, 'so much you would scarce know it. Standing on the bridge and looking up the stream the most striking object is a very large chapel which almost shuts out the hill behind'.[83] In his letters he referred disparagingly to visitors as 'B.Ts' (British tourists). Artists staying at the Royal Oak contributed anti-tourist doggerel to the visitor's book along with their drawings and cartoons. In 1866 an unidentified aficionado of long standing began his or her lengthy 'October Verses':

'I used to come to Bettws
Nigh twenty years ago.
The Oak! it was a pleasant place
With Creswick, Cox, & Co;
But then no restless Tourists
Were rushing to and fro.

The ground was all artistic,
Down by the quaint old mill
Would sit some candidate for fame,
Another on the hill
Among the heather'd moorland;
I would it were so, still!'[84]

Even as Collier described the desecration of the village in his letters, *The Art Journal* was busy promulgating Betws as a timeless Arcadia. The magazine published a new engraving of Creswick's *The Church at Bettws-y-Coed*, noting that: 'Few rural areas have been made so familiar to us by the hand of the artist as the picturesque village and neighbourhood of Bettws-y-Coed, for it is rare, indeed, to see an exhibition of paintings without some representation of this favourite resort of the "brethren of the brush".' The church, with its 'old grey walls, with the aged yew trees in the churchyard, which seem coeval with the sacred ediface, and the sylvan belt that surrounds the whole, constitute a picture at once solemn and quiet'.[85] The railway and the gasometer were not advertised.

[82]Hall, op.cit., pp.91-2. The Royal Oak was enlarged for a second time after the 1861 rebuilding. When it was sold in 1920, as 'one of the best known hostelries in Wales', there were 20 acres of grounds extending to the bank of the Llugwy. Sale catalogue, Messrs. Knight, Frank and Rutley, London, 28 May 1920.

[83]Bury, op.cit., p.27.

[84]Royal Oak visitor's book, op.cit.

[85]*The Art Journal*, 1870, p.364.

The peace and quiet of Betws had gone forever and the social scene became lively. David Cox had once been so offended by the drawing of caricatures of the vicar on the lych gate and the whitewashed church porch, that he ventured out at night to remove the offending graffiti. In the decade following Cox's death such an outburst of youthful high spirits would have seemed trivial. In November 1864 Collier noted in a letter that 'There was a great spree here on the fifth. We had no end of fireworks and a good guy and bonfire, the ceremony, of course, concluding with a grand liquoring up...', no doubt involving Whittaker and Edward Roberts of the Royal Oak.[86] Clarence Whaite was at Trefriw the same night and reported the events, with a somewhat more respectable gloss, to his father:

> *'There was a grand display of fireworks at Bettws last night; it was postponed by desire of the Welch for they said the bonfire would be burning on the Sunday and they might not have done before Sunday commenced - it was all got up by the Artists and almost regret I did not go over. There was a monster Guy twenty or thirty feet high and a large bonfire quite as large as an ordinary cottage. I believe it brought together the country folks for many miles.'*[87]

Boarding houses with English names, such as 'The Mount', 'Snowden Villa' and 'Greenbank', proliferated in Betws, almost all of them Welsh owned, and by the early 1880s the population had climbed rapidly to a peak of nearly 800.[88] Prosperous and fashion conscious English people built their own villas, some of them with a hint of Alpine style in the form of deep overhanging eaves and balconied fronts. They lived cheek by jowl with the artists. One group of substantial villas, overlooking the village and up the valley of the Llugwy, included Park Hill, home of Edwin Pettit, Ty'n-y-fron, which was occupied by Lawrence Coppard, who built a studio in the outbuilding behind the house, and Rose Hill, home of William Artingstall. George Popkin's Plas Muriau stood a few hundred yards to the north. The Plas had a particularly illustrious art history, being taken over from Popkin in 1860 by Captain William Drury Nathanial Drury Lowe, an *aide-de-camp* of Lord Cardigan.

[86] Bury, op.cit., p.23.

[87] Whaite archive, op.cit., letter dated 8 November 1864.

[88] In 1861 the census recorded a population of 509, which had risen to 784 by 1881. Ten years later it had declined to 740.

BETTWS-Y-COED, LLANRWST, CAPEL CURIG, &c. 83

CARDS OF APARTMENTS.

MR. REES P. DAVIES, GREENBANK, BETTWS-Y-COED.	MR. W. EVANS, *ELSI COTTAGE,* BETTWS-Y-COED.	Mr. D. JONES, FRONDEG, BETTWS-Y-COED.
MRS. GRACE PARRY, GLAN CONWAY HOUSE, BETTWS-Y-COED.	Mrs. ALICE HUGHES, COED-Y-FRON, BETTWS-Y-COED.	MR. R. DAVIES, *PLAS DERWEN,* BETTWS-Y-COED.
Misses M. & J. JONES, GLANDWR HOUSE, BETTWS-Y-COED.	MR. R. HUGHES, *Craig-y-don,* BETTWS-Y-COED.	MR. ROBERT HUGHES, COED GYNHELIER, BETTWS-Y-COED.
Miss E. JONES, PONT-Y-PAIR HOUSE, BETTWS-Y-COED.	MRS. JOHN OWEN, BODHYFRYD, BETTWS-Y-COED.	Mr. D. DAVIES (Exors. of) *Mount View,* BETTWS-Y-COED.
MR. I. J. HUGHES, *Snowden Villa.* BETTWS-Y-COED.	Mr. JOHN JONES, *Bod Gwynedd,* BETTWS-Y-COED.	MRS. ROBERTS, *CHURCH HILL,* BETTWS-Y-COED.
MRS. HUGHES, Melbourne Villa, FESTINIOG.	MR. HENRY PARRY, *Old Post Office,* CAPEL CURIG.	**MRS. JONES,** SALISBURY TERRACE, LLANRWST.
MRS. R. LLOYD, 2, LLEWELYN TERRACE, LLANRWST.	MRS. M. WILLIAMS, 1, LLEWELYN TERRACE, LLANRWST.	Mrs. ANN LLOYD, *Bryn Conway,* LLANRWST.

BETTWS-Y-COED.

BETTWS-Y-COED (the station in the wood) is a parish in the poor law uuion of Llanrwst, situated at the junction of the rivers Llugwy and Conway, 4½ miles from Llanrwst, 2½ from the Swallow Falls, 2½ from the Conway Falls, and 6½ from Capel Curig. Bettws-y-coed, from its admirable and romantic surroundings and position, is admittedly the most lovely village in the principality; its beauty and the facilities for angling attract many visitors during the season. Denbighshire and Carnarvonshire are united by a light and elegant iron bridge which, having been erected in 1815, is called the Waterloo Bridge. There are numerous excellent hotels and many private lodging-houses for the accommodation of visitors. By means of the Festiniog branch of the London and North Western Railway, Bettws-y-coed has direct communication with all parts of the kingdom. There are two churches of the Establishment, and chapels for various dissenting bodies. Population in 1881, 784

Post Office, Jane Jones, postmistress. Letters arrive from all parts at 7 a.m. and 4 p.m. and are despatched thereto at 10-15 a.m. and 7 p.m.
St. Michael's Church, Rev. Evan Evans, vicar
St. Mary's Church, Rev. Evan Evans, vicar
Calvinistic Methodist Chapel
Congregational Chapel, Rev. Thomas Evans
Glan Llugwy School, Miss C. Owen, mistress
National School, Robert O. Jones, master
Registrar of Births and Deaths, Daniei Jones, Glan [Conway
Police Station, Watkin Owen, sergeant
Petty Sessions are held at Police Office (monthly), Richard James, solicitor, Llanrwst, clerk to justices
Gas Works, near Railway station
Railway Station (L. & N.-W. Railway)
Coaches to Beddgelert & Llanberis from the Waterloo Hotel daily during summer
Coaches to Bangor, Beddgelert & Llanberis from the Royal Oak Hotel daily during summer

Advertisements for apartments from *Sutton's North Wales Directory*, 1889.

Opposite:
Unknown photographer,
William D.Barker, c.1880.

Below:
Ffridd Castle, Betws-y-coed,
the home of James Whittaker.

However, the Captain seems to have been a reluctant soldier, and much more at ease with artists. He bought pictures by Popkin, Harrison and Whittaker, from whom he also took painting lessons.[89] Until his untimely death, James Whittaker lived a little further north at Ffridd, where he had been succeeded by Edward Binger by 1881. Whittaker had prospered to the extent that one of his obiturists believed that he could 'sell as many pictures as he could paint, at very good prices, and had made money'. He had been able to rebuild Ffridd, which became Ffrith Castle, a substantial and idiosyncratic residence, adorned with a tower and a steeple. Nevertheless, at his death, the agent to the Voelas estate, which owned much of the surrounding land, noted that in his house 'there is not

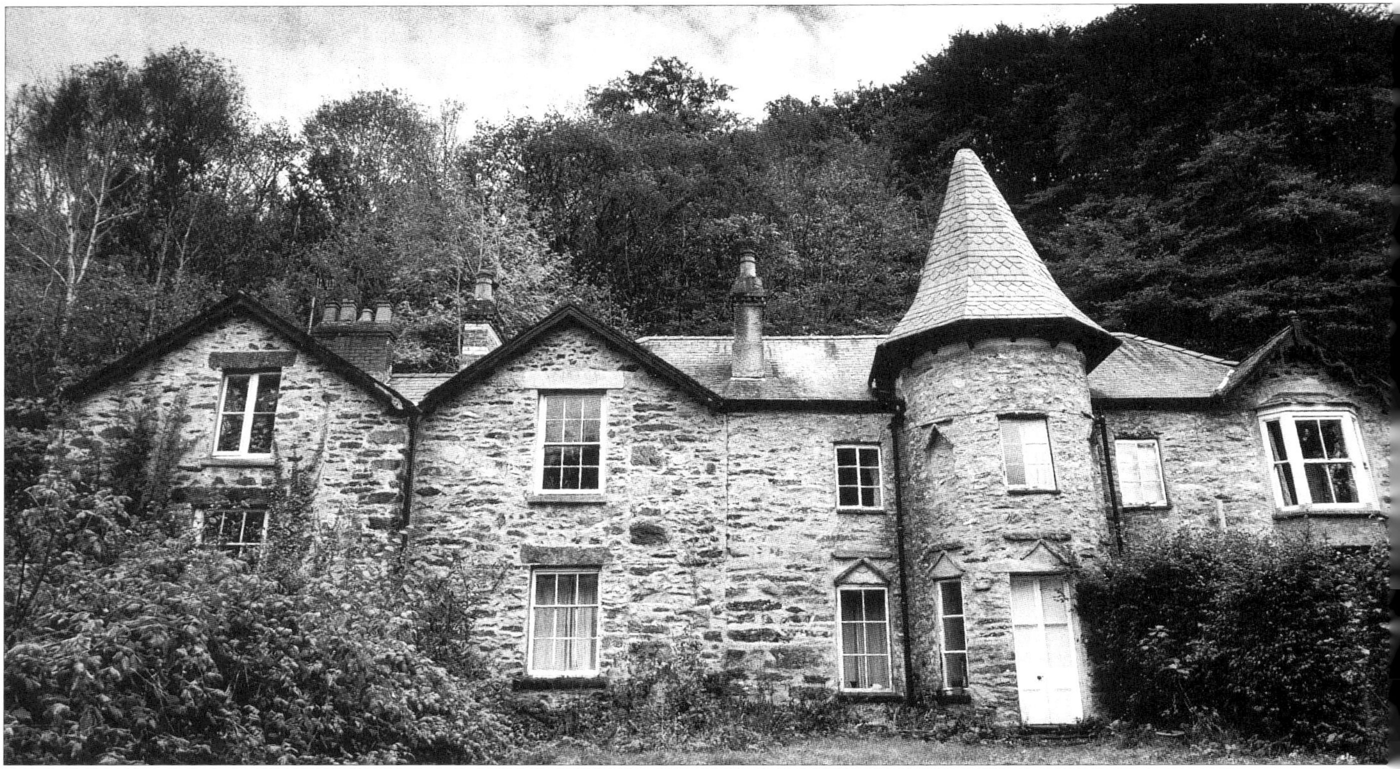

much of any value as he has sold everything he could convert into money'.[90] Whittaker's alcoholism had caused him to live his later years from hand to mouth.

No doubt recalling stories told by her father, George Harrison, Eleanor Forster believed that the artists 'added greatly to the social life of the village':

> *[They] 'got up entertainments for charities, concerts and dances among themselves and in the winter evenings a favourite form of amusement was card parties with light refreshment held at each artist's home by turn... The young bloods among them were fond of playing practical jokes on each other and some funny tales went round - one of them was challenged for a wager to run from the Royal Oak to the Old Church in his "birthday suit". He ran quite naked holding a tray in front of him and won the wager.'*[91]

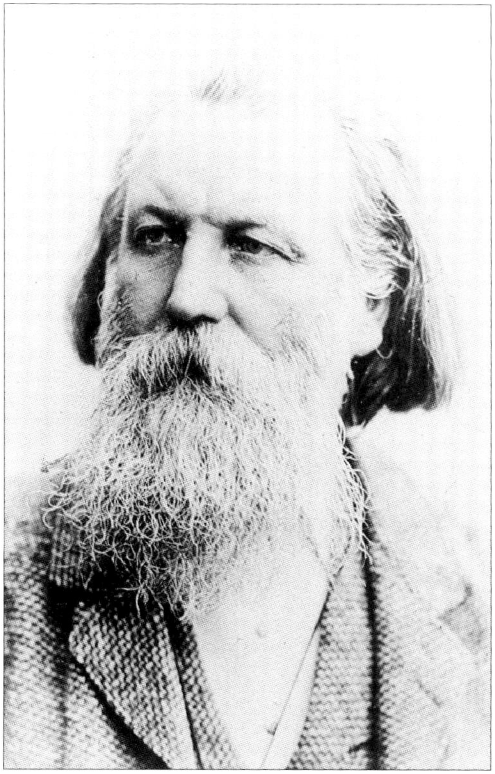

Some of the artists cut mildly eccentric figures among the respectable visitors. The painter and photographer William D.Barker, born in Salford, was 'Tall and stalwart, his strong face covered with a huge Sombrero',[92] and Edwin Pettit 'always wore a large beaver hat and a flowing tie'.[93] The artists liked to patronise local characters, such as 'Black Jack'. Eleanor Forster remembered that 'Jack's Lane (or Fordd Gruglan as it is called in Welsh) derived its name from a certain old John Jones who lived at a little farm called Gruglan, now a ruin. He was a picturesque old fellow and made a living by fishing and acting as Gilly to visitors to Bettws and occasionally sitting as model to artists.'[94]

[89] Information from the diary of W.D.N.Drury Lowe, Nottingham University Library. Lowe visited Italy in 1863 and commissioned an Italian artist, Pietro Romoli, to paint murals at his English house and a ceiling decoration at Plas Muriau in 1864. In the bedroom Drury Lowe emulated Romoli's work with a painting of his own. Another painter, James Spooner, possibly also occupied Plas Muriau for a time, though he may have lived at Muriau Farm, on the other side of the Llanrwst road. Little is known of Popkin's career after leaving Betws. He died at Exmouth in 1899. I am grateful to Lorna Schärer of Plas Muriau for making available to me her research on the house and Drury Lowe.

[90] NLW Voelas Estate Papers, B9 160, letter from A.E.Trethewy to Sir Charles Wynne Finch, 13 Sep 1876.

[91] Private archive of material relating to George Harrison.

[92] *The Manchester City News*, 29 September 1888.

[93] Harrison Archive, op.cit. Eleanor Forster wrote 'J. Pettit', presumably a mistake for the painter Edwin A.Pettit.

[94] Ibid.

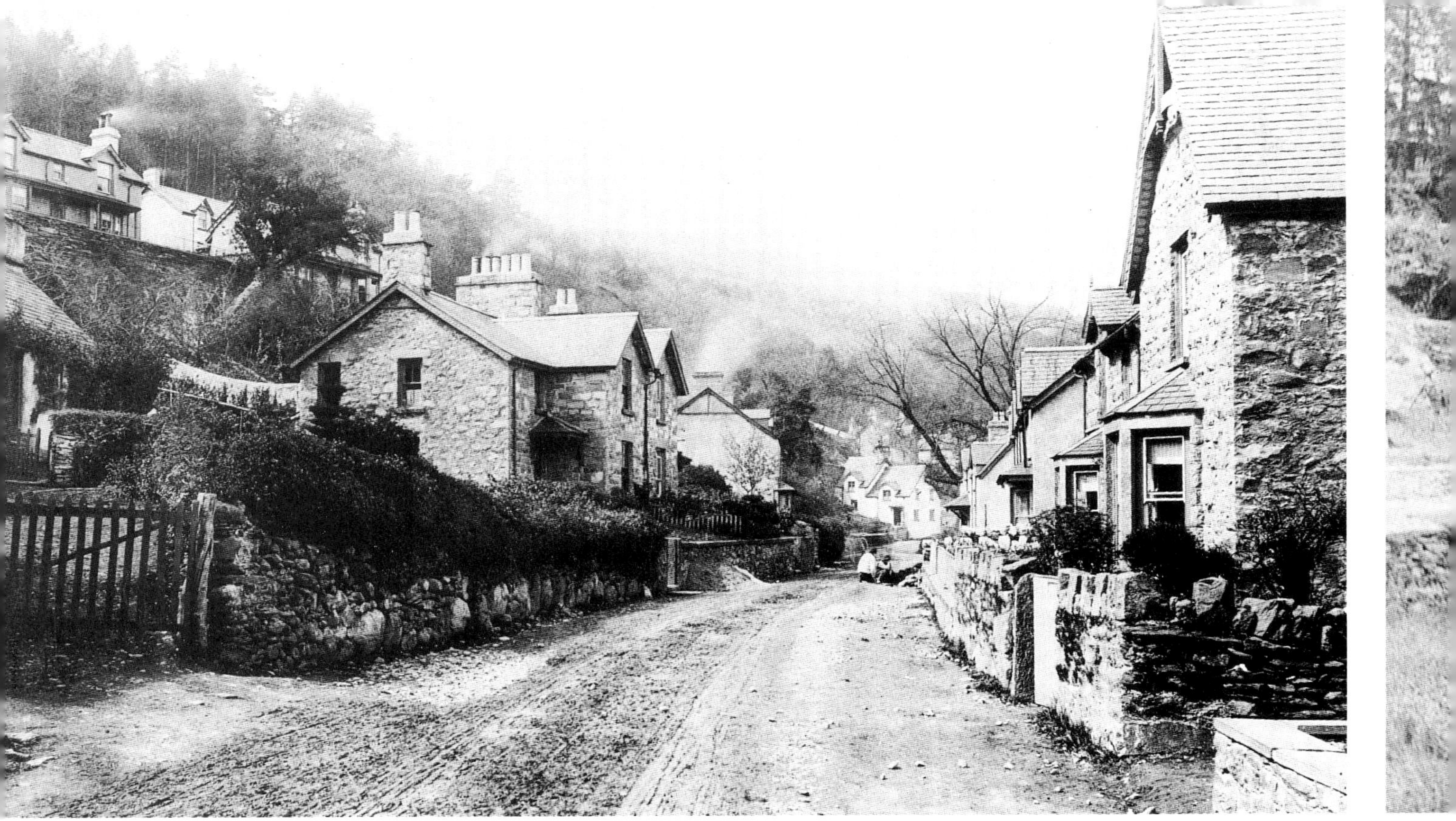

Unknown photographer,
Trefriw, c.1870

George Harrison and his family stayed in Betws, and Richard Bond remained nearby at Wern Fawr, but the location of artists in the Conwy Valley gradually became less concentrated in the village. There can be little doubt that this was the consequence of the great increase in tourism and the physical and social changes that came in its wake. Trefriw in particular grew in popularity. The painter James Atkins, originally from Warwick, had established himself at Bodlondeb by 1861 and ten years later William Barker was living at Minafon.[95] Between 1878 and 1881 at least nine other painters joined Barker in the village - considerably more than remained at Betws.[96] Trefriw was strategically placed for those artists who liked to venture up into the wild landscape of mountains and lakes that lay between the Conwy Valley and Snowdon. In 1871, Catrin Harrison, by now apparently assimilated into the English middle class, was among a party of women who joined three un-named artists who

[95]Barker lived at various addresses in Trefriw, finally settling at Plas Celyn where his daughter was still in residence in 1895 and practicing as a painter.

[96]John Paine Davies (Rowaleyn), Benjamin Fowler, Joseph Knight (Ty'n Twll), John Johnson (Fern Hill), Robert Goody (Woodbank), Henry Hilton (Fir Villa), James Moorland (Pen-y-bryn), Henry Roberts (Glandwr), and W.J.Hare (Gwydir House).

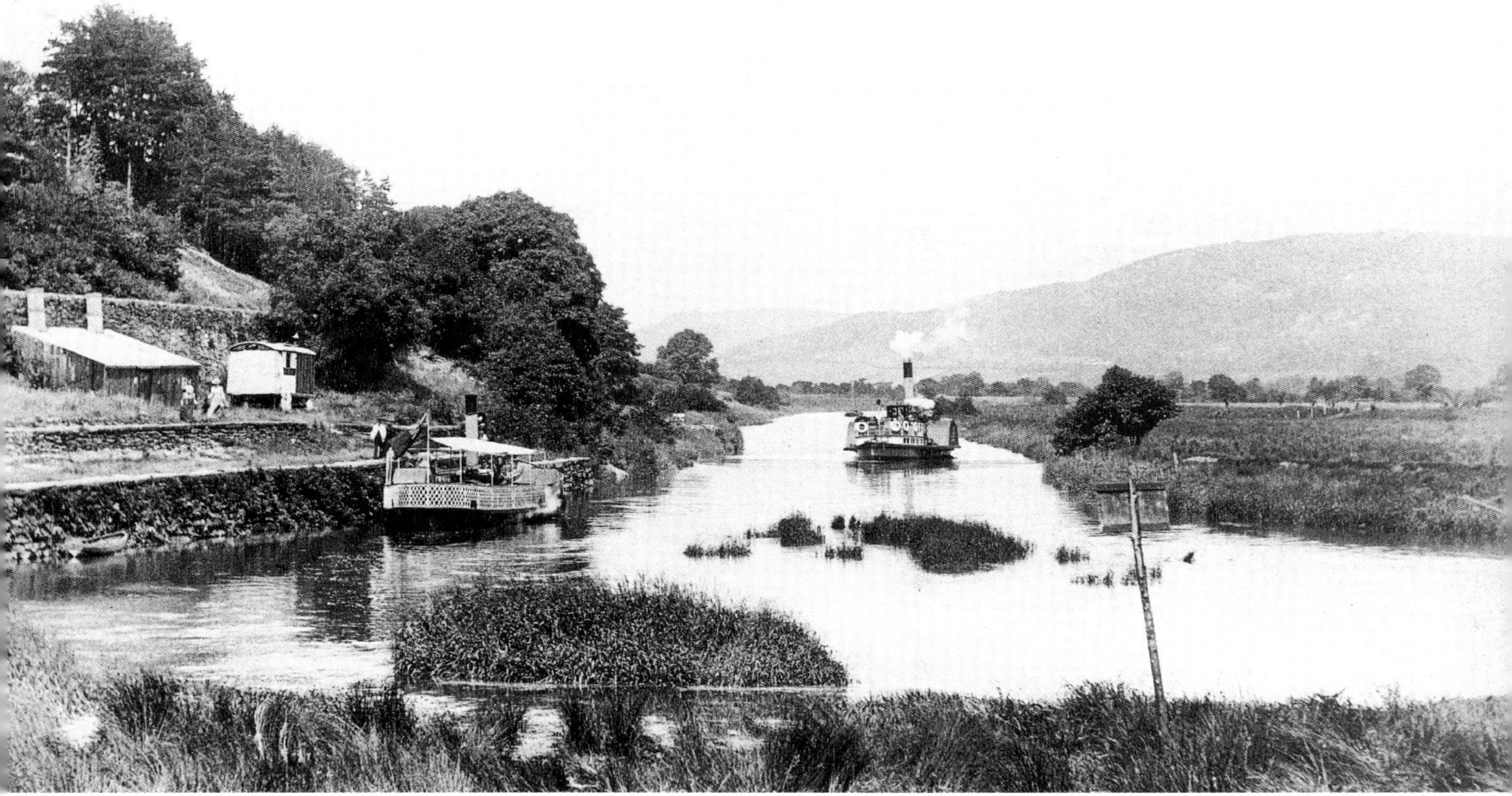

Unknown photographer,
Trefriw Quay, c.1870

had gone into the hills by this route. Their exploits were described in *The Graphic*, which helpfully prefaced its report by reminding readers that 'It is not everyone who goes to Norway for salmon-fishing, or to India for tiger-shooting':

> *'Before starting we must say that North Wales, in common with every other tourist-sought district, is divided into two parts, the part through which flows the regular tourist stream, and the part which is too difficult and mountainous for the ordinary tourist to penetrate. You may enter North Wales from several directions;... But the way that is most frequented is that which lies through the valley of the Conway. Start some morning on the little steamer which in summer goes up the river with each day tide, and after a delightful sail, during every moment of which some new scene opens in the mountain ranges on the right, you bring-to alongside the quay of Trefriw.'*[97]

[97] *The Graphic*, 18 Nov 1871, pp.486-7.

The preparations for the journey into the mountains were made on a truly Imperial scale. Having established themselves at the Waterloo Inn in Betws, the writer and two un-named artists set out for Llyn Dulyn:

> *'The necessary preparations were numerous and somewhat troublesome. First among them in importance were two canvas tents, one V shaped, the other square; then the provisions were the chief consideration. Potatoes, bread, a quarter of lamb, an enormous hunk of bacon, a frying pan, a kettle, a teapot, and a lot of tin plates and drinking utensils formed the principal portion of our* ménage. *Beside this there were the usual artistic paraphernalia of sketch books, canvas, paint boxes, and easels, and, above all, an india rubber inflating boat, the launching of which on the waters of the lake we looked forward to as a grand event in the history of Welsh exploration.'*

[98]Ibid. The names of the participants are noted on a copy of the article held in the Harrison archive, op.cit. No pictures of Llyn Dulyn were exhibited at RWS in 1871 or 1872.

After a troublesome journey with a pony cart and a guide, they arrived at Llyn Dulyn, set up camp and inflated the india-rubber boat, to take a cruise around the lake. The artists 'were in raptures with the place, declaring that the one half of its praise had not been told unto them':

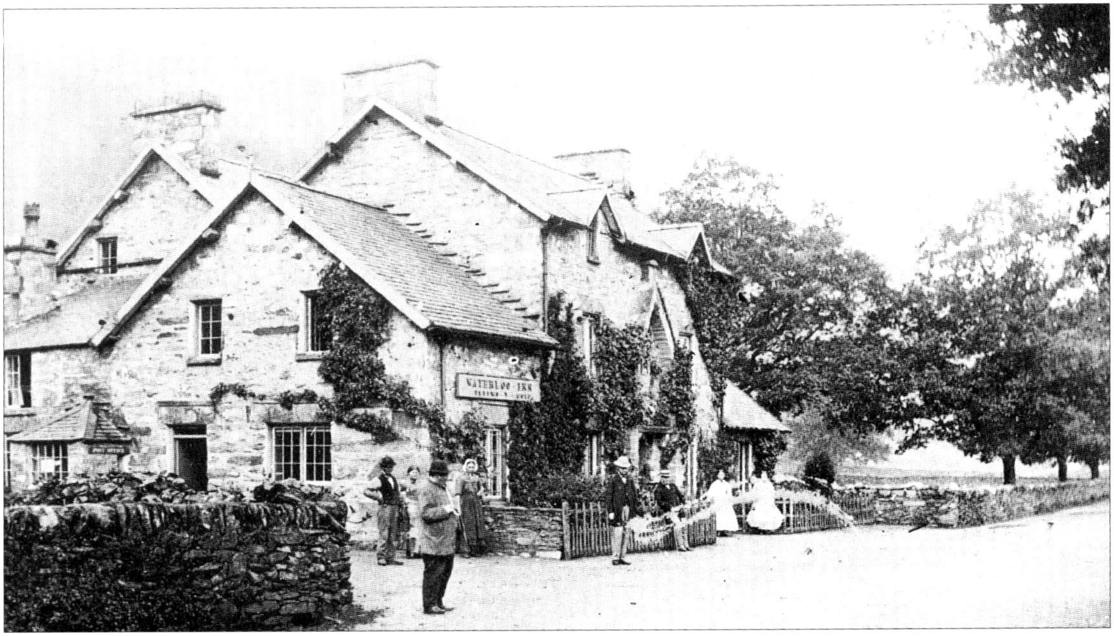

Unknown photographer, *Waterloo Inn, Betws-y-coed,* c.1880.

'Generally we rose about four and at once plunged into the icy waters of the lake, which were so cold as to be bearable only for a moment. A good deal of sketching was also done, and Dulyn will be seen at several of our next Water-Colour Exhibitions immortalised on canvas.'

The gentlemen descended a few miles from the lake to meet the ladies, Mrs Harrison, Mrs McCullach (probably the proprietress of the Waterloo Inn), and a Miss Williams, all escorted by the Rev. Ogden:

'After many mishaps and several falls, and no little amount of laughter, the whole party of us got safe to Dulyn, the ladies vowing they never could have thought it possible to travel over such remarkable roads. No sooner were we arrived than the boat was launched, and one by one the ladies were ferried across the lake and round the great rock on the other side, certainly the first of their sex who had ever made the voyage.'[98]

The intrepid painters of Llyn Dulyn have not been identified, but they were probably among the increasing number of amateurs flocking to the Conwy Valley.

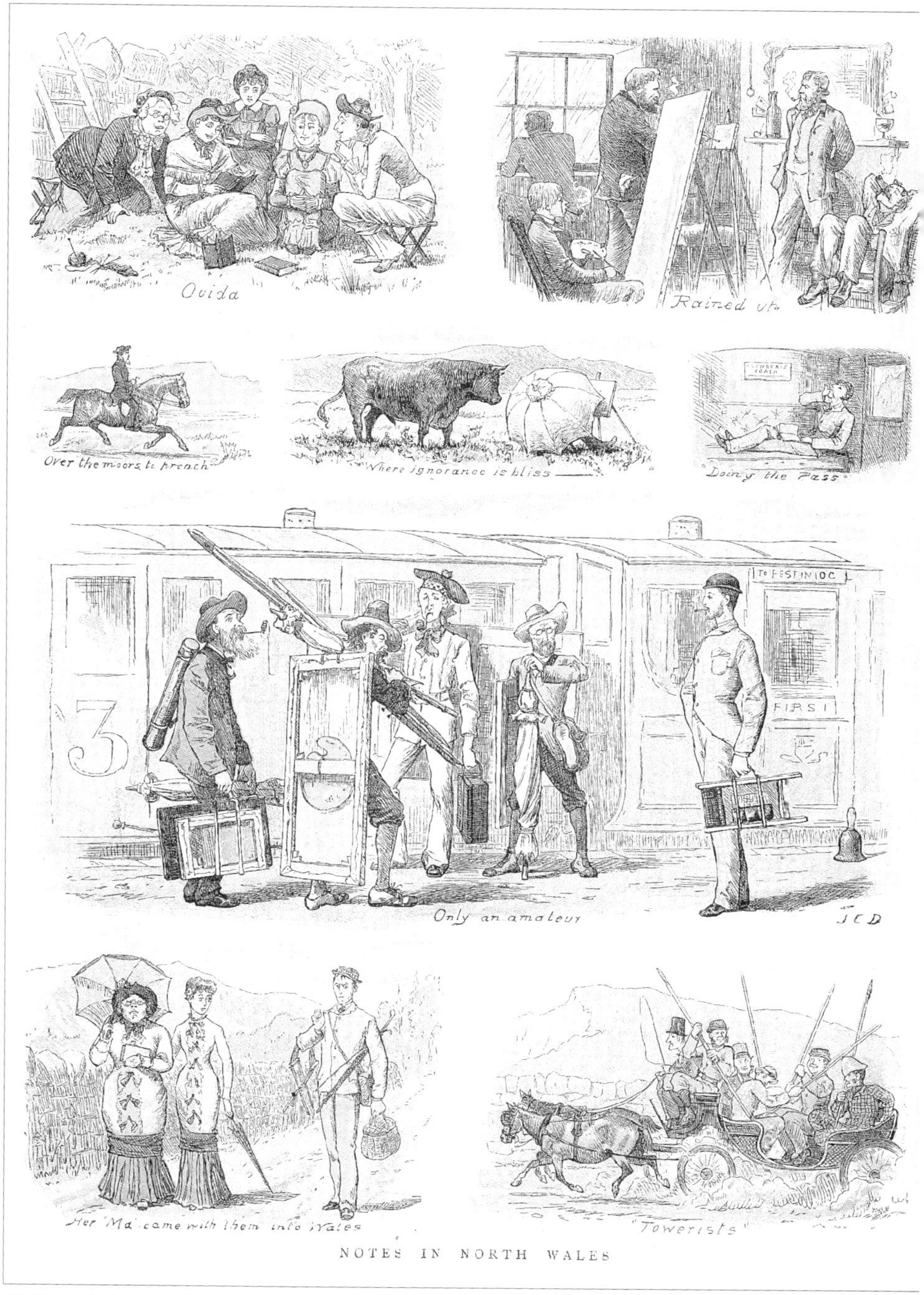

J.C.D. (probably John Charles Dollman), *Notes in North Wales*, from *The Graphic*, 1881.

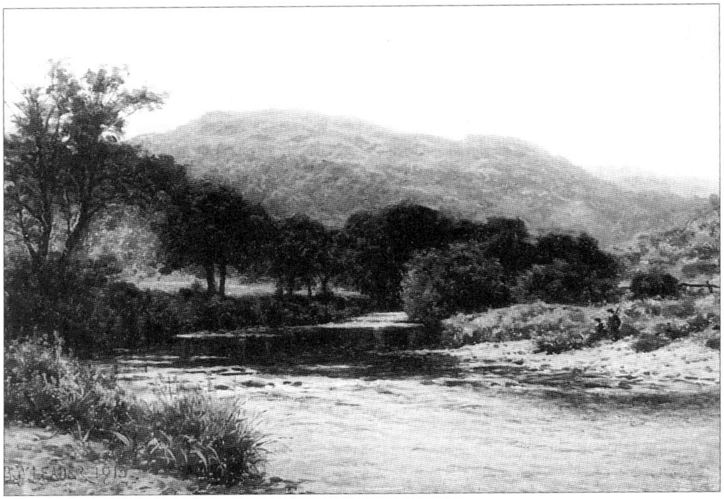

B.W.Leader,
On the Llugwy, North Wales, 1913.

Notwithstanding this influx of enthusiasts, Betws was of crucial importance in forming the artistic personalities of a new generation of professional painters in the period between the death of David Cox in 1859 and the early 1870s. Immediately prior to his first visit to the Royal Oak in the year of Cox's death, Benjamin Williams Leader had sold a picture to Creswick, and it is tempting to think that his coming to Betws may not have been entirely unrelated to this event, given the older painter's long-standing association with the village. Certainly, over the ensuing decade, the focus of Leader's activity shifted to Wales. In 1862 he moved to Whittington, near Worcester, and continued to paint in the Marches and at famous Welsh sites such as Tintern, but pictures of the river valleys around Betws became almost a trade-mark for him at this time. He would continue to paint closely related versions of pictures conceived at Betws in the 1860s until the end of his career in the new century.

Similarly, the artistic personality of Leader's contemporary, Clarence Whaite, was formed in the 1850s and 1860s in and around the Conwy Valley. However, Whaite was drawn by his romantic temperament more often to the mountains and upland lakes than to the immediate environs of Betws with its expanding social round. During term times Whaite trained in London at Leigh's Academy and at the Royal Academy. His technical development clearly reflected the two dominant forces at work in English landscape painting in the period. The force of tradition, especially watercolour tradition, transmitted directly by Cox, naturally affected both Whaite's technique and his attitudes. Like many artists who came into contact with Cox at Betws, Whaite recorded in his diary details of the Master's methods. Their influence was most apparent in his drawing directly from nature, where he practiced an open and transparent technique for most of his long career. Whaite was not unusual in this despite the mid-century fashion for particularity, opacity and high finish in works intended for exhibition. The older virtues of freshness and

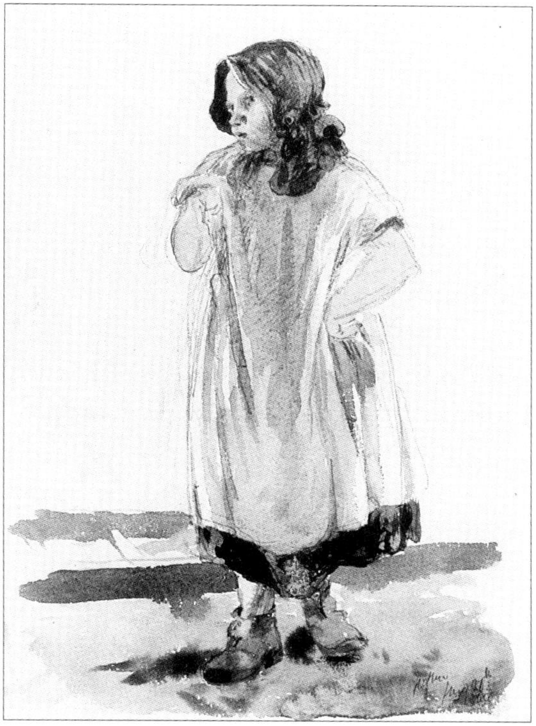

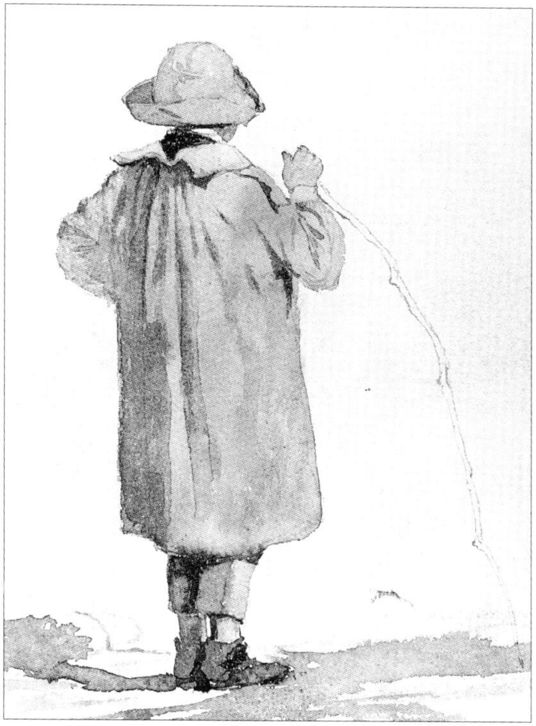

Left:
William Evans,
Boy with Smock and Staff,
c.1846

Far left:
Clarence Whaite,
Trefriw Girl, 1860.
Reproduced in colour on p.88.

immediacy of impression retained their value in the sketch, which acquired a status as a form in its own right. Thomas Collier, for instance, was among a number of painters highly regarded for their ability in this field in particular. Whaite's sketching technique in this period was strikingly similar to that of William Evans, though no documentary evidence exists to link them, and was certainly reinforced by his acquaintance with Collier and Whittaker. Contemporary observers thought Whaite was capable of retaining the freshness of his sketching in more finished exhibition works. In 1853 he exhibited *Moel Siabod* at the British Institution in London, where he was noticed by the critic of the *Art Journal*:

> *'We do not know the works of this artist, but we can attest the excellence of this picture, which appears to have been wholly studied from nature without recourse in anywise to the trick of art. The natural colour of the entire scene is most refreshing, added to which, the gradations and intervening atmosphere are exquisitely felt. It is a product of a very high character.'*[99]

[99] *Art Journal*, 1853, p.87.

The picture has not been identified, but another of the same year, *Hauling Driftwood*, almost certainly based on a Welsh drawing, tends to confirm that Whaite's early exhibition pictures were more open in manner than those which came at the end of the decade and through the 1860s, under the influence of the general move towards particularity and finish. Indeed, in the opinion of Ruskin, some of these pictures went a little too far in the direction that he himself had encouraged. In 1859 Whaite had two pictures hung at the Royal Academy, a large oil called *The Barley Harvest*, and a drawing, *Snowdon*. Ruskin was sufficiently impressed to comment upon them in his 'Academy Notes', beginning with the *Barley Harvest*:

> *'Very exquisite in nearly every respect; perhaps, take it all in all, the most covetable bit of landscape this year, and showing good promise, it seems to me, if the painter does not overwork himself needlessly. The execution of the whole by minute and similar touches is a mistake. Certain textures need to be so produced, and certain complexities of form; but the work is never good unless it varies with every part of the subject, and is different in method, according to the sort of surface or form required. Nothing finished can be done without labour; but a picture can hardly be more injured than by the quality of labour in it which is lost. Uncontributive toil is one of the forms of ruin.*
>
> *'Mr Whaite's drawing... is also lovely in conception, and right in form of cloud. It is slightly affected by the same error as the oil-painting...'*[100]

Perhaps helped by this generally favourable comment, Whaite seems to have moved for a time on the periphery of the Pre-Raphaelite circle. In 1858 a number of these artists - notably Dante Gabriel Rossetti, Ford Madox Brown and William Morris - had come together to form the Hogarth Club. Soon afterwards, they were joined by Watts and Ruskin himself.[101] Their primary purpose was to create exhibition opportunities in the face of rejection or, at best, unfavourable hanging by the Royal Academy. However, the club was ultimately more important as an exchange for new ideas and as a place where artists, writers and patrons, including those based outside London, might meet. Among the founders, George Price Boyce had the strongest connections with Betws. In his diary he recorded a number of occasions on which he discussed his Welsh works with the likes of

[100] John Ruskin, 'Academy Notes', *The Works of John Ruskin* (London, 1904), Vol.XIV, p.229-30. The *Art Journal*, 1859, p.168, echoed Ruskin's sentiments: 'When the mind is bent on one quality alone in Art, it is generally realised by the sacrifice of many others. Microscopic execution has been the desideratum of this picture, and it is carried out with a singleness of purpose which constitutes the unique quality of the work. The field is bounded by a rising ground covered with wood, the treatment of which is one of the errors induced by the passion for excessive finish.'

[101] Ruskin's membership of the club was shortlived. He resigned when a billiard table was installed. The club folded in 1861.

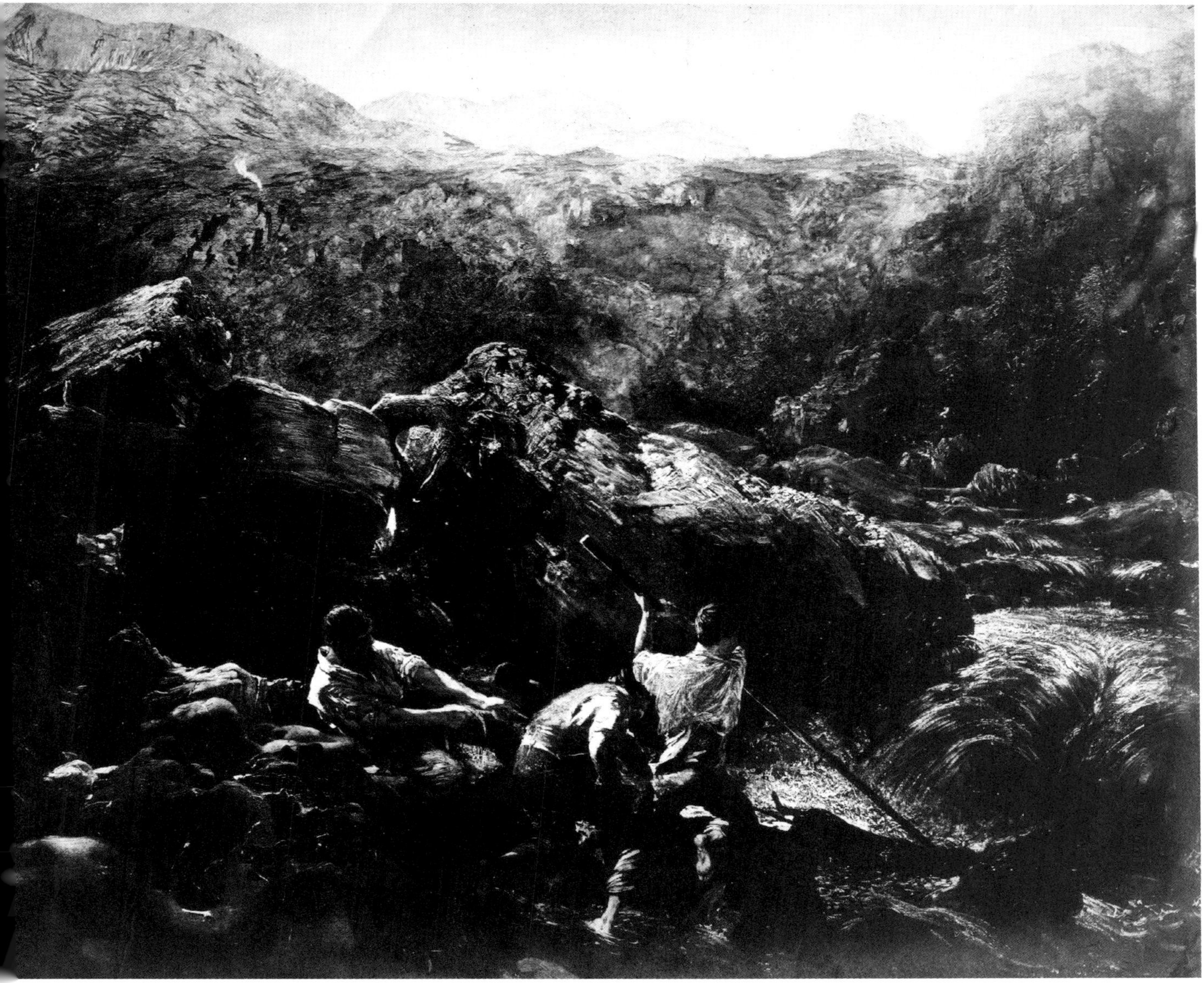

Clarence Whaite,
Hauling Driftwood, 1853.

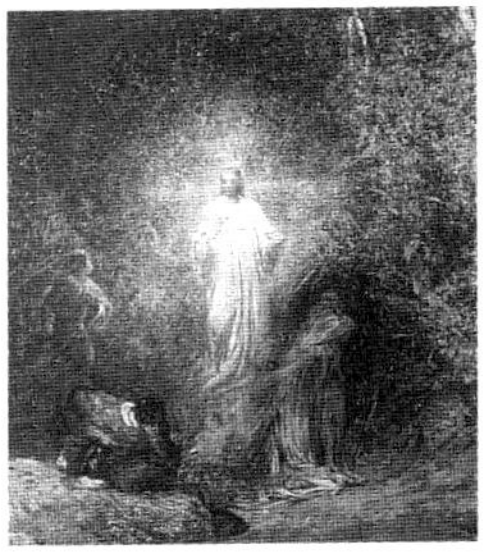

Clarence Whaite,
The Penitent's Vision,
detail, 1865.

Rossetti and Millais. By 1860 Whaite was one of the eighty members of the Hogarth Club, although precisely who among this membership was known personally to him is not clear. In fact, his inclination towards Pre-Raphaelite ideas had been manifest for some time before he became a member, and Watts would seem to have been a particular influence if subjects such as *After the Deluge* and *Lot and the Angels* can be considered representative of his ambitions. Such religious and allegorical subjects particularly attracted Whaite in this period. He began one of the most ambitious of them, *The Penitent's Vision*, in 1862, but reworked his original idea early in 1865, perhaps in response to his mother's death. He had large aspirations for the subject:

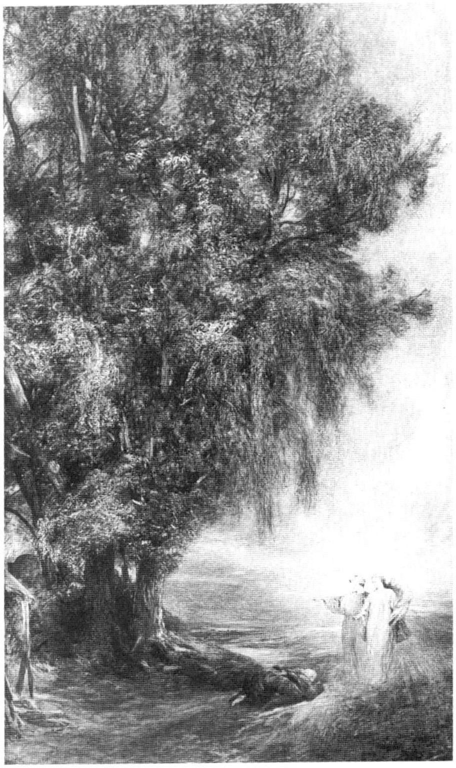

Clarence Whaite,
Lot and the Angels, 1897.
Reproduced in colour on p.93.

> *'What a sublime subject for a picture - A Christian entering the Gates of Paradise - but how overwhelming the thought of it but have been trying today to suggest the gate of heaven for Christian to enter. How timid our grandest thoughts and how poor our work is compared to the thought - Oh! grant that my mind may be so elevated that my work may be of use in teaching others.'*[102]

The picture was completed in late March, after much uncertainty and soul-searching, and was privately exhibited in Manchester to an audience whose members regarded it with mixed feelings. The *Manchester Examiner and Times* praised the landscape element highly but regarded its use 'as a vehicle for the introduction of figure' as being 'in somewhat questionable taste':

> *'Seraphic processions may occasionally sweep over Welsh hills and dales, but ordinary imaginations will find some little difficulty in accepting the idea. Now-a-days, most people prefer landscape pure and simple...'*[103]

[102]Whaite archive, op.cit., the Diary, 14 February 1865. The Whaite archive contains correspondence with Watts, but it dates from the 1880s. It is unclear when the two men became acquainted. I am indebted to David Mortimer-Jones for his detailed research on *The Penitent's Vision* and its subsequent history.

[103]*Manchester Examiner and Times*, 3 April 1865.

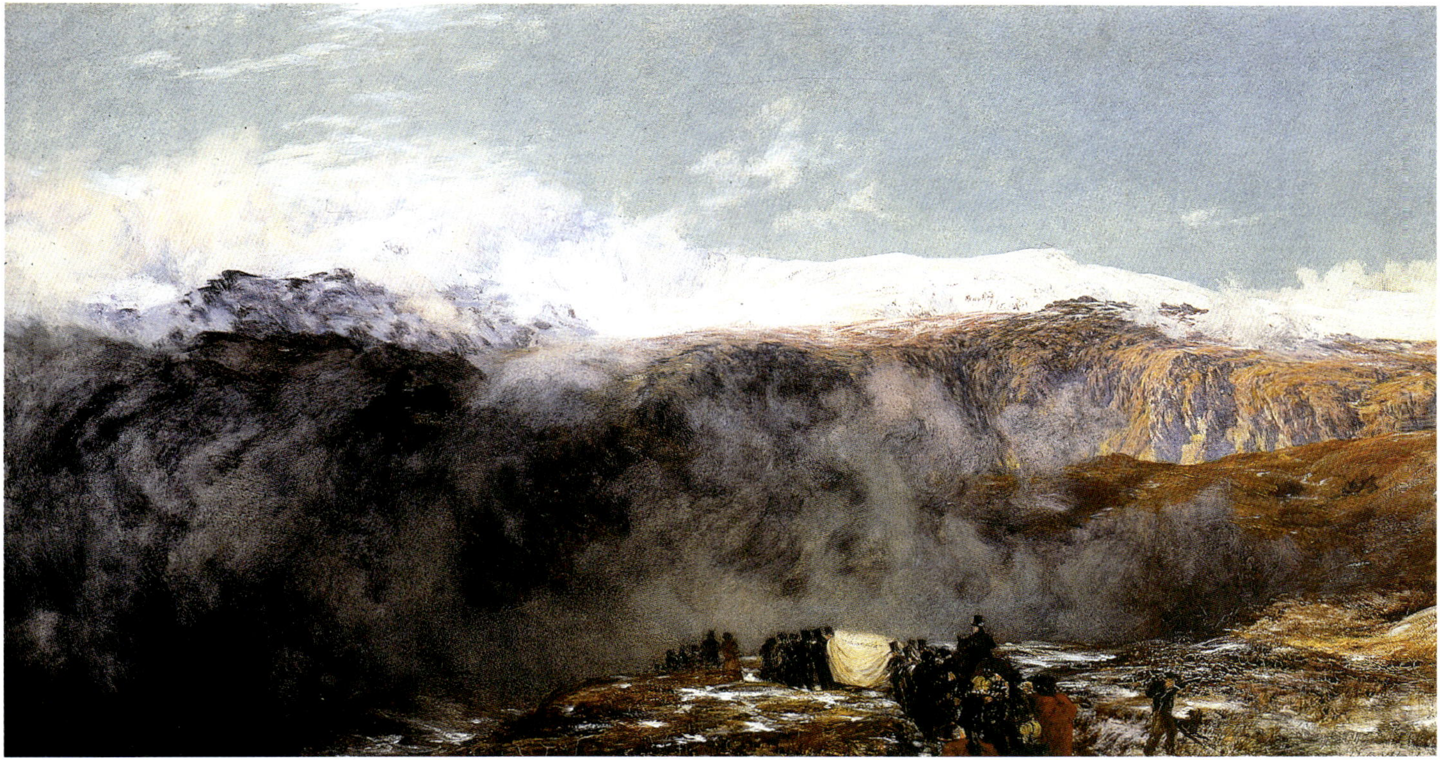

Clarence Whaite,
To the Cold Earth,
1865.

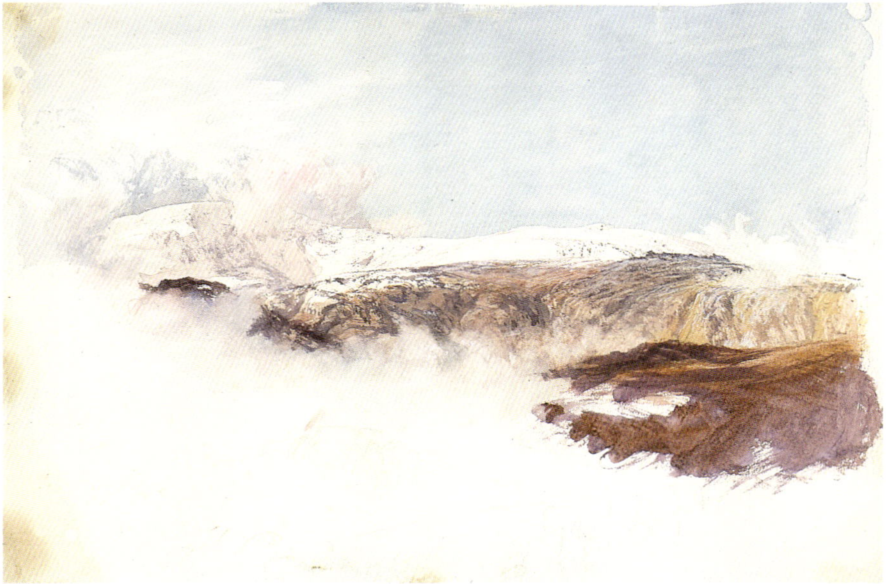

Clarence Whaite,
drawing for
To the Cold Earth,
c.1865.

Clarence Whaite, *Trefriw Girl*, 1860.

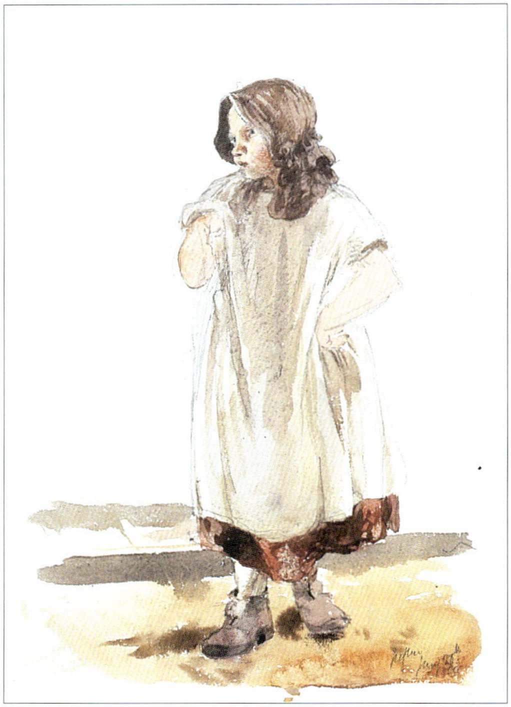

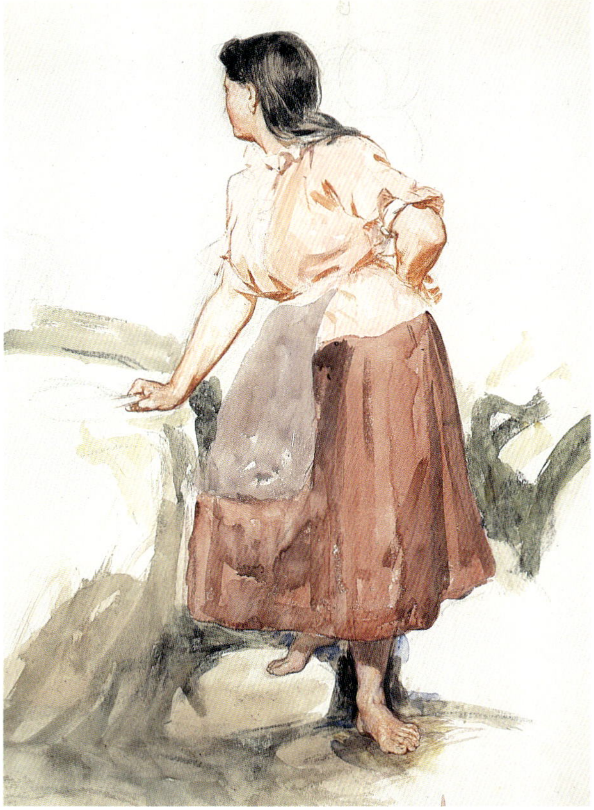

Clarence Whaite, *Young Woman on Steps*, c.1865.

Clarence Whaite, *People in a Boat*, c.1865.

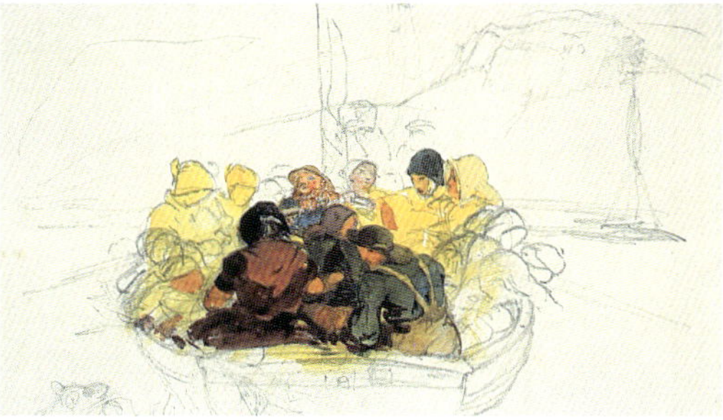

Clarence Whaite, *Old Woman, Conwy*, 1869.

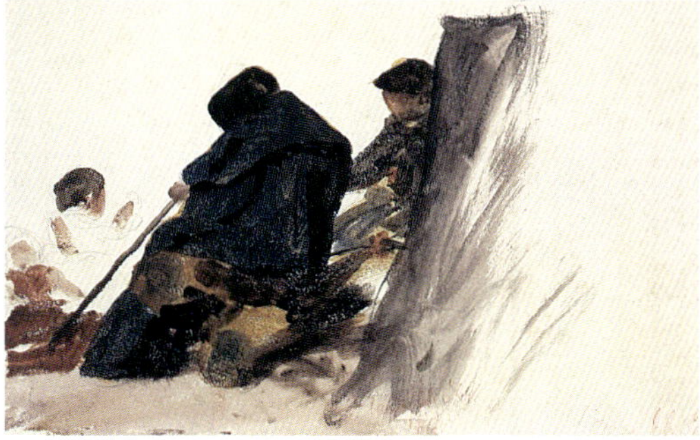

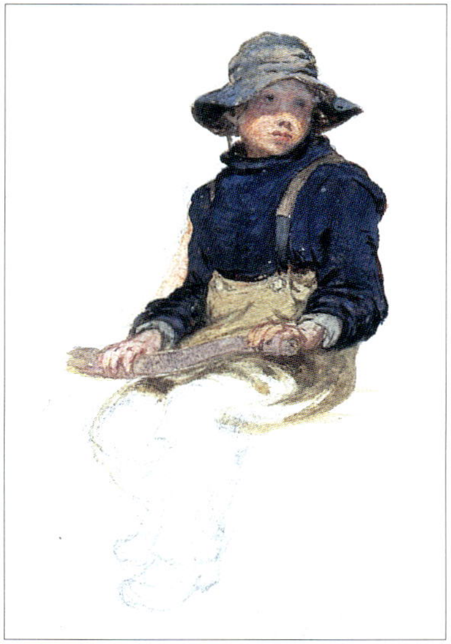

Clarence Whaite, *Boy in Blue*, c.1862.

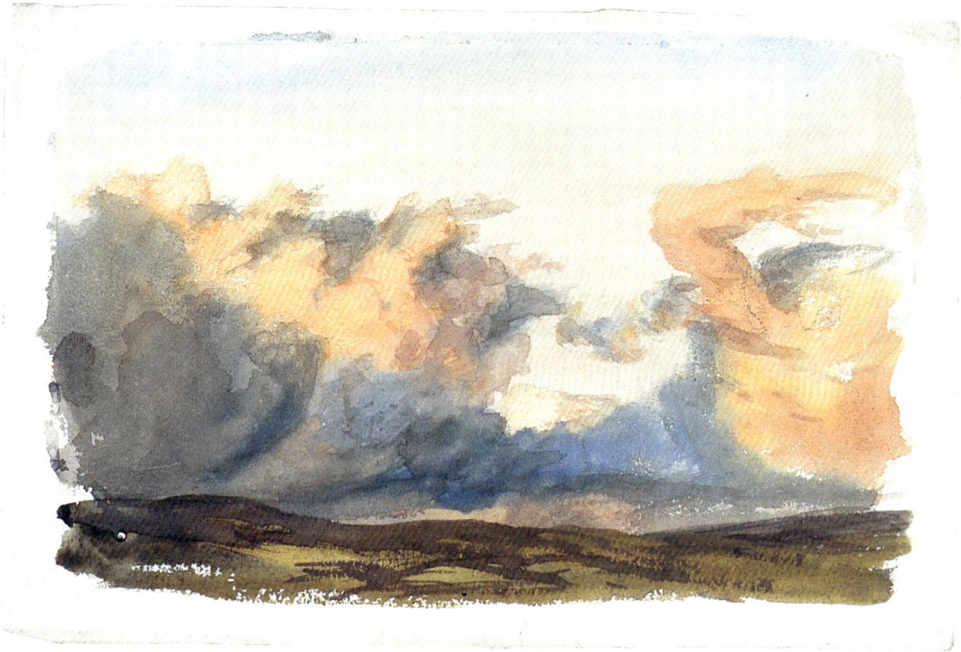

Clarence Whaite,
Sunset, 1878.

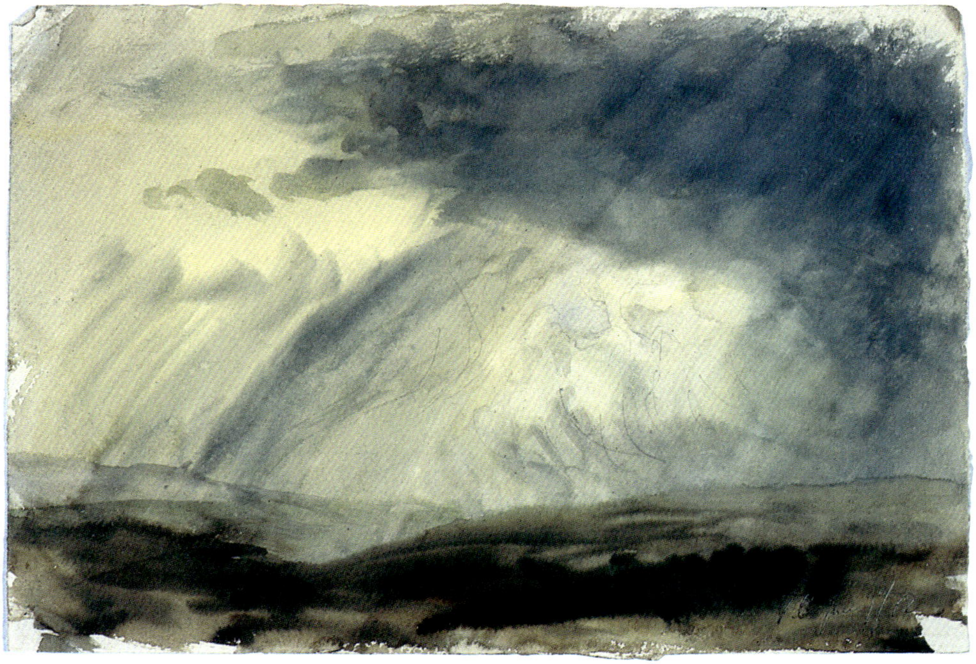

Clarence Whaite,
Rain, 1872.

Clarence Whaite,
The Rainbow, 1862.

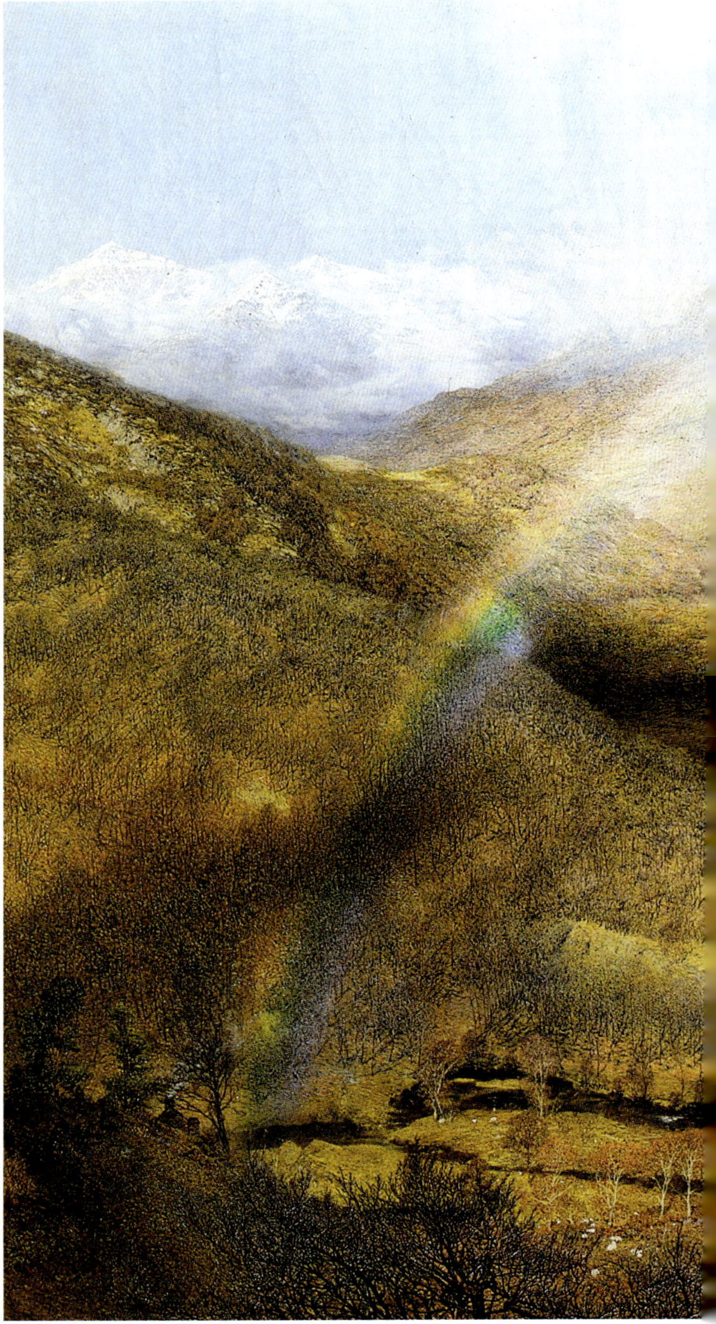

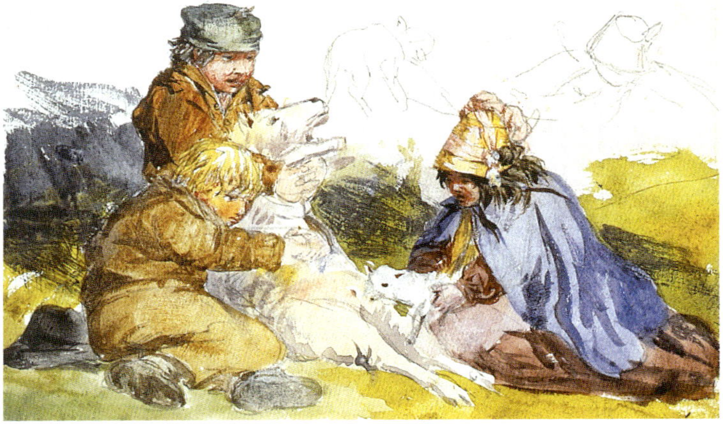

Clarence Whaite,
Children with Sheep,
c.1861.

Clarence Whaite,
drawing for *The Rainbow*,
1861.

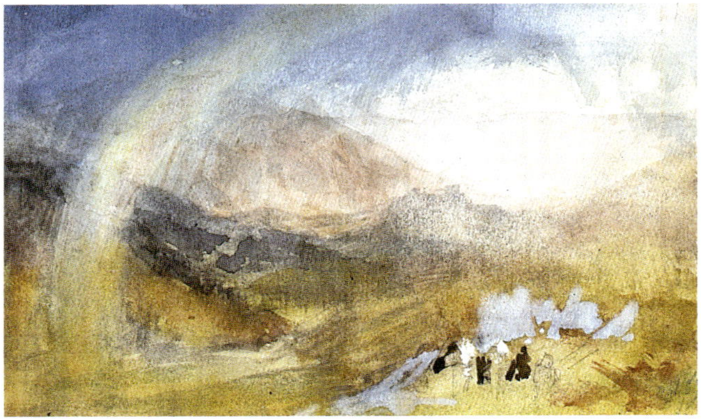

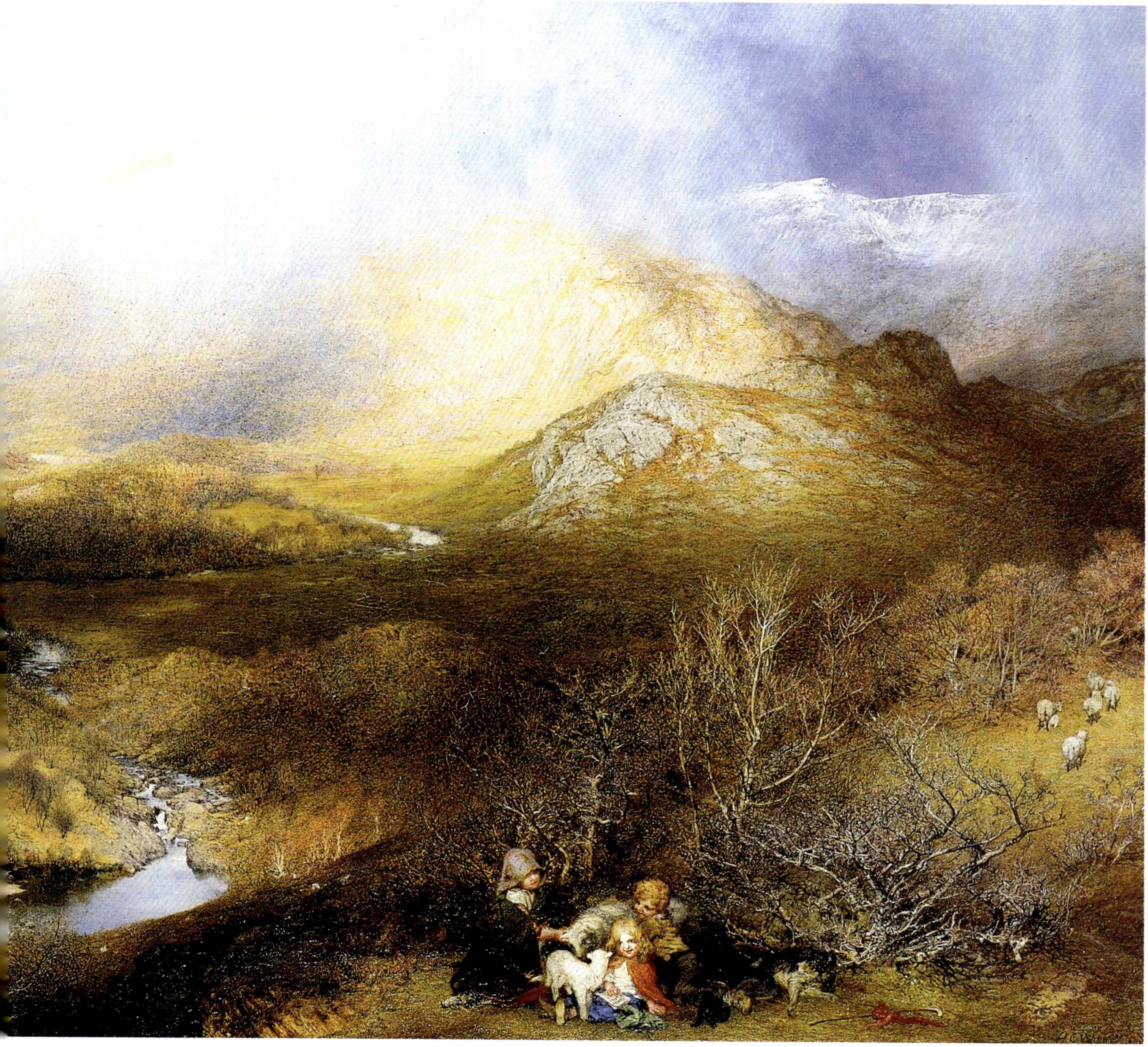

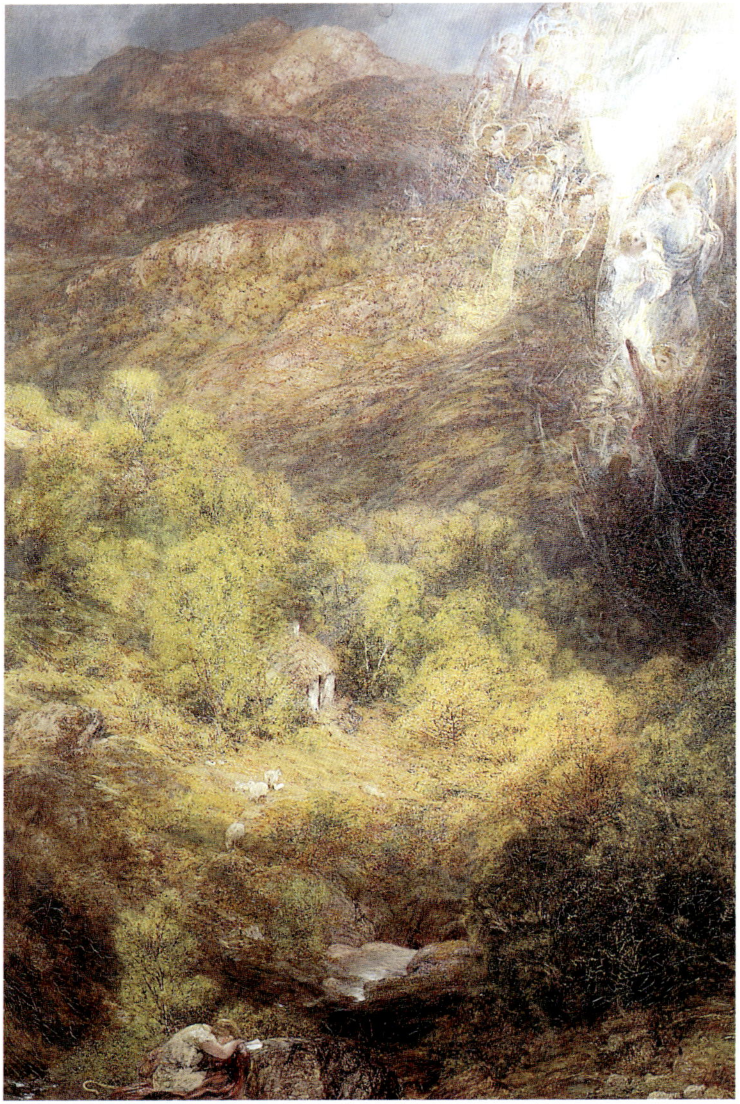

Clarence Whaite,
The Shepherd's Dream,
1865.

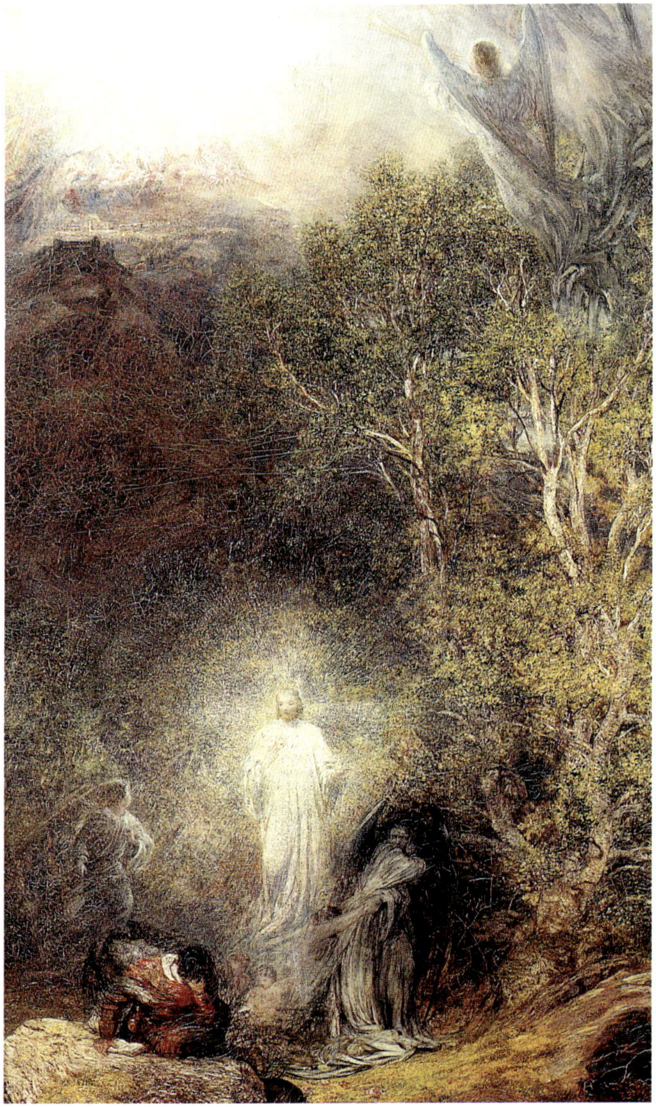

Clarence Whaite,
The Awakening of Christian,
1865.

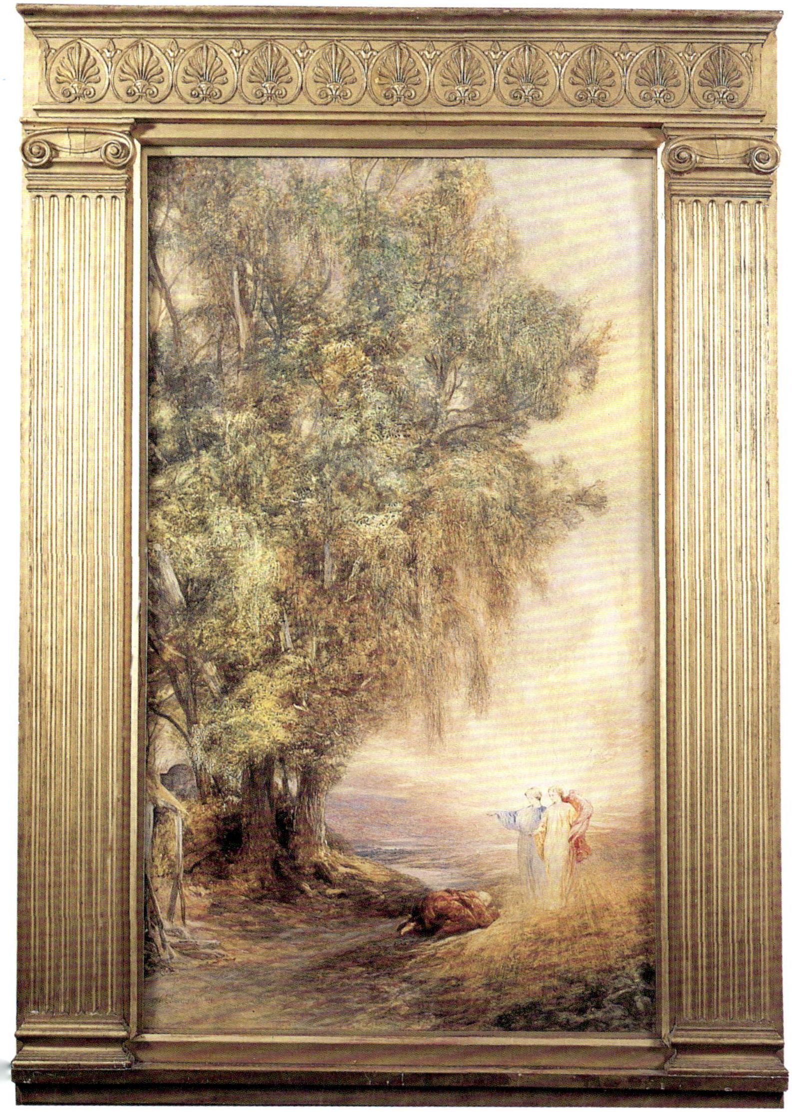

Clarence Whaite,
Lot and the Angels,
1897.

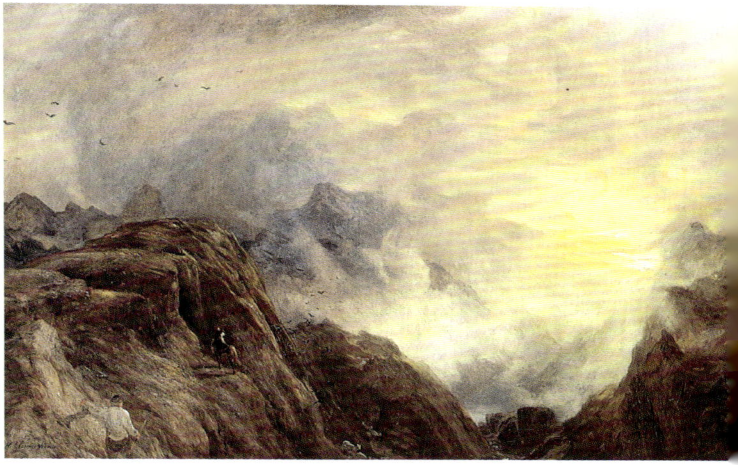

Clarence Whaite,
Mountain Vist, Sunrise,
1892.

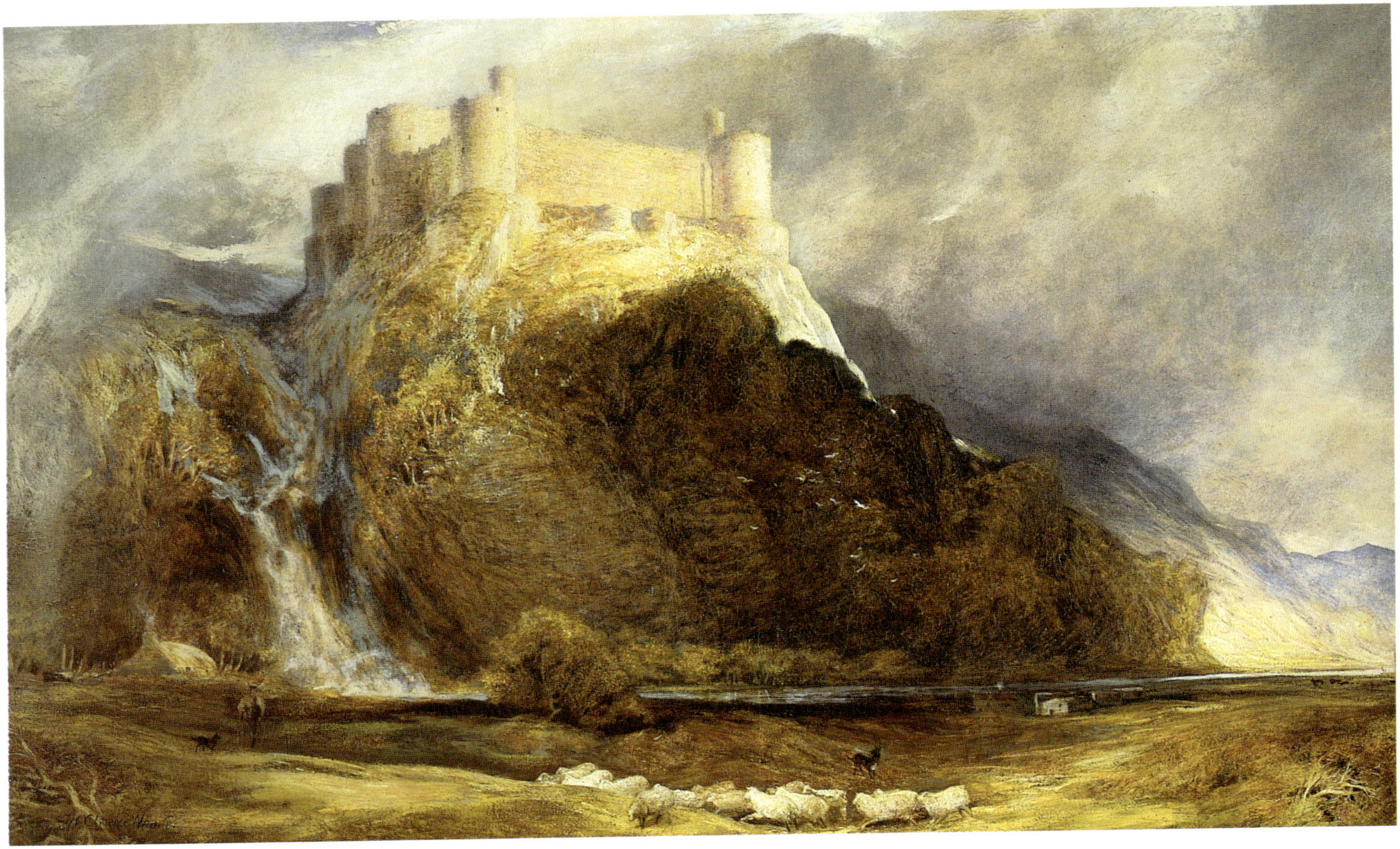

Clarence Whaite,
Harlech Castle,
'Four Square to the Winds that Blow',
1894.

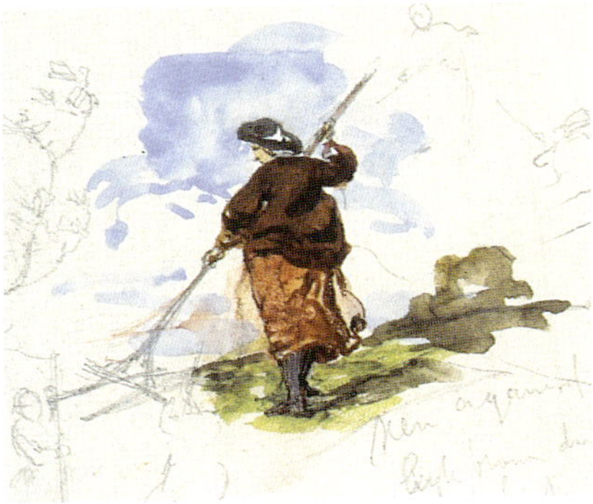

Clarence Whaite,
Men against the Sky,
c.1864.

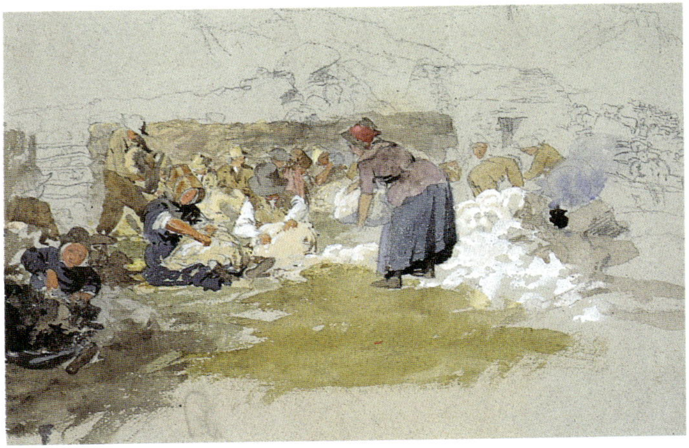

Clarence Whaite,
Shearing Sheep,
1862.

On the whole, critics were of the opinion that subject painting was not Whaite's strength, despite the fact that he had exhibited subject pictures at the Royal Academy since 1854 when *Ancient Britons surprised by the Romans* was shown.[104] There was something of a rash of such Celtic subject matter in mid-century, led in 1843 by Watts' famous cartoon for the rebuilt Houses of Parliament, *Caractacus led in Triumph through Rome*. In 1850, Holman Hunt painted *A Converted British Family sheltering a Christian Priest from the persecution of the Druids*. To what extent Whaite's interest in such subjects was furthered by his deepening affection for Wales is difficult to determine. His Arthurian pictures, such as *Arthur in the*

[104]Whaite's first two Royal Academy pictures, selected in 1851 and 1852, were Swiss landscape subjects.

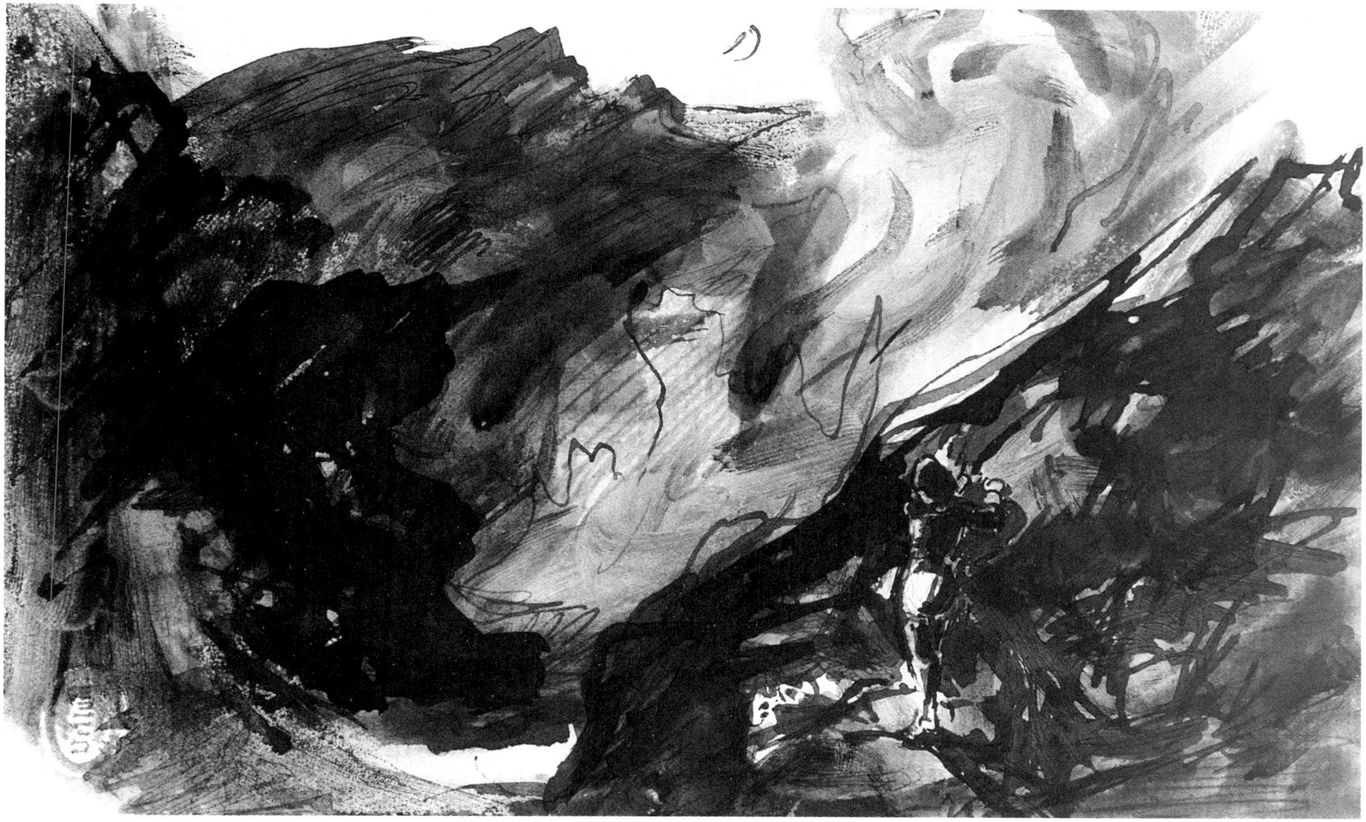

Clarence Whaite, drawing for *Arthur in the Gruesome Glen*, c.1890.

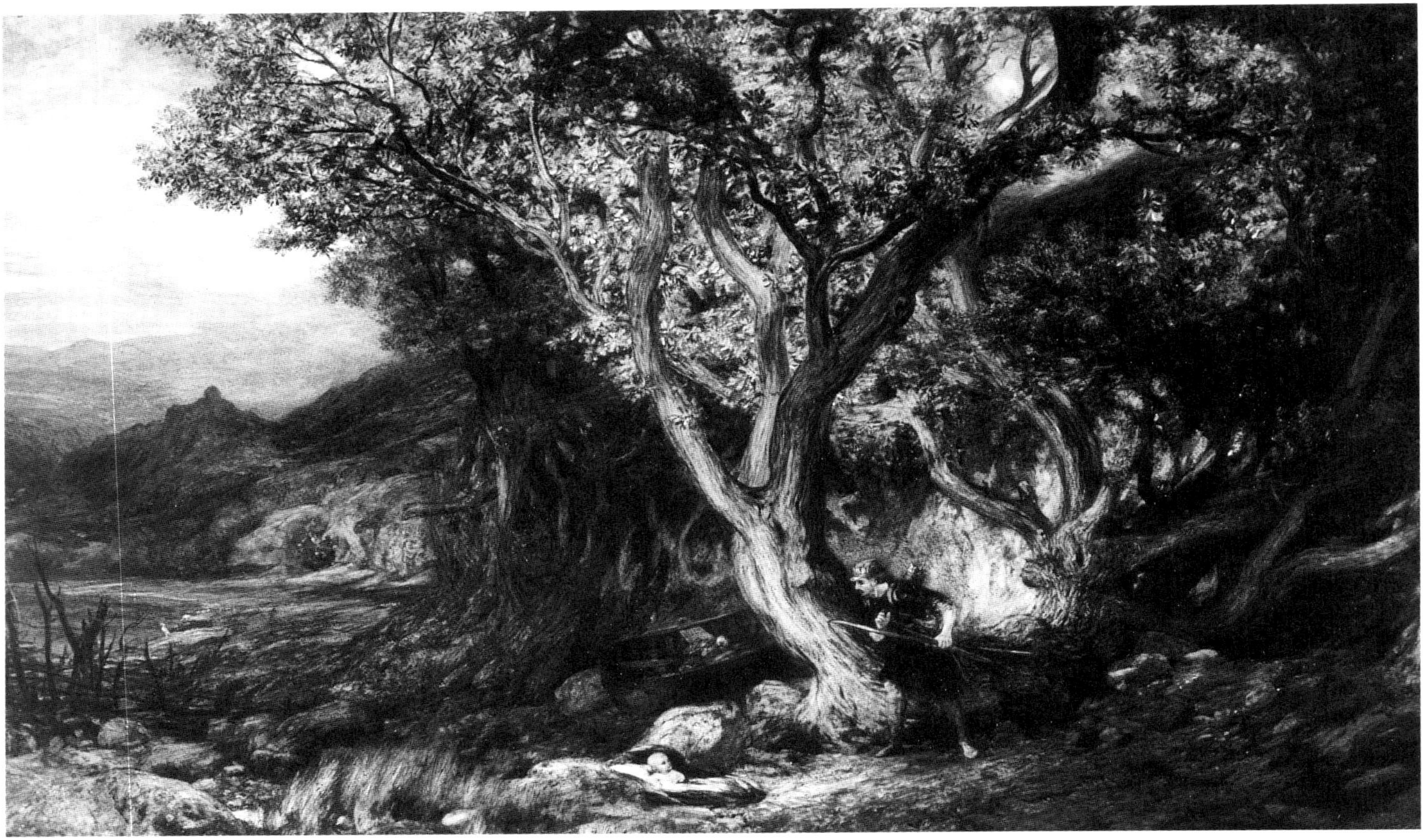

Clarence Whaite,
The Finding of Taliesin,
1875/6.

Gruesome Glen and *Aenid and Geraint at the Castle of Lanores*, may simply reflect the widespread English preoccupation with Tennyson's *Idylls of the King*. However, other subjects, such as *The Throne in the Grove*, *The Bard*, and *The Finding of Taliesin* had a particularly Welsh aspect and it is, perhaps, significant that the Taliesin picture dates from 1875, by which time Whaite had taken up permanent residence and was making the acquaintance of Welsh artists and antiquarians. Other English painters in the Conwy Valley would follow Whaite in taking up such subjects in the 1880s.

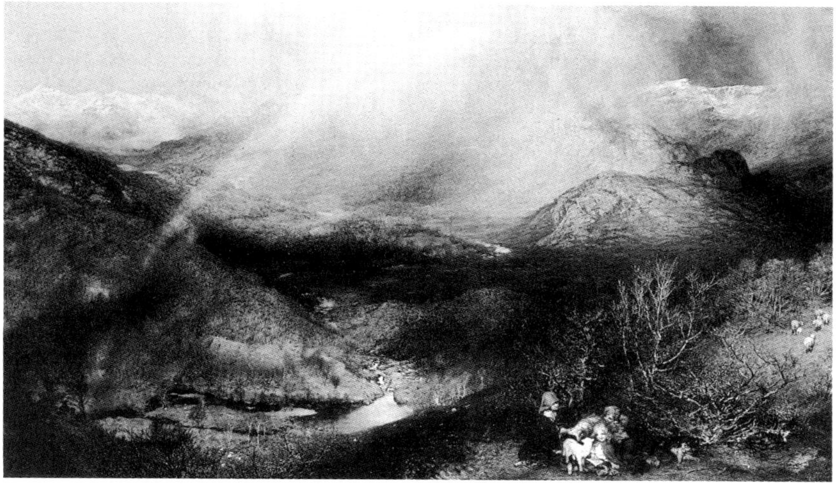

Clarence Whaite, *The Rainbow*, 1862. Reproduced in colour on p.90.

Clarence Whaite, drawing for *The Rainbow*, 1861. Reproduced in colour on p.90.

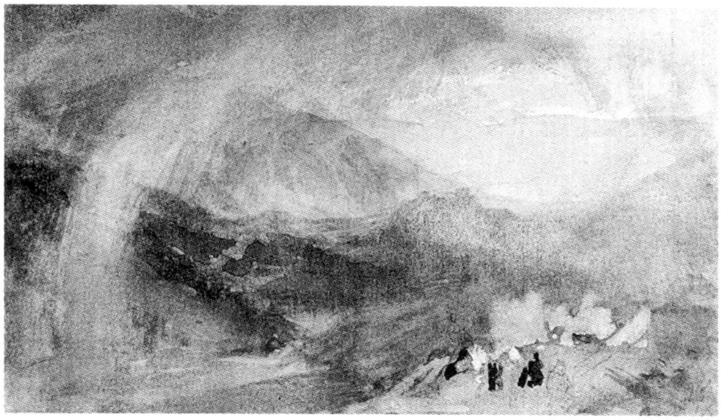

Critical approval in 1859 of Whaite's *The Barley Harvest* was followed by the successful submission of pictures to the Royal Academy for the subsequent three years, culminating in 1862 with the exhibition of *The Rainbow*. Despite its very large scale, *The Rainbow* was painted before the subject in a specially constructed studio in the mountains, where Whaite was visited by colleagues, including B.W.Leader. A number of studies for the picture have survived, drawn in the Capel Curig area in April 1861. The earliest, a water colour sketch, closely predicted the final composition, while an almost schematic black and white drawing with colour notes, dated the following day, was reversed.

Clarence Whaite, study of a *rainbow*, 1861.

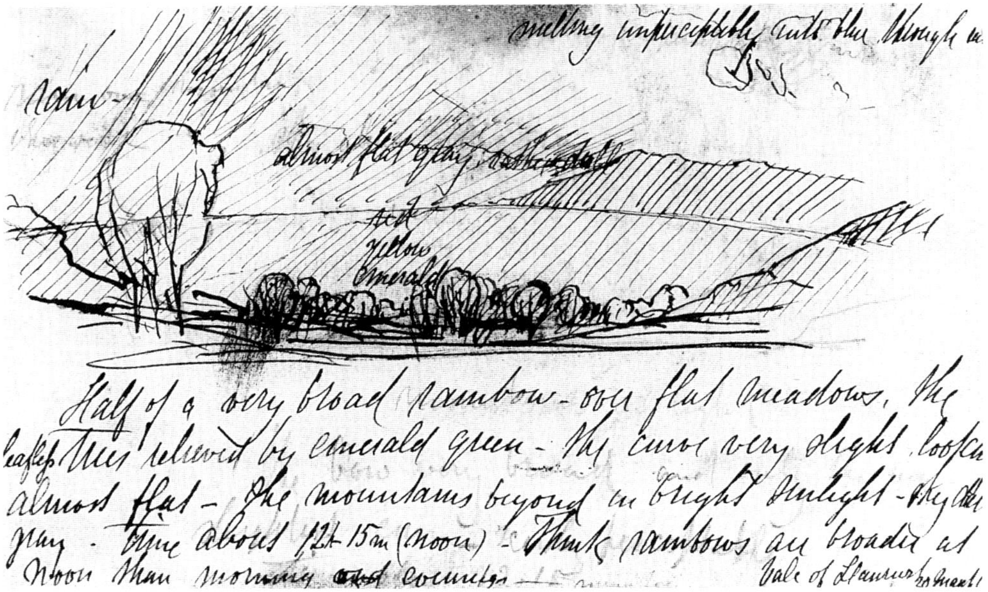

Some of the drawings included a suggestion of the foreground group which characterised the finished picture; in others the figures were omitted. A beautiful coloured drawing showed a group of three children assisting a lamb to feed from a surrogate mother. It probably recorded an observed incident though the strong allegorical undertones may suggest that it was imagined. The foreground group finally chosen by Whaite was clearly related to this drawing but simply depicted a woman and two children with a lamb.

The huge canvas was worked in many areas in minute detail, revealing a strong desire for particularity of time as well as place. According to Whaite's own account, 'It was painted on the hills above Capel Curig and I remained all winter there to set the detail for the spring foliage'.[105] Nevertheless, perhaps mindful of Ruskin's earlier strictures, the passing storm and the rainbow itself provided Whaite with the opportunity to relieve the detail with more fluid atmospheric effects, obscuring the central part of the mountain background. The critical response was enthusiastic:

[105]Whaite archive, op.cit., letter to G.H.Walker, dated 23 March 1894.

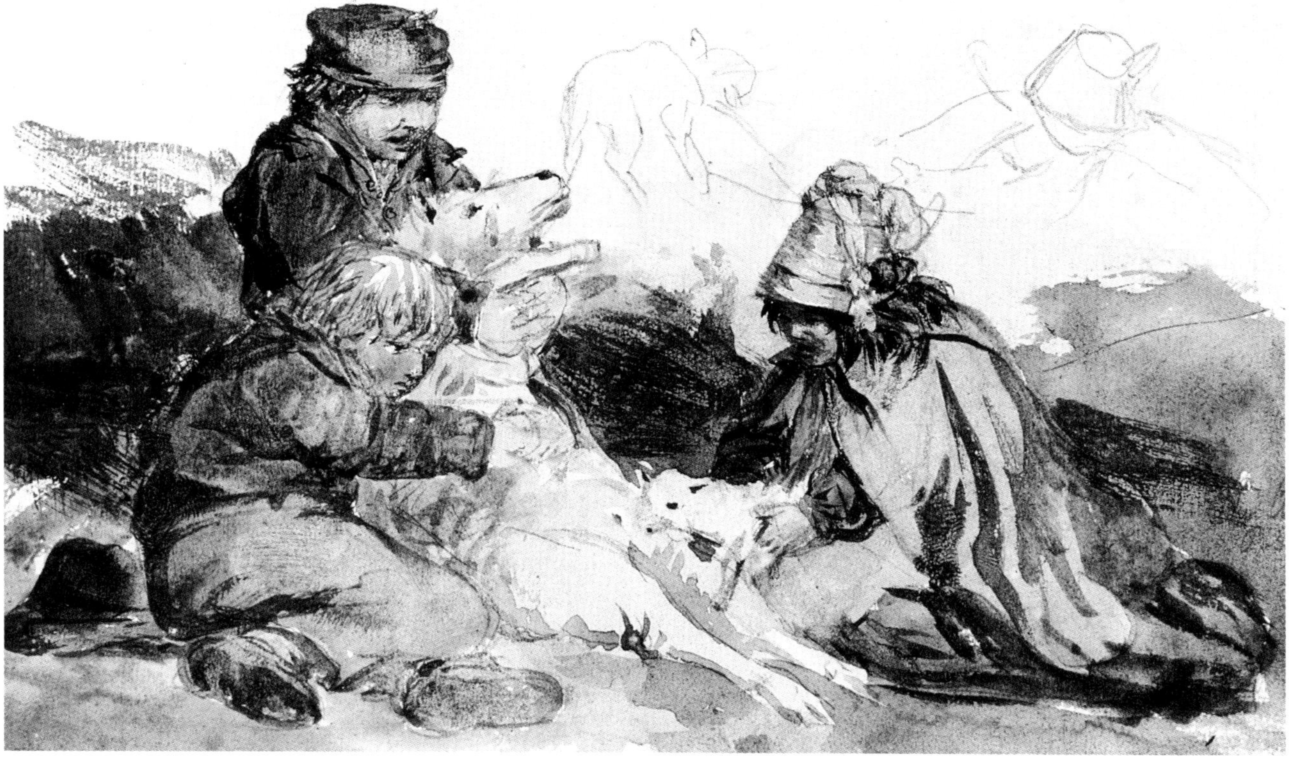

Clarence Whaite,
Children with Sheep, drawing
for *The Rainbow*, 1862.
Reproduced in colour on p.90.

'The minuteness of some of the details and the care with which they have been treated are wonderful. At the same time this care has been at no expense of freedom. The consequence is that the picture will repay study every way. Look at it from a distance, and one is surprised at the breadth of the subject, and the beautiful tone which pervades it. Examine it closely, and there is no slurring over one portion to throw another into undue prominence; but a painstaking and effective finish of every part. The texture of the cloud is perfect; the forest of trunks and branches is truth itself; and nothing can exceed the beauty of the half clothed rocks on the left, with the patches of young grass creeping over them. The picture as a whole is a finished poem of pastoral beauty.' [106]

[106] *Manchester Guardian*,
13 and 22 September 1862.

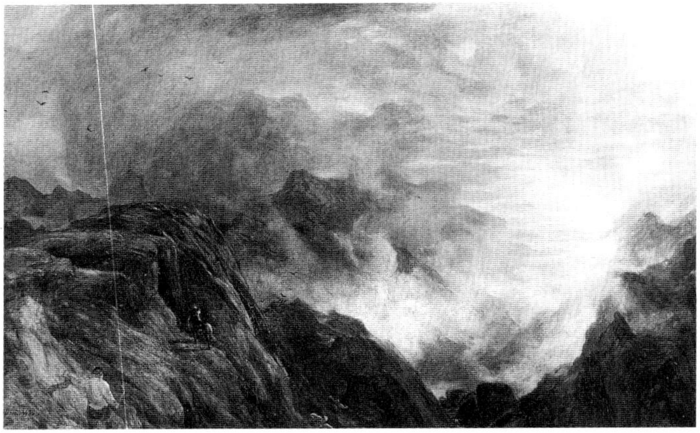

Clarence Whaite,
Mountain Mist, Sunrise,
1892. Reproduced in
colour on p93.

The expression of elevating sentiment through small figure groups in landscape settings suited both Whaite's turn of mind and his technical qualities much better than specific allegory, and he used the combination with success in many finished pictures. *Mountain Mist, Sunrise*, like *The Rainbow*, was distilled from numerous watercolour drawings, which found their final form in more than one finished oil. The scene on top of the mountains at sunrise contained within it a shepherd and his dog going to rescue a sheep trapped on a ledge below. Years later, when the picture was exhibited in Manchester, a verse by John Bell was appended to it:

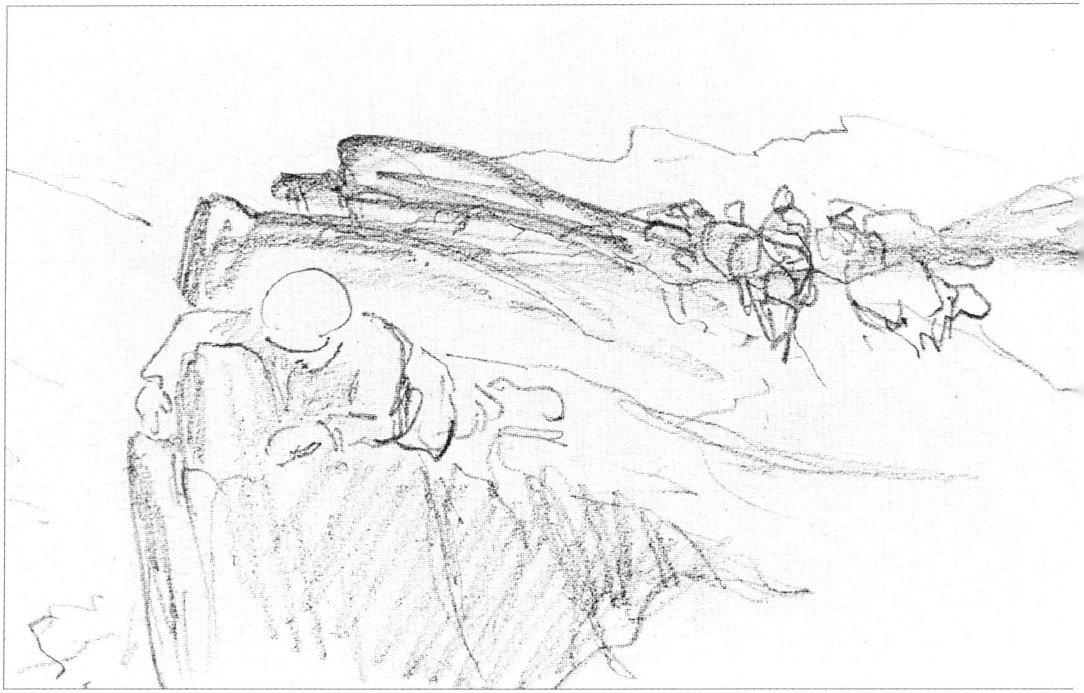

Clarence Whaite,
drawing for subject related
to *Mountain Mist, Sunrise,*
c.1892..

From the high rock the shepherd boy's ken
Searches far and wide the glen;
Aloft the guardian of the fold,
He and his dog the watch-tower hold.

The poet spoke of Cumbria, but Whaite's preparatory drawings show clearly that the scene was, for him, in Wales. A related large oil painting, *The Snowdonian Shepherd*, had the boy, once again, high on a mountain ledge, guarding the sheep below. The finished work was closely related to a pencil drawing which seems to have been taken from life.

Clarence Whaite,
The Snowdonian Shepherd, 1906-7.

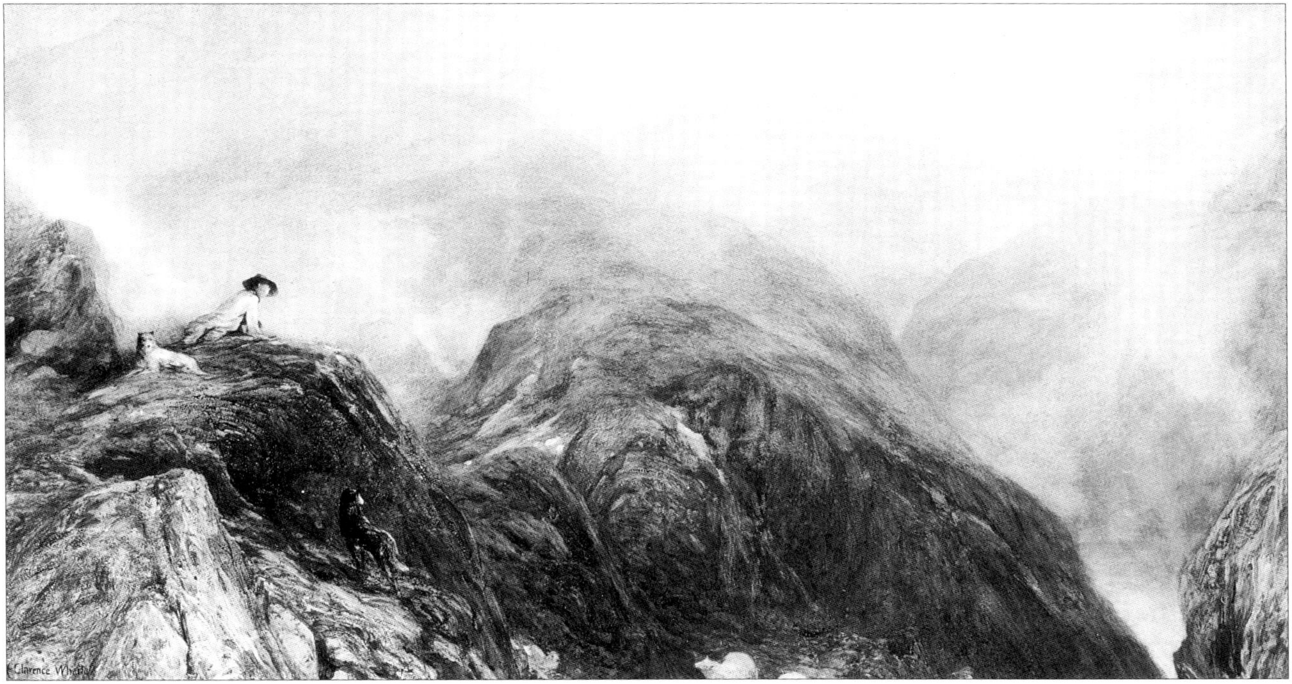

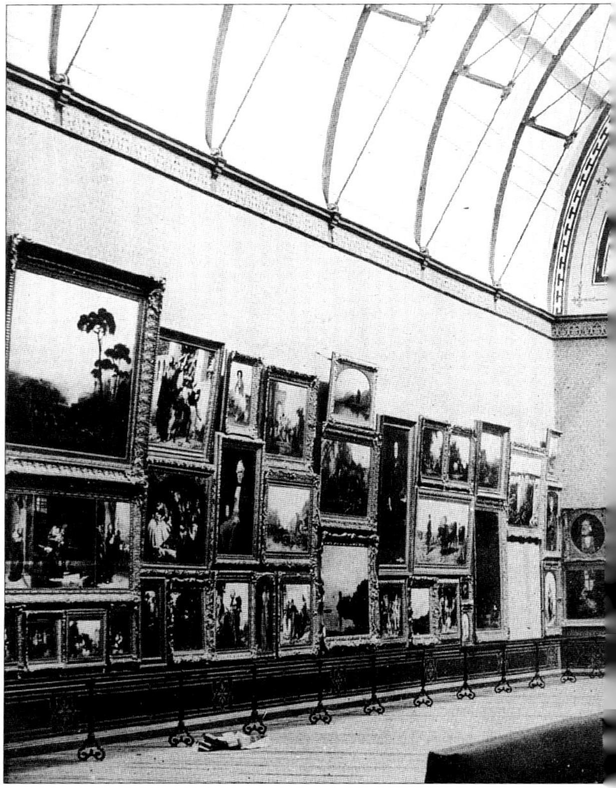

Throughout the 1850s and 1860s, Whaite spent a great deal of time in Wales but did not take up permanent residence. His family home at Stretford in Manchester remained his base, and he participated in the vigorous art life of the city. In 1859 the Manchester Academy of Fine Arts had been established, and although Whaite was excluded from the group of ten founding academicians, he was soon instated as he had, in fact, received an equal number of votes with another painter who had been granted the final place. The foundation of the Academy was the consequence of the Art Treasures Exhibition of 1857. A group of local artists had come together to organise a show of their own works to coincide with the great loan exhibition, and, encouraged by a visit from Prince Albert, they proceeded to constitute themselves on a formal basis. The city's School of Design, where Whaite had his first academic instruction, operated under the aegis of the Royal Manchester Institution, and the new Academy similarly attached itself to the older organisation.

In 1864 Whaite organised an exhibition of his works in the family's Fine Art Gallery in Manchester, consisting of 124 pictures. The prize exhibit was *The Rainbow*, priced at 400 guineas, but alongside the finished oils were shown a large number of preparatory watercolours and drawings whose subjects ranged 'from the cold stern aspect of mountain scenery under the canopy of overhanging cloud, to the richly glowing sunlight effects.'[107]

[107] *Manchester Weekly Times*, 16 July 1864.

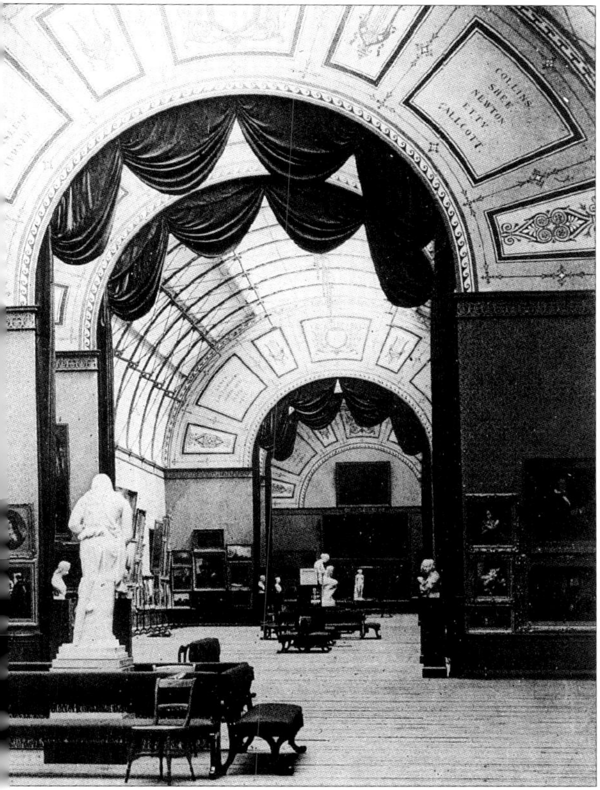

P.H.de la Motte,
Manchester Art Treasures Exhibition, 1857

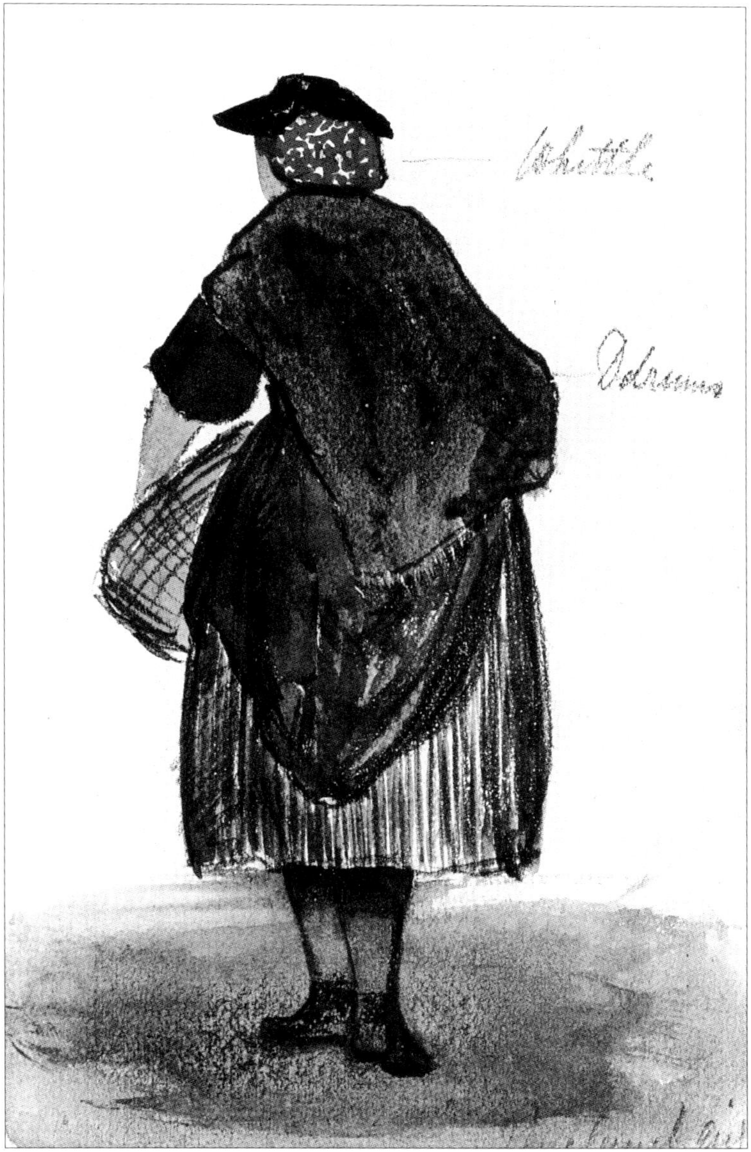

Clarence Whaite,
Penclawdd Girl,
1863

Again, press comment was favourable, with one critic expressing indignation that the Royal Academy had selected only one of Whaite's pictures for exhibition that year. In 1865 none of his pictures was shown, but despite this set-back, his visit to London in the summer to collect the rejected works was of great importance to him. On leaving the Academy he took a cab to Denmark Hill where he was received by Ruskin. He recorded in his diary that 'I was in such a nervous state I could scarce speak':

> *'When I showed him the Cornfield, he in a few minutes pointed out several faults which then looked to me very false, and I wonder how I allowed such untruth to pass. He illustrated his remarks by sketches and drawings by Turner and when put beside mine was an invaluable lesson that I can never forget...'* [108]

Despite his nerves, he left Ruskin feeling that 'nothing has occurred for many years so much to encourage and correct me than my visit'. Nevertheless, Ruskin had told him that he must make his choice between figure or landscape painting, and he did not follow this advice, continuing to paint subject pictures for many years.

In the 1860s Whaite had travelled extensively. In 1859 and again in 1863 he visited north Devon, crossing back on the steamer to work at Mumbles and the Gower. He wrote to his father that the Gower 'seems quite out of the world, and very beautiful'.[109] Like many visitors before him he drew the fishermen of the area and women gathering cockles at Penclawdd, but he recorded them with a vivid brevity and simplicity which few could equal. Nevertheless, his impression of the otherworldliness of the inhabitants of the area owed a lot to romantic wishful thinking. Local people were well aware of the market value of their picturesque attributes. On a visit in June 1858 a painter called Hamerton had not been successful 'in getting any one of the most picturesque to sit for him. On one occasion he was sketching the fire place, pot and gear where they boiled their cockles and the owner removed part of the things in doors because he refused to pay her for drawing them. He left in disgust'.[110] Whaite seems to have been blessed with greater diplomacy. In 1864 he travelled in Scotland and in 1870 to Italy, on both occasions filling sketchbooks and small notebooks with observations of general atmosphere and particular incident. Nevertheless, from these trips he always returned to the Conwy Valley and to the company of the

[108] Whaite archive, op.cit., the Diary, 15 May 1865.

[109] Ibid., letter dated 20 October 1863.

[110] Royal Water Colour Society Archive, J27/2. The incident is reported in a letter written by the painter Edward Duncan dated 8 June 1858.

artists who lived there. In the light of this continuing attraction, one of Ruskin's comments, made during their interview in 1865, seems to have been either particularly prescient or influential. Whaite recorded in his diary that Ruskin 'recommended artists living in Schools. Artists have always flourished more when living in Schools...'

Clarence Whaite, *Capri*, 1870.

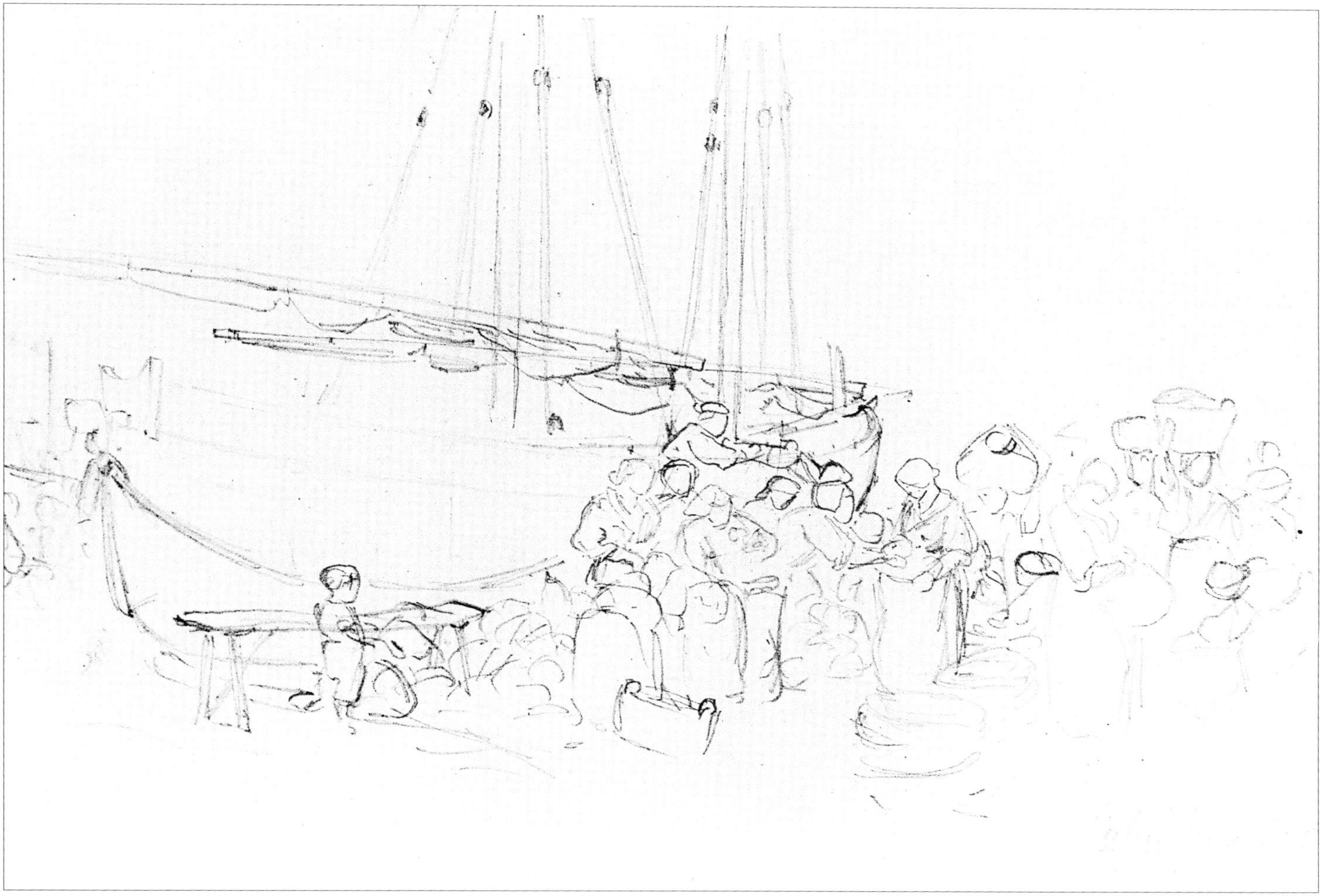

In about 1870, perhaps on his return from Italy, Clarence Whaite took Tyddyn Cynal, on the river about three miles from Conwy, for the first time. The house stood opposite Y Meddiant, where Hugh Hughes had engraved blocks for *The Beauties of Cambria*, fifty years earlier. Tyddyn Cynal became Whaite's permanent home. Six years later he married a local woman, Jane Alice Griffith of Gyffin, just outside Conwy, and soon afterwards his only child, Lily, was born.

Clarence Whaite, *Tyddyn Cynal*, c.1880.

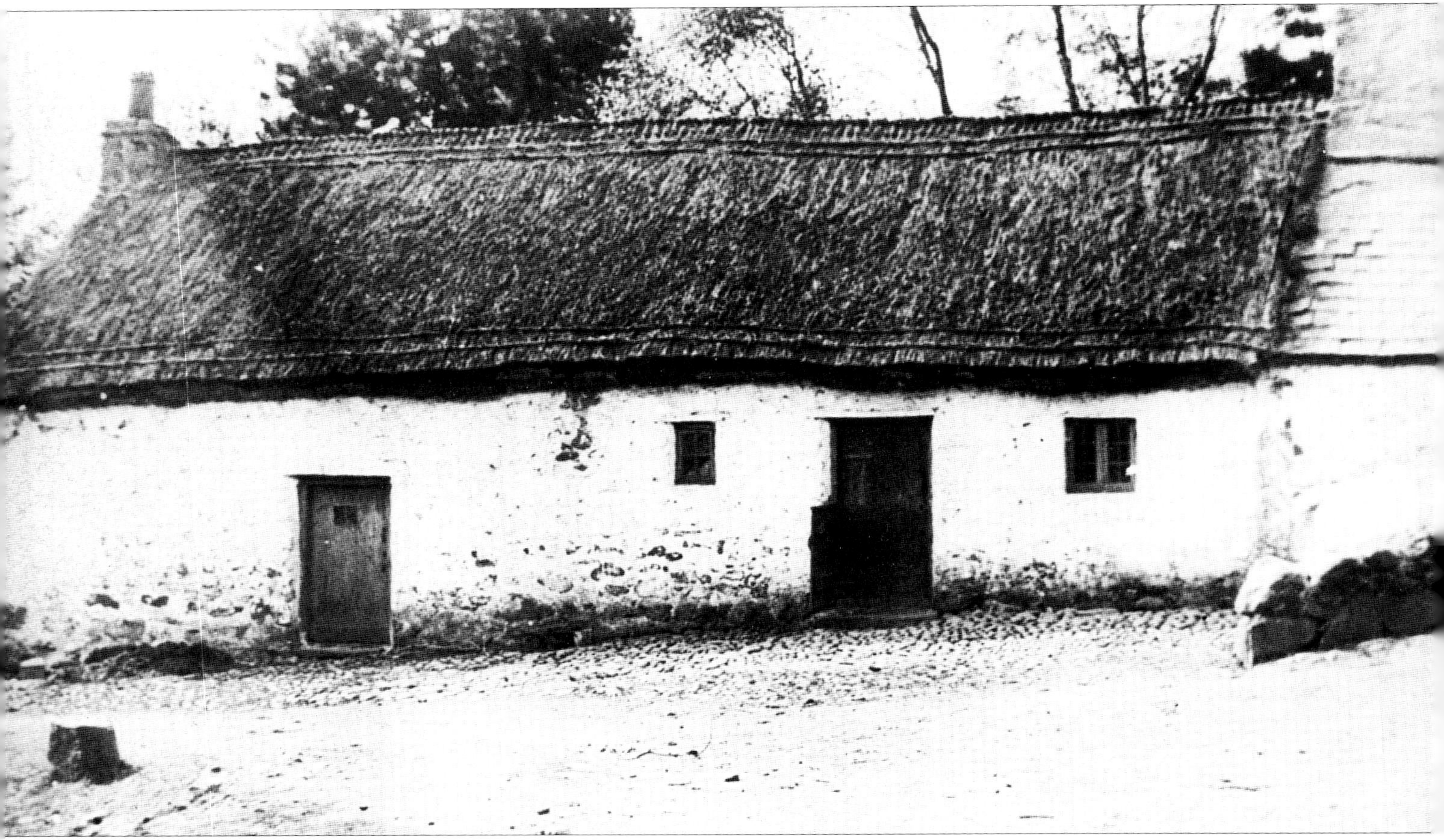

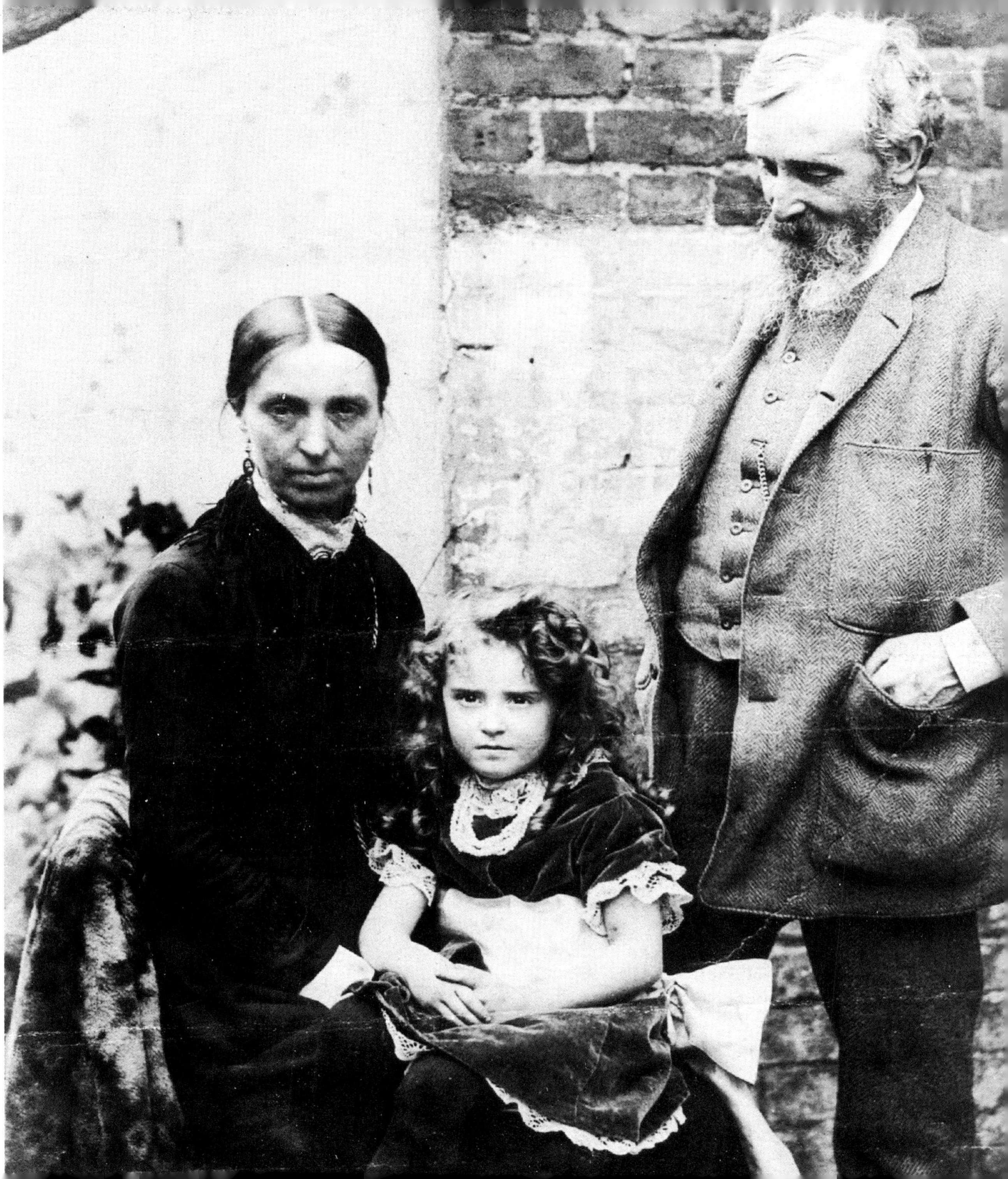

Unknown photographer, *Clarence Whaite, Jane Alice Whaite and their daughter Lily*, c.1880.

4

The Conwy Valley and progress in Welsh Art

John Thomas,
Art Treasures Exhibition,
Ruthin, 1868.

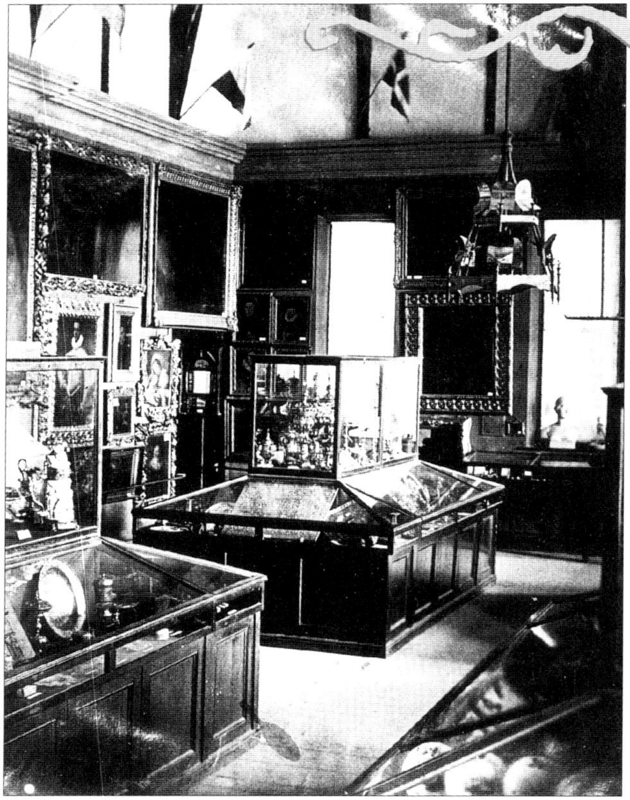

The Manchester Art Treasures Exhibition of 1857, which led to the major developments involving Clarence Whaite in that town, was not echoed in Wales for more than a decade. In 1861 a new series of National Eisteddfodau began and at Caernarfon in the following year the Social Sciences Section was inaugurated. Its broad educational aims included the encouragement of the understanding of art and craft among the public, and of potential artists in Wales. An exhibition was organised, which was sufficiently well received to encourage the committee to expand in subsequent years. Many of the leading figures in the movement were Welsh intellectuals living in London, such as the sculptor, William Davies, Mynorydd, originally from Merthyr Tydfil. However, it was under the patronage of a resident artist and connoisseur, William Cornwallis West of Ruthin Castle, that these somewhat tentative first

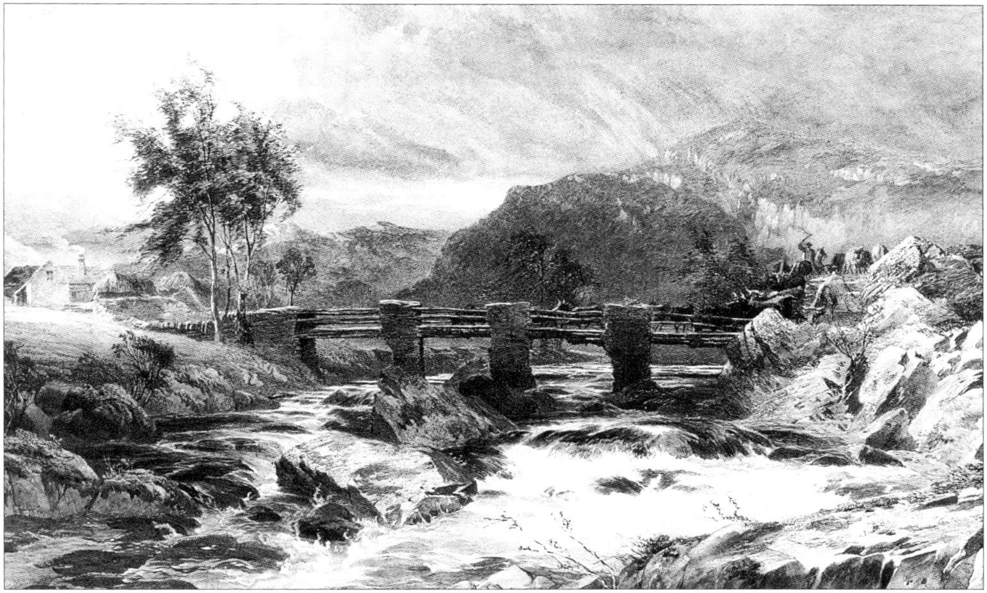

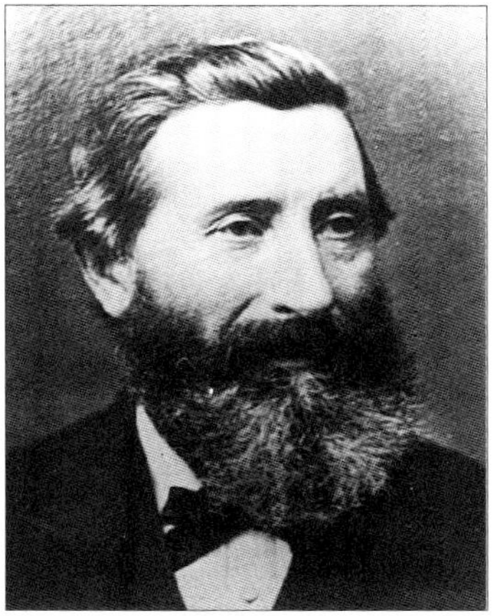

efforts were crowned by a loan exhibition on a grand scale. In 1868 Cornwallis West organised his exhibition in parallel with the small competitive exhibition at the Ruthin Eisteddfod.[111] Since it was the first major historical art exhibition in Wales, it so dominated press attention that few details of the competitions have survived. At Bangor in the following year a similar, though smaller, loan exhibition was mounted, which included works by contemporary Welsh painters and English painters resident in Wales. Notable among them were landscapes by Evan Williams of Caernarfon, who had visited the 1857 Manchester exhibition and, subsequently, wrote a review of it for the magazine *Y Traethodydd*. Also represented at the 1869 exhibition was John Cambrian Rowland, originally from Ceredigion, but who had been appointed first Principal of the Caernarfon School of Art on its inception in 1853. The painter Joseph Josiah Dodd, who lived and worked in Bangor, was well represented by landscapes, many of them owned by local, middle-class patrons. Alongside the works of these indigenous artists a number of Betws views by English painters were exhibited. These included at least two by George Wells and Joseph Charles Reed, who had been prominent figures in the artistic life of the village for some years. Reed exhibited Betws pictures at the Royal Society of British Artists in

Above:
Unknown photographer,
John Cambrian Rowland,
c.1865.

Above left:
Joseph Charles Reed,
Drovers near Beddgelert,
c.1863.

[111] For the exhibition, see *Y Chwaer-Dduwies...*, op.cit., pp.29-48.

Unknown artist, *The Loyal Incorporation of Artists*,
page from the visitors book of the Royal Oak Hotel, 1867.

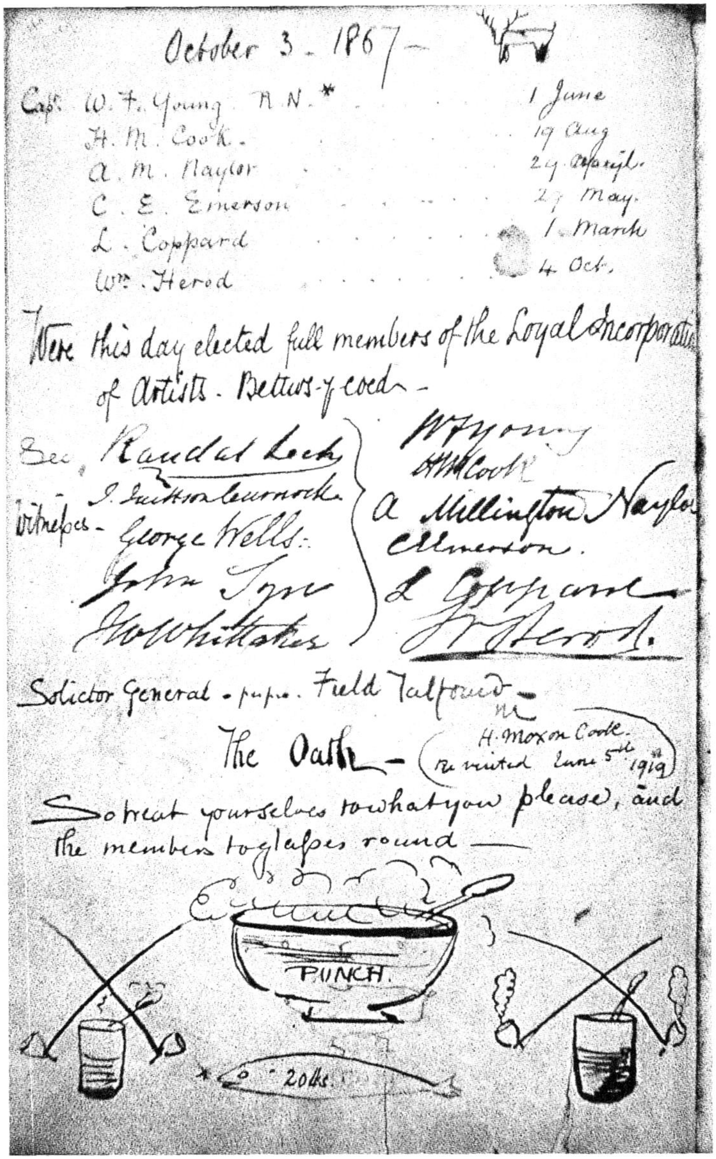

October 3 - 1867 -

Capt. W. F. Young R.N.* . . . 1 June
H. M. Cook . . . 19 Aug
A. M. Naylor . . . 24 August
C. E. Emerson . . . 27 May
L. Coppard . . . 1 March
Wm. Herod . . . 4 Oct.

Were this day elected full members of the Loyal Incorporation of Artists - Bettws-y-coed -

Sec. Randal Lock
Witnesses - J. Faithorn Cornock
George Wells
John Syer
J W Whittaker

W F Young
H M Cook
A Millington Naylor
C E Emerson
L Coppard
W Herod.

Solicitor General - p.p. - Field Talfourd -

The Oath - (H. Moxon Cooke re-visited June 5th 1919)

So treat yourselves to what you please, and the members to glasses round -

PUNCH

20lbs.

1860, and subsequently on numerous occasions at the New Watercolour Society. Wells' earliest recorded visit to Betws was in 1862, when he gave a Bristol address, but he subsequently took up residence. He exhibited his first Welsh subject at the Royal Society of British Artists the year after the Bangor exhibition and, until 1886, his works exhibited in London were almost exclusively Welsh.[112] Among his Welsh friends he counted the painter Charles Mansel Lewis of Stradey Castle, an important promoter of Welsh visual culture, especially through the Eisteddfod movement. Mansel Lewis noted a day's sketching with Wells at Betws in September 1871, and also seeing Whittaker's pictures.[113]

Since no catalogue has survived and the newspaper reports are incomplete, it is not clear how many of the well established residents of Betws, such as Whittaker and Bond, showed their work at Bangor in 1869. Nevertheless, the exhibition demonstrated the beginnings of an interaction between incomer artists in the Conwy Valley and those Welsh intellectuals and artists who sought to develop an indigenous art world based on existing institutions, notably the Eisteddfod. The local Nant Conwy Eisteddfod of 1872 was held at Betws and its publicity most unusually emphasised the artistic associations of the area, rather than literary matters. According to newspaper advertisements, Betws was 'The artist's home and the paradise of Wales'. A gold medal was offered for the best painting of 'any view in the neighbourhood of Nant Conwy'.[114] The adjudicator was the painter Randal Leche of Cardon Park, Cheshire. Leche had stayed at the Royal Oak at least as early as 1860, and exhibited the fruits of his visits in London.[115] He was the leading figure in a social club known as 'The Loyal Association of Artists' which met regularly at the Royal Oak through the 1860s. Resident and visiting artists were enrolled as members and their names recorded on mock certificates drawn in the visitors book with the club's emblems of crossed clay pipes and punch bowl. Whittaker and Wells seem to have been closely involved along with one Field Talfourd, and the lists of painters of varying status who were enrolled as members included Syer, Leader and Coppard. The inner circle clearly held non-artistic tourists in some contempt, if their doggerel is a fair guide:

> *'God save thee British Tourist*
> *From Leader, Talfourd, Leche*
> *Should you again to Bettws come*
> *Within their vengeful reach.'*

In his Eisteddfod adjudication of 1872 Randal Leche reported that 'some very excellent and beautiful work had been sent in but that most deserving of a prize was a fresh piece of Welsh painting in water colour, The Wooden Bridge at

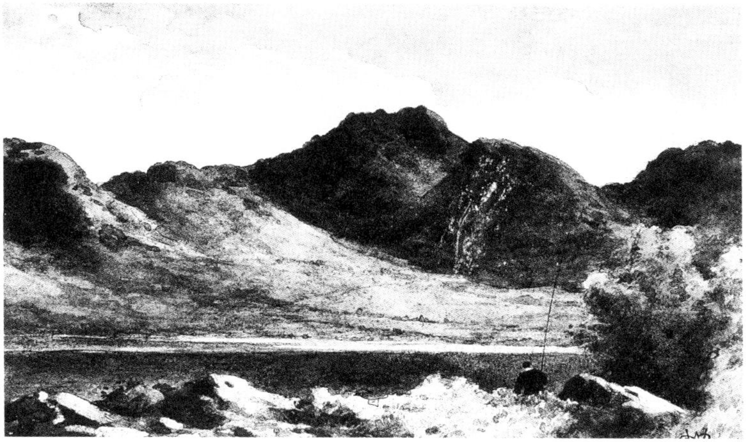

W.D.Barker, *A Lake in North Wales*, 1875.

W.D.Barker, *Trees on a River Bank*, 1879.

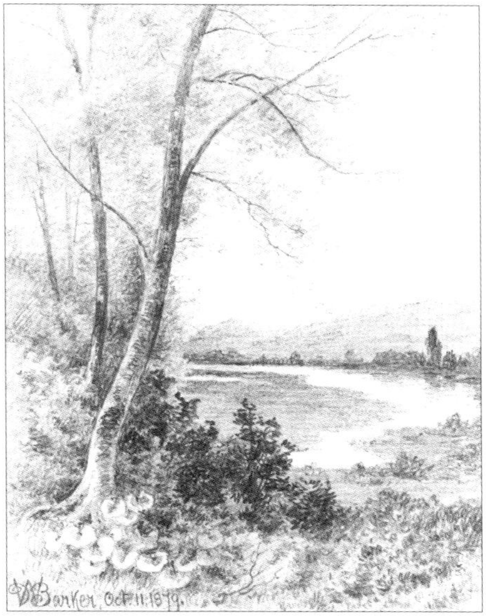

[112]Wells gave 1 Rhiwlas Villa as his address in the RA exhibition of 1888, and he was resident there at the time of the 1891 census. Rhiwlas Villa was a new terrace of little architectural distinction, one of many encrusting the steep hill behind the town.

[113]Stephanie Jones, *Charles William Mansel Lewis: Painter, Patron and Promoter of Art in Wales* (Aberystwyth, forthcoming).

[114]*Carnarvon and Denbigh Herald*, 24 August 1872.

[115]At the RSBA in 1861 and 1863, and at the RA in 1868. Randal Leche appears to have known Wells before coming to Betws, since Wells painted a portrait of a Miss Leche in 1859.

[116]*Carnarvon and Denbigh Herald*, op.cit.

[117]H.L.Mallalieu, *The Dictionary of British Watercolour Artists* (Suffolk, 1986) says that William Dean Barker exhibited 1868-1880. He showed *Afon Llugwy Tyn-y-coed* (wc) at RSBA in 1871/2.

[118]Banks was born at Kington, on the English side of the border, in 1822, but certainly considered himself Welsh. He owned Bronllys Castle and in 1850 he married Jane Emily Williams, daughter of the Rev.David Williams of Ystrad Meurig, who died in 1863. He moved to north Wales for health reasons and in 1867 married Elizabeth Maria Richards of Ynys, Anglesey.

Nant Crafnant'.[116] The painter was William Barker of Trefriw and as a result of his success he was initiated into the local Gorsedd under the bardic name Arlunydd Glan Conwy. This appears to be the first time that an English-born artist was accorded the honour and may suggest that his acquaintance with the area extended back further than his known Betws views, exhibited in London for the first time that same year, would suggest.[117]

At the 1874 Bangor Eisteddfod, the painter William Laurence Banks, who had begun his career in Breconshire but was resident by this time in Llanfairpwll in Anglesey, won a prize for a watercolour of Conwy Castle.[118] The adjudicator was J.J.Dodd. The same Eisteddfod was notable for the advertisement placed in the programme by Hugh Humphreys, the Caernarfon printer, for his Fine Art Gallery. This was probably the first establishment in north Wales to develop beyond a printers and stationers shop which also stocked engravings and into a full-blown commercial gallery. It was well established by 1877 when the Eisteddfod was held in Caernarfon and, at about that time, it was portrayed in a lithograph of Castle Square, its window well stocked with landscapes in gilt frames. Unfortunately, no details have come to light of the painters who sold work there, though the maker of the lithograph, J.J.Dodd, seems likely to have been among them.[119]

The efforts of the pioneers of the National Eisteddfod to develop a consistent policy of drawing social, scientific and visual matters into the ambit of the movement fell into disarray in the 1870s. The visual arts, in particular, shrank almost to the point of extinction. In 1876 it was Cornwallis West, once again, who demonstrated to a series of uninspired Eisteddfod committees the level of ambition and competance necessary to bear comparison with contemporary developments in other countries. In parallel with the Wrexham Eisteddfod he organised a massive Art Treasures Exhibition in a specially constructed gallery on Hope Street. In one sense, the location proved to be less than appropriate since the great critical success of the enterprise, encouraged by Royal patronage, was matched by disasterous financial failure. The costs were

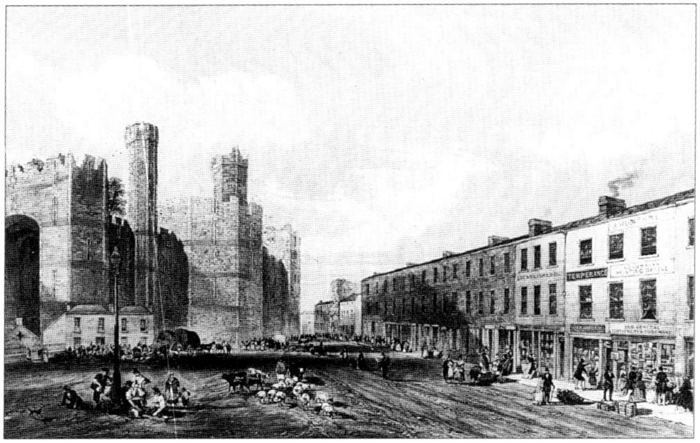

J.J.Dodd, *Castle Square, Caernarfon* - Hugh Humphreys' Fine Art Gallery to right, c.1870.

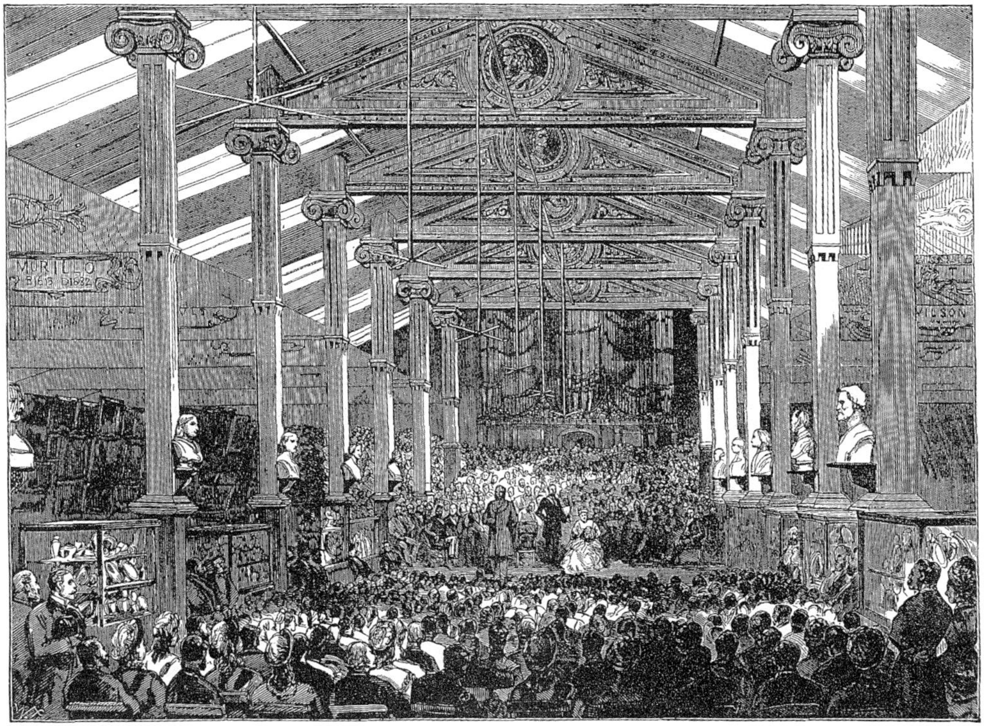

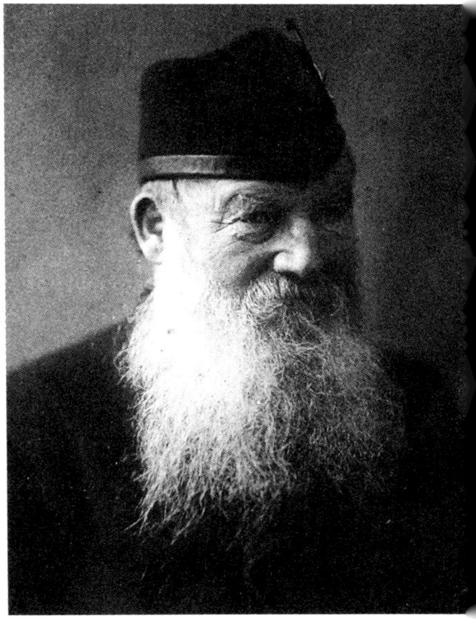

Unknown photographer,
W.L.Banks, 1893.

Unknown engraver,
The Art Treasures Exhibition,
Wrexham, 1876

born by Cornwallis West himself. Regrettably, as in 1868, information about the competitive entries in the contemporary Eisteddfod is scanty but there were certainly some Betws views, including water colours presented under the pseudonym 'Yacht', which were admired by the critics.[120] However, the importance of the Wrexham exhibition was primarily in moving forward among the younger generation the idea that there could be large exhibitions in Wales playing their part in a wider art world of professional painters and students in art schools. By this time, exhibitions had also been held in the south, notably the Cardiff Fine Art and Industries Exhibition of 1870, which was followed by a similar enterprise in 1881, both intended to raise money for the Free Library scheme in the town.

[119]Hugh Humphreys had known Hugh Hughes and owned examples of his work, of which he had published engravings. However, Hughes died in 1863 and it is not clear if Humphreys was dealing in original pictures by that time. Humphreys certainly took commissions for the painting of portraits, as well as photographs. See Peter Lord, *Artisan Painters* (Aberystwyth, 1993), p.46-7.

[120]NLW XAS 36 (Wrecsam, 1876), unidentified press cutting.

Eisteddfod art exhibitions between 1876 and 1882 were on a small scale, but, nevertheless, were significant for the gradual increase in participation of resident professional artists. In 1877 Banks was an adjudicator, and he awarded the first prize to Samuel Maurice Jones, a young Caernarfon painter. Jones was an early product of the development of public art education in Wales, having begun his training under John Cambrian Rowland at Caernarfon School of Art, before going to London in 1870. At Conwy in 1879 the art competitions were pitiful affairs but, for the first of many times, Clarence Whaite was the adjudicator. The situation at Denbigh in 1882 presented an equally unfortunate contrast between the low quality of the entries and the distinction of the adjudicator, when Hubert Herkomer was invited to assess the work, along with Edwin Arthur Norbury, a professional painter living in Rhyl. Herkomer had, presumably, been pursuaded to attend by the indefatigable Cornwallis West, who was President of the Day on which the art and craft adjudications were given.[121] The 'sleepy indolence' of the committee at Denbigh, combined with a leaking roof and a dreadful standard of work, combined to make the Eisteddfod a national embarrassment. However, things were set to develop in a dramatic fashion over the subsequent five years as the result of the combined efforts of the Conwy Valley artists in the north and a group centred on Cardiff in the south.

The increasing number of professional artists settled from end to end of the Conwy Valley, coupled with the emergence of the idea among Welsh intellectuals that educational improvement in Wales should include visual culture, provided the atmosphere in which an academy became a plausible concept. On 12 November 1881, at the Llandudno Junction Hotel, E.A.Norbury convened a meeting of interested artists. Those present under Norbury's chairmanship were W.L.Banks, now of Hendrewaelod near Conwy, John Johnson of Trefriw, Charles Potter of Tal-y-bont, and William Meredith, Joshua Anderson Hague and George Hayes, all from Manchester and who seem to have been regular visitors rather than residents. Hayes was a founder member of the Manchester Academy

[121] The origins of Herkomer's association with Cornwallis West and Ruthin are obscure. Herkomer met his future wife, Lulu Griffiths of Ruthin, in 1873 and they married in the town in 1884. The contact may have been Herkomer's patron, Charles Mansel Lewis of Stradey Castle. Both men were at Eton (though not together) where they came under the influence of Samuel Evans, the art teacher; see Stephanie Jones, op.cit.

of Arts and Meredith had become a member in 1874, providing the committee with practical experience of establishing and running such an organisation. The self-appointed committee drew up a prospectus for a Cambrian Academy, dated 26 November 1881:

> *'The Royal Academy and other institutions of a similar character have long been established in England; the Royal Hibernian Academy in Ireland, the Scottish Academy in Scotland, but Wales has hitherto felt the want of a kindred society of its own.*
>
> *'It has therefore been resolved to establish "The Cambrian Academy of Art" in the hope that such an Institution will give impetus to the further development of Art in connection with the Principality.'*[122]

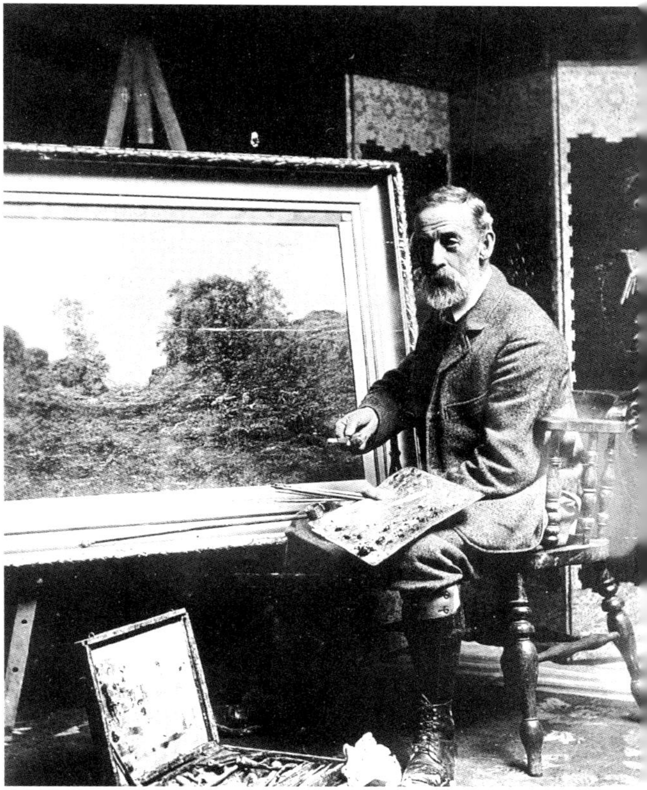

Unknown photographer,
Richard Gay Somerset, c.1885.

Despite the fact that all seven painters had been born in England, this wording suggested an intention which extended well beyond establishing an art club for north-Wales based English expatriates. Like the subject matter of some of their historical paintings, the choice of the word 'Cambrian', rather than 'Welsh', was redolent more of eighteenth-century antiquarianism than the emerging cultural and political nationalism of young Welsh intellectuals such as O.M.Edwards and Tom Ellis. Nevertheless, it is quite clear that the founding group envisaged a national role for the Academy, and foresaw the importance of attracting artists from the south as well as the north. It seems likely that Banks, given his strong national sentiments and his family connections in Breconshire, was the guiding hand behind the prospectus. Five hundred copies were distributed to attract both patrons and artists. Membership was limited to fifty, and 'confined to artists resident in or who have studied in Wales' - by which was meant artists who had worked in Wales as regular summer visitors. Eight of the founders were Manchester Academicians, although by this time some of them were resident in Wales. Notable among them were William Artingstall of Rose Hill, who became Treaurer of the Manchester Academy, and Richard Gay Somerset, who lived at Bron Haul, a fine new house close to Richard Bond's cottage, by

[122]NLW, Royal Cambrian Academy Art Records, Minute Books, 26 November 1881.

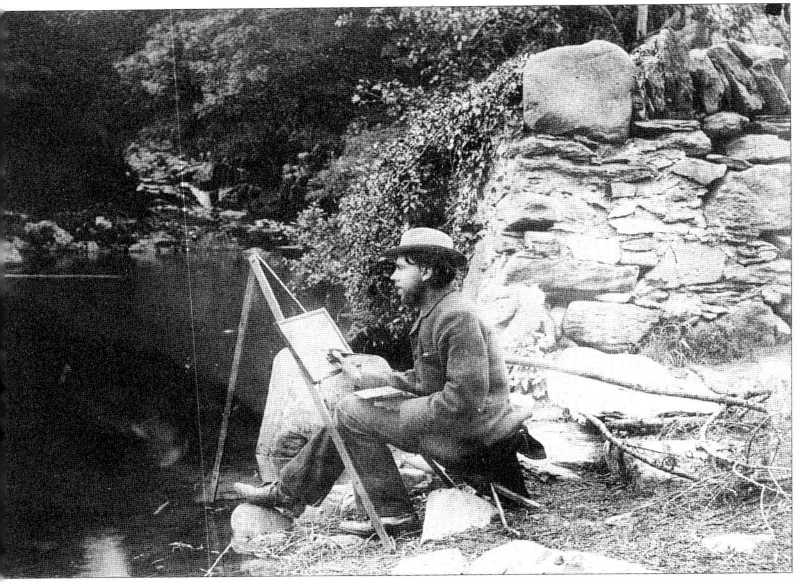

Unknown photographer, *Samuel Maurice Jones painting at Trefriw*, c.1885.

then a relic of a bygone age. Somerset's association with the Academy proved short lived, as he was expelled for unspecified misdemeanours in 1885.[123] His neighbour, Bond, though still working, was old and did not trouble to become a member. He died at Wern Fawr in 1886 at the age of seventy eight.[124] George Harrison joined the founding group, along with Arlunydd Glan Conwy and his neighbour, George Wells, whose brief career as an Academician was terminated with that of Somerset. Joseph Knight joined later. Clarence Whaite did not apply for membership until shortly after the original deadline of 1 February 1882. He was proposed by his Manchester colleague George Hayes, and was immediately accepted,

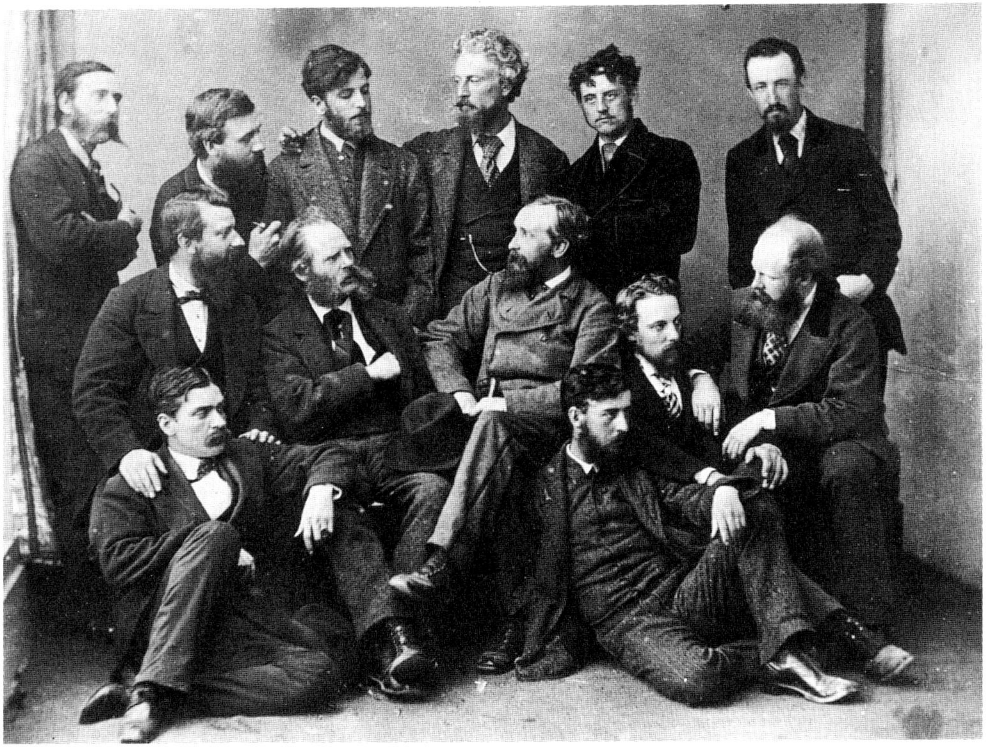

A.Ford Smith, *Royal Cambrian Academicians*, Llandudno, c.1882.

[123]Ibid., Minute Books, 21 March 1885. About 1902 Somerset moved to Bond's old house which had been bought by the Voelas Estate, substantially rebuilt and renamed Pengwern. He died in 1928 after several years of disabling illness. See NLW Voelas Estate Papers, Richard Gay Somerset letters.

[124]An obituary notice was published in *Red Dragon*, 9, 1886, p.298.

but the young Welsh painter, Samuel Maurice Jones, applying at the same time, was required to send in three examples of his work. Clearly, he was not yet a part of the network, but on the strength of his submissions was granted Associate Membership and thus became the first Welsh-born Academician.[125] There was a higher percentage of Welsh people among the early patrons, the most notable of them being Cornwallis West, who was followed by Lord Penrhyn, owner of the finest connoisseur collection in north-west Wales, and Lord Aberdare. Female applicants for membership were put off. In a meeting on 4 February 1882 Artingstall proposed that 'All lady applicants for membership or associateship be written to, including Carrie Walker, that the committee have not yet come to any determination as to the admission of Ladies'.[126]

Soon after its inception, the Academy applied to Queen Victoria for patronage and in April 1882 a letter was received from the Secretary of State 'conveying their most gracious Majesty's command that the Cambrian Academy of Art shall be styled the Royal Cambrian Academy of Art'. It seems likely that Gladstone, the Prime Minister at the time, interceded on the Academy's behalf, mainly because of his Welsh family connections though he had some taste for Welsh landscape painting. Nearly twenty years earlier he had bought an important picture by Leader, *A Welsh Churchyard*. No doubt bouyed up by Her Majesty's condescension, the members proceeded to organise the first exhibition, opened in temporary rooms at the photographer J.M.Young's Art Gallery in Llandudno on 20 June 1882. There were 129 works by 35 artists. The opening provided the first opportunity for discussion in the press of the prospects of the new institution. *The Liverpool Daily Post* reiterated the common perception of the lack of Welsh visual artists, which it regarded as paradoxical since the 1876 exhibition at Wrexham had demonstrated with its loans from Welsh houses that 'her aristocracy number some of the most liberal and cultivated Art patrons in the kingdom'.[127] The reviewer pointed out that 'the executive council... comprises only members who reside within 25 miles of Llandudno, which may be said for the present to be the headquarters of the institution. Llandudno has been selected for the purpose because it is believed to be the "art centre of Wales", and it is well known that large sums are annually spent there in the purchase of pictures...' Benjamin Woodcock's Fine Art Repository at St.George's Hall was the most prominent

[125]Jones was born in Mochdre, Denbighshire, in 1853, the son of a Calvinistic Methodist minister. He referred to himself as the second Welsh Academician, deferring to Banks as the first although the older painter had been born in England.

[126]RCA Art Records, op.cit., Minute Books, 4 February 1882. Carrie Walker has not been traced.

[127]*Liverpool Daily Post*, 19 June 1882.

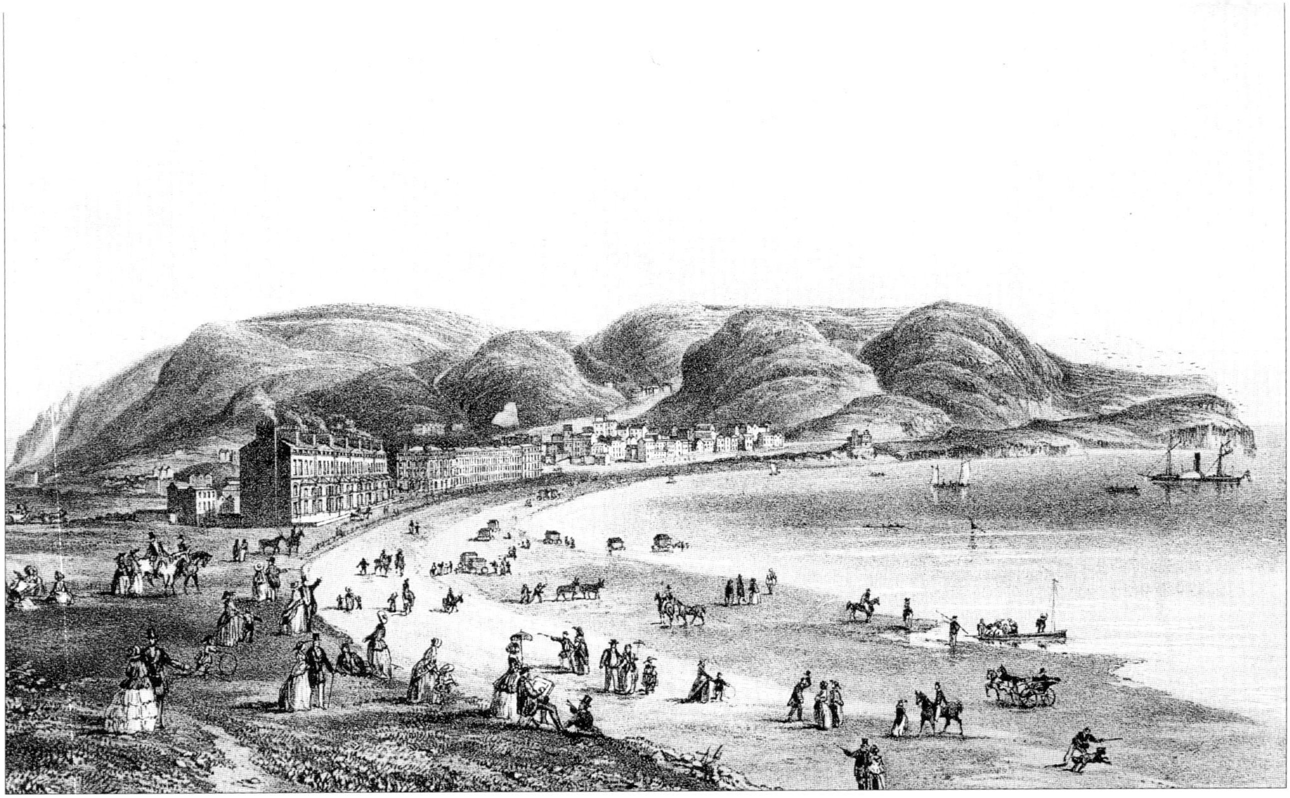

J.J.Dodd,
Llandudno Beach Scene,
1856

outlet for these sales, to which the same proprietor had added a gallery in Gloddaeth Street by 1890.[128] The Liverpool reviewer was clearly well informed of Welsh affairs, but not disposed to be generous towards the exhibition:

> *'In dealing with the initial display we must of necessity make the greatest possible allowances for the circumstances, and for all kinds of defects that are inseperable from the origination of such a scheme. But after making the greatest possible allowances and recognising all the difficulties that have to be surmounted, it would be sheer affectation to deny that it falls very far short of what should have been in some degree a representative collection and that in no respect can it be regarded as a national exhibition. It is held in a moderately-sized room over a photographer's establishment in Mostyn-street, and it contains altogether, including some very trifling sketches, only 120 works. Amongst these there are a few of the very highest value in an artistic sense, and some that are much*

[128]Trade Directories show that among his competitors were Lowe and Son (1880) and George L.Woodley (1890).

below mediocrity, while they all suffer more or less from a very inadequate and unsuitable side light. It is astonishing that such a room should have been selected for the first Welsh Academy exhibition...'[129]

Turning to individual works, the reviewer paid particular attention to subject pictures, including Norbury's *King Arthur and His Diamond Crown* and *Caractacus Leaving Britain a Prisoner*, two new works painted in the tradition of Whaite's Arthurian and Celtic subjects. Whaite himself exhibited a subject picture, though not a Welsh one. The reviewer was forced to concede that *The Nymphs of Calypso* was 'the highest effort of poetic study in the exhibition', before he or she proceeded to damn it with faint praise. The reviewer also entered the debate, still current, about finish, denigrating many works for their sketchiness, 'a degraded imitation of the French School of Corot which originated with the Manchester mannerists some time ago'. One of Anderson Hague's pictures looked like 'the filling in of a background, and is probably only exhibited as an "effect", but it is a most unpleasant one'.

Notices of the exhibition gave rise to an unfortunate dispute among the members. 'Cambria', writing to the *Carnarvon and Denbigh Herald*, appealed to that paper not to print a 'cheap advertisement in the shape of a so-called criticism in the interests of two or three members', which had appeared in Liverpool and Manchester papers.[130] A conspiracy was alleged which, amongst other things, had caused the name of 'perhaps the most eminent member of the society' to be omitted without 'the slightest notice of a very fine and important work sent in by him'. It is unclear to whom this observation referred, but the argument inspired Arlunydd Glan Conwy to write a substantial letter which not only joined the attack against partisanship in the nascent Academy, but, more importantly, threw light on the national aspirations of at least one group among the prime-movers of the institution. Having repeated the conventional wisdom that Wales was deficient in the visual arts, Barker asked:

'How is it that the Welsh boy has never taken lovingly to art? Is it because the Welsh possess no natural talent or genius? No, the reason is they have never had the chance, not even the ghost of an opportunity, of developing an inborn germ which has been lying dormant for want of proper training.'[131]

[129] *Liverpool Daily Post*, op.cit. The quoted figure of 120 works was incorrect.

[130] *Carnarvon and Denbigh Herald*, 1 July 1882.

[131] Ibid., .

Such *apologia* had been regularly offered by Cornwallis West, Mynorydd and others active in the Eisteddfod movement over the preceding two decades. The significance of Arlunydd Glan Conwy's remarks was that they emanated from a prominent member of the group that had decided upon practical action, permanently to improve the situation in the national interest:

> *'If the members of the Royal Cambrian Academy of Art will work honourably, consistently, and energetically, not selfishly, but with unity and for each other's good and for the Welfare of Wales, a grand and noble institution will be eventually formed for the development of art in the Principality.'* [132]

An increasing level of interaction between immigrant and indigenous intellectual communities in the Conwy Valley was indicated by the publication at this time of the first substantial writings in the Welsh language on the subject of the artists' colony. In July 1882 *Y Genedl Gymreig* published two pieces by O.E.Hughes, Crafnant, a neighbour of Arlunydd Glan Conwy in Trefriw, whose purpose was to 'make my fellow-countrymen aware of the importance of bringing up their children to be artists'.[133] Crafnant believed that the Conwy Valley was now the most important centre for artists in Britain, and that 'two gentlemen, who are considered in the first class of artists in this age, live here'. At the top of the valley was Joseph Knight, who had prospered sufficiently by about 1880 to build himself a substantial new house and studio, Min Afon, by the river just to the south of the Waterloo Bridge.[134] He had moved there, against the prevailing trend, from Trefriw, and lived in considerable comfort with his wife and six

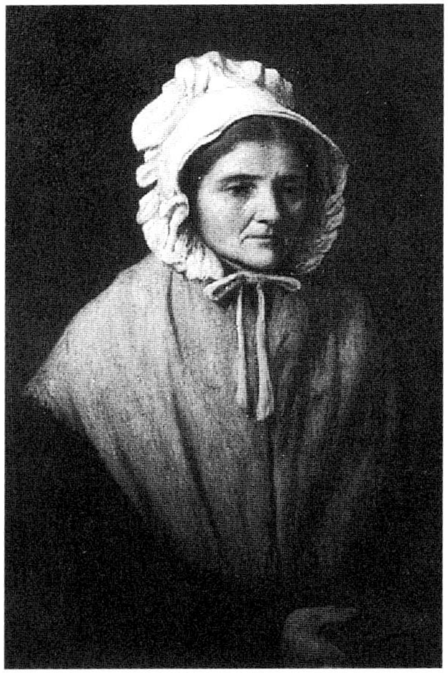

[132]Ibid.

[133]*Y Genedl Gymreig*, 5 and 12 July 1882. Only the first letter was signed 'Crafnant'. The second, a review of the first Academy exhibition, was incomplete and therefore carried no signature. Crafnant has been identified as O.E.Hughes by a letter in his hand written to Clarence Whaite on which the telegraph address was given as 'Crafnant'. There was a considerable correspondence between the two men into the 1890s.

[134]Joseph Knight (1837-1909) was not yet a member of the Academy and did not exhibit in the first exhibition.

children. The work of Joseph Knight was not universally celebrated. One zenophobic critic felt that his pictures abounded in 'all the evils of French landscape art' and that his picture *Showery Weather* showed 'the total inability of the painter to appreciate the higher qualities of landscape art.'[135] However, Knight's prosperity suggested that the high opinion of his work held by Crafnant reflected that of the majority. At the bottom of the valley lived Clarence Whaite, with whose work Crafnant seems to have been particularly familiar. The fact that some of the pictures he admired, including *The Rainbow*, *To the Cold Earth*, and *The Old Church at Llanrhychwyn*, had not been shown in public together, suggests that the two men were sufficiently well acquainted for Crafnant to have visited Whaite's studio and seen them there. In his review of the Academy's first exhibition, 'which every Welshman should visit', Crafnant particularly admired *The Nymphs of Calypso*.

Crafnant was well informed about visual culture. He had visited the 1876 Wrexham exhibition where, like Evan Williams, he admired the work of Richard Wilson. The exhibition was one of the few occasions on which many such middle-class Welsh intellectuals, who did not have access to the collections of the great houses, had been able to see his work in the original. Crafnant felt that, in his Welsh mountain landscapes, Wilson

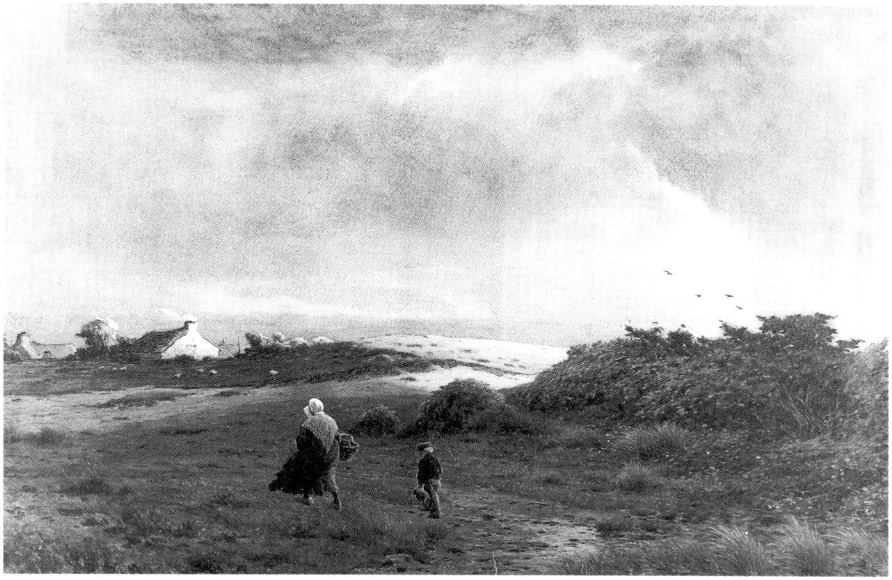

Left:
Joseph Knight,
Welsh Moorland, 1878.

Far left:
Joseph Knight,
A Welsh Grandmother,
date uncertain.

[135]*Porcupine*, 9 September 1876, p.377.

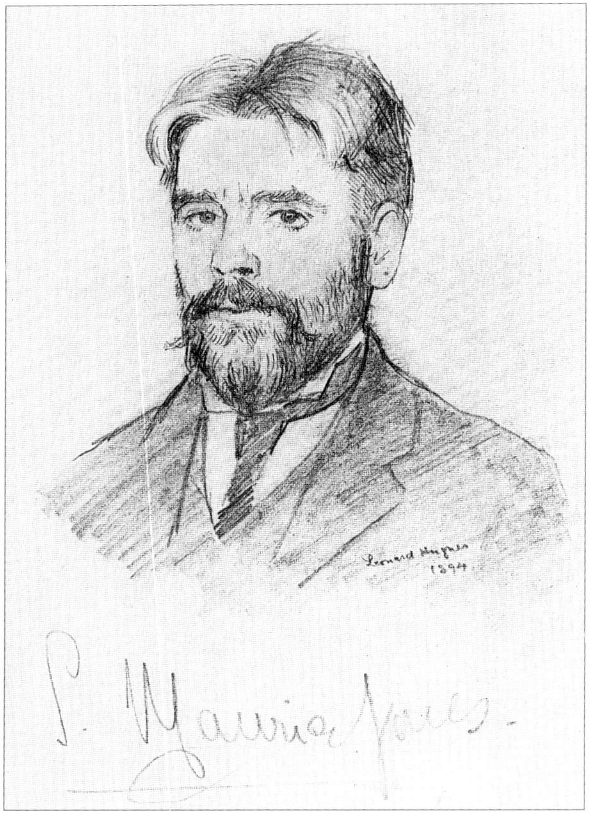

Leonard Hughes,
Samuel Maurice Jones, 1894.

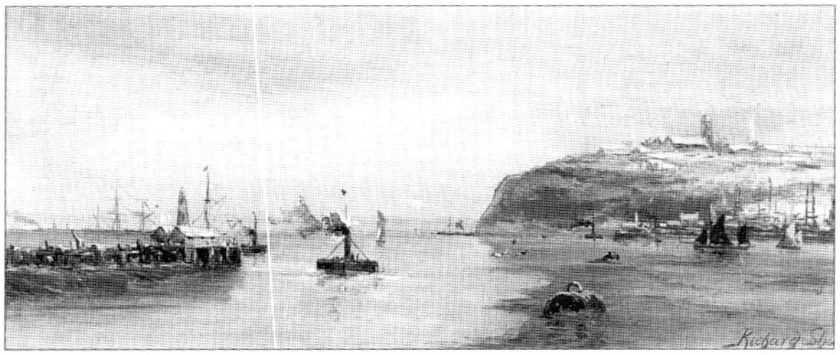

Richard Short,
Lighthouse outside Cardiff Docks,
c.1880.

'set calm to reign in the home of storms', an observation repeated in closely similar words, though with a negative gloss, by Samuel Maurice Jones in 1891, in an unfavourable comparison with Cox.[136] Like his friend, Crafnant's first love was also the work of David Cox, and in particular, *The Welsh Funeral*.

It is clear that Crafnant knew Samuel Maurice Jones very well and that they decided together that this was a suitable occasion to launch a campaign in the Welsh language on behalf of visual culture - a campaign which Jones would carry forward until the end of his life. Crafnant's second piece for *Y Genedl Gymreig* was accompanied by one written by Jones and signed 'Lluniedydd'. He opened his remarks by saying that he had 'the honour to be one of the two Welshmen, so far, to join the Academy', but his letter was significant mainly for its emphasis on the extention of the Academy's activities to the south of Wales, where, he said, it was intended to establish schools.[137]

On 9 December 1882, at the first meeting of the Council of the Academy at which Clarence Whaite was present, 'The Secretary was requested to communicate with the Mayor of Cardiff and Swansea with a view to getting up meetings at those places to further the views expressed in the prospectus'. The Chairman and the Secretary were to attend on these gentlemen as a deputation. By 17 March 1883 the painter Richard Short of Cardiff had emerged as the person who would 'initiate a movement in that town relating to the establishment of a winter gallery for the Royal Cambrian Academy of Art'. By 21 April, following the report of the Cardiff delegation, that ambition had been crucially extended:

> *'The Council of the Royal Cambrian Academy agrees to Cardiff becoming the head quarters of the Academy and that the permanent gallery and schools will be established and the annual exhibition held there.'*[138]

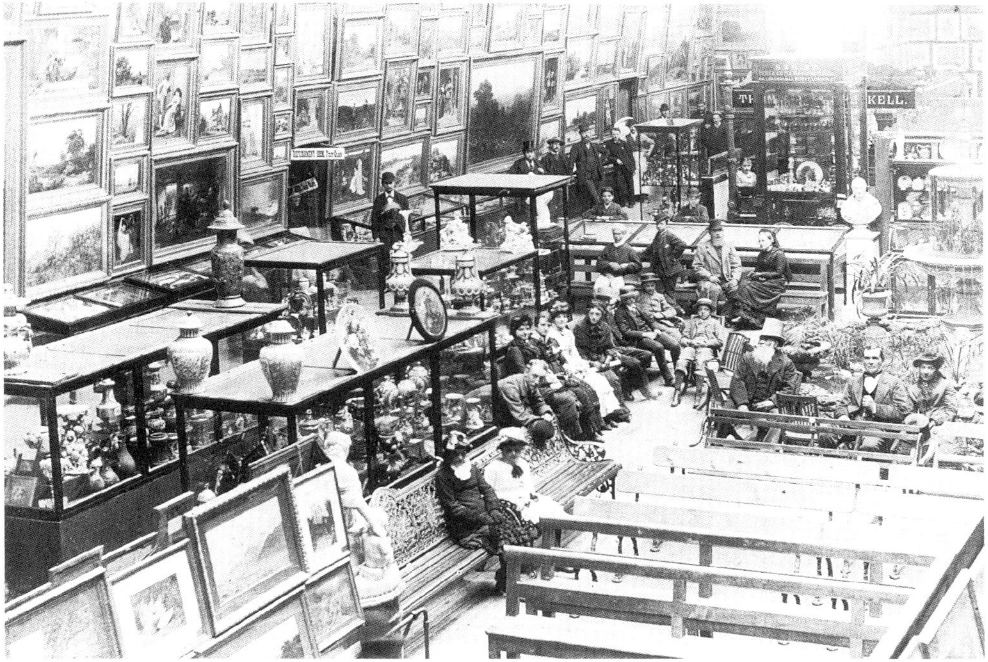

Unknown photographer,
Cardiff Fine Art and Industrial Exhibition, 1881.

Given that the founders of the Royal Cambrian Academy were all based in the north, this was a far-sighted and generous decision. It may safely be assumed that the interested parties in Cardiff had made the case for the town that was becoming, in all but name, the capital of Wales, but they were in no position to force on the founders a decision to make it the home of the Academy. It is likely that the deputation from the north had simply been impressed by the ambition, professionalism and potential resources of the Cardiff group, since they had met them at a moment of high confidence. Among them were Short, the painter and illustrator T.H.Thomas, the Cardiff-born painter B.S.Marks, presently working with great success in London, and the architect Edwin Seward, who was Honorary Secretary. Their 1881 loan exhibition of Fine Art and Industries had been a success, raising sufficient money to enable the Free Library, designed by Seward, to be opened in the following year. It provided a home for the recently donated art collection of William

[136] *Y Genedl Gymreig*, op.cit., For Samuel Maurice Jones's attitude, see Peter Lord, 'The Myth of Richard Wilson', *Gwenllian: Essays on Visual Culture* (Llandysul, 1994), p.158.

[137] Ibid, 12 July 1882, p.6.

[138] RCA Art Records, op.cit., Minute Books, 21 April 1883.

Edwin Seward,
Cardiff Free Library, c.1881.

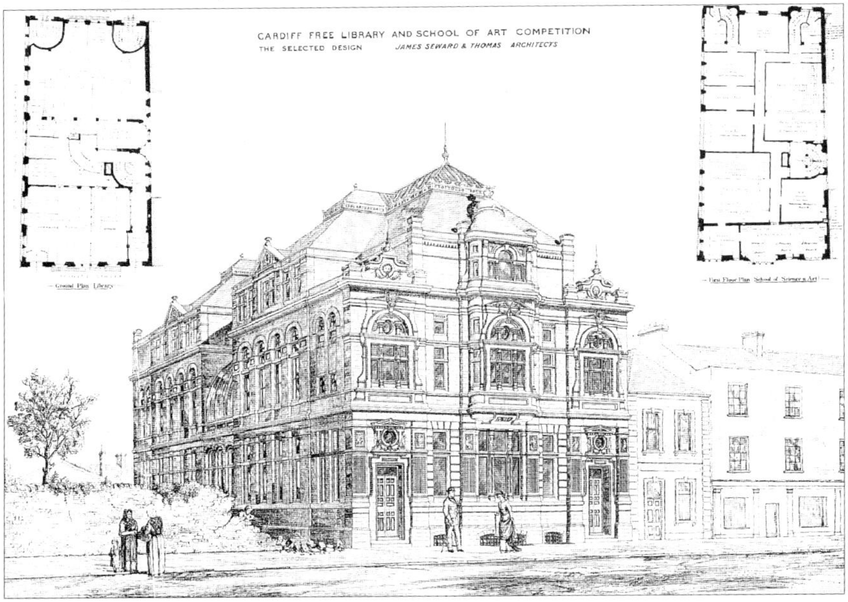

Menelaus, and also for sculpture given to the town by Milo ap Griffith following the 1870 exhibition. At the time of the visit of the Academy delegation, arrangements for the art and craft exhibition at the National Eisteddfod of 1883 were well in hand. Under the chairmanship of T.H.Thomas, it was being organised on an unprecedented scale. Unlike Cornwallis West's loan exhibitions of 1868 and 1876, and the two earlier Cardiff exhibitions, the Eisteddfod exhibition was to be composed only of contemporary work and was competitive in nature. In addition to Thomas, Marks and Seward, the energetic organising committee included Frederic Ternon of the École Centrale in Paris, and from the town itself, the painter Peter Price and J.Pyke Thompson, the collector.[139] At the meeting on which the Cardiff delegation reported back to the Academy on 21 April 1883, several of these individuals, notably Thomas, Seward, and Price, along with Richard Short, were immediately elected members, and in the catalogue of the Cardiff Eisteddfod exhibition, the letters RCA appeared after their names. All but one of the committee established in Cardiff to campaign for the Academy were drawn from this Eisteddfod group. The competitions were differentiated by medium and divided between open classes and those confined to residents of Wales. Set subjects, which had always been a constraint on professional artists submitting their work, were abandoned. The art adjudicators were L.Alma Tadema, one of the leading London painters of the day, and a well-known critic, Frederick Wedmore. The exhibition was sponsored by the *Western Mail*, and, as a consequence, received good publicity. The result was an entry of nearly five hundred works, far beyond that achieved by the Academy in its first exhibition the previous year, or in its contemporary second exhibition at Rhyl.

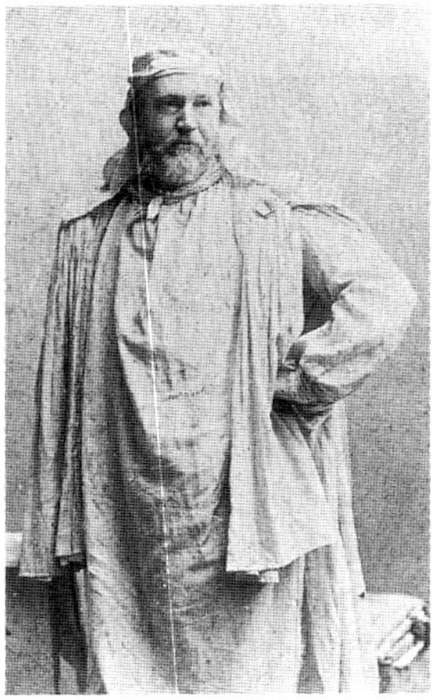

Unknown photographer,
T.H.Thomas in Eisteddfod Robes,
c.1883.

By bringing together organisers, competitors and public, the Eisteddfod provided an ideal opportunity for discussing the prospects of the Academy and the state of the art world in Wales in general. At the prize giving, Frederick Wedmore congratulated the group on their energy and enterprise and saw 'good reason to believe that this fresh start, together with the settlement of the National Academy of Art - the Royal Cambrian Academy - at Cardiff, will do much for painting and draughtsmanship in Wales'.[140] Academicians had done well in the classes for residents, J.C.Salmon of Tal-y-bont, one of the founders, taking the watercolour prize and Richard Short coming second in the oil painting. Leonard Hughes, shortly to become a member, took the third prize. The winner of the gold medal for the best work in all competitions was Milo ap Griffith, and both he and B.S.Marks were invited to give papers at the Cymmrodorion meeting held in connection with the Eisteddfod. Griffith struck a somewhat sour note, prompted by his own difficulties in gaining commissions in Wales: 'With reference to the Academy which it was proposed should be located at Cardiff, he wished to ask them what they intend to do with those students who might eventually become accomplished artists.' With an eye on developments in Manchester and Birmingham, he proposed to the Cymmrodorion that 'If they intended the arts to be a success here in Wales something should be done, besides establishing institutions for teaching, to collect the works of art of their living artists into a gallery, and, if they could, make it a national one'.[141] Despite his reservations, Milo, and also Mynorydd, the sculptor who had pioneered art in the first series of National Eisteddfodau in the 1860s, were elected full members of the Royal Cambrian Academy in February 1884. They joined B.S.Marks, elevated from associate status.

[139]Pyke Thompson was the Chairman of Spillers grain company, and lived at Penarth His collection mainly comprised watercolours.

[140]*Transactions of the Royal National Eisteddfod of Wales* (Cardiff, 1884), p.478.

[141]*Proceedings of the Royal National Eisteddfod of Wales* (Cardiff, 1883), reprinted from *The Western Mail*, p.40.

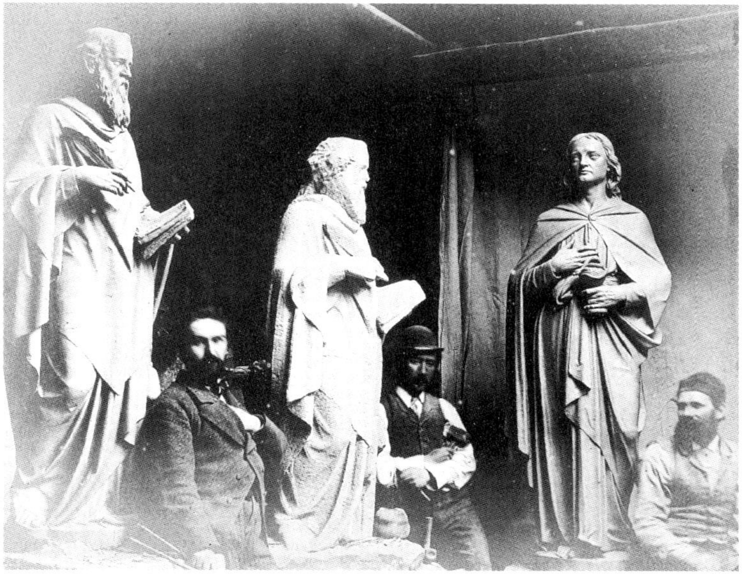

Unknown photographer,
Milo ap Griffith (left) in his studio with statuary for Bristol Cathedral, c. 1875.

The two centres of energy thus united, the prospects for developing the Academy into an important national institution which would act as a focus of practice, patronage and criticism in an indigenous art world, seemed good. Buoyed up by the success of the Eisteddfod, the Cardiff group proceeded to organise a large-scale loan exhibition which would provide the initial finance for building a permanent home for the Academy. The exhibition was mounted at Cardiff Public Hall and opened in February 1884. There was a grand procession of civic dignitaries and Academicians, no doubt organised by T.H.Thomas, who had a *penchant* for such events. On behalf of Cardiff, the Mayor recited the litany of famous Welsh artists - Inigo Jones, Richard Wilson, John Gibson and, striking a more contemporary note, Owen Jones - to illustrate what giants the nation might produce, given the educational advantages offered by the English, Scottish and Irish Academies. Also echoing the conventional progressive sentiment of the day, he regarded a somewhat different aim as perhaps the most important:

> *'...viz, to give the toiling thousands of our race the opportunities of coming in contact with the productions of the best painters and artists - a privilege now enjoyed by the few who can afford to travel long distances in order to gratify their taste and fancy... I believe in the elevating power of true art.'*[142]

E.A.Norbury spoke for the Academy, again making the case for the new development by the example of the Scots and the Irish.

The display had only been rivalled in size in Wales by Cornwallis West's Wrexham Art Treasures Exhibition of eight years earlier, and unfortunately the results were much the same - a combination of critical acclaim and financial disaster. It is possible that audience fatigue, as much as philistinism, was to blame, following the exhibitions of 1881 and 1883, though accusations of indifference on the part of prominent local citizens who might have led public opinion were voiced. The failure did not initially undermine the Academy financially, since the loss was born by the Cardiff organising group. Nevertheless, it dealt a blow to the credibility of Cardiff as its future home, especially in the minds of some

[142] *Western Mail*, 15 February 1884, p.3.

English-born Academicians who had little enthusiasm for national aspirations. From a Cardiff perspective the prestige of the Academy was tarnished, a fact which would have serious repercussions over the succeeding few years. In September 1884 the Council of the Academy instructed the Chairman to prepare an article about the proposal for the journals *The Artist* and *Y Cymmrodor*. Norbury delegated the task to T.H.Thomas who wrote in the immediate aftermath of the financial failure at Cardiff. His article, entitled 'The Royal Cambrian Academy and its Educational Scheme', provided the best insight into the intentions of the activists in the first years of the Academy's existence, and also into the tensions which lay under the surface. It is significant that Thomas devoted the larger part of his article to explaining the national 'problem'. In his view, it arose both because of an ancient estrangement between north and south Wales, and because of the preponderance of English-born artists among the founders. Nevertheless, Thomas's attitude was unequivocally inclusive, since many of these English-born artists, who had first come to Wales as visitors, had chosen to take up residence and thus became 'by love of her and by denizenation, artists of Wales'.[143] Furthermore, some Welsh artists were to be condemned for their unwillingness to participate. Irrespective of the origins of the Academy he believed that 'No movement can be started without serious thought, much labour, and considerable risk, and the wise and only just course is to aid in the effort made by whatever section of our numerically small Welsh Art world'.

From the position of a Welsh-born artist, Thomas encouraged those among his compatriots who saw the institution as alien to act in the national interest by participating. Many of the English-born founders, notably Arlunydd Glan Conwy and Norbury, soon joined by Whaite, had already demonstrated that they took a strongly national view, but it is clear that a number of other English artists were less than enthusiastic. It may well be that moves made by some members in 1885 to establish a separate institution - the Artists' Club - were indicative of these internal tensions. The Club was formed among the Trefriw painters, who may have revised their priorities in view of the fact that the Academy was to be built in Cardiff. Among the more prominent members of the Club were their President, Charles Potter, along with J.H.Cole, Peter Ghent, J.C.Salmon and Benjamin Fowler. All these painters were also Academicians, but they were joined by a few non-members.

[143] T.H.Thomas, 'The Royal Cambrian Academy and its Educational Scheme', *Y Cymmrodor* VII, 1886, pp.78-88.

They organised an exhibition of their works in Liverpool which, in stark contrast to the Cardiff fiasco, raised £400 to build 'a handsome stone Gothic club-house, of Early English pattern, at Tal-y-bont':

'This delightful spot attracts the brethren of the brush as much by its picturesque and ever-changing scenery as by its comparative isolation, for the railway has never penetrated the west side of the Conway. Here a great number of the leading artists have settled, and they have for some time past felt the need of a club which will afford conveniences for study as well as for social intercourse.'[144]

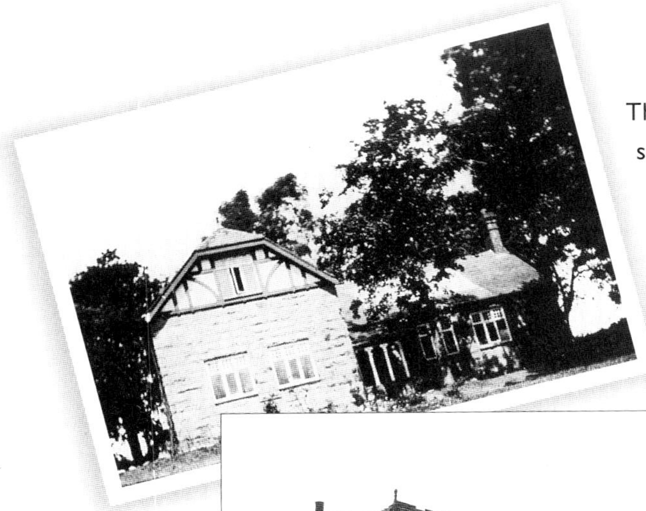

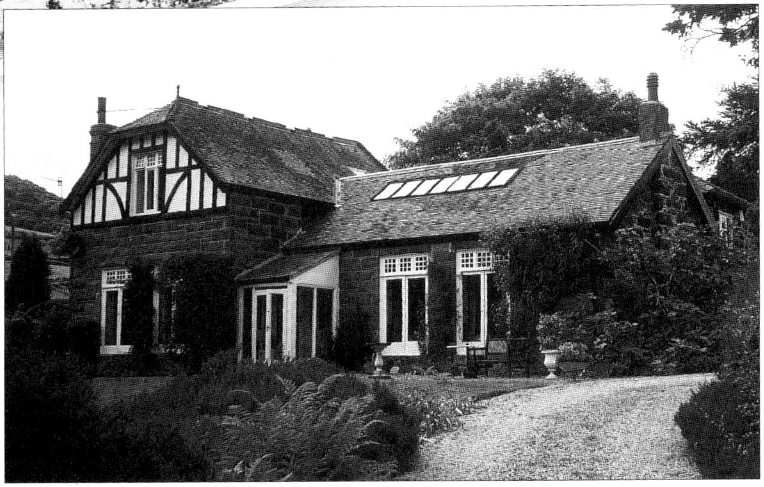

Above: Unknown photographer, *The Artists' Club, Llanbedr-y-cenin*, c.1920.

Right: The Artists' club rebuilt as a private house.

Benjamin Fowler, the Secretary, said that 'a good many of the artists thereabouts felt the importance of studying from rustic models, and they had hitherto used a classroom for this purpose':

'They, however, felt the necessity of a better room to work in, and they made a number of contributions in pictures to an exhibition in Liverpool, which realised the necessary funds for building a club-house. When it was completed they had no doubt they would all spend many a pleasant and profitable hour in it. This was one of the most beautiful sites in the valley of the Conway, and he thought their club would form the nucleus of an artists' colony in that locality. It would also be of advantage to the artists in their business, for it would give the many visitors to the Conway Valley an opportunity of encouraging and advancing the landscape art of the day.'[145]

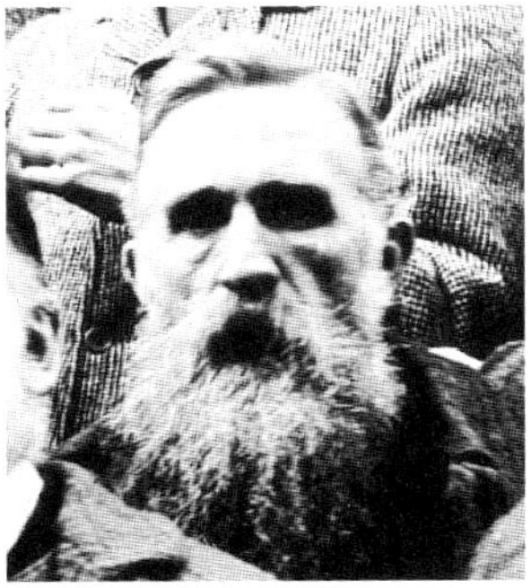

Unknown photographer, *Benjamin Fowler*, c.1897.

A prominant figure in the Liverpool art world, Alderman Samuelson, laid the foundation stone. In his address he made reference to the fact that 'there were so few Welshmen members of the Academy, and felt certain that in the face of a movement such as this the blemish would soon be removed from the Welsh nation'. However, he also referred to a 'proposed affiliation with the South Wales University College, and he hoped that members would never depart from the establishment in their own beautiful locality, and if there was to be any affiliation let it be with the North Wales College'.[146] In the circumstances, this was an unhelpful proposal, but one which elicited loud applause.

Late in 1884, or early in 1885, Clarence Whaite had visited Cardiff on behalf of the Council of the Academy, where, presumably, he spoke with Richard Short, T.H.Thomas Edwin Seward and others of the Cardiff committee. Whaite reported that he 'was much pleased at what he saw and heard there as to the progress made in favour of the Academy'.[147] Despite the failure of the loan exhibition, a proposal for an exhibition of Academy work, to be organised in association with the South Wales University College, had been mooted by Short. Subsequently, Norbury and Banks were deputed to 'proceed to Cardiff... with Carte Blanche to make arrangements for an Exhibition'.[148] Thomas, Seward and Whaite were emerging as the most active proponants of the creation of a national institution in Cardiff, and the three men became life-long friends at this time. Whaite himself was increasingly important in the Council of the Academy, and the minutes of the meeting to which he reported on the Cardiff situation were the first to be signed by him. At the following meeting on 4 February 1885 he was unanimously elected President.

The Academy entered into the second Cardiff exhibition with sufficient confidence to appoint J.L.Treharne as Professor of Anatomy, and J.Pyke Thompson and C.W.Ingram as Honorary Lecturers of the new institution. Unfortunately, the second exhibition repeated, on a smaller scale, the fiasco of the first. From the beginning the enthusiasm of reviewers for the works shown was tempered by pessimistic hints about its likely success with the public:

[144]Unidentified press cutting in NLW Samuel Maurice Jones Papers. The club was opened in the summer of 1886, see note in *Red Dragon*, 10, 1886, p.174. Contrary to the published descriptions, it was located at Llanbedr-y-cennin, not Tal-y-bont.

[145]Ibid.

[146]Ibid.

[147]RCA Art Records, op.cit., Minute Books, 7 January 1885.

[148]Ibid, 21 March 1885.

Right:
Clarence Whaite,
The Shepherd's Dream, 1865.
Reproduced in colour on p.92.

Far right:
Clarence Whaite,
The Awakening of Christian, 1865.
Reproduced in colour on p.92.

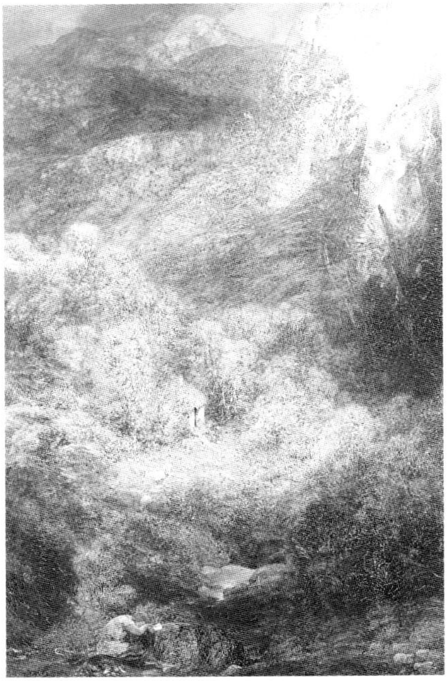

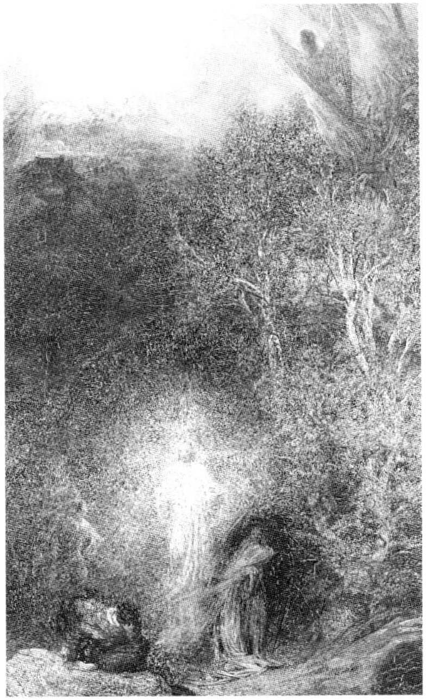

'There on the walls of the College buildings is a collection of modern paintings never before equalled in Wales. Such a show as this in any of the English large towns would have a continuous flow of visitors, and not a few buyers. We trust this may be the case now in Cardiff....' [149]

The main attraction in the exhibition was G.F.Watts' *The Daughter of Herodias*. Watts was frequently claimed as a Celt, if not as a Welshman, by patriots in the period, and accepted associate membership of the Royal Cambrian Academy.[150] After Watts, Clarence Whaite was given the most detailed review in the press. Among works shown by the President were *The Penitent's Vision*, which, by this time, he had cut into two parts, entitled *The Awakening of Christian* and *The Shepherd's Dream*. Writing for *The Welsh Dragon*, 'Hypolite' believed that 'There is an exquisite refinement of manner and treatment about everything that emanates from the studio of Mr. Whaite, of which this picture [*The Shepherd's Dream*] is a good specimen. The scenery is from the favourite painting land of North Wales, and shows high rising ground, covered with spring foliage, rugged too in parts. A shepherd asleep, and his dream, a faint gleam of iris-tinted angels seeming to float down from the sky, half lost among distant trees and melting away into the blue of heaven'. [151]

[149] *Red Dragon*, 8, 1885, p.252.

[150] Watts was not, however, a founding Associate as suggested in the membership list published in *A Centenary Celebration* (Conwy, 1982), where he is given as J.F.Watts. This may result from confusion with a later Academician, James Thomas Watts. The same list omits the name of Samuel Maurice Jones, who was, indeed, a founding Associate. For perceptions of Watts' nationality, see the entry in Mardy Rees, op.cit. p.136.

[151] *Red Dragon*, op.cit., p.253. 'Hypolite' is untraced, but in other articles in *Red Dragon* indicates that he or she wrote from Swansea. The Royal Academy had initially rejected *The Penitent's Vision*, but in 1884, after its division into two halves, Whaite submitted it again. Both halves - *The Shepherd's Dream* and *The Awakening of Christian* - were accepted!

[152] Ibid., p.502.

[153] Ibid., 7, p.464.

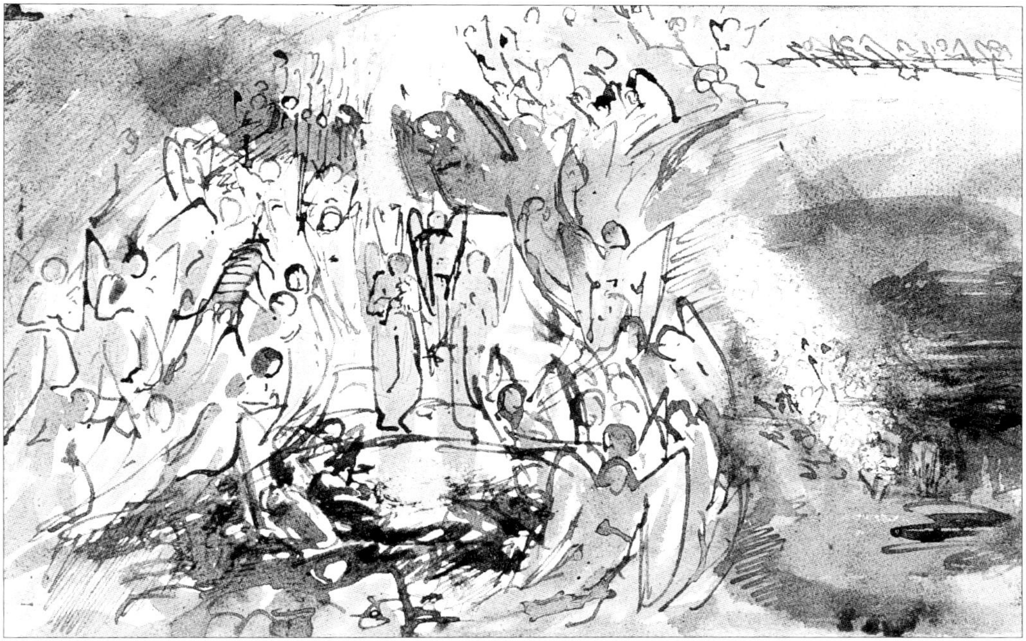

Clarence Whaite, *Angels before the Gates of Paradise*, c.1865.

Such major attractions, along with works by less well-known Academicians such as Harrison ('very nice and faithful'), Banks and Barker, as well as contributions from invited artists such as Charles Mansel Lewis, failed to attract the crowds. Hypolite believed that 'Were a movement like this one well taken up and heartily entered into, it might be made the centre of a new Welsh School of Painters', but such hopes were not to be fulfilled. When the exhibition closed on 26 September, the committee had sold only half as many tickets for its Art Union, intended to defray the costs, as it had expected. It was decided to proceed with the draw and the result was a loss of £224, leaving the Academy itself in deficit. Nevertheless, despite 'the want of interest taken in it by local gentlemen',[152] the committee decided to press on with its plans. The arrangement made with the College had been to hold exhibitions for three years, the rooms to be rented for £100 per annum, in the expectation that 'At the expiration of that time... the Royal Cambrian Art Society [sic] will have established a permanent home in Cardiff'.[153]

George Harrison, *Crafnant Pass*, date uncertain.

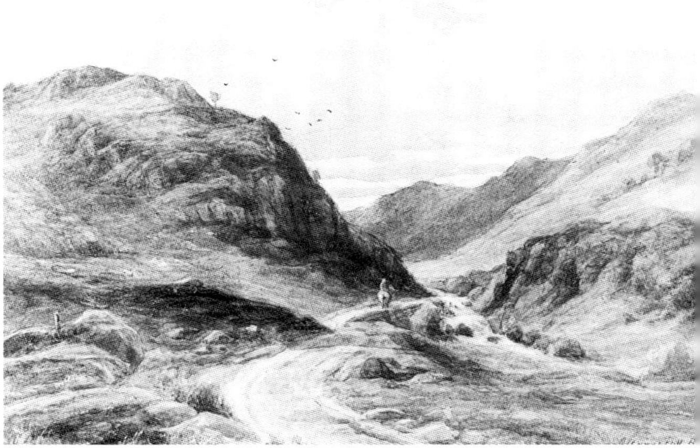

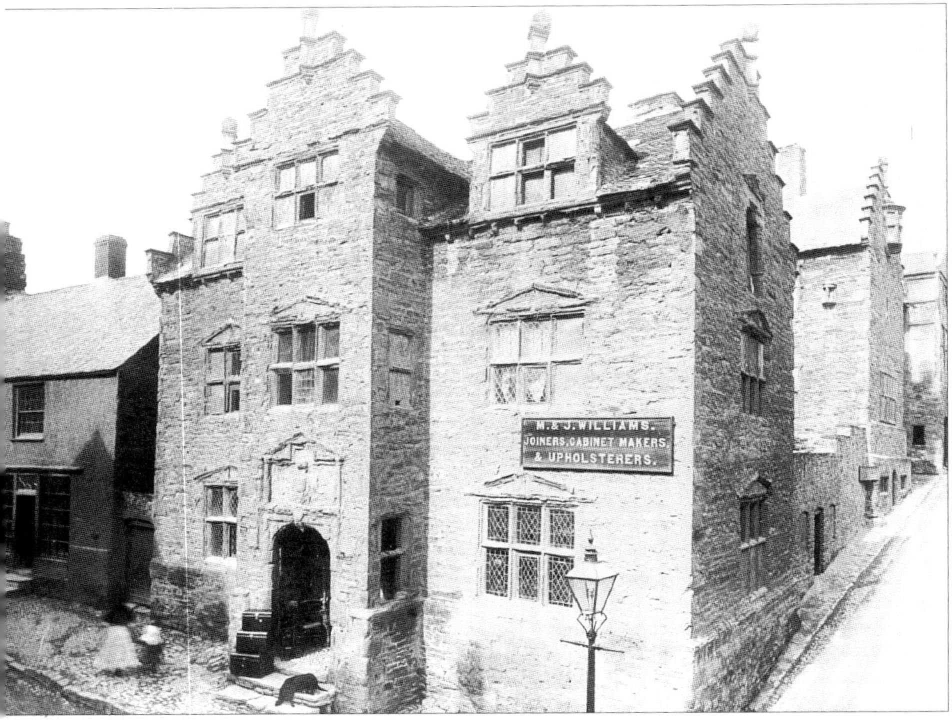

Unknown photographer,
Plas Mawr, Conwy,
c.1880.

However a serious dispute now arose with James, the Registrar, compounding an already difficult situation. The Council of the Academy resolved 'that the Secretary be empowered to communicate with the members of the South Wales University College Council individually placing before them the conduct of the Registrar of the college in connection with the allotment of rooms for exhibition purposes, his demand for a gratuity and his altering the agreement'. From this point, attitudes among some of the northern Academicians began to harden from indifference to opposition to the Cardiff scheme. On 14 November 1885 a special meeting was convened, addressed by T.H.Thomas. The following resolution was passed:

'With regard to the position of affairs at Cardiff this meeting is of the opinion that the Academy are morally and honourably bound to carry out their engagement with Cardiff, and are prepared to do so, so soon as Cardiff has carried out her side of the agreement in providing the accommodation promised and until that is done all matters must remain in abeyance. That in the meantime, the Head Quarters of the Academy be in North Wales.'

Clarence Whaite made the case for gaining Lord Mostyn's agreement to occupy Plas Mawr in Conwy, which he owned, and by June the following year the Academy was installed in the ancient house.

At the National Eisteddfod of 1885, in Aberdare, Cornwallis West made reference to recent developments, taking a somewhat pessimistic view. Despite his support for the Academy, he believed that 'its usefulness must necessarily be limited... Without a permanent home with schools and professors, it can effect but little'. Cornwallis West considered that it would be 'difficult for a country so small as Wales to support with any chance of profit an institution such as a Royal Academy of Painting, which requires so much that can only be obtained in large centres of population'.[154] In holding this metropolitan view, he was not, of course, at odds with the activists within the Academy itself, and, demonstrating a remarkable degree of tenacity, the Cardiff group made one further and very determined attempt to locate the Academy in the town. The opportunity was provided in 1886 by the government's encouragement of projects to celebrate Queen Victoria's jubilee in the following year. Two building proposals were mooted in Cardiff, the first for the University College and the second for the Science and Art Schools. Edwin Seward perceived an opportunity to resuscitate the Academy scheme and raised the matter in the newspapers:

> *'Extension of the schools has become an imperative necessity, and I can quote continual cases in which students have been turned from the doors through lack of working facilities... But even the shortcomings of the schools can be called efficient in comparison with the meagre scope yet given for art gallery purposes. As a fact, Cardiff has no Art Gallery, for it is only by some sort of happy accident that the rooms at the top of the Library Buildings have obtained recognition as such.'*[155]

Seward proposed that a new gallery could be ably managed for the town by the Royal Cambrian Academy. In addition, 'Free training would be given by the Academicians to eligible students in oil and water colour painting, modelling, sculpture, architecture, &c., subjects which the curriculum of no local institution (except the Science and Art School) even contemplates at present.' Seward was able to draw on the example of the young William Goscombe John to strengthen his case:

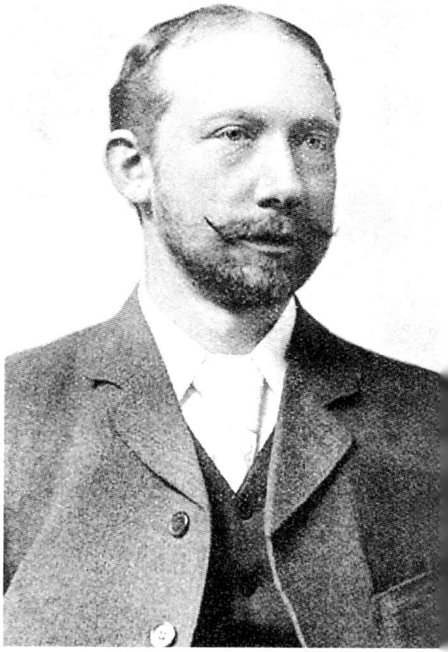

Unknown photographer,
Edwin Seward, c.1890

[154] Cornwallis West, 'Inaugural Address to the Cymmrodorion Section of the National Eisteddfod of 1885', *Annual Report of the National Eisteddfod Association* (London, 1885), p.36.

[155] Whaite archive, op.cit., unidentified newspaper cutting, 1886.

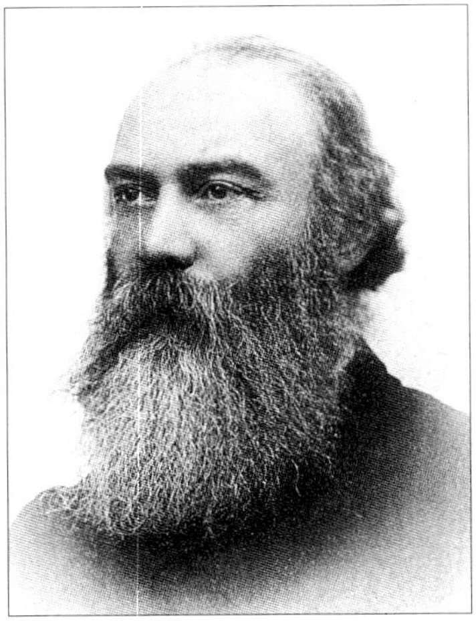

Unknown photographer,
Charles Jones,
c.1880

'The effect of such opportunity as this on the lives of students and on the arts they are destined to practice can be foreseen in the praiseworthy success which your issue of Saturday last chronicles of Mr W.G.John, a student at the Cardiff Art School... who has obtained the silver medal of the Royal Academy and £20 for life modelling.'

Seward proposed 'a National Academy or National Institute' comprising a number of existing national and local societies, such as the Cardiff Naturalists Society and Library (with which T.H.Thomas was much involved), to be headed by the Royal Cambrian Academy. The project soon became known as the National Institution and Seward explained his concept in a series of letters and articles in newspapers and magazines. The Mayor of Cardiff, Morgan Morgan, was sympathetic and in December 1886 the Academy received an invitation from the Town Clerk to participate. However, at a public meeting convened in January to discuss the jubilee, it became clear that the supporters of the College building scheme were not going to give way gracefully to the Institution. The Rev.Dean Vaughan, supporting the College, was of the opinion that 'there was nothing particularly appetizing in the thought of a number of struggling societies being suddenly lifted up into a position of national prominence'.[156] Nevertheless, the proposal to develop the Institution, whose chief co-operating organisations were to be the Royal Cambrian Academy, the Science and Art Schools, and the Free Library, Museum and Art Gallery, was carried. A committee was established to co-ordinate the scheme with the town council, many of whom were veterans of the original Academy proposal of 1884, including Seward, Thomas, Short, and Pyke Thompson. Milo ap Griffith and B.S.Marks, from whom letters of encouragement had been read out at the meeting, were also co-opted. The Academicians were particularly active in soliciting support from distinguished names, and shortly afterwards letters in favour of the scheme from the painters Alma Tadema and Charles Jones appeared in the Cardiff papers. [157]

Although it sought to include many other elements, there can be no doubt that the Institute scheme was primarily a means of establishing the Royal Cambrian Academy in Cardiff, and that the prime-movers were Cardiff-based Academicians. Nevertheless, their vision was a truly national one and was not motivated simply by self-interest. It was explained by Seward in detail in an article in the magazine *Red Dragon*:

[156] *South Wales Daily News*, 7 January 1887.

[157] *Western Mail*, 20 and 22 January 1887. Charles Jones (1836-92) was a native of Cardiff and a successful painter. He was known as 'Sheep Jones' because of his fondness for this subject. He became an Academician and exhibited regularly at Conwy. T.H.Thomas knew him well enough to visit when in London; see NMW Artists, Persons and Places files, letter from Jones to Thomas dated 1889. This letter also conveys 'kind regards' to Thomas from 'B.L.', that is, Benjamin Williams Leader.

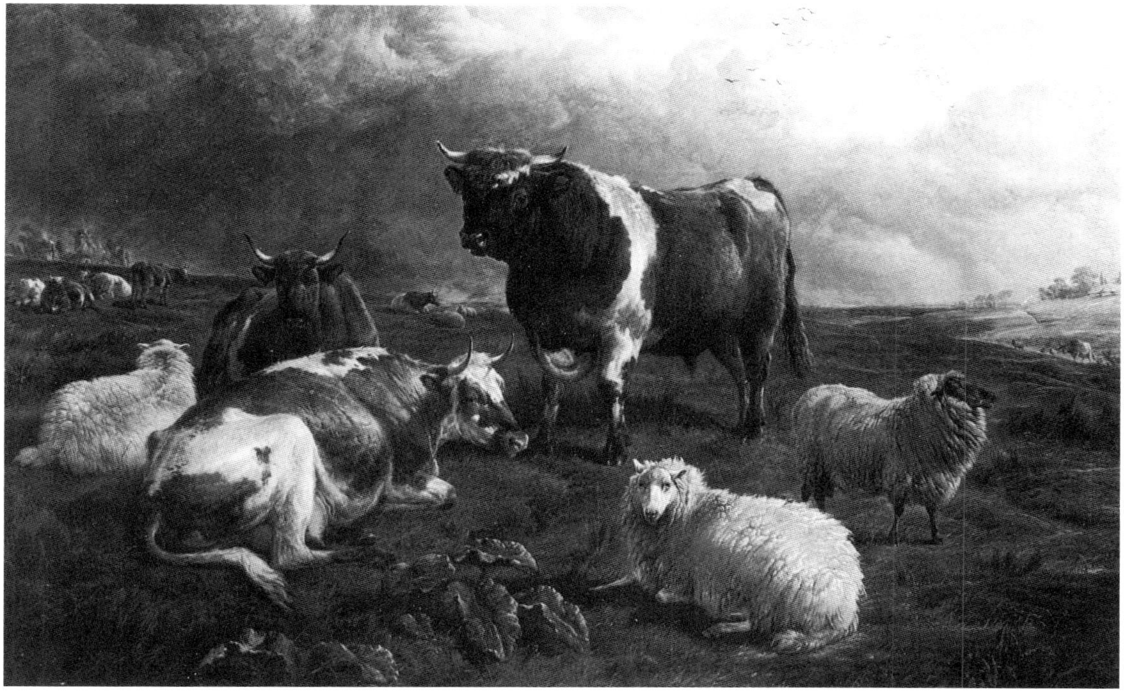

Charles Jones,
Repose,
1879.

'Associated with a National Institute of Wales, true national character and aim should attach to the Royal Cambrian Academy, and in a centre of population, and, consequently, of opportunity, like Cardiff, it can become a truly powerful agency for good - a possibility quite remote if its operations had remained confined to the means and development afforded by summer visitor or Manchester patron in the North.'[158]

However, others in Cardiff who were of a more parochial turn of mind and who were determined to further the College building scheme, had yet to admit defeat. Bitter differences of opinion surfaced at the second meeting of the co-ordinating committee. The opponents of the National Institution were led by a town councillor, Dr.Charles Vachell, who said that 'it was perfectly clear the whole scheme was got up to provide rooms for the Royal Cambrian Academy'. The ensuing fracas was reported by the *Western Mail*:

[158] *Red Dragon*, 11, 1887, p.169.

'If they really wished the public to put their hands into their pockets the best thing was to ask for subscriptions for the Science and Art Schools. But if they came forward and asked the public to bolster up a totally impecunious society. - (Mr.Seward:No.) - Dr.Vachell repeated his remark, adding that the Royal Cambrian Academy was a society that had made its effort in North Wales and had broken down and failed. - (Mr.Seward:No.) - Because they had broken down there they came down to South Wales to see if the people of Cardiff could be more easily gulled than the people of North Wales.

'Mr.SEWARD: Order. "Gulled" is not a word to use in a public meeting.

'Dr.VACHELL, That is my opinion, however. Continuing, he said the scheme never originated with the societies proposed to be embraced in the institute. The Royal Cambrian Academy had tacked them to their tail so as to get what they wanted...'

The argument was pursued in the local newspapers, where the financial consequences of the failure of the two Cardiff exhibitions proved to be an Achilles' heel to the scheme. In early 1887 Banks, by this time Honorary Treasurer as well as Secretary to the Academy,[159] canvassed the support of Lord Tredegar both for the Institute scheme in principle, and also for financial support. Banks asked Tredegar to direct any financial donation through Conwy, in an attempt to improve the financial credibility of the Academy:

'To the friends of the Institute about £1500 have been subscribed, chiefly by Lord Bute, Mr J.D.Llewelyn, and the Mayor of Cardiff... May I very respectfully venture to suggest that if your Lordship contemplates subscribing towards the National Institute of Wales, a great privilege would be bestowed on the Royal Cambrian Academy by your kindly permitting any announcement of your Lordship's wishes to be made through myself...'[160]

It appears that nothing came of this appeal and, while the committee continued to negotiate with the Council for an appropriate site in the Hayes, sniping from the newspapers, emanating in particular from a correspondent signing 'Wales', undermined confidence. In early September, an irritated Edwin Norbury responded on behalf of the Academy:

'SIR, - I have read the great self elected's long letter in your issue of the 6th inst. carefully through several times, and cannot arrive at any conclusion respecting its object except that

[159] A.Brandish Holte, the original Treasurer, resigned from the Academy under a cloud in November 1883, having lied to the Council about a letter to the press which he at first denied writing.

[160] RCA Art Records, op.cit., Letter Book 8, March, 1887.

the writer, from some sinister motive, designs by wilful perversion of facts, on the one side, to bring the Royal Cambrian Academy into discredit as far as he can with so much of the Cardiff public as may be induced by his vulgar abuse to accept his untruths, and, on the other side, to persuade the Academicians to cease "to cling to the town like blood-suckers," to cease "to lick the dust and to grovel for Cardiff to receive it," and to decline any further "kicks and rebuffs at the hands of the Cardiff public" (as represented, presumably, by himself), and so give Cardiff up in disgust... He says:- "They use the word 'Royal' in the same way and with the same authority as tailors, paper-hangers, hairdressers, dealers in cats' and dogs' meal, publicans, and pill vendors used." I do not know anything about the way in which the useful and industrious tradespeople to whom he refers may or may not use, or be authorised to use, the term. But I do know that the Royal Cambrian Academy has the same title to the word 'Royal' that the Royal Academy has...'[161]

Royal Cambrian Academy Jubilee Album, 1888.

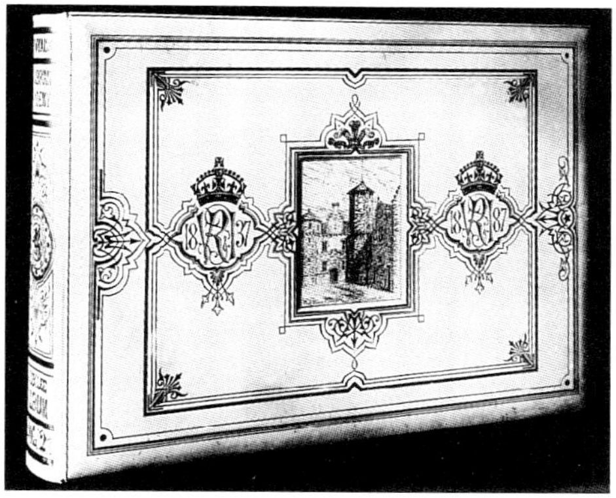

The *Western Mail* continued to publicise the views of 'Wales', whose anti-northern animus also infected other newspapers. In 1888, the editor of the *South Wales Echo* reported that 'sundry rumours have reached me here that all is not well with the Cambrian Society of Artists':

'There had been a serious row about the bad management of the North-Walians, or at any rate, Northerners, who came down here to arrange for and superintend the exhibition. The combination, which consists of work-a-day artists, are said to have been put to the expense of £500 on the Cardiff exhibition item alone. The other row arises out of the Jubilee testimonial. No less than £200 was expended on the album which was presented to the Queen. Of course, these sums burdened a young society very much, and some of the men are said, I hope not truly, to be shaking the dust off their feet on the floor of their Conway house at Plas Mawr...'[162]

Various groups of supporters endeavoured to rebut the accusations of self-interest and of the Academy's inability to raise funds in support of the Institute, which had been made by 'Wales' and others. However, the scheme was fatally wounded, and although discussions continued for some time, eventually it fell into abeyance along with any serious aspiration to locate the Royal Cambrian Academy in Cardiff.

[161] *Western Mail*, 17 September 1887.

[162] *South Wales Echo*, 21 April 1888. The album contained examples of works by leading Academicians and had, indeed, been a controversial matter.

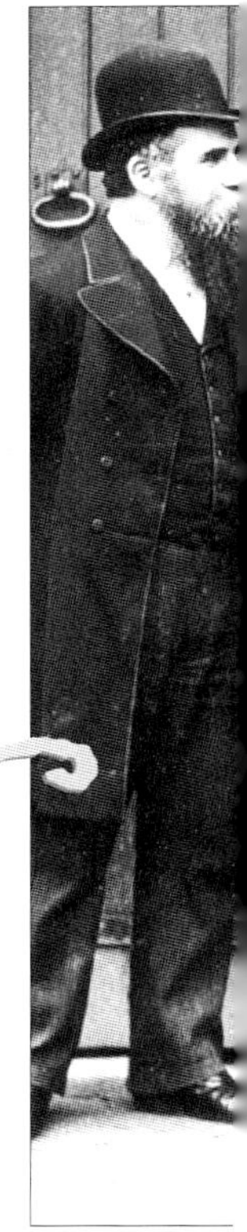

5

Yr Arlunfa Gymreig — *the* — *Welsh Studio between 1880 and 1914*

Despite the failure of the various Cardiff schemes, throughout the 1890s and the early years of the new century Clarence Whaite endeavoured to maintain a national dimension in his own career and also, whenever possible, in the development of the Academy. Many of the Cardiff group, drawn together by the exhibitions and campaigns of the 1880s, became formally associated as the South Wales Art Society in 1888. The chair was taken by T.H.Thomas with Edwin Seward as his deputy, while Pyke Thompson and B.S.Marks sat on the committee. Clarence Whaite was among the distinguished names from beyond south Wales who publically lent their support to the new group. From the first exhibition in September 1888, Whaite not only exhibited regularly with the Society but, along with Banks, encouraged other Academicians to do likewise and so maintain links between the north and the south. Rumours of emnity between the Society and the Academy were denied by Whaite in a letter to Herkomer in 1895: 'The South Wales Art Society is not at all antagonistic to the Royal Cambrian Academy', he remarked, adding that 'It was started and held together by our member and our one honorary member of it'.[163] Earlier in the year, Whaite had written to T.H.Thomas, offering him hospitality at Tyddyn Cynal when he came to a Council meeting, and remarking that 'I always feel a pleasure when you are with us, telling us what is doing in art circles in South Wales'.[164]

[163] Whaite Archive, op.cit., Letter Books, Whaite to Herkomer, 10 August 1895.

[164] Ibid., Whaite to Thomas, 17 January 1895.

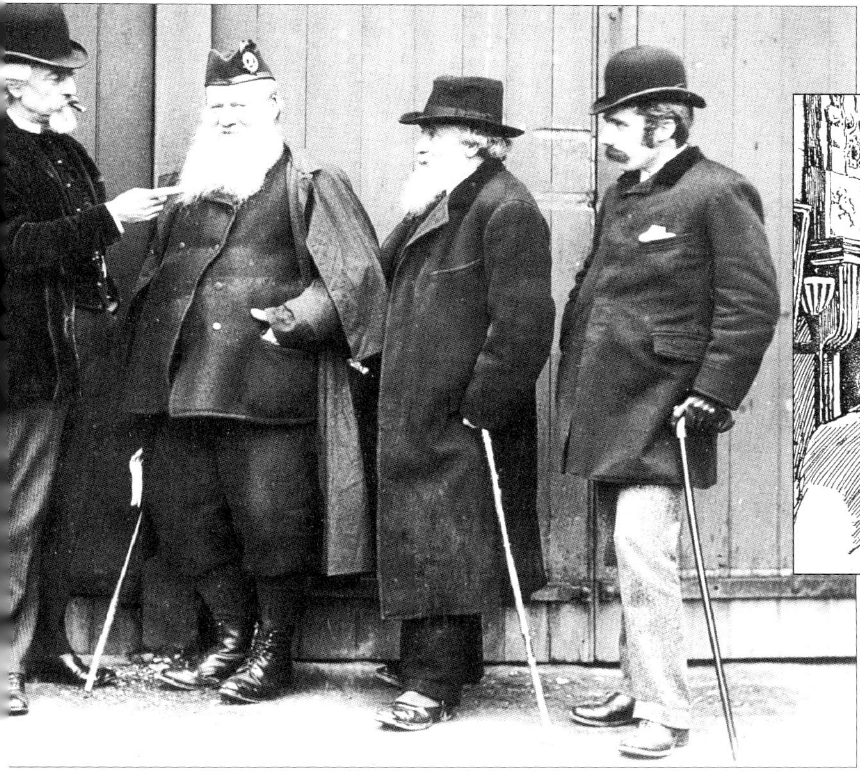

Unknown photographer,
Royal Cambrian Academicians, including Watson, Banks and Whaite, c.1890

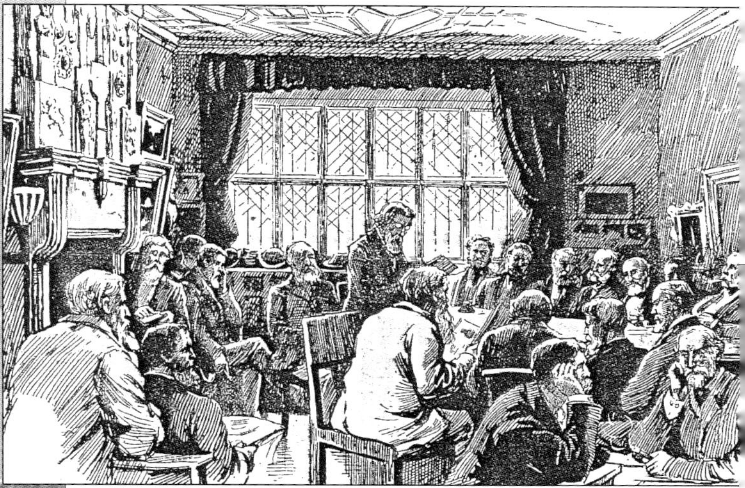

T.H.Thomas,
Council Meeting of the Royal Cambrian Academy addressed by Clarence Whaite,
1890

There was, indeed, much to discuss since moves were afoot at this time both to relocate the Cardiff Museum in a new building, to be designed by Edwin Seward for a site in Cathays Park, and to establish a National Museum. Pyke Thompson had been elected chair of the Council's Fine Art sub-committee and had given part of his collection on loan. On 26 November 1895 Whaite wrote to Seward that he 'was much pleased to receive your letter [and] to hear you are making a start with the new municipal art gallery in Cardiff which some day will be a great Art Centre - and if it is a success of course that the Royal Cambrian Academy should have a footing there. Can you suggest any action we might take to forward an interest or do you think such is possible? I know it is a very long question and I am reluctant to go into it but your letter opens the subject...' [165]

[165]Ibid., Whaite to Seward, 26 November 1895.

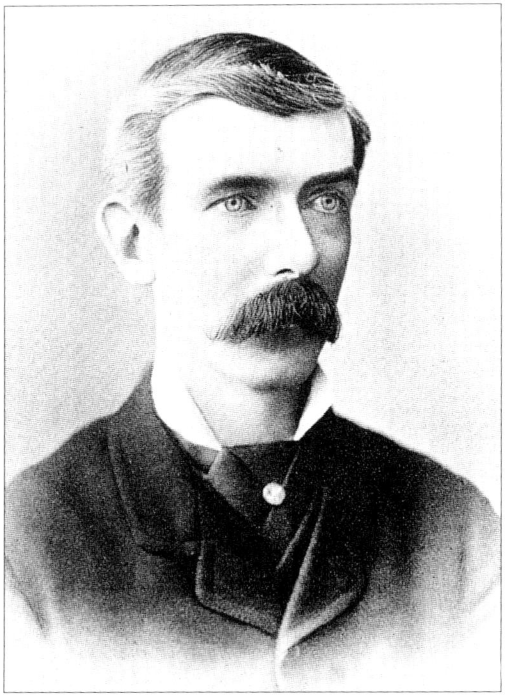

Unknown photographer,
James Pyke Thompson,
c.1870-5.

Pyke Thompson died in 1897 but left his art collection and £6000 towards the new museum and gallery project. It became clear that the Cardiff municipal scheme could easily evolve into the proposed National Museum, but dissent from other parts of Wales over its location in the town became a stumbling block to progress. On the occasion of the presentation of a memorial to Parliament on the matter in 1902, Whaite briefly ventured into the controversy, suggesting to the Cardiff authorities that two museum sites, one in the north and one in the south, might answer the question. In his reply, the Town Clerk of Cardiff, J.L.Wheatley, pointed out the shortcomings of this proposal:

'The initial difficulty which all concerned with this movement for Wales must unite in clearing up, is the one which has so far effectually prevented Parliament from giving due heed to this National Claim, viz, the separation of Local interest which has hitherto been evident in the matter. The chances are that any Grant made will be hardly sufficient to deal properly with one Institution; if such Grant should unfortunately be halved the result must necessarily be quite inefficient for each, and the proportion and dignity of a National Establishment would continue to be lacking.

'It has become evident therefore that the first step is that of united pressure from Wales as a whole to Parliament on behalf of a National Grant, it being a fair and clear understanding on all hands that the question of location is a separate one which will be fully opened to, and settled by arbitration.' [166]

Power and influence were centred in Cardiff and the Academy was essentially a spectator to the campaign which led to the granting of a charter for the National Museum in 1907.[167] Nevertheless, Academicians Seward and Thomas, who were both deeply involved with the movement, did their best to maintain their contact with Plas Mawr during this period. For instance, in April 1890 they travelled to Conwy to assist in hanging the annual exhibition, staying with W.L.Banks, and when the Honourary Secretary and Treasurer died, three years later, it was they who attended his funeral at Talgarth on behalf of the Academy.

[166] Ibid., Wheatley to Whaite, 5 March 1902.

[167] The evolution of the Cardiff scheme, designed by Seward, into the National Museum led to a serious dispute with the architect, who was passed over for the new building.

Thomas provided both text and line drawing for the obituary published in the *Weekly News*. Over the subsequent ten years the pressure of advancing age and the intensity of his life in Cardiff rendered Thomas a less frequent visitor to the north, but his friendship with Whaite remained close. In January 1904 Whaite wrote to him that he 'was pleased to hear there is a chance of seeing you at our annual meeting, it will look like old times seeing you with us...' [168]

The Art and Craft Exhibitions of the National Eisteddfod provided another occasion on which the art worlds of north and south kept in contact. Prior to the Eisteddfod at Llandudno in 1896, Thomas and Whaite were in correspondence about a proposal, made by the President, that the Academy should be more closely involved with organising the exhibitions. Thomas believed that conflicts of interest might arise, given that many of the competitors would be Academicians, and instead proposed 'the donation of a yearly sum (say £20 or £25) in the nature of a scholarship tenable for two or three years which should be strictly for the furthering of the art education of the winner'.[169] Nothing seems to have come of this idea, but the Eisteddfod of 1896 was the starting point for one important development in the Welsh art world which, once again, had its roots in the artists' colony. At the Eisteddfod a special committee under Lady Augusta Mostyn was established to organise women's contributions to the Art and Craft Exhibition. Presumably, this committee had been set up sometime in 1895, and was therefore contemporary with - and closely related to - the establishment of the Gwynedd Ladies' Art Society in the same year. Despite the presence of a number of women artists in the Conwy Valley, the Royal Cambrian Academy had not revised its early decision to refuse to consider women for membership. Under the presidency of Augusta Mostyn, the Gwynedd Ladies' Art Society held its first exhibition in Conwy in 1895. The second exhibition, in the following year, was given a substantial, illustrated notice in the the magazine *The Artist*, a degree of recognition outside Wales which Eisteddfod exhibitions had seldom achieved. A number of the women involved in this movement were the daughters of Academicians, notably Clara Knight, Maud Salmon and Lily Whaite. Maud Salmon married another Academician, Frank Beswick, but exhibited under her maiden name. Clara Knight went to Manchester to train, returning to Wales in about 1900. She exhibited at the Royal Academy and in Liverpool, but like most of her contemporaries, depended mainly on Plas Mawr to show her work.[170]

[168]Whaite archive, op.cit., Letter Books, Whaite to Thomas, 11 January 1904.

[169]Ibid, Thomas to Whaite, 23 January 1896.

[170]It seems that Clara Knight and Lily Whaite were at school together, and that their respective fathers knew each other well, despite a serious falling-out in 1895. Clara Knight showed 100 times at Plas Mawr, 18 times at the Walker Art Gallery in Liverpool, and 6 times at the Royal Academy. She was eventually granted membership of the Royal Cambrian Academy. Lilian Woodcock, a landscape painter, seems to have been among the most active of the founding group of the Gwynedd Ladies Art Society.

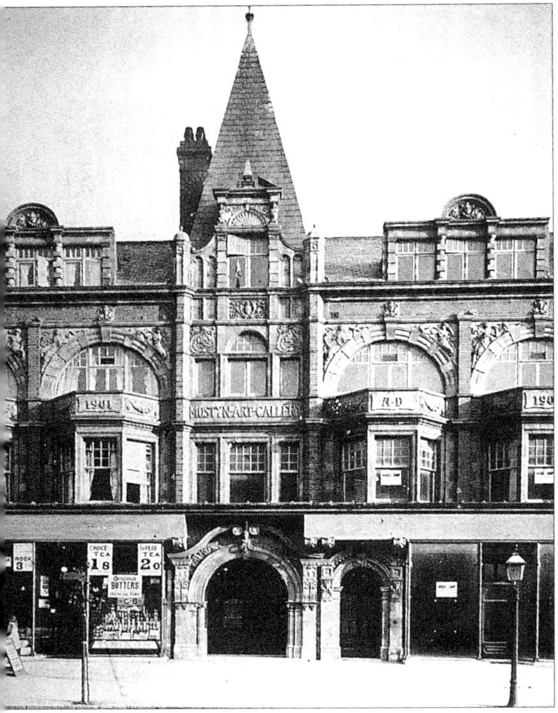
1901
MOSTYN·ART·GALLERY
A·D

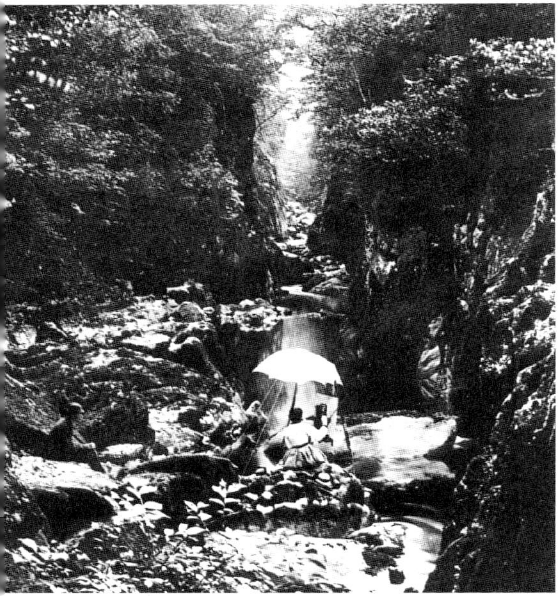

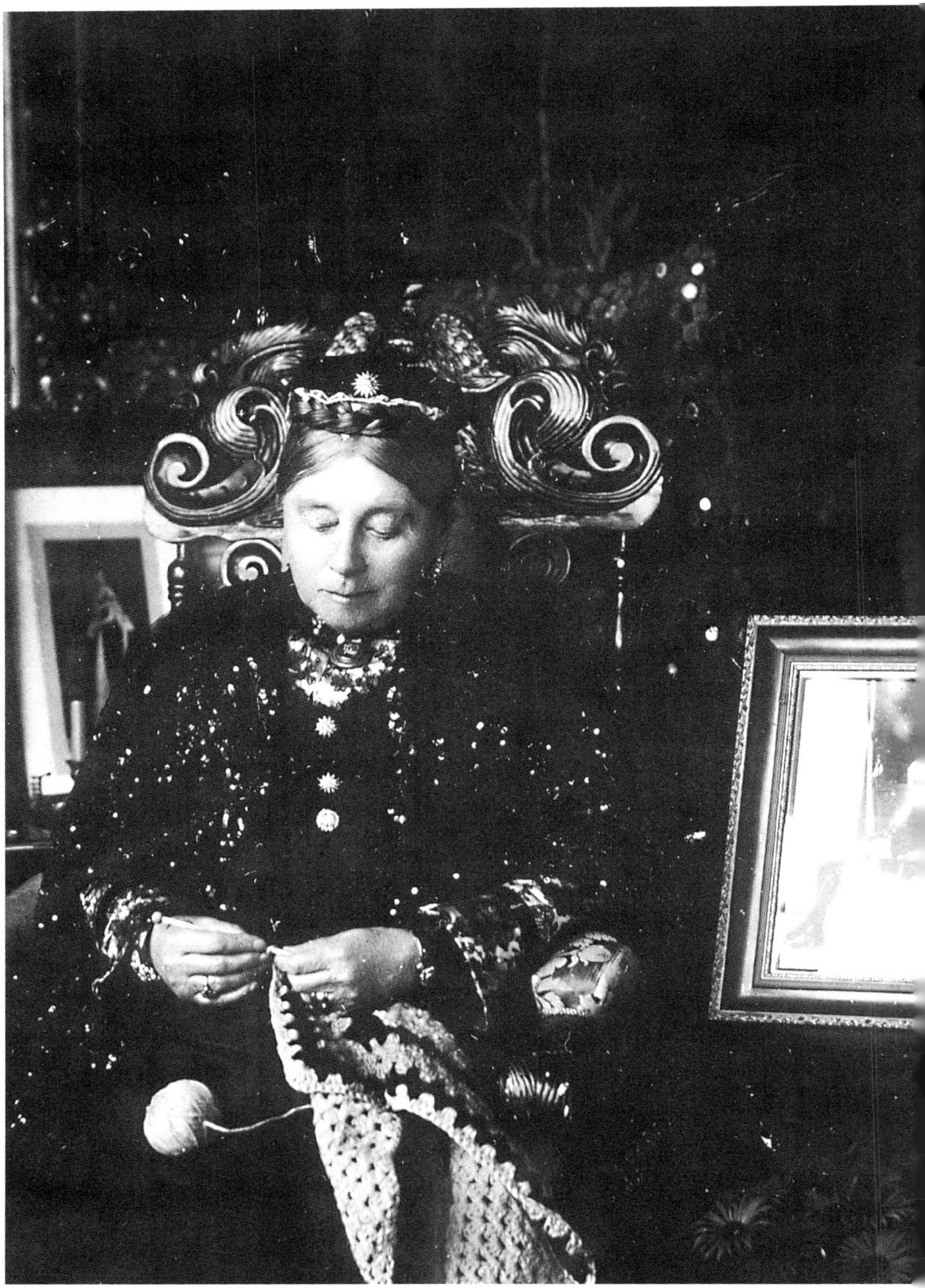

Left:
Unknown photographer,
Augusta Mostyn, c.1900.

Far left, top:
G.A.Humphreys,
The Mostyn Art Gallery, c.1902.

Far left, bottom;
Unknown photographer,
Bettws-y-Coed - Ffos Noddyn (the Fairy Glen), c.1880.

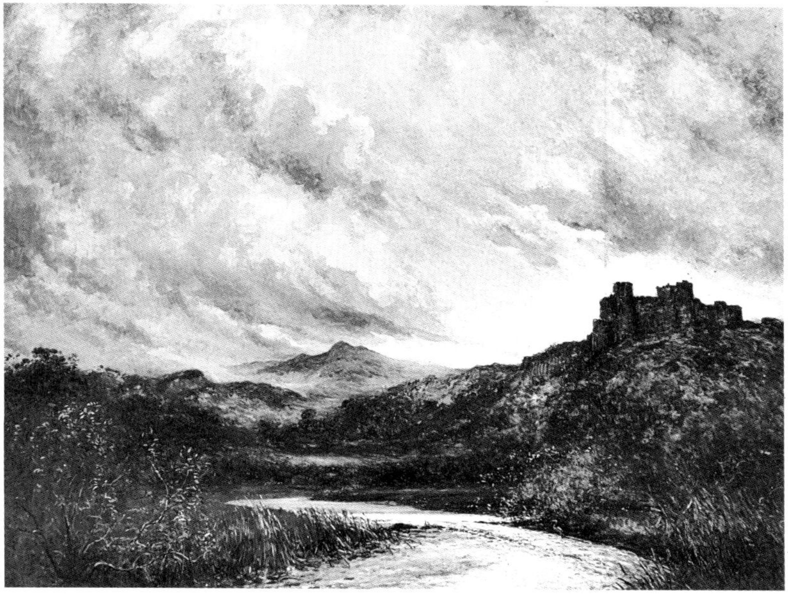

Clara Knight,
Valiant Heritage - Harlech Castle at Dusk,
c.1927.

By 1900 the Academy had slightly modified its attitude to women artists. In a newspaper review of the exhibition for that year, the author remembered to 'pay my compliments to the young ladies who have been admitted to the exhibition for the display of fruit and flowers subjects'. [171]

Perhaps in response to this reluctance on the part of the Academy to open its doors fully to women artists, Augusta Mostyn pursued the development of the Gwynedd Ladies' Art Society with a remarkable act of patronage. On the site of the 1896 Eisteddfod exhibition in Llandudno she constructed an elegant art gallery to display the work of the Society. In August 1900, the local newspaper reported that 'the new home of the Gwynedd Ladies' Art Society, which Lady Augusta Mostyn is errecting in Llandudno, is approaching completion. It is a commodious building, splendidly lighted and ventilated'.[172] The Mostyn Art Gallery, the only gallery in Wales dedicated to the exhibition of the work of women artists, was opened by Lady Augusta's son in 1902. Despite the fact that it was by far the best exhibition space in the north, the internal appointments were not to everyone's taste. Lily Whaite wrote to her father in London that she wanted to send 'a good drawing to Llandudno this year as Lord Mostyn is opening the place and most likely will bring friends with him'. In the event, she exhibited six works, 'but I did not like any of them in the Gallery. The walls are painted such a horrid red colour, it kills everything, except some green pictures I saw there, and it made them look greener'.[173]

[171] *Carnarvon and Denbigh Herald*, 17 August 1900.

[172] Ibid., 31 August 1900. The newspaper also noted that 'the removal of the headquarters from the old borough of Conway will be keenly felt in more than one quarter'. The Royal Academy in London had initially accepted women members on its establishment in 1768, but failed subsequently to elect a woman until 1922. The Society of Women Artists was founded in London in about 1855, but did not acquire its own gallery until 1987.

[173] Whaite Archive, op.cit., 9 April 1902; 16 April 1902.

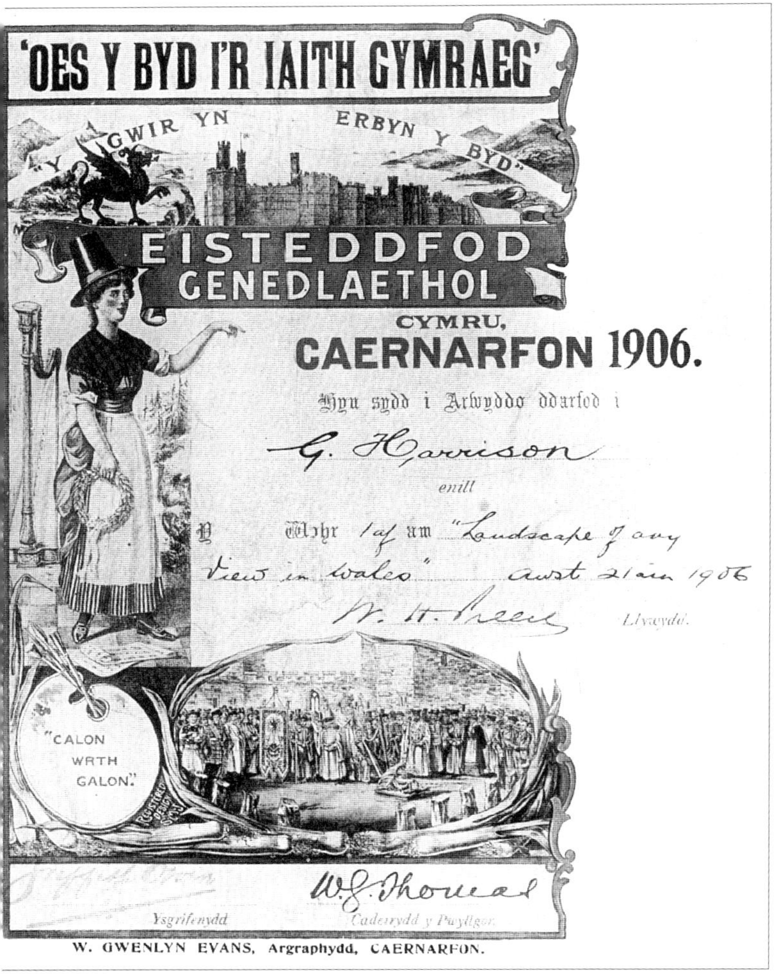

Samuel Maurice Jones, *Certificate of the National Eisteddfod at Caernarfon*, 1906, (awarded to George Harrison).

In 1906 painters associated with the artists' colony and the Academy were again prominent in the Art and Craft Exhibition of the National Eisteddfod, held at Caernarfon and organised by Samuel Maurice Jones. Clarence Whaite was among the adjudicators and George Harrison was a prize-winner. The loan collection exhibited in Caernarfon included pictures by Whaite, Samuel Maurice Jones and Leonard Hughes, as well as works representative of a new generation of Welsh painters, including Christopher Williams of Maesteg and John Kelt Edwards of Blaenau Ffestiniog. Whaite had encouraged both these young men in the development of their careers. By 1896 he was in touch with Christopher Williams, then studying at the Royal College of Art, and in 1898 he gave Kelt Edwards a letter of introduction to the British Academy in Rome, despite having 'a poor opinion of it'.[174] When Williams followed Edwards to Rome in 1905, he wrote to Whaite, who, in his reply, recalled his own visit there in 1870:

> *'I thank you very much for your interesting letter. Having spent twelve month[s] rambling about Italy [I] have seen most you describe. I also send you my congratulations on your marriage for having your bride with you gives an additional charm to your visits... I was in South Italy during the summer months but could not recommend it to you - but rather, not later than the middle of May, after that it is very dangerous to an Englishman - and I feel its effects to this day...*

[174]Ibid., Letter Book, 8 February 1898. Whaite also encouraged the painter A.E.Elias.

'I hope your journey will inspire you with the very highest feeling for Art and on your return we may see much good work to do honour to our Principality.'[175]

Whaite's encouragement, along with that provided by a wider network of intellectuals associated with the Celtic revival of the period, was of crucial importance in the development of Williams' career. He had already painted the first of the series of pictures in which he made use of a particularly Welsh iconography, the portrait of the Archdruid, Hwfa Môn, dressed in the regalia designed by Herkomer. The commission was probably associated with the Eisteddfod of 1904, held at Rhyl. In November of the following year, on his return from Rome, Williams was again in the north, painting Professor John Morris Jones at Bangor, from where he wrote to his wife that he had been 'steeped in Celtic ideals, flooded with early Welsh history and pre-Arthurian tales and mythology':

[175]Ibid., Letter Book, 10 March 1905. Surprisingly, Williams did not become an Academician. Kelt Edwards joined in 1898. On 19 January 1898 Whaite wrote to T.H.Thomas that he had had 'two or three letters from your friend Edwards at Bl.Festiniog, and you may rely upon me doing all I can to ensure his election'.

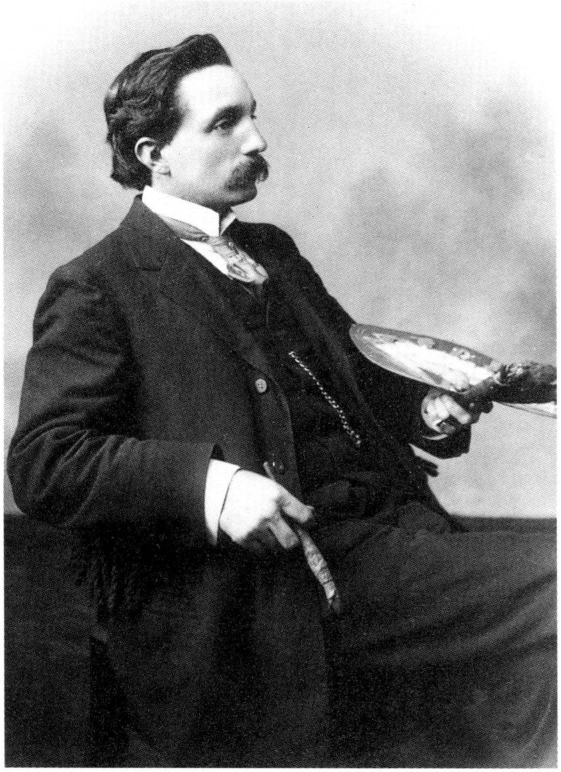

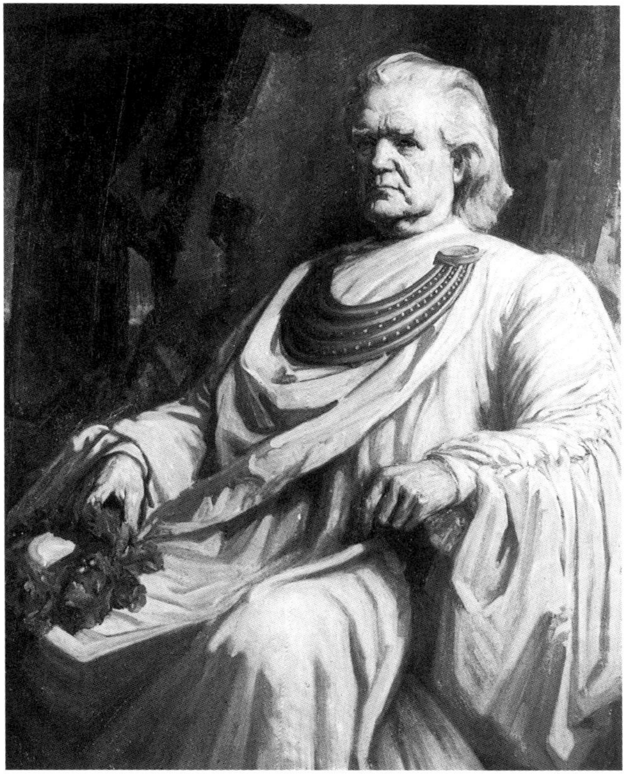

Far left: Unknown photographer, *Christopher Williams*, c.1905.

Left: Christopher Williams, *Hwfa Môn*, 1904.

Unknown photographer,
Leonard Hughes, c.1890.

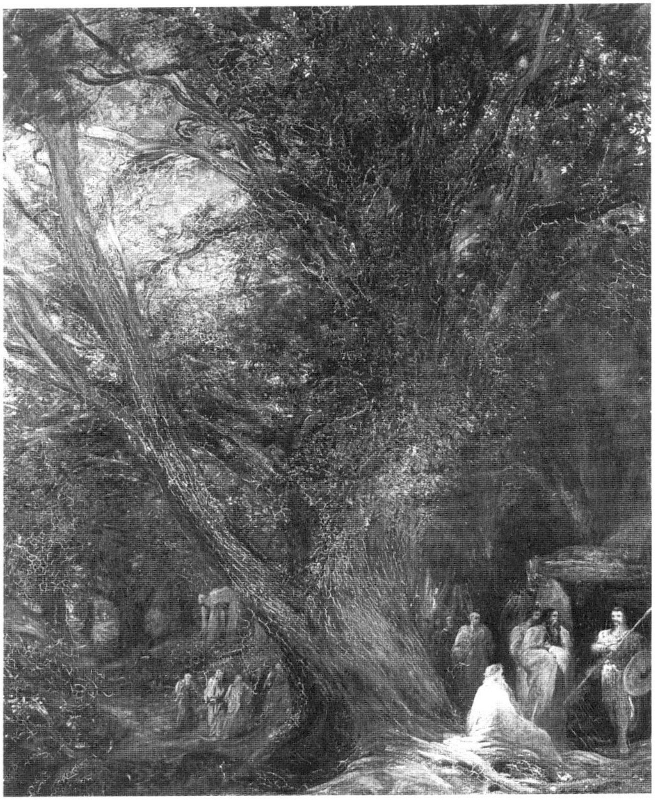

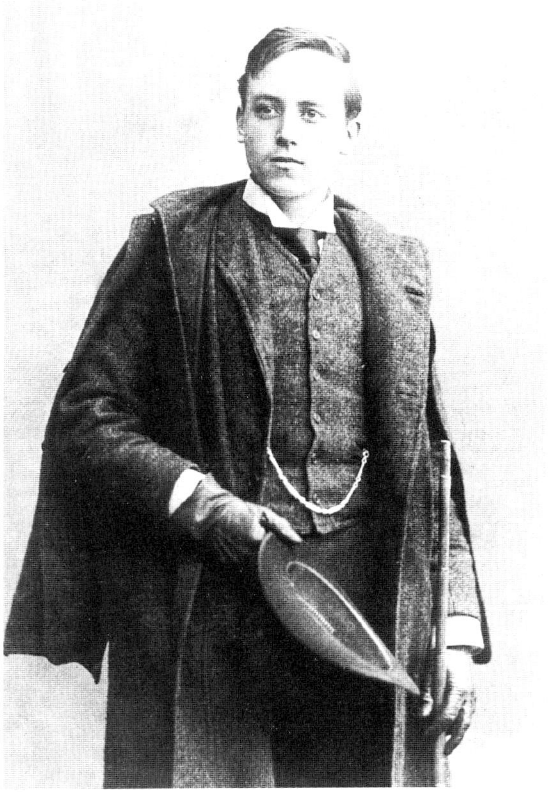

Clarence Whaite,
The Archdruid:
A Throne in a Grove,
1898.

'The Mabinogion has been in constant use, so also has Lady Charlotte Guest's Red Book and the Black Book of Carmarthen. I have plenty of subjects for painting, three of which I shall soon tackle. It is a gold mine untouched and full of Welsh fire and imagination.'[176]

Williams' enthusiasm eventually resulted in his three Mabinogi pictures, *Ceridwen, Branwen* and *Blodeuwedd*, and in his large allegory, *Wales Awakening*, which have tended to appear in Welsh art culture as isolated specimens of the kind of national mythological painting practiced more extensively in other small European countries in the period. However,

[176]Quoted in A.D.Fraser Jenkins, *Christopher Williams Centenary, 1873-1973* (Cardiff, 1973), p.7.

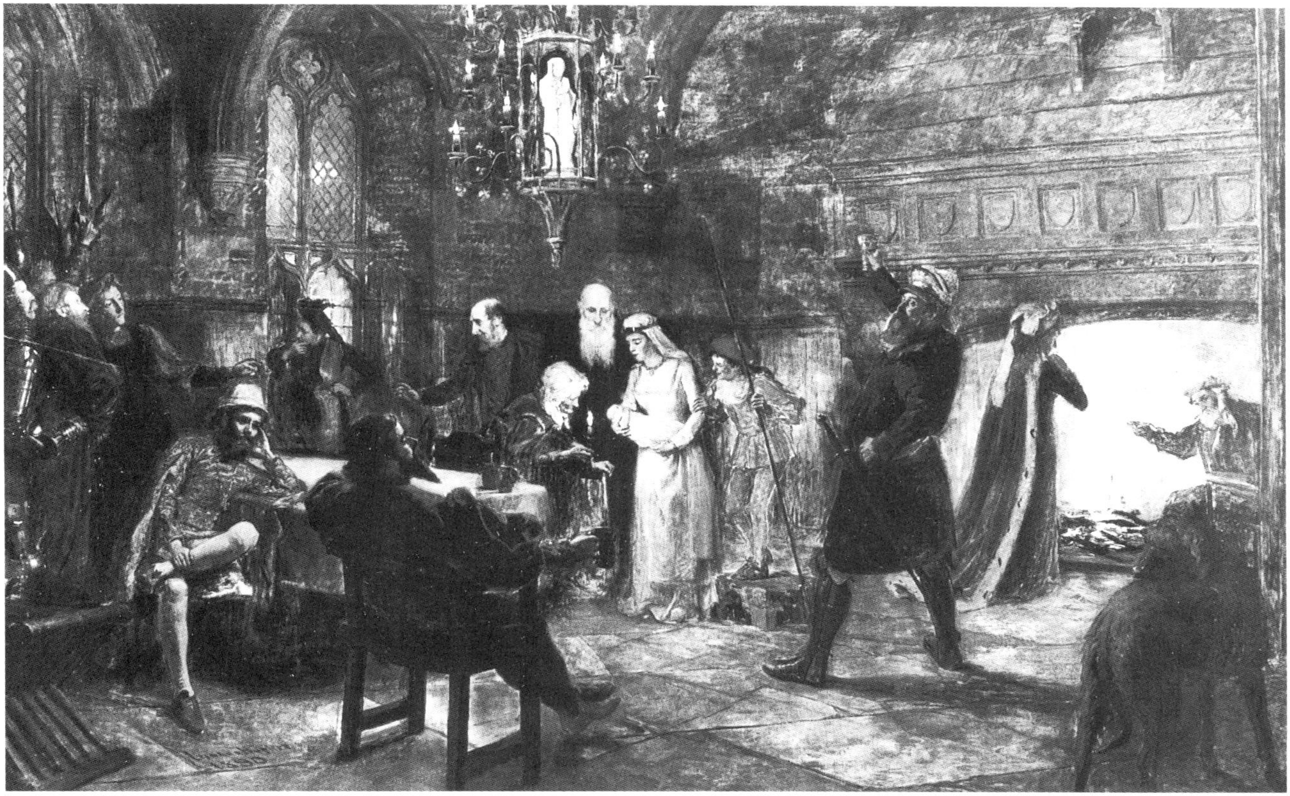

Leonard Hughes,
Myfanwy, 1890.

these pictures should be seen in the light of the Celtic and historical works of the painters of the Conwy Valley, which - unlike Williams' works - largely dissappeared from view in the twentieth century. When Williams visited the 1906 Eisteddfod at Caernarfon, both as exhibitor and as fellow adjudicator with Clarence Whaite, he would have seen the President's own contribution to the loan exhibition, entitled *The Archdruid: A Throne in a Grove*. Among the other exhibitors was Leonard Hughes, who had also painted historical and mythological subjects. His *Myfanwy* had been awarded the prize at the Bangor Eisteddfod of 1890 by Whaite himself. On the same visit, Williams might also have seen, either in the

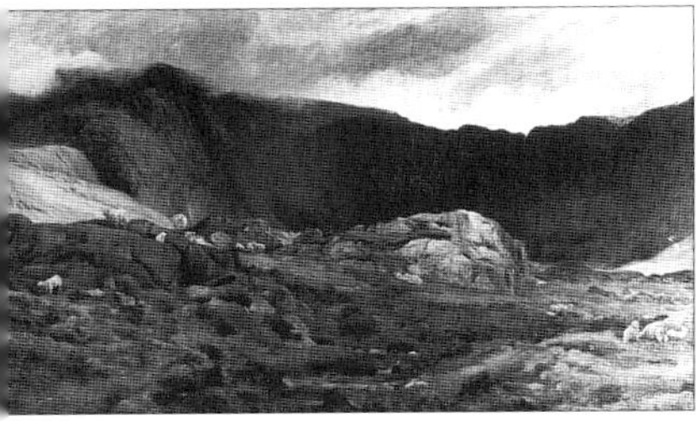

Charles Mansel Lewis,
The Devil's Kitchen, 1882.
Reproduced in colour on p.151.

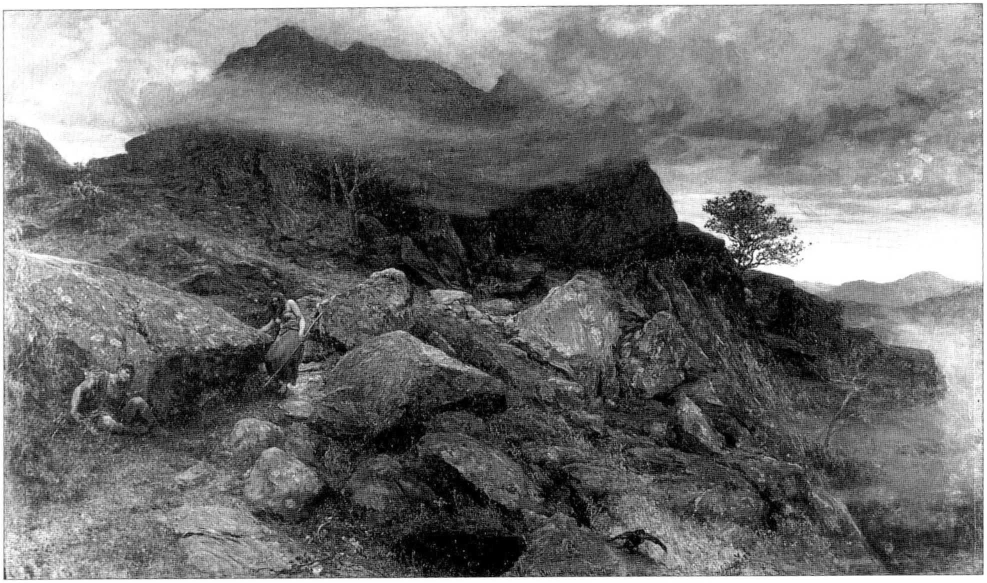

Hubert Herkomer,
Found, 1884-5.

artists' studios or at Plas Mawr, Whaite's *Arthur in the Gruesome Glen*, Norbury's *King Arthur and His Diamond Crown* and *Caractacus Leaving Britain a Prisoner*, painted in the early 1880s, and Henry Measham's picture of the last battle of Llywelyn ap Griffith, probably painted in 1882.[177] Given the celebrity of the painter, he may well also have been aware of Hubert Herkomer's Welsh pictures. His first working trip to Snowdonia with Charles Mansel Lewis in 1880 had resulted in the painting of *The Gloom of Idwal*, exhibited in London the following year. Although the painting was a landscape it is clear that, for Herkomer, the mythological associations of the site were crucial to its meaning. In 1884, following a further visit with his patron, Herkomer painted *Found*, a subject picture in the 'Ancient Britons' genre, clearly set in the same landscape. Although, as he pointed out, the Mabinogi had not been extensively used by Welsh artists, Williams was not the isolated painter of the Welsh Celtic revival that he has come to appear, but the inheritor of a tradition of Celtic and national subject painting practiced by Royal Cambrian Academicians, most of whom were based in the Conwy Valley, and their friends.

[177]Measham's picture was seen at Plas Mawr in 1894 by R.J.Williams. See *Wales*, ed. O.M.Edwards, 6, 1894, p.78. In the same year as the Eisteddfod, the Mostyn Gallery showed an exhibition which included works by Burne Jones, Ford Maddox Brown, and other prominent painters in the English art world. It was opened by Harold Rathbone, who remarked that 'Almost everything to be seen in the exhibition has something to do with Celtic life or sentiment. The same principles are at work in all art, whether poetry, music, painting or pottery'.

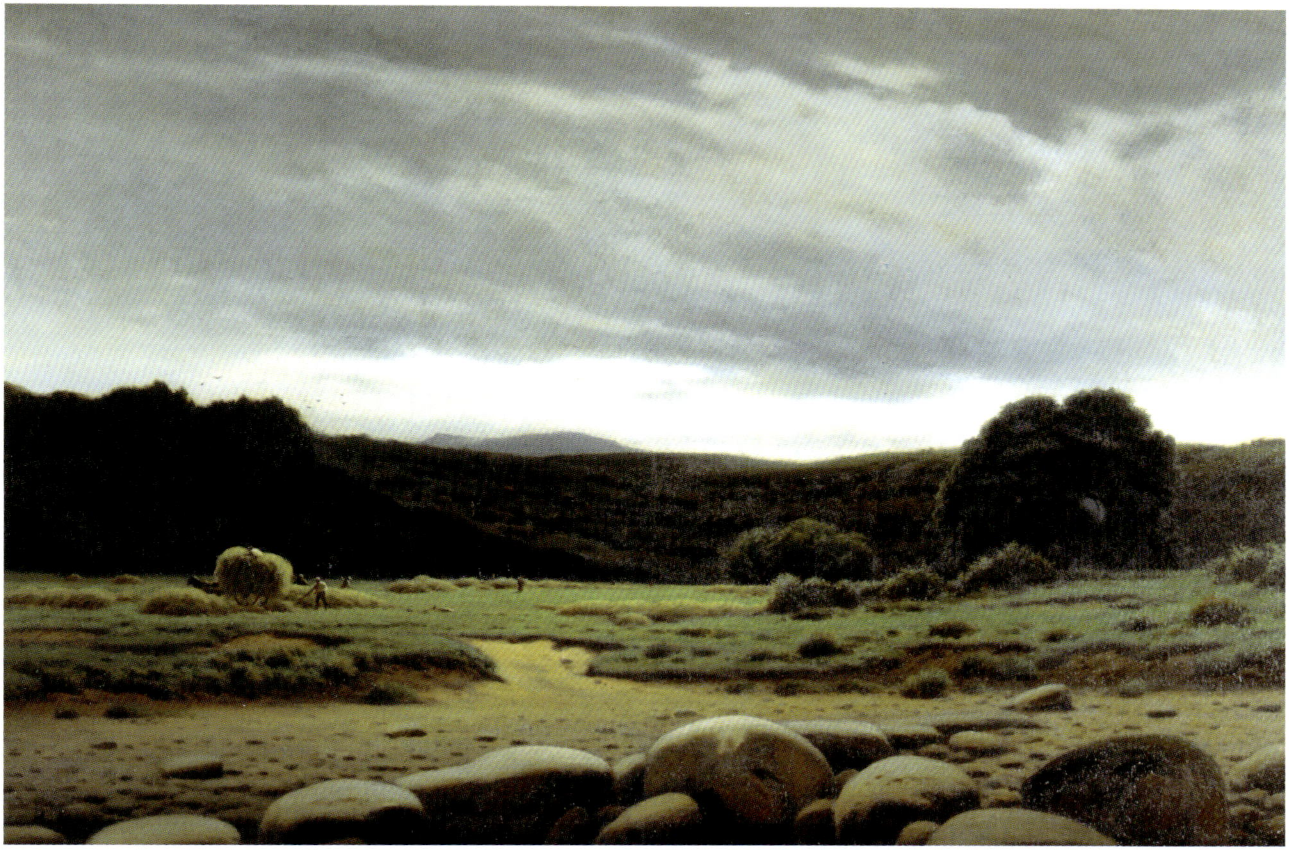

Joseph Knight,
Showery Weather,
1876.

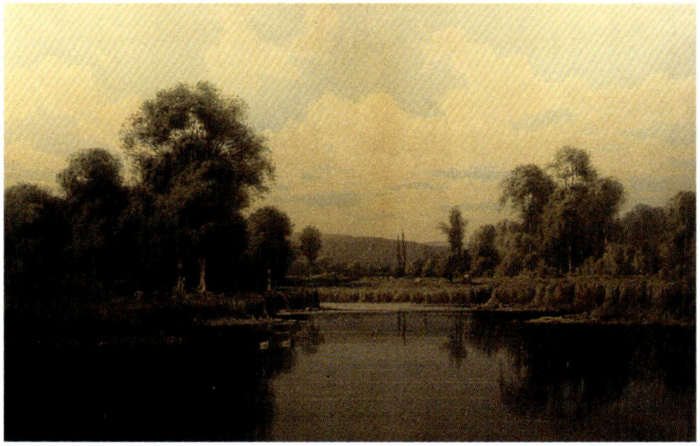

W.D.Barker,
Tranquility,
undated.

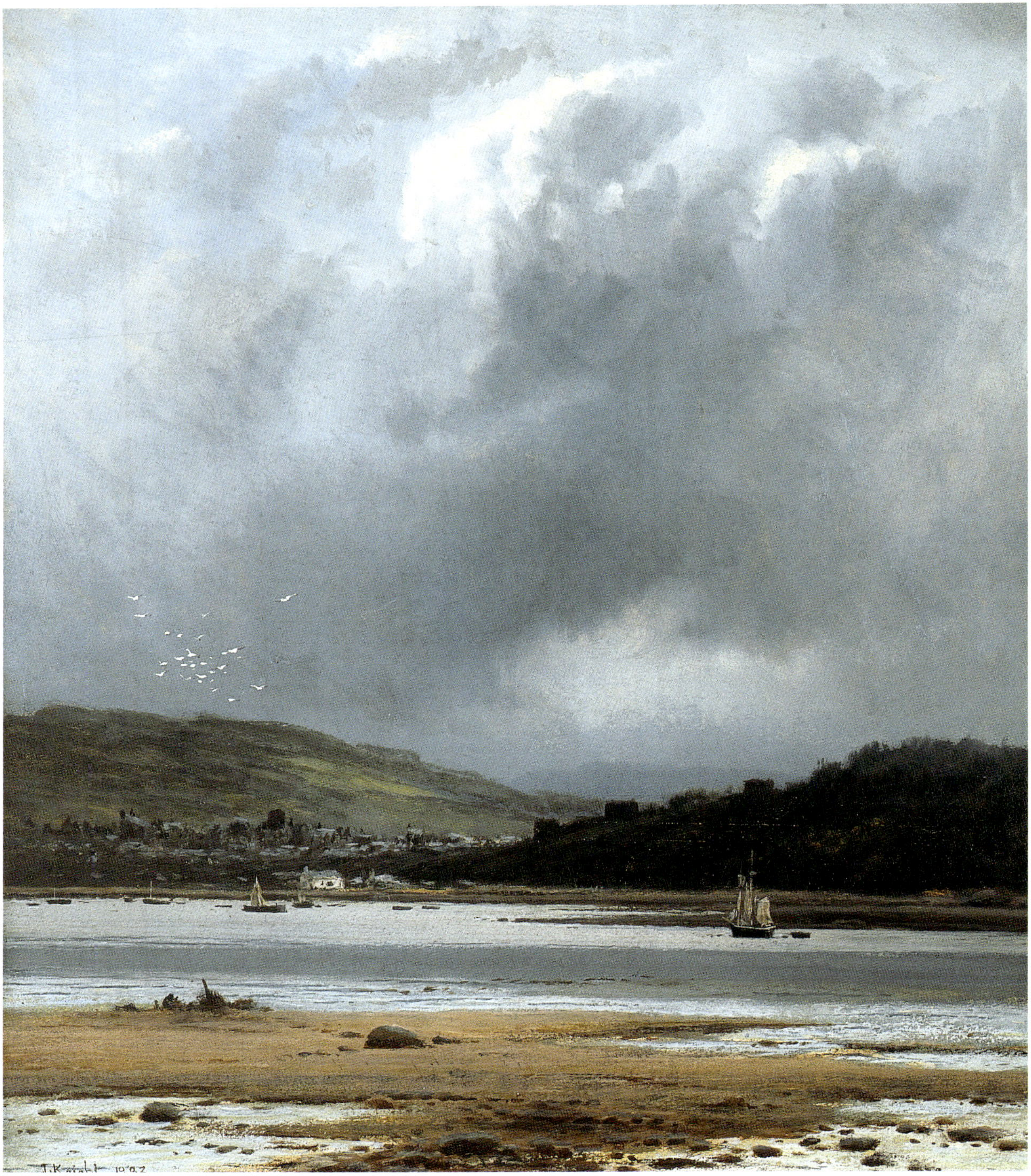

Joseph Knight,
Conwy, 1883.

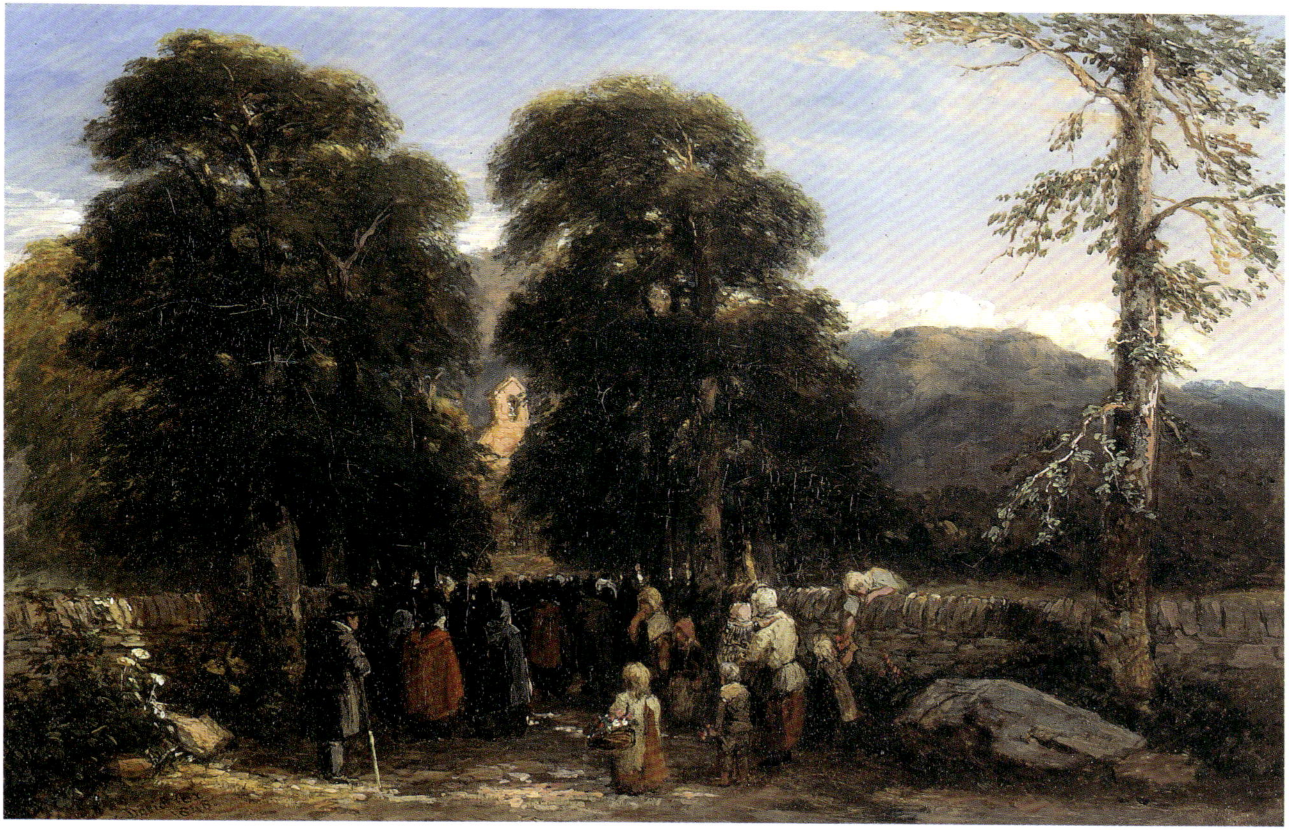

David Cox,
The Welsh Funeral,
1848.

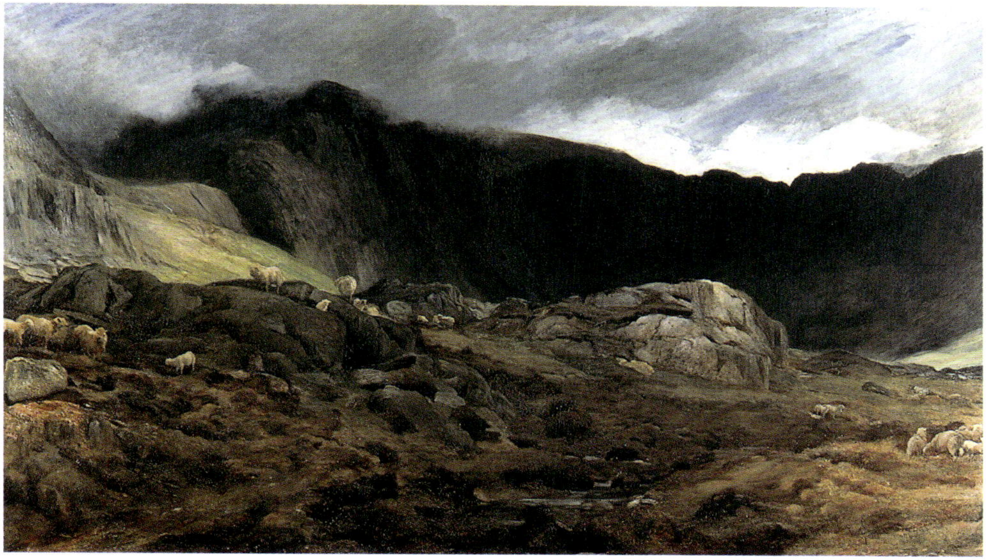

Charles Mansel Lewis,
The Devil's Kitchen, 1882.

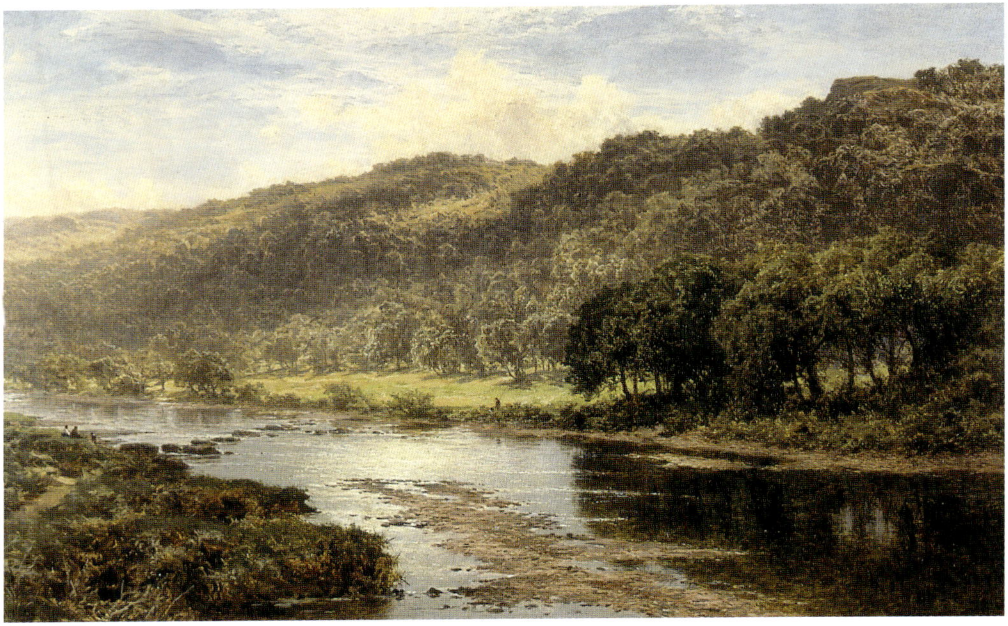

Benjamin Williams Leader,
View on the Llugwy,
1903.

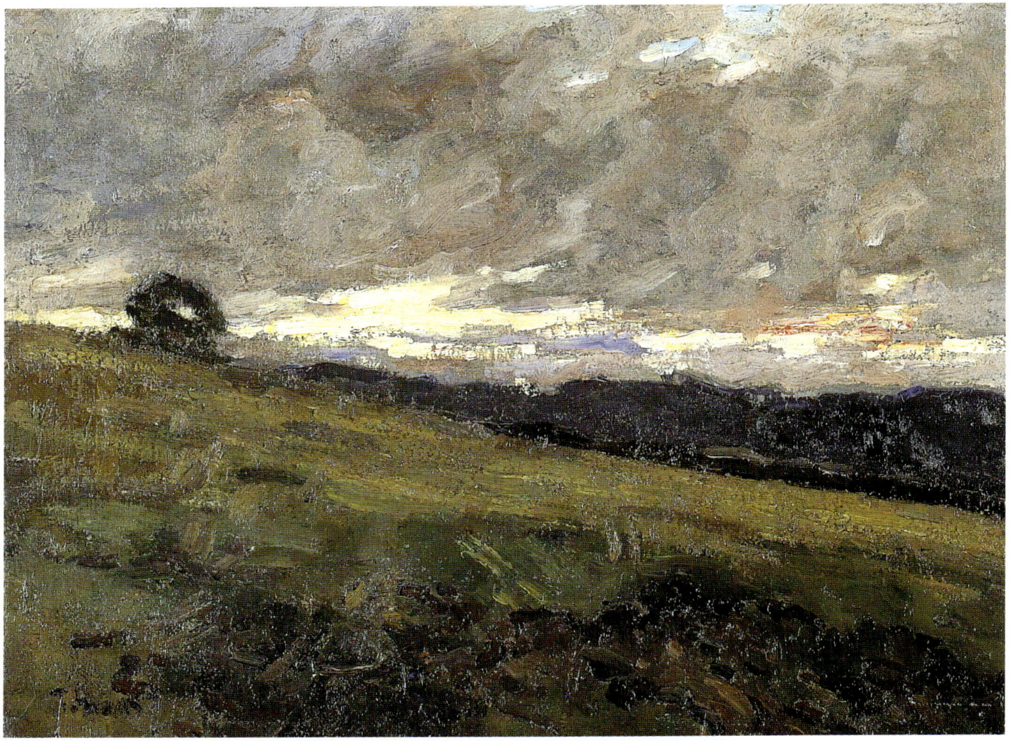

Timothy Evans,
Stormy Evening,
Dyffryn Conwy,
date uncertain.

The Celtic enthusiasm of the period was part of a wider antiquarianism which informed the attitudes and activities of Academicians. Whaite and the architect Harold Hughes became involved with a number of restoration projects, notably at Gyffin Church and at Conwy Castle. In 1902 they jointly prepared a design for Queen Eleanor's Tower in the castle, supposedly the baptismal room of Edward II, which his descendent, the future King George V, had been shown by Whaite on a visit in 1899.[178] The restoration occasioned one of the more curious responses from a Welsh-born intellectual to an incomer artist. In March 1902 Gwilym Cowlyd, proprietor of Gorsedd Geirionydd (set up in opposition to the recognised Gorsedd over which Hwfa Môn held sway), wrote a letter to Whaite, which - albeit in an extreme form - revealed the prevalent fascination with things Celtic:

> *'The mysteries that hath been hid from ages and from generations are now to be made manifest in Caerleon and the Kymry - in the primary seat of Kymric priority = Conwy. You are going to restore that unique pivot in which the whole earth revolves - Alleluiah. The Holy Spirit be with you, guiding you in all good and goodness. You are one of the twelve Cymric Primary Elders of the Order of Righteousness. God hath led you to Conwy - He led you to have your Bardic name - Caerleon, (the ancient see of Bardism.) He led you to be President of a Cambrian Soc in "Plas Mawr" - which is the oldest Plâs in the oldest town - for Cyffin means the originale...'*[179]

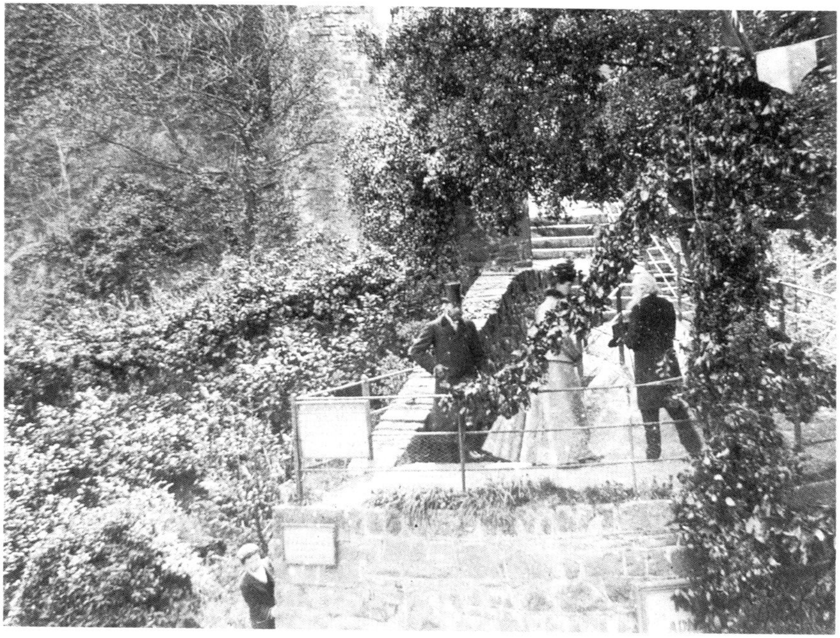

Unknown photographer, *Clarence Whaite and the Duke and Duchess of York at Conwy Castle*, 28 April 1899.

[178] *Building News*, 4 April 1902. The design included a window to be made by Fred Shields. Hughes was not happy with the quality of some of the work. On 26 May 1902 he wrote to Whaite: 'Much of the work they have been doing in the castle lately I regret from an archaeological point of view.' Whaite Archive, op.cit.

[179] Ibid., Gwilym Cowlyd (William John Roberts, 1827-1904) to Whaite, 15 March 1902. Whaite was made a member of the Gorsedd at the National Eisteddfod in Brecon in 1896.

Unknown photographer, *Bygones in the National Eisteddfod Art and Craft Exhibition at Caernarfon*, 1906

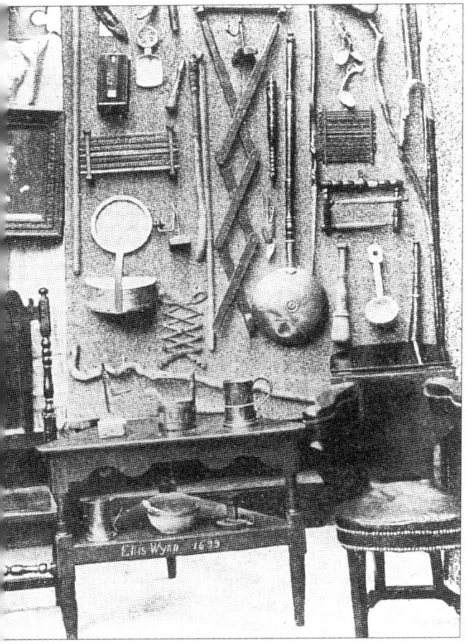

Whaite and Harold Hughes had earlier set about the restoration of Plas Mawr, and, in particular, the sixteenth-century plasterwork. They sought advice in this matter from Lady Augusta Mostyn, who was currently restoring her own house, Gloddaeth, and as a consequence the Academy employed the same firm of restorers. The project also resulted in the publication in 1888 of a beautiful volume of description and engravings entitled *Plas Mawr, Conway*, by the Academy's honorary architects, Arthur and Herbert Baker.

Harold Hughes was also interested in domestic architecture, and published a pioneering study, *The Old Cottages of Snowdonia*, in 1908.[180] This interest in the lives of ordinary people, as well as of the aristocracy, was shared by George Harrison and T.H.Thomas, who communicated regularly by letter. Folk history was a new and expanding field, and Thomas and Harrison collaborated in the collection of rural craft objects, known to them as 'bygones'. Exhibitions of such objects were a regular feature of the Eisteddfodau of the period, including Caernarfon in 1906. Efforts to acquire objects for preservation were not always successful, as in the case of a milk churn driven by a dog wheel, still in use in a village near Betws. Eleanor Forster remembered that 'My grandfather, the late George Harrison RCA, painted a sketch of the wheel... About the time the sketch was painted, an artist friend of his, Mr Thomas Henry Thomas, of Cardiff, went to Bwlch Iocynn and asked William Williams if he would consider selling the churn to the Cardiff Museum, and replacing it with more modern equipment. He turned down the offer saying it had served its purpose for so many years that he saw no reason to churn any other way.'[181] Other attempts to acquire bygones for the Cardiff Museum were more successful, and the collection eventually passed to the new National Museum where part of it was displayed in the 1920s in a reconstructed farmhouse kitchen. The collections of Harrison, Thomas and others, notably T.C.Evans, Cadrawd, eventually formed the basis of the Museum of Welsh Life at St.Fagans.

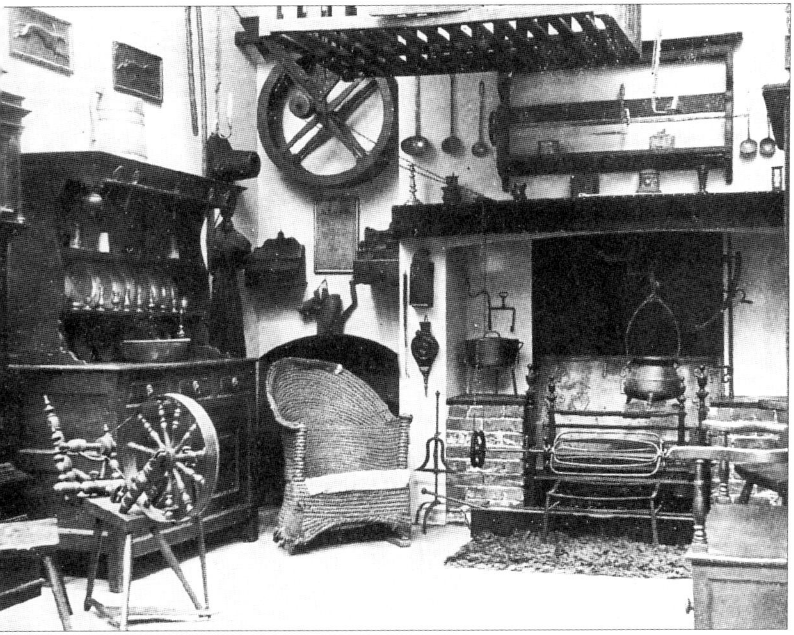

Unknown photographer, *The Welsh Kitchen at the National Museum*, 1929.

Thomas's interest in folk life extended to the illustration of two books written by his American friend Wirt Sikes - *British Goblins* and *Rambles and Studies in Old South Wales*. Thomas chose a painted version of one of these illustrations, *Shui Rhys led away by the Tylwyth Teg*, as his contribution to the Academy's Jubilee Album. However, in general, the enthusiasm for folk life did not transfer itself to large-scale Welsh painting. At Betws, a long standing tradition of drawing the local people continued, and, as we have seen, at the opening of the Artists' Club at Tal-y-bont, 'opportunities for the study of rustic models' were sighted as one of the *raisons d'être* of the group.[182] Clarence Whaite had produced such studio studies since the 1860s, as well as hundreds of beautiful water colour notes of the life of the common people drawn in the mountains, at fairs and markets, and in the town of Conwy. However, in subject pictures painted for exhibition, his figures remained small and visually subordinate to landscape and to atmospheric effect. It was the search for 'truth' in these effects which had sent Whaite to paint even very large-scale works, such as *The Rainbow*, in the open air and by which critics tended to judge the quality of Welsh landscape art in general. They did not associate Betws pictures with the figure, either in allegorical or realist terms. Only one painter of the new generation represented at the Caernarfon Eisteddfod exhibition in 1906 made folk life a central theme of his work and it is significant that he seems not to have been attracted to Betws. By this time, Carey Morris of Llandeilo was moving in Welsh art circles, exhibiting at the South Wales Art Society as well as in the National Eisteddfod, and socialising in London with Christopher Williams and Herkomer. However, his early career sheds light on the declining status of the artists' colony in the Conwy Valley among young painters at the end

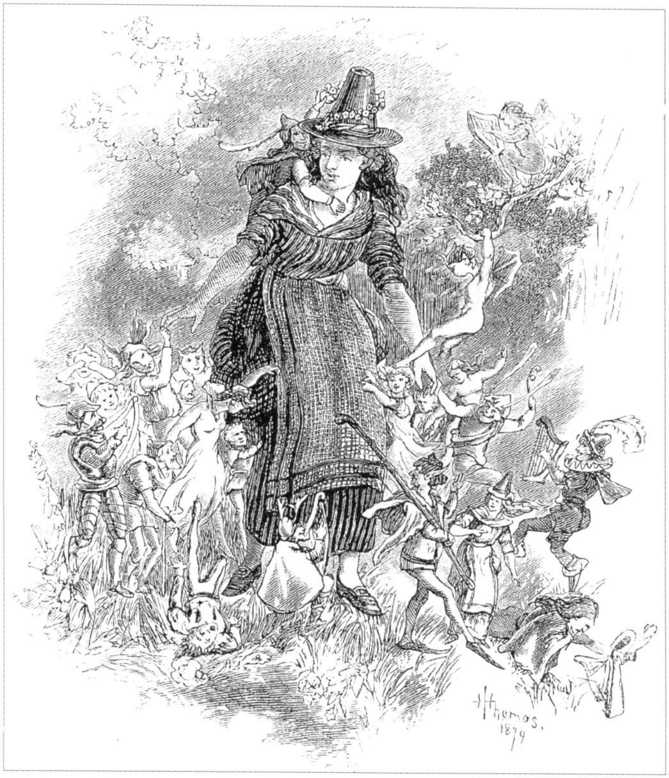

T.H.Thomas, *Shui Rhys led away by the Tylwyth Teg*, 1879, illustration for Wirt Sikes, *Welsh Goblins*.

[180]H.Hughes and H.North, *The Old Cottages of Snowdonic* (Bangor, 1908). Among the cottages described was Whaite's Tyddyn Cynal.

[181]Harrison Archive, op.cit.

[182]Alderman Samuelson, NLW Samuel Maurice Jones Papers, op.cit.

of the nineteenth century. After training at Carmarthen and then in London, Carey Morris went to work at the artists' colony in Newlyn, Cornwall. Young painters had begun to gather at Newlyn in the early 1880s. A number of them had worked together in Paris and in Brittany, and it was their experience in those places that lay behind their philosophy of painting in the open air with 'unflinching realism'. Their work owed much to Millet, Courbet and, in particular, to Bastien-Lepage. They received a mixed reception when they first showed their work in London, but general critical acclaim soon followed, especially after the exhibition of Stanhope Forbes' *A Fish Sale on a Cornish Beach* at the Royal Academy in 1885, and they came to be recognised as a new English movement. Many Newlyn painters set the common people and their working lives at the centre of their exhibition pictures, and it was this development which caught the mood of the period.

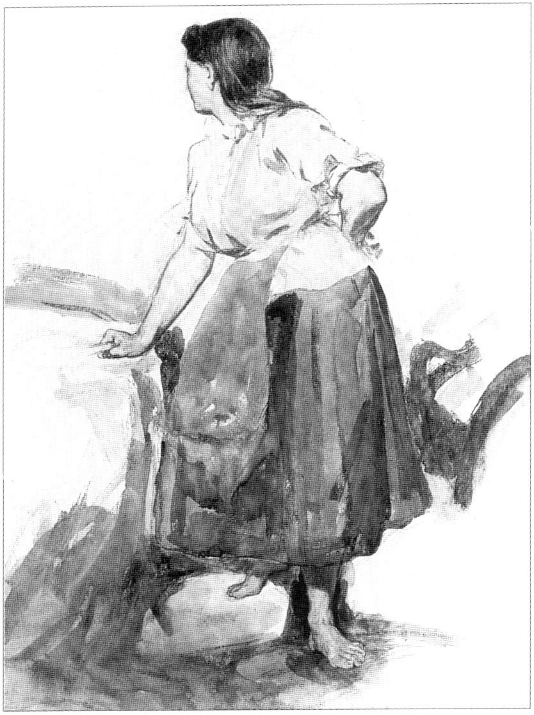

Clarence Whaite, *Young Woman on Steps*, c.1865. Reproduced in colour on p.88.

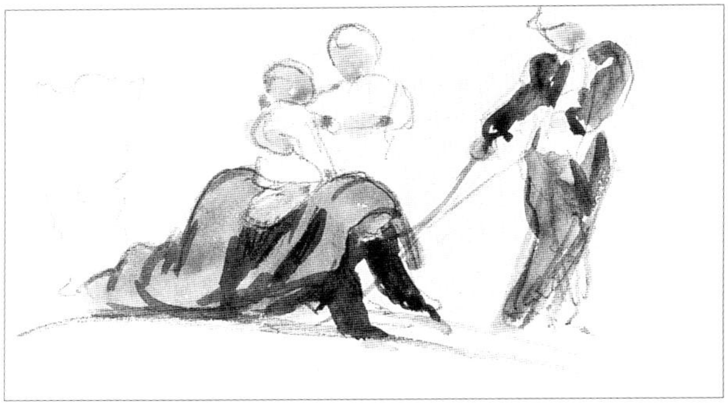

Clarence Whaite, *Play*, c.1865.

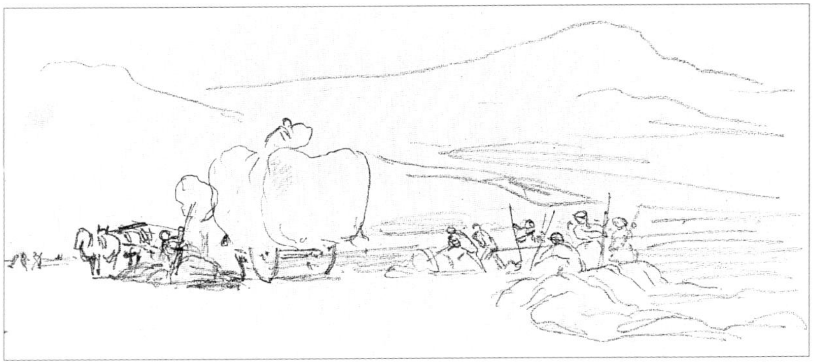

Clarence Whaite, *Bringing in the Hay*, c.1865.

The ideas of Ruskin and Morris about the dignity of labour had, of course, found their way into visual art at an earlier date through the Pre-Raphaelite movement, but the new painting was part of the more specific interest in the study and celebration of Folk Life. In pictures such as *The Welsh Weavers* Carey Morris reflected the Newlyn philosophy through Welsh eyes, but apparently with little knowledge of, or interest in the precedents offered by painters working in his own country.

Only one Welsh artist of Morris's generation seems to have painted regularly in the area. Timothy Evans was born in Llanbedr-y-cennin, near Ro-Wen, in the kind of circumstances celebrated by the Newlyn painters. In 1922 he wrote: 'I was born in a cottage, and my father was a shoemaker. I know what it is to struggle against Poverty...',[183] and, perhaps because of his early acquaintance with the unpleasant realities of what the Newlyn painters

[183]Quoted from an unidentified source in a note by Isaac Williams, appended to T.H.Thomas's copy of Mardy Rees, op.cit., in NMW.

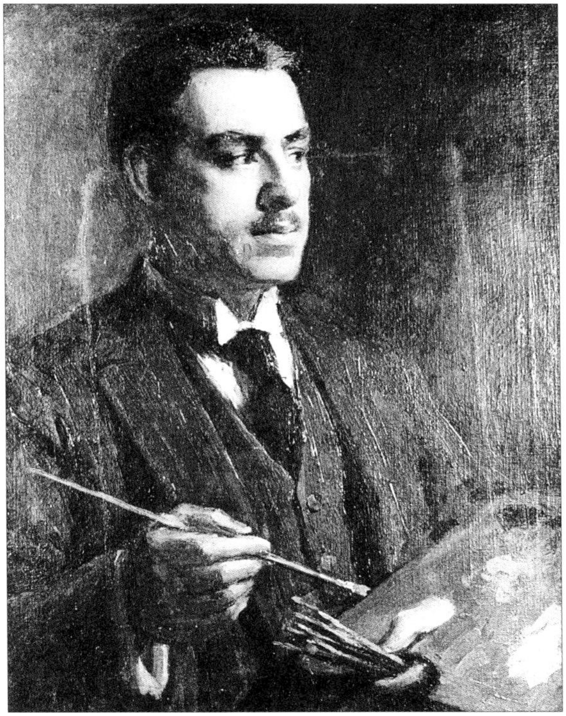

Carey Morris, *Self-portrait*, c.1900.

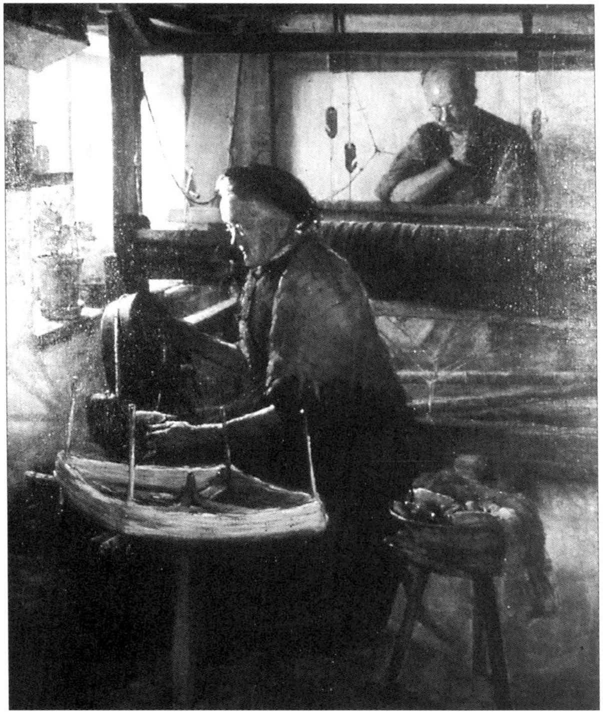

Carey Morris, *The Welsh Weavers*, c.1910.

Right:
Unknown photographer,
Timothy Evans,
c.1910.

Far right:
Timothy Evans,
Stormy Evening, Dyffryn Conwy,
date uncertain.
Reproduced
in colour on p.152.

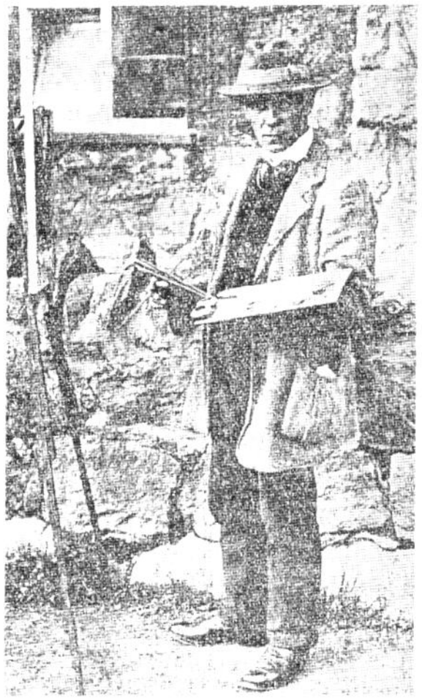

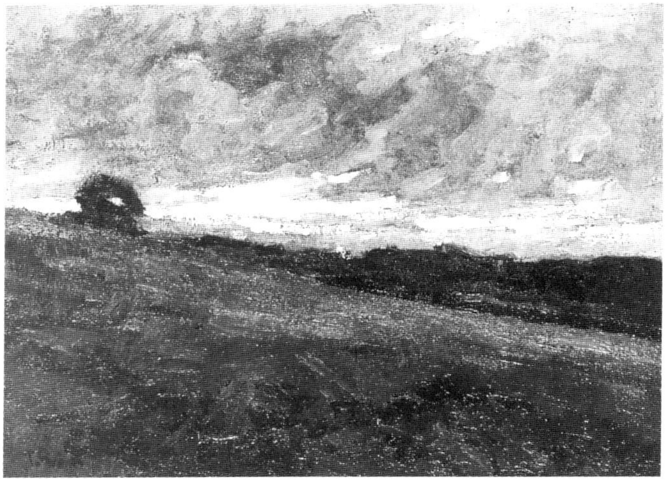

Timothy Evans,
Passing Showers,
date uncertain.

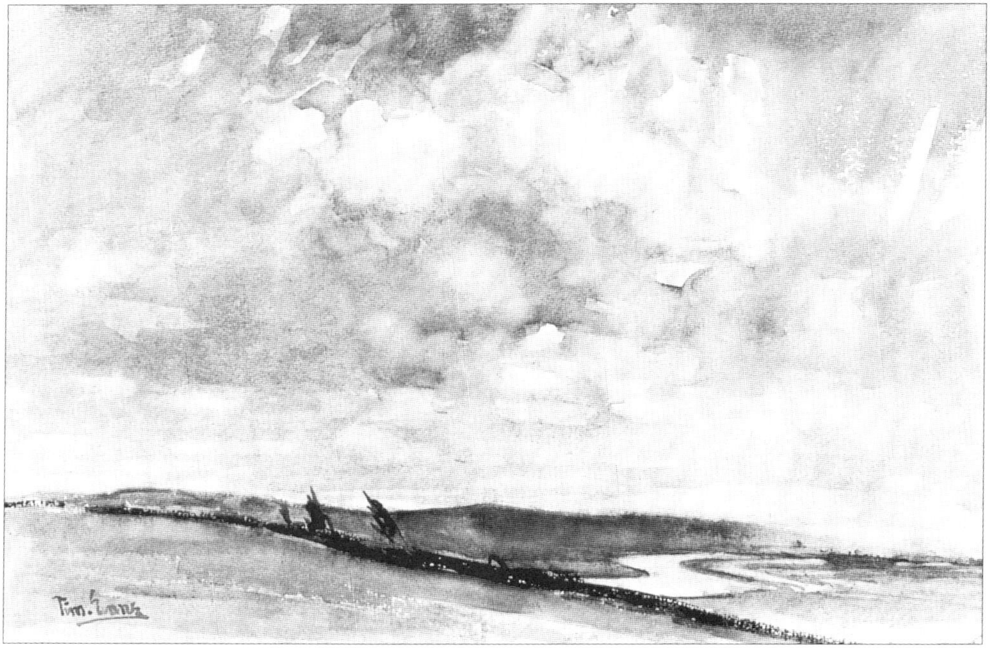

romanticised, he chose not to paint the life of the common people from among whom he had emerged. His work reflected the emphasis on pure landscape given by the older painters. Evans became a close friend of Kelt Edwards and the two men travelled together on the Continent, studying in Paris and Rome. However, although Evans visited Wales regularly and won more National Eisteddfod competitions than any other artist, he chose not to return home to live, and made his career in London.

In its early years the Academy attempted to establish an art school to encourage and develop young indigenous talent such as that of Timothy Evans. At Newlyn, the school established by Stanhope Forbes and his wife Elizabeth attracted dozens of young painters to Cornwall, including Carey Morris, in the early years of the twentieth century. By comparison, the well-intentioned efforts of the Academy were a complete failure. For instance, in 1890 it was decided that Norbury and Salmon should teach a twice weekly class, but no pupils at all were forthcoming at elementary level and only one at advanced. The Council resolved to establish an 'Artizan's Class' at a reduced fee of 5/- a term. The results were equally depressing. At the beginning of 1891 Norbury raised the question of art in the context of the Intermediate Education Act and suggested that the Academy should develop a teaching prospectus. In October it was resolved that 'Teaching should include drawing from the flat, model drawing, and drawing from the cast'. Arrangements were also made for an advanced class in oil and water colour from the draped figure. Special terms were offered to schools but only two applications were received and the scheme was discontinued. Fitful efforts of this kind were made by the Academy through the early years of the new century, but came to little. In the 1880s and 1890s few young painters took up permanent residence in the Conwy Valley, although Betws retained its high reputation as a place of artistic resort from England, occasionally reinforced by articles in the art press about the village or the Academy. In 1889 the *Liverpool Daily Post* reported that:

> *'There is probably no more interesting exhibition of paintings in England to the artist and the connoisseur than that at Plas Mawr in Conway... This annual exhibition of the Royal Cambrian Academy is practically at the present time the home and headquarters of English*

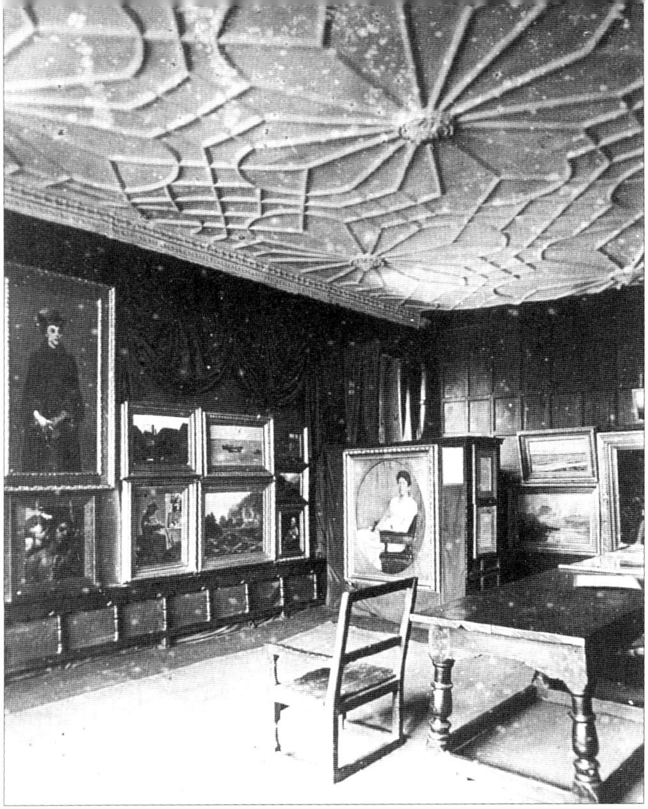

Unknown photographer, *Exhibition at Plas Mawr*, c.1910.

landscape art, for although it is not extensive, it contains some of the best pictures painted by the artists whose home is in Wales and in addition to these fine specimens of our "National Art", which is essentially landscape, there are some of the best productions of the acknowledged masters of our time.'[184]

Despite the confused sense of national identity manifested in this eulogy, the Academy reproduced it as a poster. Similarly, in 1896 *The Artist* published a substantial and generally complimentary notice of the Academy's first exhibition in its new Victoria Gallery, constructed at Plas Mawr. Both Herkomer and Burne-Jones contributed important works to boost the status of the show. Two years earlier, in a more general piece, the *Art Journal* had maintained that, for north Wales at least, Betws remained 'the capital for the artist; easels and umbrellas and sketching tools stand at every corner, while cameras of all the oddest shapes and sizes seem part of the necessary impedimenta of every tourist'. Even the railway had become 'an object of beauty, and no longer a point for discussion and dislike'.[185] The article was copiously illustrated by Clarence Whaite, by then 68 years of age, and was notable for one of the few references made in print to the activities of the Artists' Club at Llanbedr-y-cennin:

> *'At this point the traveller is now near Tal-y-Bont, an artists' club on the hill-side, and half-way to Conway. Every autumn an exhibition of pictures is open, the works being contributed by the forty enterprising members who form its constituency. Some day, perhaps, they will take their exhibition to Bettws, for it is no easy matter to induce visitors to spend time and money in driving so far as Tal-y-Bont is from a railway station. During the winter, life classes are said to be held in the club, and certain it is, that in their mountain loneliness, these excellent artists must have plenty of time for study.'*[186]

[184] *Liverpool Daily Post*, 9 June 1889.

[185] D.C.T, 'Bettws-y-Coed', *The Art Journal*, 1894, pp.267-71.

[186] Ibid., p.270. Whaite was paid £21 for his illustrations.

The Art Journal, 1894, 'Bettws-y-coed', illustrated by Clarence Whaite

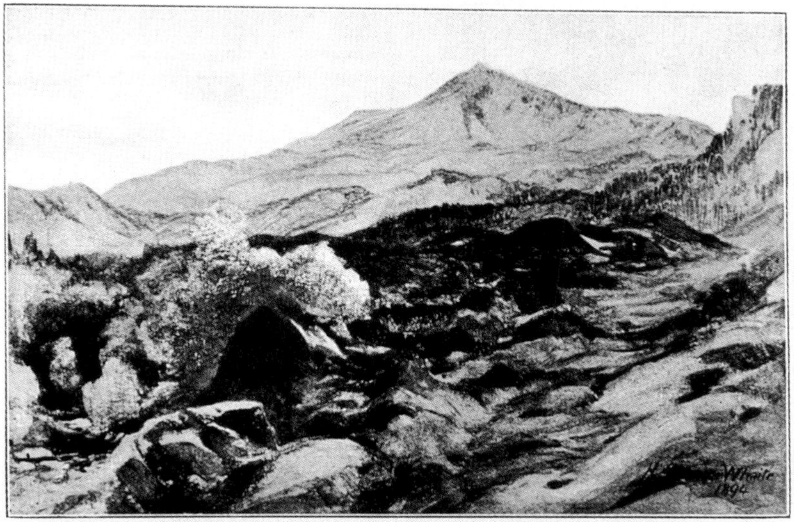

MOEL SIABOD FROM THE LLEDR VALLEY. DRAWN BY H. CLARENCE WHAITE, P.R.C.A.

BETTWS-Y-COED.

BETTWS-Y-COED is one of the resting-places for those of artistic temperament. At some time or another every artist and every art-lover has been there, if only for a single day. Since David Cox made it his chief resort, more than fifty years ago, Bettws-y-Coed has steadily increased in artistic fame. All the waterfalls have been painted, every valley has had its masterpiece, and almost every rock can be found in one picture or another.

Within recent years, Bettws—to give the simple name affectionately inscribed in the hearts of the whole Welsh world—has been considered too picturesque to be acceptable to the younger generation of advanced artists; but to those who do not care for scenery which is only pretty —and, therefore, probably namby-pamby—a morsel of special advice may be given. If fortune or fate leads you to Bettws, and you wish to draw the lesser known and unconventional, go up the hills behind the village and paint the moorlands a thousand feet above the houses. Lake Elsi, one of the calmest of placid

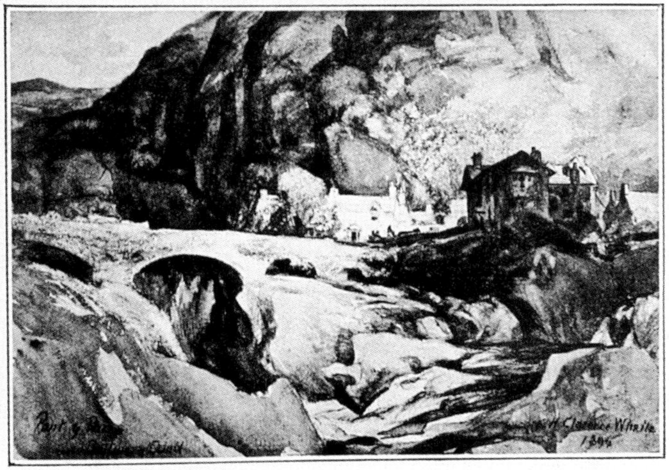

PONT-Y-PAIR, BETTWS-Y-COED. DRAWN BY H. CLARENCE WHAITE, P.R.C.A.

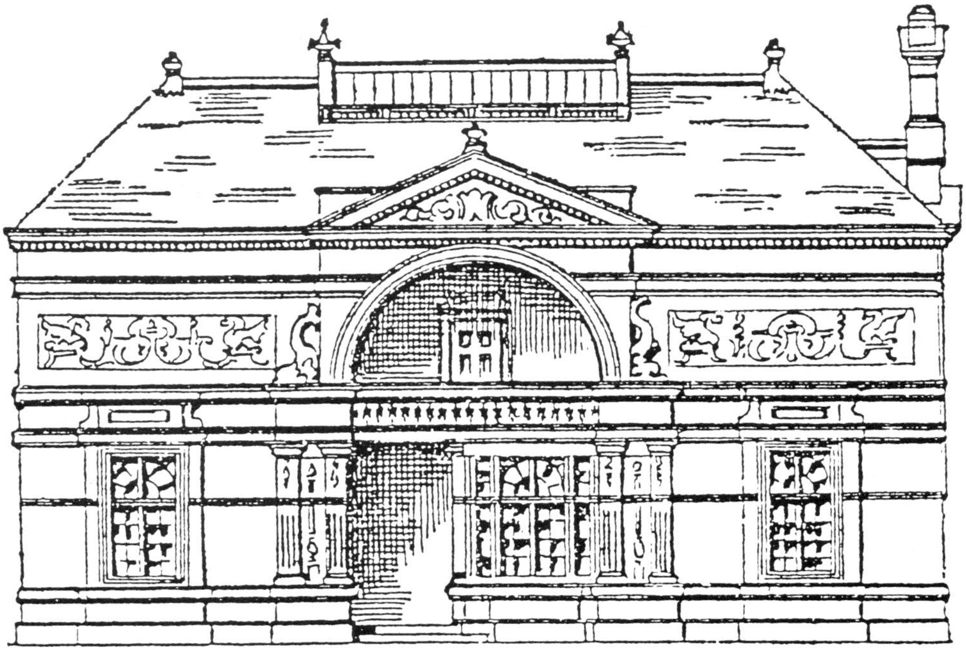

Edwin Seward
Turner House Gallery,
1887.

In fact, the Artists' Club had, by the 1890s, built up a membership of about 150, with its 'non-resident members' from outside the immediate area. A number of Cardiff painters such as Parker Hagerty had joined though not T.H.Thomas or Edwin Seward. The Club's social activities, and particularly the smoking concerts, were not to everyone's taste. In 1889 George Crozier wrote to Whaite having heard that certain members of the Club and the Academy were proposing to introduce this form of entertainment at Plas Mawr. 'I do not think myself that your own feeling would prompt you to simulate the level of the Talybont Club with its "Hot Pot" suppers', he remarked, 'but if once an innovation of the proposed kind was made there is no telling what would follow.' [187]

The *Art Journal's* observations on the inaccessibility of Tal-y-bont to the average tourist emphasised the dispersed nature of the artists' colony, strung out between Llandudno, the fashionable sea-side resort, Conwy with the Academy at Plas Mawr, Llanbedr-y-cennin with the Artists' Club, Trefriw, where most of the artists lived, and Betws itself. The artists' colony at Newlyn was much tighter, with the painters living and working in a small

[187]Whaite archive, op.cit., 17 December 1889. The Artists' Club survived until the Great War but was disbanded shortly afterwards. The building was sold and converted into a private house.

area around the school, and by 1895, a gallery devoted to their work had also been opened. The artists' colony in the north German village of Worpswede benefitted from a similar confirmation of their group identity in the form of a gallery. Augusta Mostyn's initiative in Llandudno, echoing that of Pyke Thompson, who had commissioned Edwin Seward to construct a somewhat smaller gallery at Penarth in 1887, demonstrated that patronage on this scale was available in Wales before the Great War. Had the efforts of either patron been directed to Betws, for the display both of a permanent collection of representative works and to sell new productions by the artists, some more dynamic sense of group identity might have been encouraged. As it was, the only gallery that was opened at Betws was a small commercial venture by one Thomas Spinks, established in about 1910, of which little is known.[188]

In its article of 1894 the *Art Journal* had all but conceded that Betws was living on a reputation won in the past, and that its artists were now perceived as outmoded, when it remarked that 'Within recent years, Bettws... has been considered too picturesque to be acceptable to the younger generation of advanced artists'. The teaching prospectus at Plas Mawr was antiquated and the school was in the wrong place. The fashion was for painting in the open air, before the subject, and study indoors which could be related directly to it. In Conwy, the Academy could not offer that sense of immediate involvement with the working life of the common people, so characteristic of Newlyn, because the potential subjects were miles away, up the valley. Furthermore, they were now not so easily found in Betws itself, which had become a sea of respectable boarding houses. The leading painters were ageing, and among them there was no charismatic figure like Stanhope Forbes, inspired with new ideas, to attract young followers. This was the role that Cox had fulfilled in the days when Betws was newly discovered by artists and unspoiled. The result, in the 1850s and 1860s, had been the kind of excitement among young painters now enjoyed at Newlyn, and which had drawn Clarence Whaite and Benjamin Williams Leader, among many others. Leader had not taken up residence, and Whaite, for all his Cox-like generosity of spirit and interest in the new generation, did not cut the figure in the English art world of his great predecessor. Neither did he have the reputation of Leader or of the younger Stanhope Forbes. Whaite kept a studio in London and was,

[188]The gallery became a shop, though Spinks' slate sign survived into the 1980s. One of the victims of the Cardiff fiasco had been an offer of financial support from the brothers Cuthbert and J.R.Grundy to construct a gallery. Their patronage was eventually redirected to Blackpool, although Cuthbert remained an active supporter of the Academy and, indeed, succeeded Clarence Whaite as President.

indeed, a prominent figure in the Royal Watercolour Society by this time, but had failed in his attempt to become its president. His English reputation remained at its strongest in the north west, where in 1892 he was appointed President of the Manchester Academy. Charles Jones wrote from London to congratulate him, though with a word of warning: 'I trust most sincerely you wont let it interfere with your presidentship of the RCA...'.[189] Whaite was well known and well liked. However, although he occupied a respectable position in the heirarchy of contemporary artists, obsessively discussed by critics in the period, it was high only in the second division.

[189]Whaite Archive, op.cit., letter from Charles Jones, 21 February 1892. Jones regretted that Whaite had not called to see him at the Savage Club when last in London, 'to have a good chat... about the RCA and other matters'.

Despite the prestige of Benjamin Williams Leader, whose works continued to depict the area, by 1890 Betws was considered *passé* by young artists. In 1888 William Barker's obituarist noted that he had 'maintained to the last the Bohemian freedom in costume and manners which used to characterize artists, but which has latterly given way to the conventionalities and monotony of modern "respectability"', and this, indeed, was increasingly the image that Betws presented to the world. The artists' colony was not, on the whole, the kind of phenomenon conjoured up by that appelation in the *fin de siécle* period. It had had its occasional high-jinks and a share of heavy drinkers such as Whittaker, but it had never been truly Bohemian. Neither had William Evans' ascetic existence at Ty'n-y-cae become a model. The tone for life at Betws had been set by Cox's high seriousness and Protestant reserve, which evolved into solid respectability as the *nouveaux riches* of the English manufacturing towns made it their favoured resort. Their attitides went hand in glove with those of a middle-class chapel-going Welsh community, who prospered in the resultant tourist trade. Among the artistic community, Catrin Harrison, daughter of the village blacksmith, if she had ever been a picturesque

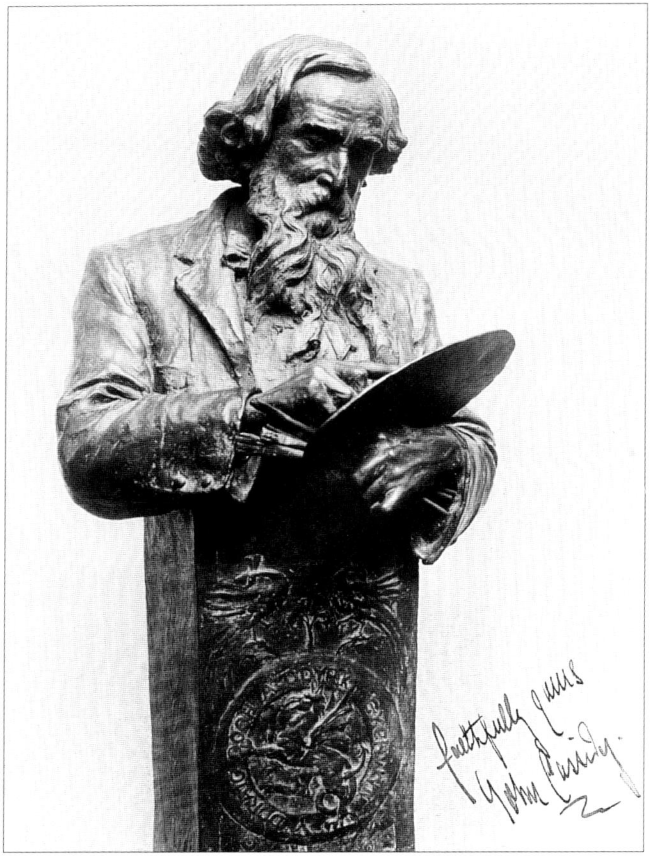

John Cassidy,
Clarence Whaite, 1897-8.

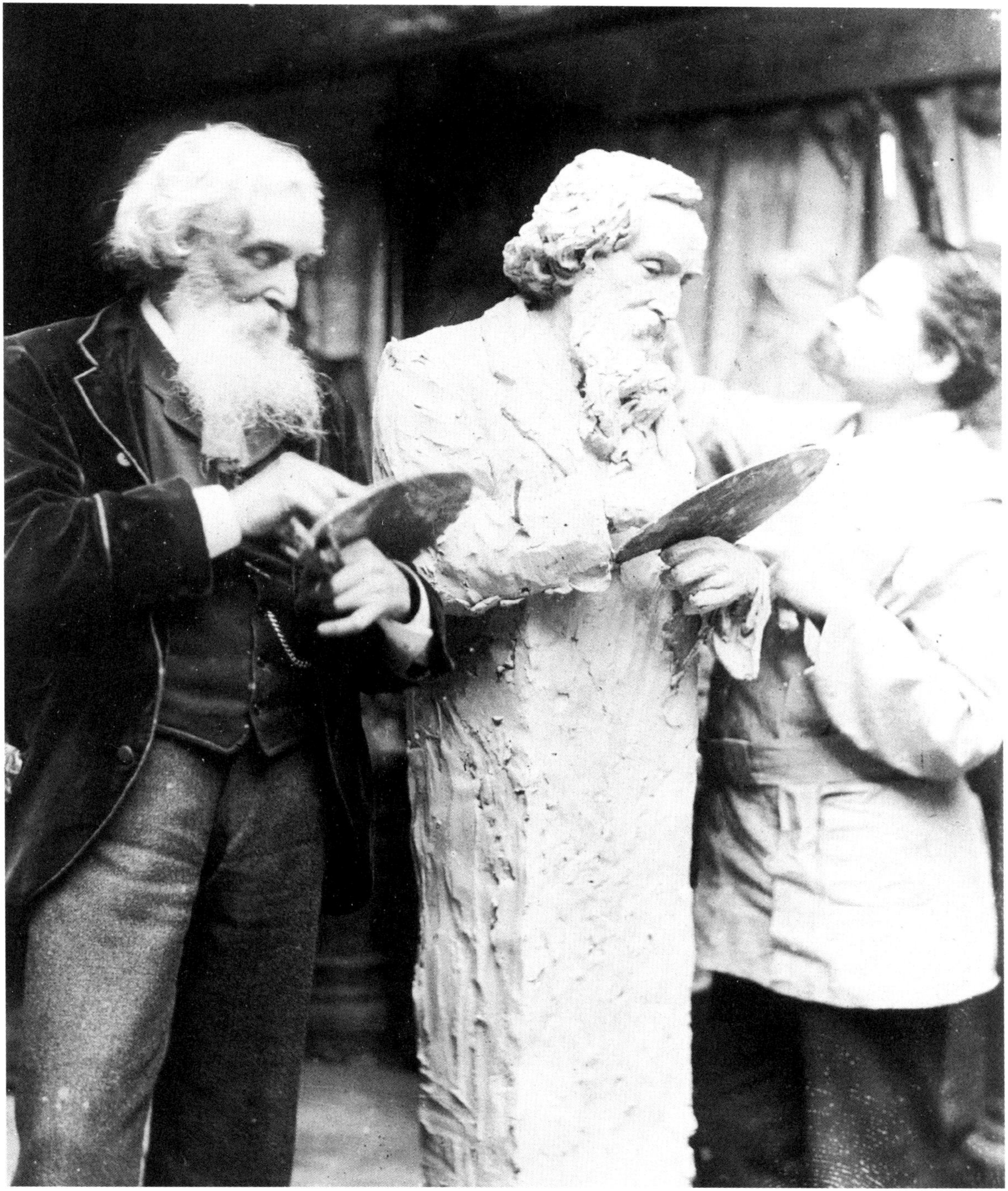

Unknown photographer, *Clarence Whaite with the sculptor John Cassidy and portrait bust, c.1896-7.*

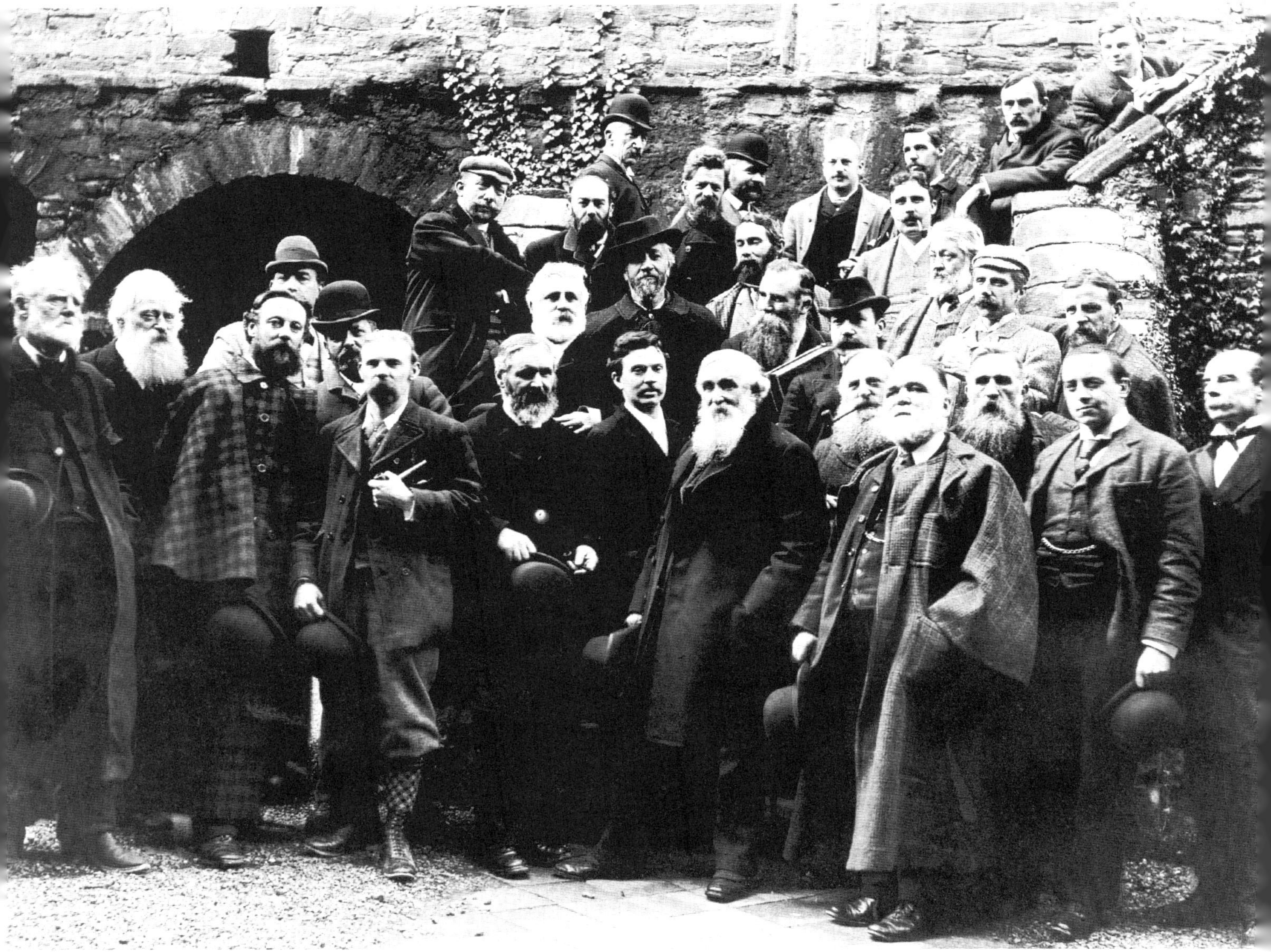

Unknown photographer,
Royal Cambrian Academicians at Plas Mawr, c.1897.

peasant, was by now a respectable Victorian lady. In the early 1890s the Harrisons left Tŷ Gwyn and crossed the river to live at Joseph Knight's former residence, Min Afon.[190] It was probably there that they were photographed *en famille*, with Catrin encased in matronly satins. This image denoted respectability rather than prosperity. Joseph Knight had been among the most successful of the artists and had made money, but Harrison had not. In 1908 he sent a drawing to the National Eisteddfod at Llangollen, *A Winter Piece on the Conway*, and two weeks later wrote to his friend Clarence Whaite, who was, once again, the adjudicator, hoping that it would 'merit a prize. It would help me a good deal in these hard times'.[191]

[190]Knight was recorded in both the 1881 and 1891 census as resident at Min Afon. Harrison was living there by 1893. It was later occupied by the amateur painter and musician, Alfred Rodellad, and frequented by Edward Elgar.

[191]Whaite Archive, op.cit., 2 August 1908.

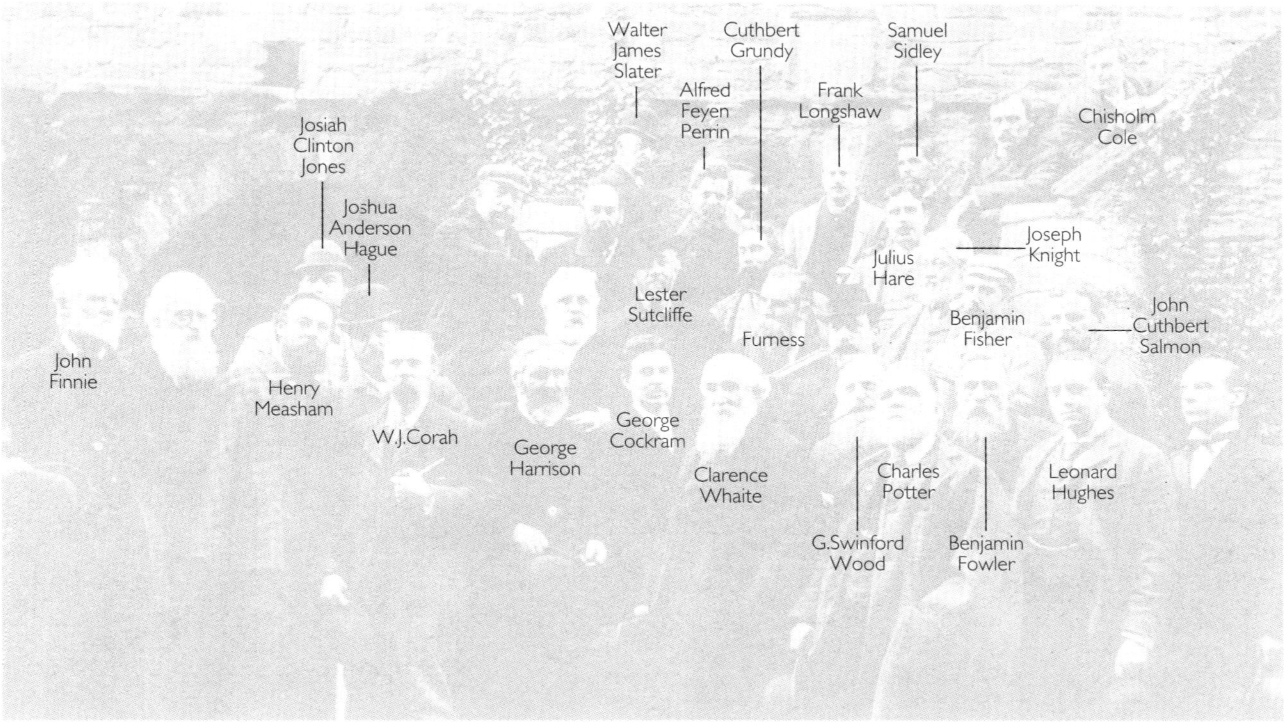

Unknown photographer, *George and Catrin Harrison and their two daughters*, c.1890.

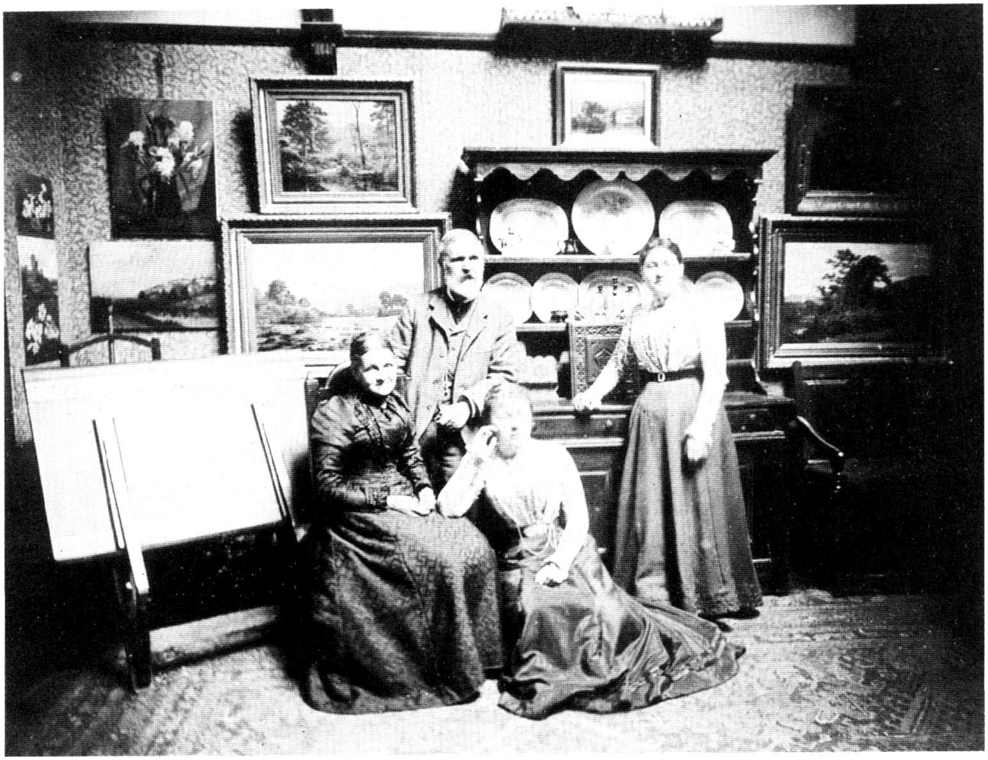

George Harrison, *Ruined Cottage*, 1863.

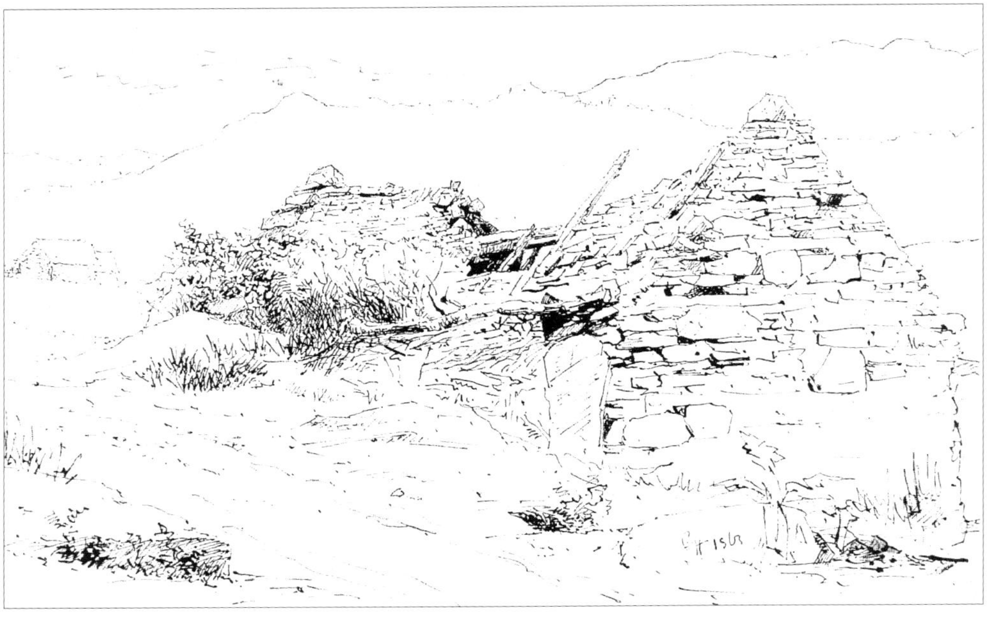

Perhaps the most crippling deficiency which prevented Betws developing from an artists' colony into a school of painting was the absence of a coherent philosophical standpoint and aesthetics. Following the Cardiff fiascos of 1884 and 1885, Academicians did not show again as a group outside Conwy until 1900. In the summer of that year an invitation was received at Plas Mawr from the the Director of the South London Art Gallery at Camberwell (which had been erected by J.Passmore Edwards, patron of the Newlyn painters), to mount an exhibition of Royal Cambrian Academy work.[192] J.R.Furness, Curator at Plas Mawr, succeeded in a very short time in organising a show of 141 works by 44 members, which opened at Camberwell on 15 November. Most of the prominent Academicians participated, led by Clarence Whaite who showed six oils, including *Mountain Mist - Sunrise*. This exhibition appears to have been the only occasion on which the Conwy Valley painters were shown together outside Wales before the Great War, and it came far too late for the kind of work that they were making to have a collective impact on the London art world. However, it was just at this belated stage that attempts were being made in Wales to define a common philosophical thread which would tie the painters of the area together, and transform them from a professional group into an aesthetic school. The attempt was made by a number of Welsh intellectuals working mainly in the Welsh language.

The new Welsh criticism was motivated by patriotism and, like the effort to develop art institutions in Cardiff, came from within the broader national movement at the end of the nineteenth century.[193] T.H.Thomas expressed the spirit of the time in 1902, when he wrote about the purpose of the proposed National Museum:

> *'Besides the enormous educational advantage a National Museum would afford... we have also an opportunity which, in this direction, can never again occur, of proclaiming that the Cymry are a nation, and of building another mole to strengthen our boundary against which for ever beat waves of influence, both mighty and insiduous.'*[194]

[192]Edwards subsequently constructed the Whitechapel Picture Gallery.

[193]The movement also saw the first attempts to develop Welsh art history. T.H.Thomas was engaged in research on indigenous painters, notably Hugh Hughes, before the turn of the century, and in 1912, the first book on the subject, *Welsh Painters, Engravers and Sculptors* was published. The author was the Rev.T.Mardy Rees but his information came from the research of the circle of art enthusiasts around Thomas.

[194]T.H.Thomas, 'A National Museum for Wales', *Young Wales*, 1902, p.145.

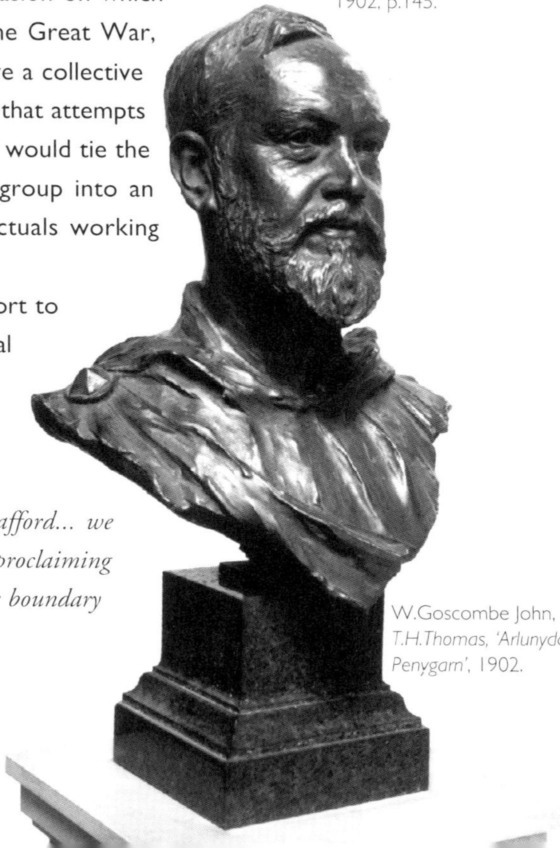

W.Goscombe John, *T.H.Thomas, 'Arlunydd Penygarn'*, 1902.

The widespread perception of the deficiency of the indigenous culture in visual art[195] weakened the national argument, which maintained that Wales could be a complete and self-governing entity within the world-wide Imperial family of nations. Welsh intellectuals were faced with the problem of identifying an art which by its distinctness and distinction both presented a particular Welsh quality to the world and could be promoted as the equal of English work. Since the patriotism of most of them did not transcend a belief that conventional English values represented the peak of civilisation, these two requirements operated against each other. They were unwilling to go beyond London and identify Wales with the modernism of continental Europe, despite the fact that, at the very moment of their attempt to define a Welsh School, two Welsh painters - Augustus John and J.D.Innes - were leading the way in precisely that direction. Neither were they ready to propose a central place in the national culture for visual conventions from outside academic art, despite their intense interest in folk life. That step, taken by Iorwerth Peate and his contemporaries, was still twenty years in the future. They were left with academic landscape painting, and particularly that associated with Betws, as the only Welsh art product that had high status in England - and with the difficult paradox that, with the exception of Wilson, most of the best work had been produced by English-born artists.

Within their common patriotic framework, members of the intellectual community responded in somewhat different ways. Echoing T.H.Thomas's attitude, expressed in his justification of the Royal Cambrian Academy in 1886, Tom Ellis, the greatest of the nationalist leaders of the period, was reluctantly inclusive of English artists. Addressing the Cymmrodorion in 1897 on the subject of 'Domestic and Decorative Arts in Wales', he drew attention both to the importance of contemporary landscape painting and to the perceived detachment of the painters of the Conwy Valley from the indigenous culture, which resulted in a failure to take advantage of the prestige which their products could bring the nation:

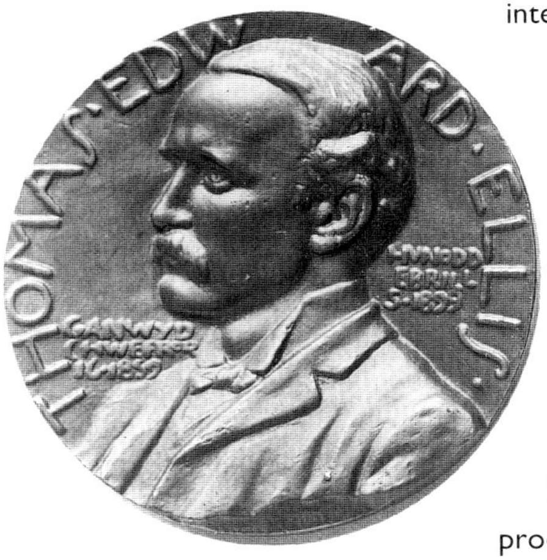

W.Goscombe John, *Tom Ellis medal*, c.1902.

'Before I touch upon my actual subject, I ought to refer to one other point. That is the change which has come over Wales in one respect during the last thirty or forty years in the fact that artists - not, I am sorry to say, as a rule Welsh artists, but artists from outside - have from time to time lived and settled down in Wales, in order to interpret the scenery and life of Wales. My feeling in regard to them is one rather of sadness that the interpretation of the beauty of the landscape and of the life of Wales should be left to artists from outside, and that their products should be for a public outside Wales.'

Mindful of the moves afoot to develop a gallery in Cardiff, Ellis tellingly observed that:

'Their pictures do not pass through the mind or the heart of Wales, and this must be so, until we have a municipal gallery or galleries or national gallery or galleries, where the products of these artists, who have seen the loveliness of Wales, can be exhibited for the wise enjoyment of the Welsh people. As it is we have neither galleries nor artists of our own, nor any means, except the wealth and good fortune and taste of an individual Welshman here and there, of securing for our people either temporarily or permanently, the artistic interpretation of the landscape and life of Wales by artists who come and live in Wales or who settle down there for a season.'[196]

Samuel Maurice Jones, writing six years earlier, had expressed similarly ambiguous sentiments in the face of the paradox of a Welsh art which was not made by Welsh-born artists, but had done so in less conciliatory terms. In 1891 Jones coined the expression 'Yr Arlunfa Gymreig' - the Welsh Studio - to describe Betws, and built his analysis of its meaning around the work of David Cox. In his view, Cox had captured not only the visual quality of the place but, most importantly, its underlying spirit. However, unlike T.H.Thomas and Tom Ellis, he regarded much of the work that had been produced after Cox's death as a betrayal of the Master's understanding. He observed, with deep disapproval, that it was not unusual to see in English art exhibitions 'Coed Carreg y Gwalch adapted by the painter as a scene through which one of Shakespeare's main characters wandered'.[197] The 'students of the brush' were everywhere in Betws, disturbing the tranquility of the place and perverting its indigenous culture:

[195]For an analysis of this perception, see Peter Lord, *The Aesthetics of Relevance* (Llandysul, 1992).

[196]T.E.Ellis, 'Domestic and Decorative Arts in Wales', *Transactions of the Honourable Society of Cymmrodorion*, Session 1896-7, (1898), pp.16-17. This paper was considered sufficiently important to be posthumously reprinted in *Young Wales*, July 1899.

[197]Jones's perception was not new. The author of *The Gossiping Guide to Wales* (London, 1872), remarked that 'To reach the Fairies' Glen you turn off to the right between the Fish Inn and Bettws, and a short and pleasant walk brings you to a spot that might well be transferred to canvas for a representation of *Midsummer's Nights' Dream*.'

'And in order to satisfy foreigners who visit the studio, one finds a host of John Bull's idolators ready to bow down before his princely majesty, and to exchange the old words to fit the lips of the gentry. Nowadays, Pont ty hyll, Pont y Pair, Llyn y bod, Ffrith goch, and various others, are things of the past. According to the latest revised reading one must ask for Uglyhouse Bridge, Luniebod, Pont pare, and Betsi Coed.' [198]

Three years later the *Art Journal*, in its article about the Betws artists' colony, manifested all those Anglo-centric perceptions which so angered Jones:

'The road on the other side of the Conway is in Denbighshire, Bettws itself being in Carnarvonshire. Nearly three miles along this road, down the river, lies Llanrwst, a prosperous Welsh village, whose little ones are ignorant of English and whose men and women seem to translate their words from the Welsh. The unexpectedness of the enormous use of the language of consonants brings forth characteristic expressions of surprise from every English-speaking visitor; theoretically we all know that Welsh is a living language, but it is only in a village like Llanrwst that one realises the hold that Welsh has on the ordinary people. When railway notices are headed "Rhybudd," followed by various unpronouncable words, when shop-signs and window-tickets are incomprehensible save when they carry a numeral, and when, most astonishing of all, lengthy advertisements appear in newspapers in Welsh, then the British traveller begins to feel like a stranger in his own island. This holding to a hereditary language is only a sentiment, for sooner or later the young folks are compelled to master English; but it is a pretty sentiment, and one we would not willingly let die.' [199]

Samuel Maurice Jones felt that Cox, despite his English birth, had transcended such attitudes. Using what seems, in retrospect, an unfortunate comparison, he believed that 'It could be said, with much appropriateness, that the brush of the painter David Cox tells as much of the life and customs of the Welsh sixty years ago as does the pen of the Welshman H.M.Stanley of the manners and customs of the inhabitants of Central Africa in our time'.[200]

[198] Samuel Maurice Jones, 'Yr Arlunfa Gymreig', *Cymru Fydd* IV (1891), p.27.

[199] *The Art Journal*, op.cit., p.270.

[200] Samuel Maurice Jones, op.cit., p.22.

[201] Ibid., p.24. Typical of many popular poems expressing such sentiments was Gwilym Marles 'Mynwent Cwmwr Du', originally published in 1863. When O.M.Edwards published a collection of the poet's work in the series 'Cyfres y Fil' in 1905, Samuel Maurice Jones provided illustrations for the book. Jones also drew a Welsh funeral to illustrate 'Llan y Mynydd', *Cymru'r Plant*, V (1896), p.250. T.H.Thomas illustrated the same subject for D.Davies, *Echoes from the Welsh Hills* (London, 1883).

Cox's empathy with the spirit of the place he painted reached its apotheosis in *The Welsh Funeral*. The genesis of the picture has become obscured by myth, but it appears that the painter was moved by witnessing the evening funeral of a young local girl at the churchyard in Betws. *The Welsh Funeral* assumed considerable importance in the minds of Welsh critics before the Great War for reasons that were, once again, shot through with the ambiguities of contemporary patriotism. Enthusiasts believed that the painting truly conveyed the particular essence of the Welsh soul. For Jones it was 'a picture of death passing through the middle of the beauty of life', a sentiment redolent of a century and a half of Nonconformist religious prose and poetry in the Welsh language.[201] However, of equal importance was the fact that the picture achieved extraordinary popularity in England, presenting an image of Welsh piety assiduously cultivated by generations of Welsh religious and political leaders in rebuttal of the accusations made by the government's Commissioners for Education. The first version of the picture was painted in 1848 while the controversy surrounding the publication of their Blue Books, the previous year, was at its height. The contrast between the contemporary perceptions of the Commissioners and those of Cox and his friends was, indeed, remarkable. In the 1844 edition of *Wanderings and Excursions in North Wales*, Roscoe had described an incident which took place at the Royal Oak:

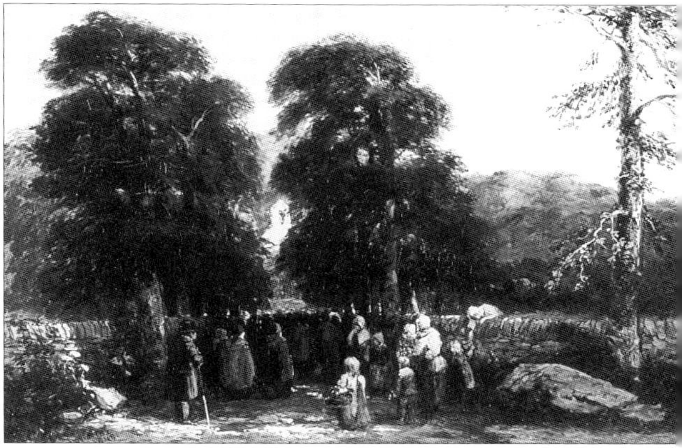

David Cox,
The Welsh Funeral, 1848.
Reproduced in colour on p.151.

David Cox,
drawing for The Welsh Funeral, c.1848

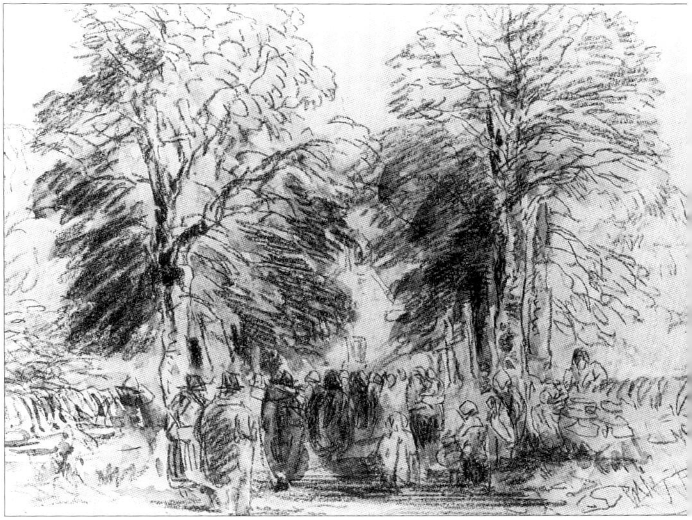

> *'I was surprised on my return at the gathering of many visitors in the family room of mine host at the Royal Oak, and the more than usual order and gravity that prevailed throughout the domicile; but the secret was revealed when I heard the voice of some one reading, with "solemn air," the words of Holy Writ. The clattering feet of the little party announced another movement, and the same voice then rose in reverential prayer, deepening into pathos, and advancing into impassioned earnestness, as the varied subjects of his supplication seemed to engage his attention... The whole of the service was*

conducted in the Welsh language, of which I did not understand a word, and I could therefore only judge of the several parts by the tones and action of the speaker. I was greatly affected with the circumstance at the time, especially by the thought, ordinary enough in itself, but which at that moment came with extraordinary force to my mind, that He, the great Father of all, could perfectly understand the prayer of his children, to what tribes of earth soever they might belong, and with whatever language they might address the throne of his Mercy.'[202]

Although there is no reason to doubt the veracity of Roscoe's account, his description of the virtue of the Welsh folk, based on an experience at the Royal Oak, certainly depended on the exercise of considerable selectivity.[203] The landlord of the Royal Oak himself presented substantial and well-known evidence to the contrary. Sometime in the mid 1860s, Samuel P.Jackson wrote of the disappointments of his stay at the inn because 'the landlord is dying':

'There are no "fashionables" at present - as the landlord is too ill to stand them. Said landlord I must tell you has gone the way of all landlords and drunk out his vitals. Mrs Roberts certainly made a most unfortunate match in marrying him. But the knowing ones say that she is not likely to profit from the experience, and already "spot" our future host.'[204]

On the other hand, George Price Boyce had been impressed by Welsh piety. In 1852, near Betws and in the company of David Cox, he 'stopped to listen to some simple and moving singing, in the Welsh chapel'.[205] These kind of comments emanating from the circle of Cox certainly disposed Welsh writers of the late nineteenth century favourably towards them, and the fact that Cox himself was a Nonconformist and known for his piety, reinforced their high opinion of him in particular. *The Welsh Funeral* had not been an instant success with the English public, though another of the ex-patriate Betws painters, Frank Topham, had perceived its quality from the beginning. William Hall noted of the picture's early history that 'The large water-colour drawing of this subject, exhibited at the Pall Mall Gallery in 1850 - a truly magnificent production - strange to say, did not find a ready

[202]Roscoe, op.cit., p.214. The minister was a Calvinistic Methodist, 'with which the Principality abounds', noted the author.

[203]Among the many additions made by Roscoe to the second edition of his volume in 1844 was the observation, occasioned by advertisements he saw at Llanrwst for temperence houses and coffee rooms, that 'Wales has often been spoken of for its national sobriety'. Ibid., p.194.

[204]Undated letter to J.J.Jenkins, Royal Watercolour Society archive, J102/1.

[205]Boyce, op.cit., p.10.

purchaser there, although its price was extremely low. Mr.Topham, the eminent artist, induced a prizeholder in the London Art Union to make a choice of it for his prize of £50; but this individual soon became tired of it (not being pretty enough for his taste), and, Mr.Topham, disgusted, doubtless, took it off his hands, giving him the money, which most likely pleased him a great deal better'.[206]

However, in 1862, the Art Union published a version of *The Welsh Funeral* as an engraving and the immediate popularity of the picture was reinforced by the emergence of a rash of related works by other artists. In 1863 Leader exhibited *A Welsh Churchyard* at the Royal Academy, which was considered 'very striking in its masses of huge yew-trees, almost black, standing over the dusky grey tombs like mourners, the evening sky luminous behind them, and still glowing on the distant hills.'[207] As we have seen, the picture was bought by that pillar of Protestant rectitude, the Prime Minister, Mr Gladstone, and hung at his home in Hawarden, Flintshire. Creswick's picture of the same scene, published in 1870 as an engraving, has also already been noted. By this time, Betws-y-coed possessed the most celebrated graveyard in Europe. Five years earlier Clarence Whaite had painted *God's Acre*, which was exhibited at the Royal Institution. The *Manchester Guardian* reported that it 'is a scene in a Welsh churchyard, with a finely conceived unity in the plain edifice, the old protecting trees, the rustic worshippers, and their last resting place'.[208] Whaite extended his exploration of the theme a stage further in the same year of 1865 with a picture whose original title, *To the Cold Earth*, by stages evolved into *The Welsh Funeral*, truly reflecting the element of homage to Cox which it is difficult not to suspect lay at the back of the painter's mind. *To the Cold Earth* was described in detail by the art critic of a Manchester newspaper:

> *'The subject is a Welsh funeral. The grim messanger knocks at the cottage of the lithe and hardy Cambrian mountaineer, as surely though less frequently perhaps, as at the cellar of the pale denizens of the courts and alleys of crowded cities. When a funeral occurs among these primitive people the scattered villagers for miles around assemble to pay their last token of respect to the departed. Mr Whaite has depicted the funeral procession passing over the windings of the snow-clad mountains to the village churchyard. The idea is exceedingly poetical and is well worked out, the mist and snow of the mountain tops being well executed.'*[209]

[206]Hall, op.cit., p.93.

[207]Lewis Lusk, 'B.W.Leader, R.A., *The Art Annual*, 1901, pp.21-2. Leader painted at least one other version of the same subject.

[208]*The Manchester Guardian*, 10 October 1865. The title refers to Longfellow's line, 'This is the field and acre of our God'.

[209]*The Courier*, 1 April 1865. This picture and *God's Acre* were contemporary with *The Penitent's Vision*, which, as noted above, p.86, may well be related to Whaite's mourning for his mother, as well as the wider vogue for such subjects at the time.

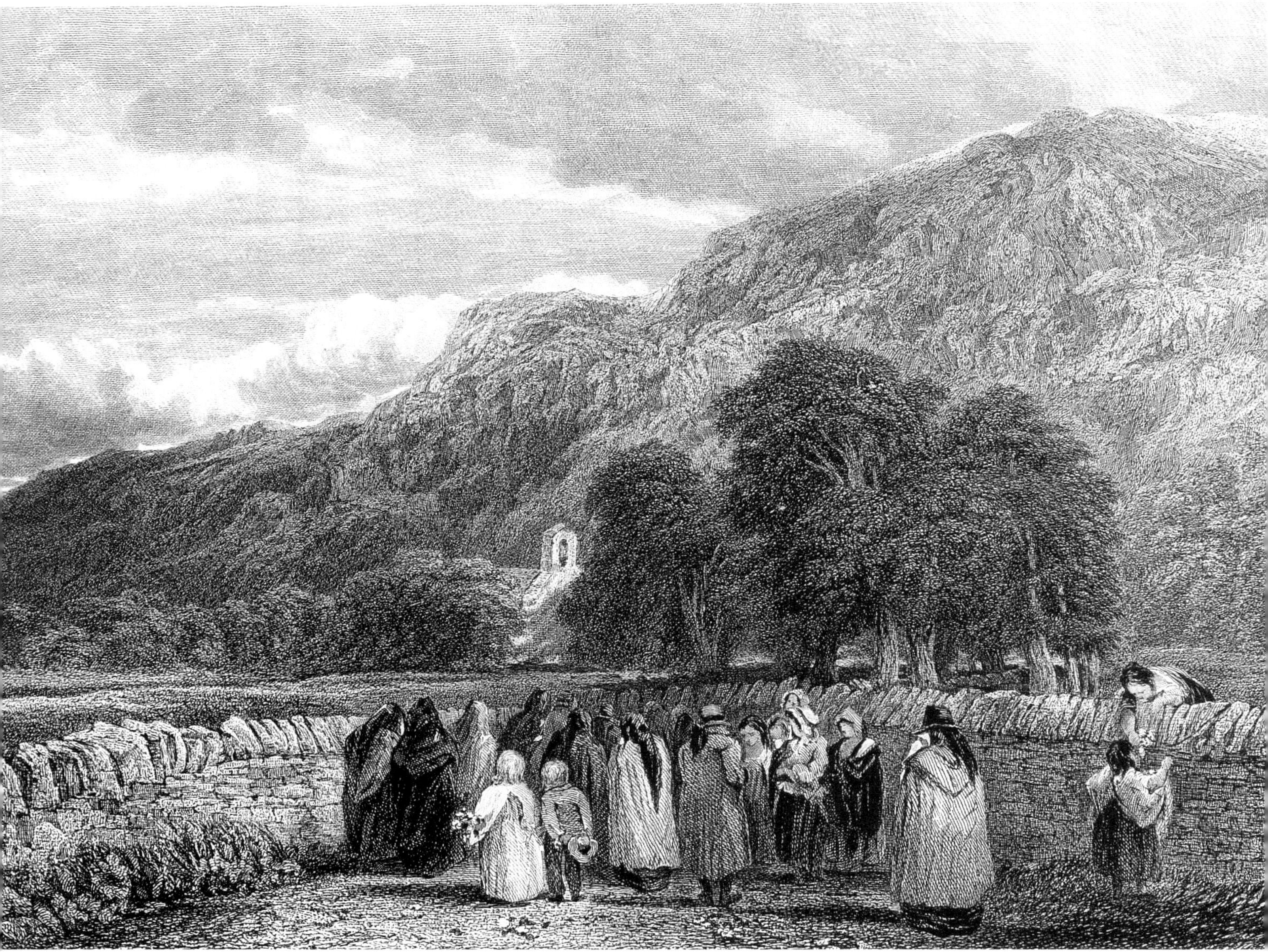

Engraving after David Cox, *The Welsh Funeral*, 1862.

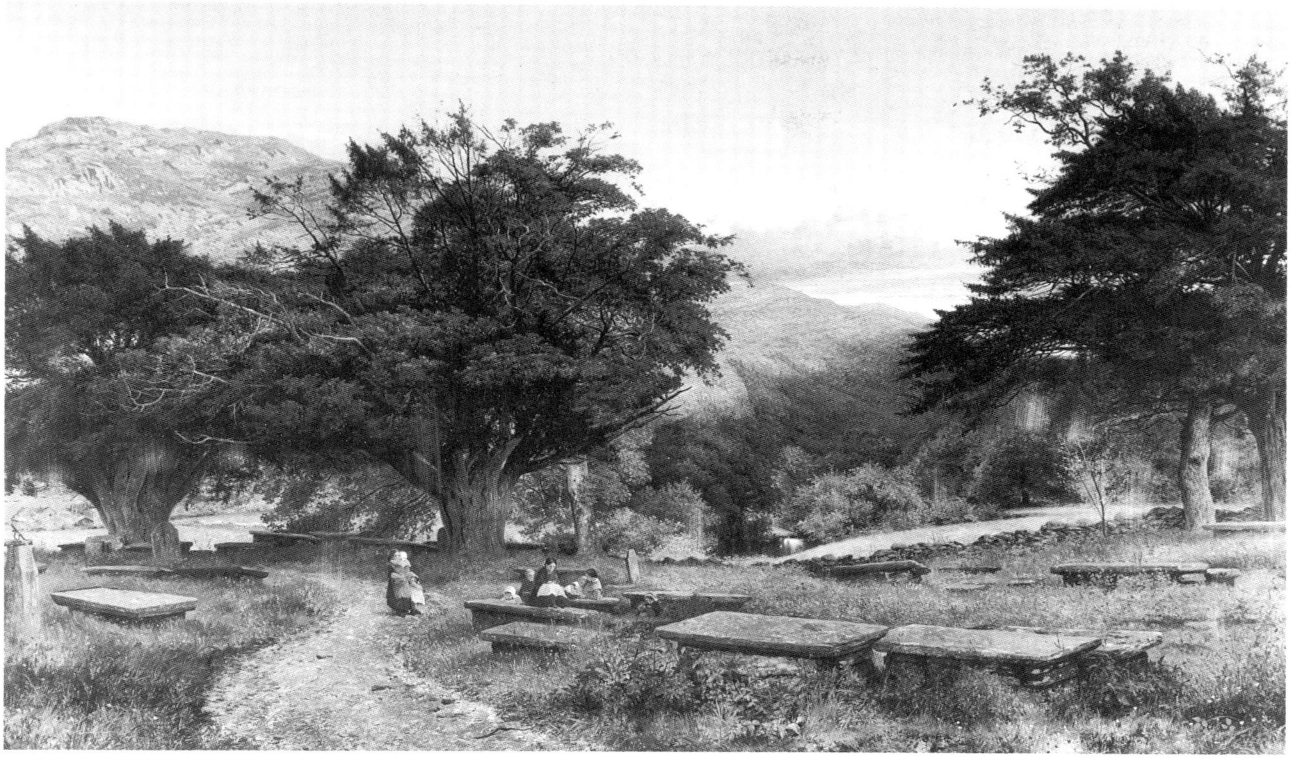

B.W.Leader
A Welsh Churchyard,
1863

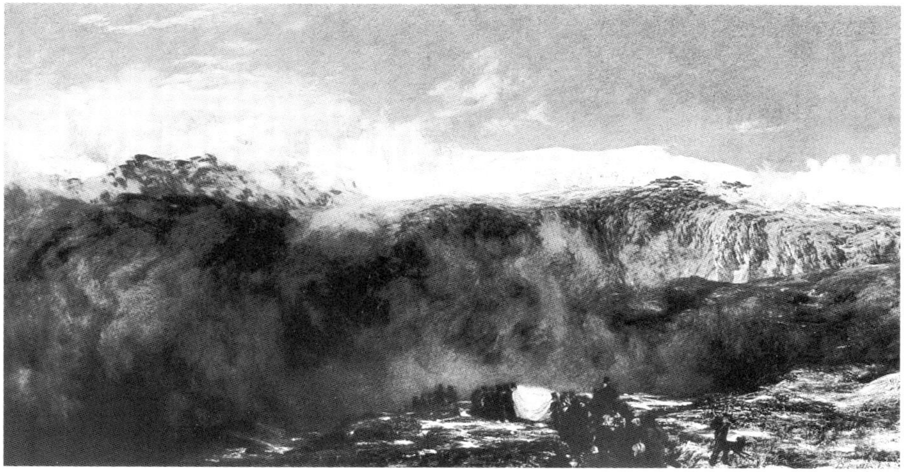

Clarence Whaite,
To the Cold Earth, 1865.
Reproduced in colour on p.87.

Simply asserting the insiderness of Cox and the influence of his Welsh works did not, of course, entirely meet the needs of nationalist critics. There remained the perplexing question as to precisely how the English-born painter had become one with both the natural world and the indigenous culture of Betws. In the absence of a convincing explanation of this phenomenon, it would not be possible to construct a national aesthetic on the basis of his work. In another age, the question might have been answered simply in terms of the genius of the man. At the beginning of the twentieth century, however, critics adopted a more scientific approach. They found their answer in that uneasy union between the rational and the mystical, so characteristic of the period, which proposed that persistent racial characteristics were manifested in human behaviour. Such characteristics were carried in the blood from generation to generation and were to be discerned in many aspects of culture, including art works. This mysticism expressed in the language of reason had a particularly strong resonance for Welsh Nonconformists, echoing the way in which they prided themselves on the rationality of their religious practice, notwithstanding its foundation on an inner revelation which transcended the mind. The empathy of the English Cox with Wales was to be accounted for by his birth and upbringing near the border and his contact with the mystical River Severn, which had drawn him to Wales. The leading proponent of this view, and the critic who went furthest towards defining a national aesthetic based mainly on the landscape painters associated with Betws, was Thomas Matthews of Llandybie. Writing in O.M.Edwards' magazine *Cymru* in 1911, Matthews made a determined effort to Celticise Cox, going so far as to imply Welsh blood by spelling his name Dafydd Coch. Unlike Samuel Maurice Jones, Matthews extended the phenomenon to other English-born landscape painters working in the Conwy Valley, in an attempt to draw them unequivocally into the ambit of the indigenous culture. He was particularly concerned with the work of the most celebrated contemporary practitioner, Benjamin Williams Leader:

Unknown photographer,
Thomas Matthews, c.1910

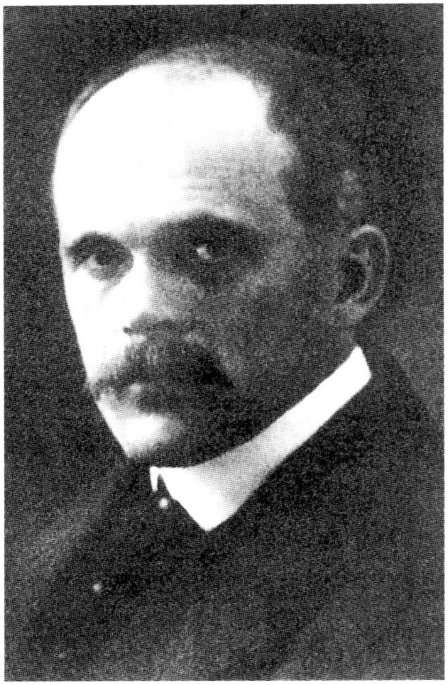

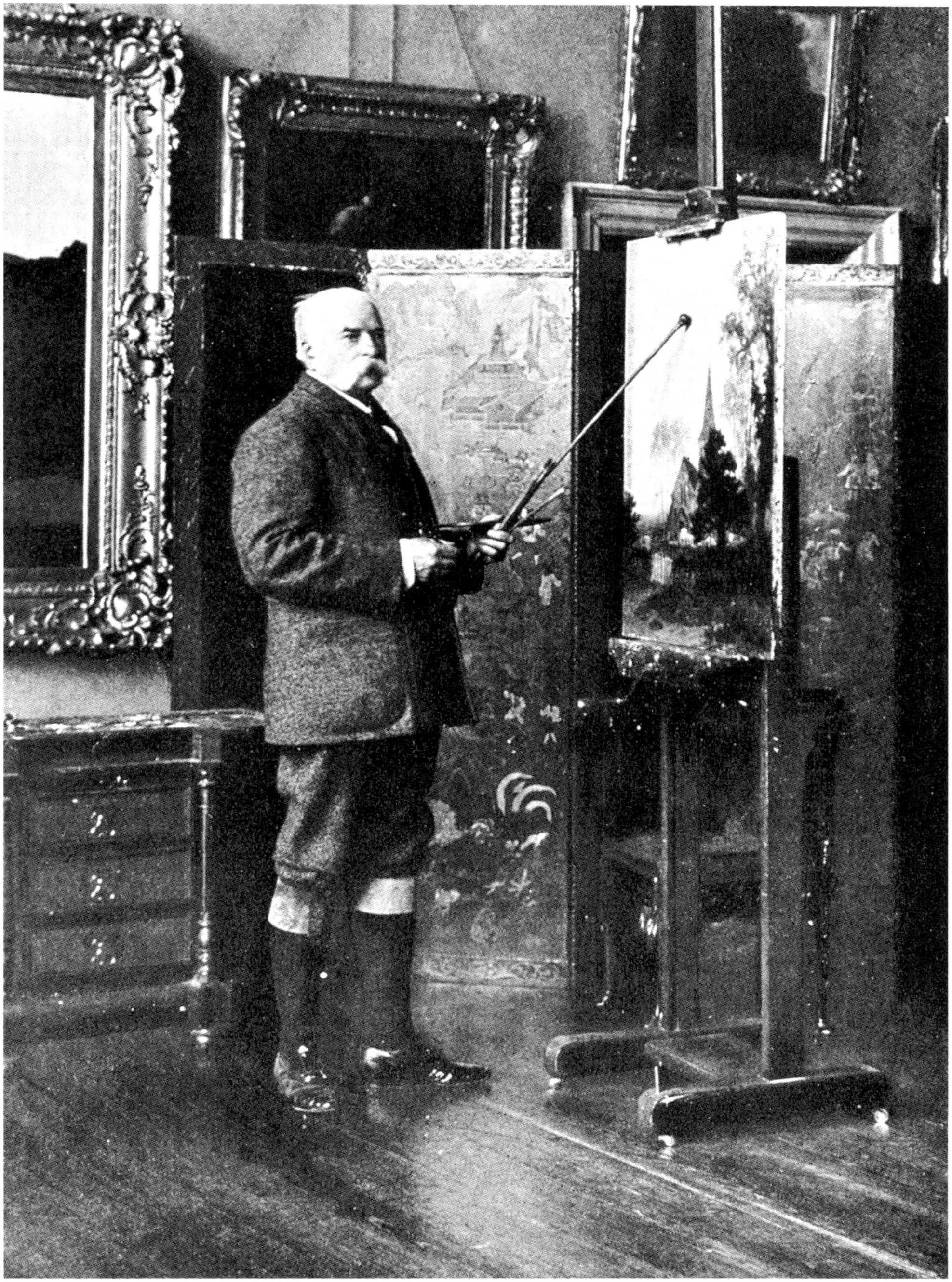

Unknown photographer,
Benjamin Williams Leader,
c.1900

'Some critics say that no-one apart from David Cox (or Coch) manifests his Celtic origins more obviously than Leader. Although he was born near Worcester on the Severn, it is as if the goddess of the river had given him an instinct to turn to the mountains of his country for strength. Like many others, he came to her bosom, and was generously rewarded by her.'[210]

Ironically, Matthews was probably led to his nationalist interpretation of Leader by an English critic, Lewis Lusk, who had written at length about the painter in *The Art Annual* for 1901. Lusk drew particular attention to *The Welsh Churchyard* since it brought out 'the Celtic strain of poetry', which he believed was manifested in this work, and in others, by a particular tonal quality which he called 'the amber note':

'It is a peculiarly Western British quality, and is very characteristic of Mr Leader's work... I use the term West Britain, in preference to the term West England, because so much of the Severn and Wye country still bears the half effaced stamp of Wales. Besides, there is a very strong Celtic strain in the artist's family, and in many of the spots by the Severn you shall find that the names have been originally moulded by the Welsh tongue... During the middle ages the Welsh marches extended far along the river... The essence of all this Celtic region pervades Mr Leader's style as it does that of David Cox.'[211]

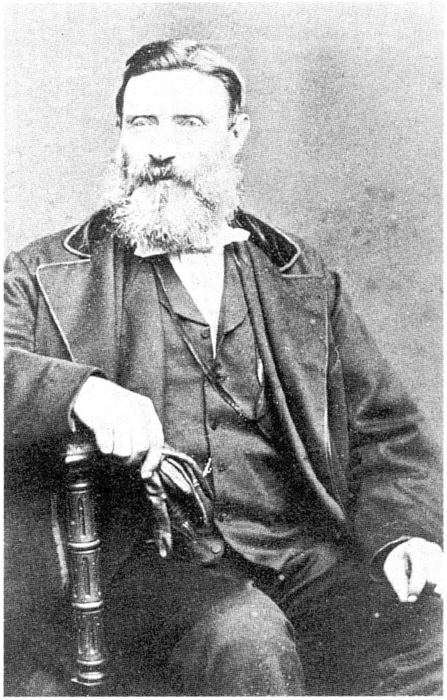

Matthews developed his Celticist theory by drawing both on Welsh literary tradition and the cherished myth of the inherent poetic nature of the Welsh people. He also drew upon the esthetics of the painter Evan Williams, heavily informed by Nonconformist religious ideas. Williams had written his first essay on art as a

[210]Thomas Mathews, 'Celf yng Nghymru', *Cymru*, ed.O.M.Edwards (1911), p.209.

[211]Lewis Lusk, op.cit., p.30. Leader's family name was in fact Williams and his father was of Welsh descent. The painter changed his name because he felt that Williams was not sufficiently distinctive in the competitative English art world.

[212]Calvin, *Institutes*, III, 10, 2.

direct response to the Blue Books. Before its publication in the magazine *Y Traethodydd* in 1848, no substantial theoretical writing on art had been available in the Welsh language, and Williams intended his article to counter the accusations made by the Commissioners about the ignorance of monoglot Welsh speakers. The author developed his ideas over three decades of writing in the same magazine. Williams was not only a professional painter and a writer, but also a Calvinistic Methodist minister, and steeped in the Puritan tradition. He could not take visual art for granted, since that tradition had come to regard it with suspicion as being a distraction from the inner knowledge and contemplation of God. In fact, Calvin himself had stated quite clearly in *The Institutes* that God had granted the things of the natural world not simply to meet human needs but also for human pleasure.[212] Taking his cue from Calvin, rather than from Bowdlerised tradition, Williams constructed a rational justification for landscape painting based on the idea of its moral

Left:
Unknown photographer,
Evan Williams,
c.1875.

Below:
Clarence Whaite,
Just Arrived by the Sloop,
1889.

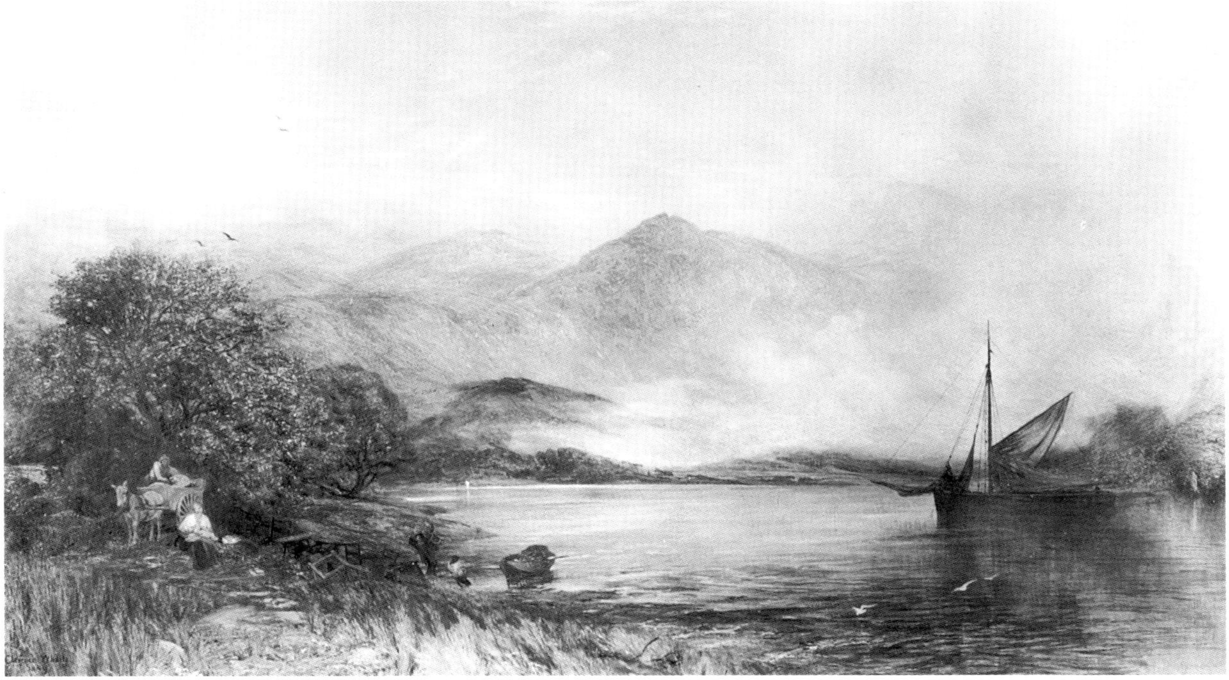

and spiritual utility. The artist was 'a fitting leader for all who would be introduced to the presence of nature in all its forms and its wonderful effects, which are certainly intended to add to the enjoyment of life, and to elevate the mind to the creator.'[213] Since nature was the handiwork of God, in meditating upon it human beings came as close to the deity as they might in this world. Landscape painting enabled nature to be carried into the private home and the public gallery, for meditation to continue. However, the essential requirements of the landscape painter were humility and truthfulness to the appearance that nature presented, so that the sin of idolatory - of mistaking the picture of God's handiwork for God himself - was avoided.

The meaning and definition of beauty in nature became, therefore, the central question in Evan Williams' aesthetics. This was hardly unexplored territory, of course, and he deployed the arguments of many of the great writers of the past. That he did so for the first time in the Welsh language would have been sufficient to make his work worthy of note, but that he wrote from a particularly Welsh Nonconformist standpoint made it of especial importance. Williams deployed a Classical argument of archetypes, leading him to the construction of hierarchies of individuals and categories, their beauty judged by their resemblance to the archetype.[214] The virtue of the Classical writers was their rationality. Nevertheless, as a Christian, it was necessary for Williams to demonstrate the limitations of their pagan philosophy, overlaying it with the mystical experience of God within the individual, which was the definitive Nonconformist idea. Classical art was objectively magnificent, but had no transcendent quality, and could not, therefore, exert a moral influence: 'It is, in truth, extraordinary as a manifestation of the mind, but not of the mind in its truest and most sacred context', he observed. The role of the artist was 'Not to make a detailed imitation of something and nothing more, but to insinuate ideas into the mind, ideas of a poetic nature, that are likely to impress themselves on the imagination'. For only in the imagination might God be approached:

> *'Art is concerned mainly with ideas which treat of beauty and sublimity; and in addressing these ideas, sympathy for them is aroused, and the most wonderful human feelings are disclosed.'* [215]

[213]Evan Williams, 'Natur a Chelfyddyd', *Y Traethodydd* (1867), p.38.

[214]Evan Williams believed, for instance, in the superiority of the European races, remarking that 'the white skin, as we call it, is more beautiful than the black skin, because it shows the signs of living energy more obviously'. Evan Williams, 'Y Gelfyddyd o Arlunio', *Y Traethodydd* (1848), p.363.

[215]Ibid., p.166.

This was a description of the Methodist meditation on the nature of Christ - the excitement of the soul and the revelation in this world of those things closest to God in human nature. Art was a force for human improvement, the 'wise enjoyment' proposed by Tom Ellis in his lecture to the Cymmrodorion in 1897:

> *'The chief service of the fine arts is the rational pleasure that they give to the mind, and their influence in its elevation and education through the truths and beauties of nature... A good picture is nature reflected by a human medium to address the human mind'.* [216]

In Evan Williams' own landscape painting, as in that of many of his much more distinguished contemporaries, the results of the superficial stress on objectivity were an unpretentious visual restraint which it was easy to confuse simply with conservatism.[217] The essence of the picture was not its abstract visual quality, and its success was not to be judged in formal or technical terms, though those things were important. Composition and colour were to be organised on rational principles which could be clearly defined and which respected nature as God's handiwork, on which no improvement could be made. Since no liberties were to be taken with reality, works which demonstrated this restraint were praised by critics who shared Williams' philosophy for their 'faithfulness', 'truthfulness' or 'sympathy'. However, it was the ability of the picture to act as a prompt for transcendent ideas and patterns of thought which determined its quality. It was for the observer to make the imaginative leap by contemplation of the painted token of natural beauty, to beauty itself. Beneath the surface rationale of the great painting lay an imaginative impulse which soared above the constraints of this world, as the warmth of the inner response to God transcended the conventions of worship in the Nonconformism of the period.

This philosophy was expressed by Thomas Matthews in a freer and more romantic way than by Williams. Matthews was writing from within a confident national movement, whereas his predecessor's work had been marked by the defensiveness of those who experienced the trauma of the Blue Books. Matthews was prepared to drive a wedge between English and Welsh aesthetics, implying that the realism of contemporary English landscape was decadent since it lacked transcendent qualities. Williams had dispproved of Turner on similar grounds. The great English painter was decadent and arrogant because

[216]Evan Williams, 'Sefyllfa Celfyddyd ym Mhrydain', *Y Traethodydd* (1865), p.426.

[217]Few of Evan Williams' landscapes have survived. One extant group of pictures of mountain subjects in Snowdonia are of excellent quality and quite distinct in style from the painter's rather wooden portraits. They survive in a private house in Wales, for which they were bought when new, but unfortunately, they have not been made available for reproduction.

he attempted to image the transcendent and to imitate the internal experience of God in nature. In this tendency, which Williams associated with Puseyism and the Oxford movement, Turner expressed his Englishness. His work was contrasted unfavourably with the outward rationality of Wilson, laid over an inner warmth of poetic feeling characteristic of the Welsh soul.[218] Thomas Matthews developed Evan Williams' analysis by comparisons made between visual art and the imagery of Welsh poetry. In his opinion, 'The painter must also be a poet':

'Is there not something more in a picture than the purely literal? Is it not better to have something which elevates us above the common things of life? Is it not better to have something,-

"Man never saw
More beautiful
In swoon or sleep?"[219]

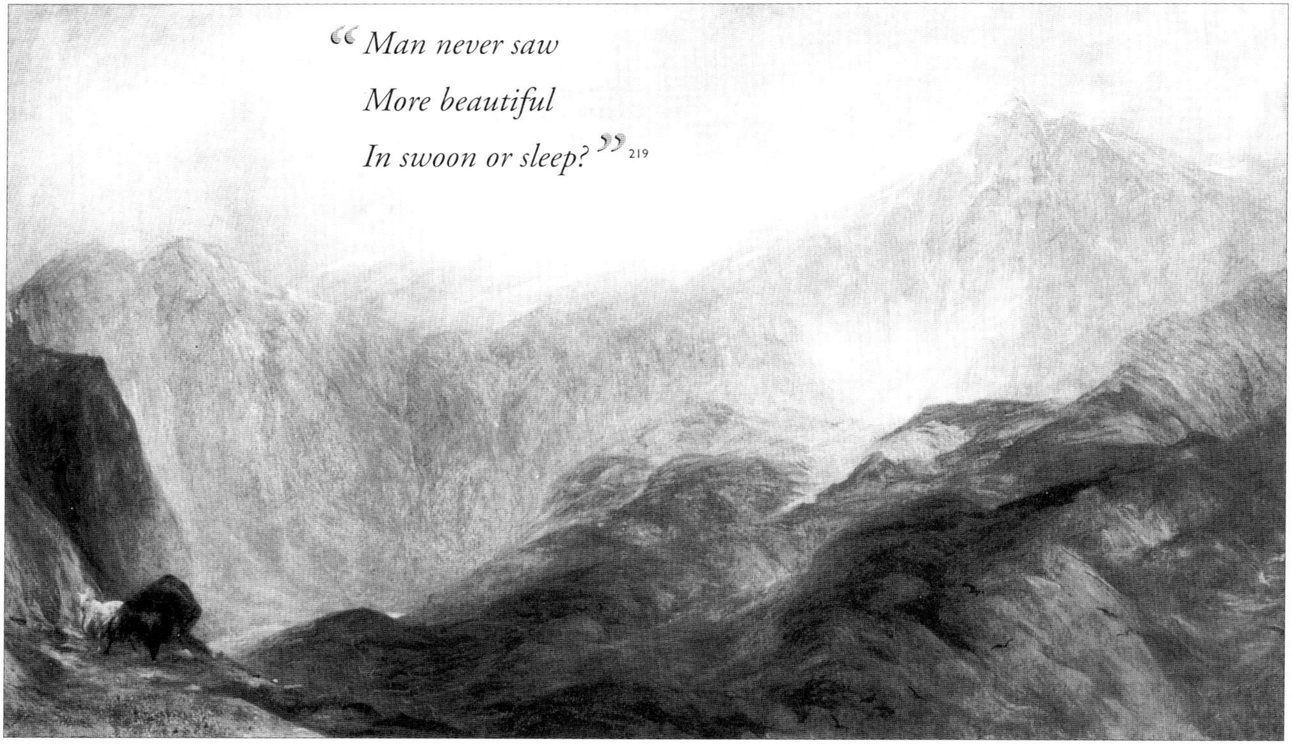

Clarence Whaite, *Snowdon*, 1910-11.

[218]Evan Williams, 'Arddangosiad Trysorau Celfyddyd', *Y Traethodydd* (1857), pp.336-8.

[219]Nas gwelodd dyn/Eu mwynach erioed/Mewn llesmair na hun.

Because only in this way will we go from step to step until we come in all things to the perfection which lies before Him. For this reason, the highest aspect of painting is not the ideal of the school which is so renowned in England today - although perhaps it seems so to the Philistine and the narrow-minded. This is why the prize in the Colwyn Eisteddfod was given to a picture of a field of turnips. Nearly everything in the picture which is relevant to the craft of the artist is, indeed, correct; but it lacks that highest aspect of art.' [220]

The unfortunate painter, associated by Matthews with the decadent English school, was Timothy Evans.

Matthews made extensive use of the work of Islwyn in his comparative analysis of contemporary painting. He once remarked that 'In the same way as Islwyn is the poet of "The Storm", Leader is the poet of "Peace"'. However, in the following example, in which Matthews extended his argument from Leader to include Clarence Whaite, he took a poem of the fifteenth century. The pictures he discussed were shown in the 1911 Academy exhibition at Plas Mawr:

'Some pictures stand very much higher than the others, and this is only natural. Here we see the deep sympathy of B.W.Leader, - or Elidir, as it should be spelt, - in his "After the Storm." The flood of the river Llugwy flows to the sea in the Autumn, and the mist up on the mountain top fleeing before the wind - and showing better times at hand. This is one of the best pictures of this famous artist.[221] *With this, a picture of similar sympathy with nature, "Snowdon" by the President of the Academy. The Queen of Snowdonia is hidden by snow. It is wonderful with what finesse he has succeeded in conveying the might of the mountain, the snow-terror to the mountain-dweller, and the awsome beauty of the snow on the dismal precipices; the beauty of*

A silver garment of ice for a moment,
The coldest quicksilver in the world;
A cold cloak, sad the waiting,
The sadness of hill, and valley and ditch...
A thick steel slip, weight of a landslide,
A paving greater than the sea grave.' [222]

[220] Thomas Matthews, 'Celf yng Nghymru', *Cymru*, ed. O.M.Edwards, 1911, p.15.

[221] Lewis Lusk had been moved to even greater mystical heights by Leader's *The Old Holyhead Road*: 'To our charmed eyes had come, not a picture, but a vision. A wild mountain country had suddenly appeared - one purple summit half veiled by the scudding clouds of a distant storm. There beneath it lay the green vales, all steaming with mellow light of a late afternoon - nearer, an old mossed bridge of warm grey, almost as massive as Stonehenge - it was the Holyhead Road, gleaming wet, winding like an old silvery serpent away into the mystery of the hills, and, bounding toward us till it seemed as if it would come thundering out over the frame and wash down the whole place - a mighty amber - foaming torrent!' Lusk, op.cit., pp.9-10.

[222] Matthews, op.cit., p.110. Matthews seldom indicated the authorship of his extensive quotations, which were sometimes obscure, but, in this case, the poem can be identified as 'Yr Eira' (The Snow) which he would probably have considered to be the work of Dafydd ap Gwilym. Most scholars now consider it to be the work of an unknown poet of the fifteenth century (perhaps Ieuan ap Rhys ap Llywelyn), and the preferred reading of the text differs from that given by Matthews and here directly translated, see *Dafydd ap Gwilym Apochrypha*, ed. Helen Fulton (Llandysul, 1996), pp.114-5 and 226-7.

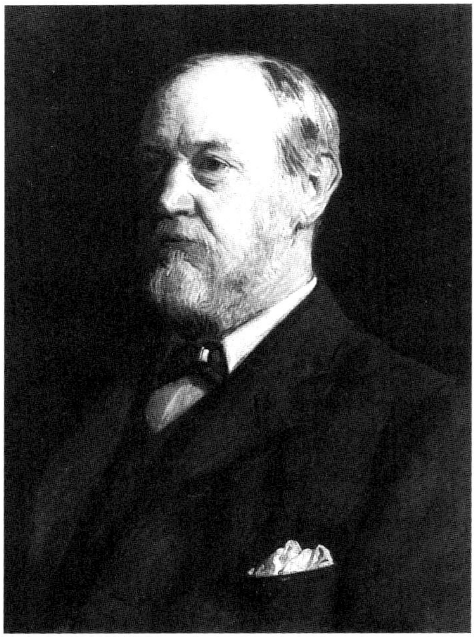

Christopher Williams,
T.H.Thomas,
1902.

However fanciful the pseudo-science of its Celtic genes, the Protestant mysticism of Thomas Matthews defined a philosophy which truly encompassed the beliefs of many of the painters of the artists' colony. Clarence Whaite can certainly be counted among them, although since he was not a theoretician, the written evidence to justify such an assertion is limited to the privacy of his diary and suggestive titles for pictures, such as *A Leaf from the Book of Nature*. Had Matthews' aesthetics and criticism been published sixty years earlier, when Whaite had first come to Betws, they might have provided a common intellectual framework which could have transformed the artists' colony into a school. A third generation of painters might have been attracted to the area to take up and develop such ideas. However, the confidence which enabled Thomas Matthews to identify latent common values and translate them into a national aesthetic came too late for Betws and for Wales. In 1912, the year after Matthews defined his aesthetics in the magazine *Cymru*, Clarence Whaite died. His friend T.H.Thomas survived him only by three years, by which time the National Movement as a whole had been overwhelmed by the Great War.

When Clarence Whaite met David Cox at Betws in 1852 there was no evidence of a Welsh art world, but by 1886 T.H.Thomas was talking in a quite unselfconscious way about just such a thing. This was a remarkable transformation, and it had been engineered primarily by those two groups of artists and intellectuals based in Cardiff and in the Conwy Valley whose efforts were linked together by the long and distinguished career of Clarence Whaite. They deserve greater respect and recognition for their achievement than they have been given by the art historians of the twentieth century.

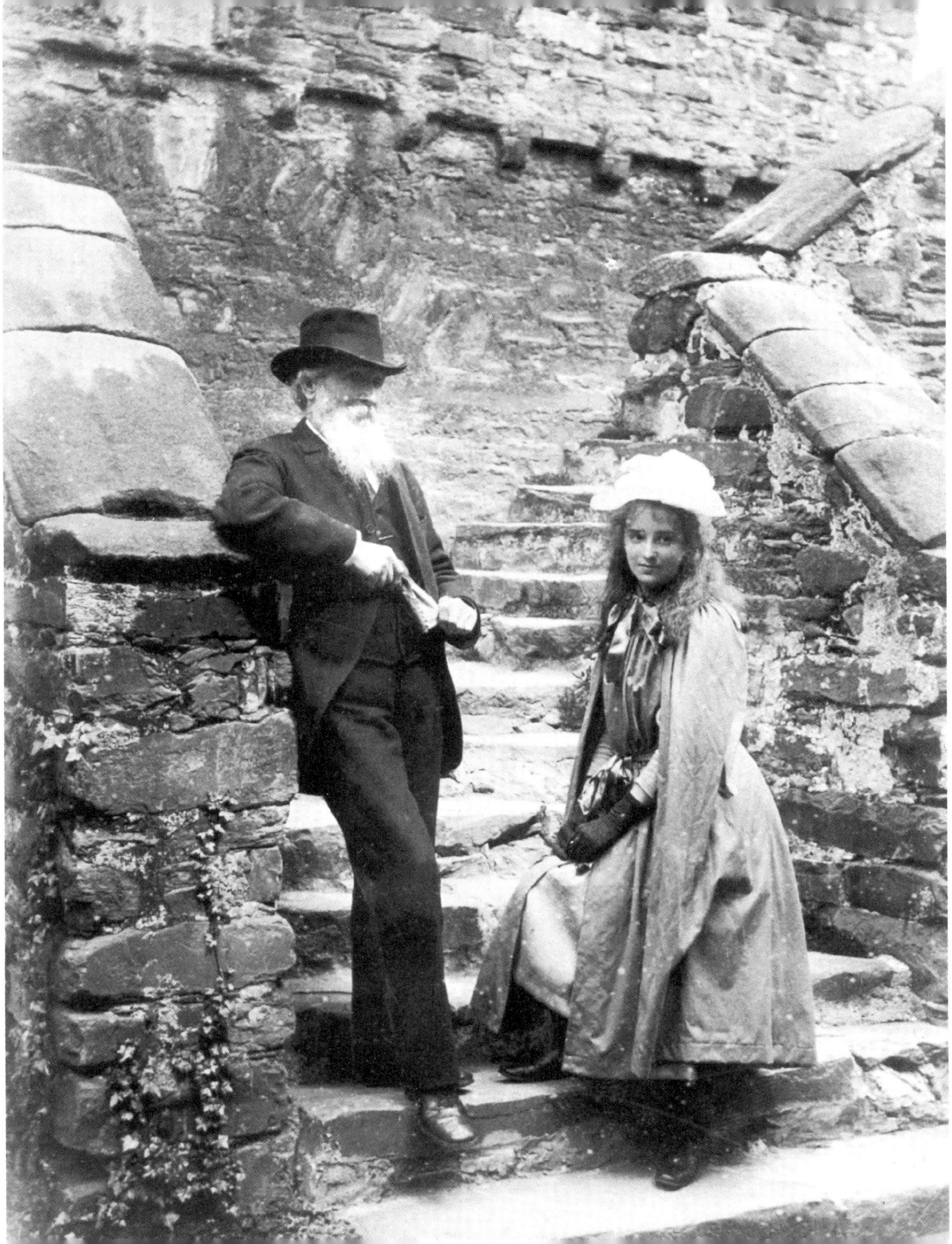

Unknown photographer, *Clarence and Lily Whaite on the steps at Plas Mawr*, c.1890

Index

(Black and white illustrations are noted in bold type; colour illustrations are noted in bold type underlined)

Acknowledgements

Reproductions by courtesy of private collectors and the National Library of Wales, with the exception of the following:

Ashmolean Museum, Oxford: 173
Birmingham Museums & Art Gallery: 15, 48, 67, 151
Board of Trustees of the National Museums and Galleries on Merseyside (Walker Art Gallery, Liverpool): 149, 150
Bristol Museums and Art Gallery: 53
The British Museum: 16, 43, 44
Caernarfon Town Council: 147
City of Nottingham Museums; Castle Museum and Art Gallery: 87, 90, 91
City of Salford Museums and Art Gallery: 120
Denbighshire Record Office: 108
Fitzwilliam Museum, Cambridge: 40
Guildhall Art Gallery, Corporation of London: 177
Gwynedd Archives Service: 180
Manchester Central Library - Local Studies Unit: 102-3
Manchester City Art Galleries: 111
The Martyn Gregory Gallery: 43, 83
The National Museum of Wales: 30, 39, 52, 60, 109, 125, 131, 140, 145, 152, 158, 169, 170, 184
The Royal Cambrian Academy: 77, 115, 128, 134, 146, 166
Sefton MBC Leisure Services Department, Arts and Cultural Services, Atkinson Art Gallery: 149
Tate Gallery: 148
V&A Picture Library: 43, 52, 62, 64, 121
The Whitworth Art Gallery, University of Manchester: 101
The Witt Library, Courtould Institute of Art: 57
Yale Center for British Art: 29, 41, 42, 44, 54

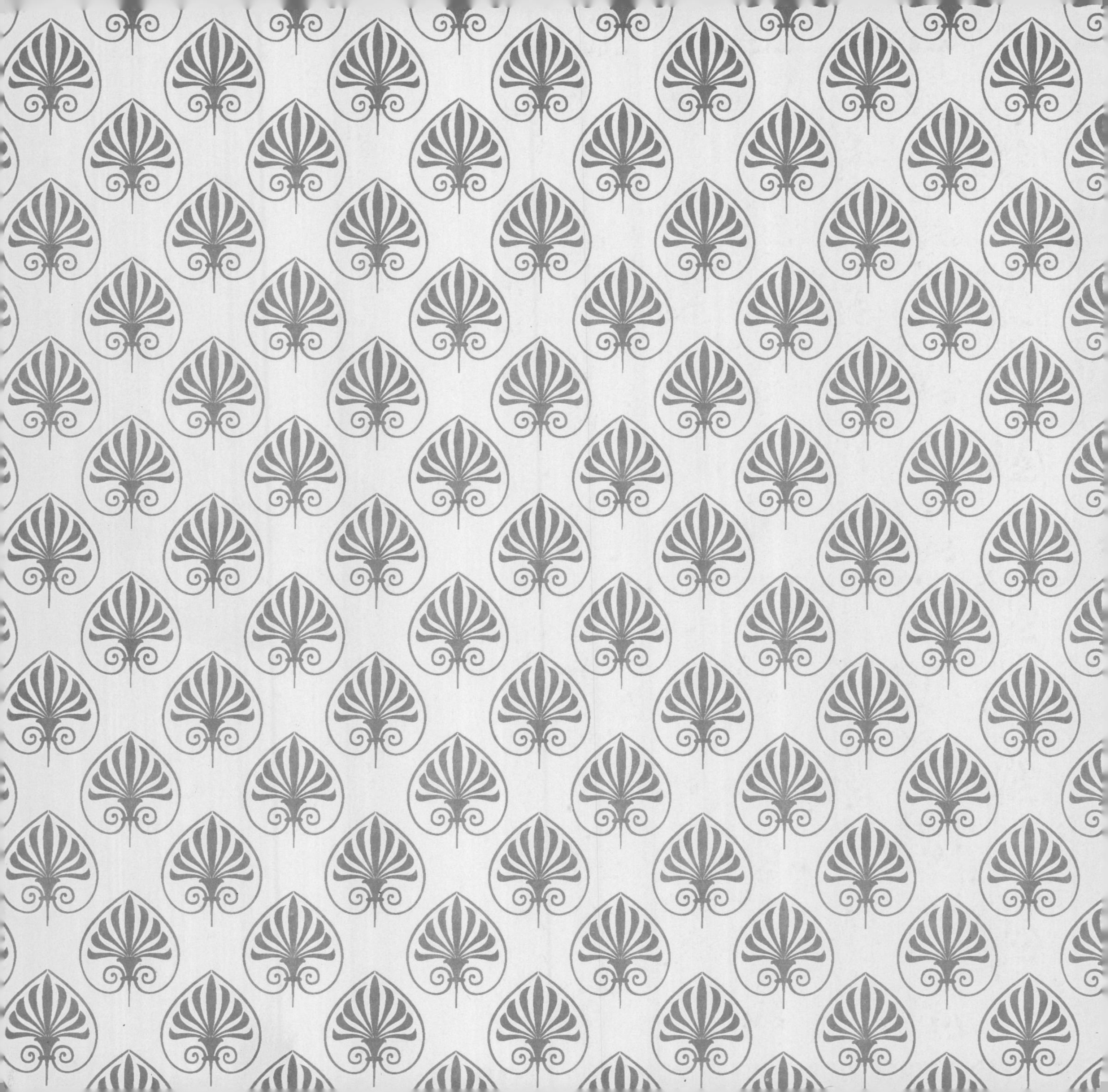